It's another great book from CGP...

If you can read this, you obviously know a fair bit about English Language.
But to do well at GCSE, you'll need to be able to analyse it in a lot more detail...

Not to worry. This brilliant CGP Revision Guide covers all the reading and writing skills
you'll need — each backed up with exam-style texts, questions and student answers.
And of course, it's all perfectly matched to the new AQA course.

As if that wasn't enough, we've also included fully worked exam papers with graded
answers, plus an exam advice section with a detailed guide to all the questions!
So now you've got no excuse not to mind your language.

CGP — still the best! ☺

Our sole aim here at CGP is to produce the highest quality books —
carefully written, immaculately presented and dangerously close to being funny.

Then we work our socks off to get them out to you
— at the cheapest possible prices.

CONTENTS

CONTENTS

Published by CGP

Editors:
Emma Bonney
Joe Brazier
Emma Crighton
Anna Hall

With thanks to Holly Poynton, Matt Topping and Nicola Woodfin for the proofreading.
With thanks to Laura Jakubowski for the copyright research.

Acknowledgements:

AQA material is reproduced by permission of AQA.

With thanks to iStockphoto.com for permission to use the images on pages 27, 34, 61, 67 & 78.

Letter on page 30 to Princess (later Queen) Victoria from King Leopold I of Belgium, August 1832, from The Letters of Queen Victoria, Volume 1 (of 3), 1837-1843.

Extract from The Snow Child by Eowyn Ivey on page 68 © 2012 Eowyn Ivey. Reproduced by permission of Headline Publishing Group & Reagan Arthur Books/Little Brown and Company.

First interview on page 81 adapted from "Of the life of an orphan girl, a street-seller", London Labour and the London Poor, volume 1 by Henry Mayhew, published in the 1840s.

Second interview on page 81 adapted from "Of children sent out as street-sellers by their parents", London Labour and the London Poor, volume 1 by Henry Mayhew, published in the 1840s.

Every effort has been made to locate copyright holders and obtain permission to reproduce sources.
For those sources where it has been difficult to trace the copyright holder of the work, we would be grateful
for information. If any copyright holder would like us to make an amendment to the acknowledgements,
please notify us and we will gladly update the book at the next reprint. Thank you.

ISBN: 978 1 78294 369 3
Printed by Elanders Ltd, Newcastle upon Tyne.
Clipart from Corel®

Based on the classic CGP style created by Richard Parsons.

Exam Structure

Understanding the structure of your exams can take some of the stress out of sitting them. If you know what you're up against, you'll have a massive head start, leaving you free to run off into the sunset with all the marks...

You will sit two different papers

Unfortunately, your 'explorations' won't actually involve leaving your desk.

1) Paper 1 is called 'Explorations in Creative Reading and Writing' — it focuses on fiction.

2) Paper 2 is called 'Writers' Viewpoints and Perspectives' — it focuses on non-fiction.

3) You will have 1 hour 45 minutes for each paper.

4) Both papers are split into two sections — Section A covers reading, and Section B covers writing.

5) Each paper is worth 50% of the GCSE.

Both papers have five questions...

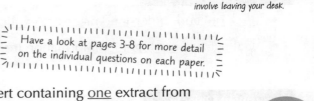

Have a look at pages 3-8 for more detail on the individual questions on each paper.

For paper 1, there will be a question paper and a separate insert containing one extract from a work of literary fiction — it will be from either the twentieth or twenty-first century.

You should spend the first 15 minutes reading through the source and the questions.

Section A: Reading is worth 40 marks. It has four questions:

- Question 1 is worth 4 marks. You should spend about 4 minutes on this.
- Questions 2 and 3 are worth 8 marks each. You should spend about 9 minutes on each of these.
- Question 4 is worth 20 marks. You should spend about 23 minutes on this.

Section B: Writing only has one question (there'll be a choice of tasks, but you only need to do one):

- Question 5 is worth 40 marks. You should spend 45 minutes on this.

For paper 2, there will be a question paper and a separate insert containing two non-fiction sources — one from the nineteenth century and one from either the twentieth or twenty-first century (whichever wasn't used in paper 1).

If you have any time left at the end of the exam, use it to check through your work.

You should spend the first 15 minutes reading through the sources and the questions.

Section A: Reading is worth 40 marks. It has four questions:

- Question 1 is worth 4 marks. You should spend about 4 minutes on this.
- Question 2 is worth 8 marks. You should spend about 9 minutes on this.
- Question 3 is worth 12 marks. You should spend about 14 minutes on this.
- Question 4 is worth 16 marks. You should spend about 18 minutes on this.

Section B: Writing only has one question:

- Question 5 is worth 40 marks. You should spend 45 minutes on this.

"How did you find the exam?" "It was just on the table..."

Make sure you've really got your head around this page, especially the number of marks available for each question — if you allow just over one minute per mark, you'll be on track to get everything finished in time.

The Assessment Objectives

If you've got the basic structure of the exams covered, now's a good time to get your head round each of the questions in more detail. First up, the background to what the questions are about — the assessment objectives.

Each assessment objective refers to a different skill

1) The assessment objectives are the things that AQA say you need to do to get good marks in the exam.

2) They'll come in handy when you're working out what you need to do for each of the questions — there's more on how each of the assessment objectives apply to the individual questions on pages 3-8.

3) These exams test assessment objectives 1 to 6. Here's a brief description of each of them:

Assessment Objective 1

- Pick out and understand pieces of explicit and implicit information from the texts.
- Collect and put together information from different texts.

Assessment Objective 2

- Explain how writers use language and structure to achieve their purpose and influence readers.
- Use technical terms to support your analysis of language and structure.

Assessment Objective 3

- Identify different writers' ideas and perspectives.
- Compare the methods used by different writers to convey their ideas.

Assessment Objective 4

- Critically evaluate texts, giving a personal opinion about how successful the writing is.
- Provide detailed evidence from the text to support your opinion.

Assessment Objective 5

- Write clearly and imaginatively, adapting your tone and style for various purposes and audiences.
- Organise your writing into a clear structure.

Assessment Objective 6

- Use a wide variety of sentence structures and vocabulary, so that your writing is clear and purposeful.
- Write accurately, paying particular attention to spelling, punctuation and grammar.

Understanding the assessment objectives is the key to success...

Once you're up to speed on all these assessment objectives, check out the next six pages. They'll show you how to successfully unleash this new knowledge on each of the questions so you know what to expect.

Paper 1 — Questions 1 and 2

The first question on paper 1 is pretty straightforward — you just need to do a bit of fact-finding. Question 2 requires a bit more thought, but it's a great opportunity to show off your analytical skills. Oooh... flashy.

You need to find four facts for question 1

1) Question 1 will test the first part of <u>assessment objective 1</u> — it will test your ability to <u>find</u> information or ideas in the text.

2) Most of the information you'll be asked to find will be <u>explicit</u> (it will be obviously written out in the extract), but keep an eye out for <u>implicit</u> information too (information that needs to be worked out from what is said in the text).

3) The <u>question</u> will usually look something like this:

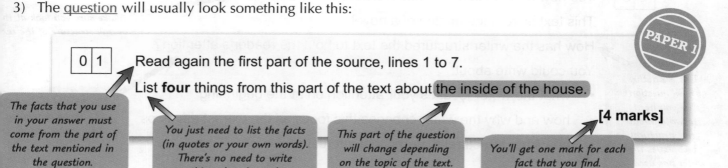

| 0 | 1 | Read again the first part of the source, lines 1 to 7. |

List **four** things from this part of the text about the inside of the house.

[4 marks]

The facts that you use in your answer must come from the part of the text mentioned in the question.

You just need to list the facts (in quotes or your own words). There's no need to write anything else about them.

This part of the question will change depending on the topic of the text.

You'll get one mark for each fact that you find.

PAPER 1

Question 2 is about the effects of language on the reader

1) This question will test the <u>language</u> part of <u>assessment objective 2</u> — you'll need to write about how the writer uses <u>language</u> to achieve <u>effects</u> and <u>influence</u> the reader.

The structure part of assessment objective 2 will be covered in paper 1, question 3 (see page 4).

2) The <u>question</u> will usually look something like this:

| 0 | 2 | Look in detail at lines 11 to 20 of the source. |

Make sure you only analyse this part of the text.

How does the writer use language to describe the atmosphere in the room?

You could include the writer's choice of:
* words and phrases
* language features and techniques
* sentence forms.

For questions that ask 'how' the writer has done something, you need to write about the methods the writer has used and their effect on the reader. In this case you need to focus on the effects of the writer's language on the reader.

Make sure your answer includes quotes that demonstrate each of the things mentioned in the bullet points.

Try to use technical terms to describe the writer's use of language.

This part of the question will change depending on the purpose of the text.

[8 marks]

PAPER 1

It's like the world's dullest treasure hunt...

Ok, so it's an exam not a treasure hunt, but finding those four golden facts is super important. Question 1 is a great opportunity to pick up some easy marks before you have to tackle the more complex questions.

Paper 1 — Questions 3 and 4

Question 3 is a pretty similar deal to question 2, except it's about structure rather than language.
After that though, you're into the big leagues — question 4 weighs in at an impressive 20 marks...

Question 3 asks about the writer's use of structure

1) This question will test the <u>structure</u> part of <u>assessment objective 2</u> — you'll need to write about how the writer uses <u>structure</u> to achieve <u>effects</u> and <u>influence</u> the reader.

2) The <u>question</u> will usually look something like this:

> 0 3   You now need to think about the **whole** of the **source**.
>
> This text is from the ending of a novel.
>
> How has the writer structured the text to hold the reader's attention?
>
> You could write about:
>
> • what the writer focuses your attention on at the beginning
>
> • how and why the writer changes this focus as the extract develops
>
> • any other structural features that interest you.
>
> **[8 marks]**

Make sure you look at the overall structure of the text

This part of the question will change depending on the purpose of the text

This is another 'how' question — you need to write about the structural techniques the writer has used to produce the desired effect on the reader.

Make sure your answer includes examples of each of the things mentioned in the bullet points.

Try to use technical terms to describe the writer's use of structure.

You need to give a personal judgement for question 4

1) This question will test <u>assessment objective 4</u> — you'll need to <u>evaluate</u> the text <u>critically</u> and give a <u>personal response</u>.

Question 4 is synoptic — which means you'll need to use everything you've learnt across the whole course to answer it properly.

2) The <u>question</u> will usually look something like this:

> 0 4   Focus this part of your answer on the second half of the source, **from line 18 to the end**.
>
> A student, having read this section of the text said: "The writer has created a very lifelike set of characters. You feel as if you really get to know them."
>
> To what extent do you agree?
>
> In your response, you could:
>
> • write about your own impressions of the characters
>
> • evaluate how the writer has created these impressions
>
> • support your opinions with references to the text.
>
> **[20 marks]**

Make sure you only analyse the part of the text.

This statement will be tailored to the specific text. It'll usually focus on the writer's techniques and their effect on the reader.

You need to write about your own opinion of the text and the methods the writer has used to make you feel like this.

Make sure you provide lots of evidence to back up your points.

It's time to get up close and personal...

To get all the marks for question 4, you need to provide a personal evaluation of the text and back it up with detailed evidence — use a range of short examples from the text to show what you've based your opinion on.

Paper 1 — Question 5

By the time you've got to question 5, you're halfway. The reading is behind you, but the writing is still to come...

You only need to do one of the tasks for question 5

1) Question 5 is a <u>creative writing</u> task that will test <u>assessment objectives 5 and 6</u> — examiners will be looking for you to produce an <u>interesting</u>, <u>well-organised</u> and <u>accurately written</u> piece.

2) There will be a <u>choice</u> of tasks, but you only need to do <u>one</u>.

3) The tasks will usually be on a <u>similar theme</u> to the text from the <u>reading</u> section.

4) The <u>question</u> might look something like this:

This question is worth 40 marks, so you need to write quite a lengthy answer — making a plan will help you to make sure your answer is well organised.

Question 5 is the only question in the writing section.

Section B: Writing

You should spend about 45 minutes on this section of the paper.

You are advised to plan your answer.

Write in full sentences.

Leave enough time to check your work.

 0 5 You are going to enter a creative writing competition.

You will be judged by a panel of your teachers.

Either:

Write a description suggested by this picture:

The question will always give you a specific purpose, form and audience — you need to show that you've adapted your writing style to match these.

Make sure you only do one of the tasks.

One of the tasks will ask you to respond to a prompt. It might be a picture, a scenario or a statement.

Or:

Write the opening part of a story about camping in a remote location.

(24 marks for content and organisation
16 marks for technical accuracy)

[40 marks]

You should make your writing as engaging as possible — try to use a wide variety of structural features and vocabulary. There's more on this on pages 54 to 57.

Loads of the marks for this question are awarded for assessment objective 5 — so you need to make sure your writing is clear, imaginative and well structured.

There are also quite a few marks available for assessment objective 6 — make sure you've used Standard English throughout your answer and your spelling, punctuation and grammar are accurate (see pages 16 and 17).

I like what you've done here. It's... err... creative...

This is your chance to show your creative side — the examiners want you to show that you can be imaginative. Make sure you use lots of descriptive language and try to produce as interesting a piece of writing as possible.

Paper 2 — Questions 1 and 2

Paper 2 starts with a couple more fact-finding questions, but this time there's a twist. In question 1, you'll have to avoid some sneaky falsehoods, and in question 2 you'll need to summarise information from both sources.

You need to find four facts in question 1

1) This question will test the first part of assessment objective 1 — you will need to show that you can find information or ideas in the text.

2) The question will usually look something like this:

PAPER 2

| 0 | 1 | Read again **source A**, from lines 1 to 11.

Choose **four** statements below which are TRUE.

You can only pick out facts from this part of the text.

• Shade the boxes of the ones that you think are true

• Choose a maximum of four statements.

There are 4 true statements and 4 false statements. You just need to pick out the 4 true ones.

It's important that you only select four statements.

A   Aaron's parents think he goes to football every Thursday. □

B   Aaron would like to be better at sport. □

C   Aaron really likes board games. □

D   Aaron admires his brother. □

E   Aaron has a good relationship with his parents. □

F   Aaron enjoys school. □

G   Aaron is a high-achiever at school. □

H   Aaron likes living in Manchester. □

The facts might be implicit or explicit. Look at the tone of the text for help with the more implicit ones.

You'll get 1 mark for each true statement you find. **[4 marks]**

Question 2 asks for facts from both sources

1) Question 2 will test both parts of assessment objective 1 — it will test your ability to find information and ideas in two sources and summarise what you find.

2) The question will usually look something like this:

PAPER 2

| 0 | 2 | You need to refer to **source A** and **source B** for this question:

Pick out bits of implicit and explicit information to support your points. Remember to include quotes.

Use details from both sources.

Write a summary of the differences between Jane and Mrs Silverton.

[8 marks]

The question is asking you to summarise information from both texts — use linking words to show you're thinking about both texts together.

The question will always ask about something that both texts have in common — it might be a topic or a pair of characters.

Some of those 'facts' are as fake as Father Christmas...

For these questions, you need to show that you've really understood the texts. Don't get led astray by any seductive false statements, and try to make really perceptive links between the sources in question 2.

Paper 2 — Questions 3 and 4

Question 3 on paper 2 is pretty similar to question 2 on paper 1 — it's all about how the writer has used language. Question 4 is about attitude — and I don't mean the it's-7am-of-course-I-don't-want-any-breakfast kind.

Question 3 covers the effects of the writer's use of language

1) This question will test the <u>language</u> part of <u>assessment objective 2</u> — you'll need to write about how the writer uses <u>language</u> to achieve <u>effects</u> and <u>influence</u> the reader.

2) The <u>question</u> will usually look something like this:

> | 0 | 3 |
>
> You now need to refer **only** to **source B**, the entry from Jenny's diary.
>
> How does Jenny use language to express her frustration?
>
> **[12 marks]**

PAPER 2

This is another 'how' question, so you need to write about the techniques the writer has used to achieve their purpose. Have a look at paper 1, questions 2 and 3 for other examples of 'how' questions.

Your answer should include lots of quotes and technical terms to back up your points.

Try to refer specifically to particular words, phrases, language features and techniques.

This part of the question will change depending on the purpose of the text.

Question 4 asks you to compare perspectives

Question 4 is synoptic — which means you'll need to use everything you've learnt across the whole course to answer it properly.

1) This question will test <u>assessment objective 3</u> — you'll need to <u>identify</u> and <u>compare</u> different writers' <u>attitudes</u> and <u>perspectives</u>, and <u>how</u> they're conveyed.

2) The <u>question</u> will usually look something like this:

> | 0 | 4 |
>
> For this question, you need to refer to the **whole of source A** together with **source B**.
>
> Compare how the two writers convey their different attitudes to dieting and healthy eating.
>
> In your answer, you could:
>
> - compare their different attitudes
> - compare the methods they use to convey their attitudes
> - support your ideas with references to both texts.
>
> **[16 marks]**

PAPER 2

Make sure you cover everything mentioned in the bullet points — you need to write about what the writers' attitudes are and how they are similar or different.

Make sure you give quotes and examples from both sources.

Try to identify how the writers have used language and structure to show subtle differences in their attitudes. This will show the examiner that you've really understood the text.

This part of the question will change depending on the topics covered in the texts.

Hmmm... I'm sure I've seen this before...

Question 3 is very similar to question 2 on paper 1, but don't forget — it's worth quite a few more marks. Question 4 is your chance to bring all your skills together and really show that you've understood the texts.

Section One — Exam Basics

Paper 2 — Question 5

And last but definitely not least, it's time for paper 2, question 5. It's another whopping 40 mark writing task, but this time it's about giving your own perspective on a theme.

The last question is a writing task

1) Question 5 is a <u>writing</u> task that will test <u>assessment objectives 5 and 6</u> — examiners will be looking for you to produce an <u>interesting</u>, <u>well-organised</u> and <u>accurately written</u> piece.

2) You'll need to write in the <u>form</u> of a <u>non-fiction text</u>, such as a newspaper article.

3) The question will ask you to give your <u>own perspective</u> on a similar <u>theme</u> to the one covered in the <u>reading section</u> of the paper.

4) The <u>question</u> will usually look something like this:

Joe's perspective on the issue was: 'from above'.

Question 5 is the only question in the writing section.

Section B: Writing

You should spend about 45 minutes on this section of the paper.

You are advised to plan your answer.

Write in full sentences.

Leave enough time to check your work.

This question is worth 40 marks, so you need to write quite a lengthy answer — making a plan will help you to make sure your answer is well organised.

PAPER 2

The task will usually ask you to respond to a prompt. It might be an opinion, a scenario or a statement.

0 5 'School uniforms are a pointless expense. They are never worn correctly, they are uncomfortable and they restrict pupils' creativity.'

Write a letter to your headteacher, in which you persuade them to agree with your point of view on this statement.

(24 marks for content and organisation
16 marks for technical accuracy)

[40 marks]

The question will always give you a specific purpose, form and audience — you need to show that you've adapted your writing style to match these.

Loads of the marks for this question are awarded for assessment objective 5 — so you need to make sure your writing is clear, imaginative and well structured.

There are also quite a few marks available for assessment objective 6 — make sure you've used Standard English throughout your answer and your spelling, punctuation and grammar are accurate (see pages 16 and 17).

Your true colours need to do more than just shine through...

They need to be glaringly obvious in this question. Your own point of view is pretty important here, but you also need to make sure the way you deliver it is well-suited to the purpose, form and audience of the text.

Section One — Exam Basics

Planning Answers

Now you know all about what to expect from the questions, the next few pages will help you with the basics of how to answer them. First up, what to do before you start scribbling away at the answers...

Read the questions carefully and calmly

1) You should give yourself <u>15 minutes</u> to read through the <u>questions</u> and the <u>texts</u> at the start of the exam.

2) Always <u>read the questions</u> before the exam texts — that way, you'll know what to look out for.

3) Make sure you're clear about what the questions are <u>asking</u> you to do by <u>underlining</u> the <u>key words</u>.

| 0 | 2 | Write a <u>summary</u> of the <u>differences</u> between the two <u>main characters</u>.

4) Once you've read the questions, carefully <u>read</u> through the <u>texts</u>. It's a good idea to <u>highlight</u> key <u>words</u> or <u>phrases</u> that will help you to answer the questions — but don't spend ages doing this.

Remember, it's your exam paper and you can write on it if it helps you.

Jot down your main ideas before you start writing

1) Don't spend <u>too much</u> time planning. You don't need to do a plan for the simple <u>fact-finding</u> questions, but you might want to jot down some <u>points</u> and <u>highlight</u> the texts for some of the other <u>reading</u> questions. You <u>should</u> do a plan for the <u>writing</u> questions on both papers.

2) Don't go into too much <u>detail</u> — just get your <u>main ideas</u> down, and <u>outline</u> the <u>structure</u> of your answer.

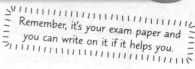

| 0 | 5 | 'Modern music glorifies violent and criminal lifestyles and should be banned.'

Write a speech, to be delivered in your school assembly, in which you argue for or against this statement.

PLAN

Para 1 — Intro

Make sure your points are linked to the question — think about purpose, form and audience.

"My fellow students" etc. don't listen to critics - we're currently in golden era of music.

Para 2 — Not all modern music glorifies violence - give examples.

Para 3 — It's not just modern music - old music did this too. Give examples.

Para 4 — People aren't robots - won't just become violent by listening to music.

Para 5 — Ban = bad for freedom of expression. Censorship. Slippery slope etc.

Para 6 — Conc

Briefly outline the focus of each paragraph.

Critics = out of touch. Haven't really listened to much 'modern music'.

Modern music = celebration of choice.

Make sure you're clear about which side you're arguing for before you start.

To save time, write in note form.

A plan is like a nice hot water bottle...

... useful and comforting when you need it, but you don't need it all the time. You won't need to plan for every question, but it's a good idea to make a brief plan to help you tackle some of the longer answers.

P.E.E.D.

You can have loads of great ideas in your answers, but you won't get good marks unless you explain and develop them properly. That's where P.E.E.D. comes in — use it wisely my young apprentice...

P.E.E.D. stands for Point, Example, Explain, Develop

To write good answers for the longer reading questions (2-4 on both papers), you must do <u>four</u> things:

1) Make a <u>point</u> to answer the question you've been given.

2) Then give an <u>example</u> from the text (see page 11 for more on this).

3) After that, <u>explain</u> how your example backs up your point.

4) Finally, <u>develop</u> your point — this might involve saying what the <u>effect on the reader</u> is, saying what the <u>writer's intention</u> is, <u>linking</u> your point to another part of the text or giving your <u>own opinion</u>.

"That wasn't really the kind of back up I was thinking of..." thought the sergeant.

The <u>explanation</u> and <u>development</u> parts are very important. They're your chance to show that you <u>really understand</u> and have <u>thought about</u> the text. Here are a couple of <u>examples</u>:

PAPER 2

0 3 How does the writer use language to show how she feels about school dinners?

This is your <u>point</u>. → The writer feels quite angry about school dinners. She says school food is "pallid, tasteless pap". ← *This is your <u>example</u>.* The word "pap" has a disgusted sound to it. It emphasises how appalled she is at the low quality of the food. ← *This bit is your <u>explanation</u>.* I think the writer's intention is to show *This is where you <u>develop</u> your point further.* → that it isn't surprising that school dinners are unpopular. She is implying that schools should provide food that isn't disgusting if they want children to eat it.

PAPER 1

0 3 How has the writer structured the text to show how he is feeling?

This introduces the main <u>point</u> of the paragraph. → The writer sounds as if he is confused. For example, he starts each paragraph with a question, giving the impression that he doesn't ← *A structural feature is the <u>example</u> here.* *This <u>explains</u> the effect of the example.* → understand what's happening to him. This is reinforced by the writer's use of flashbacks throughout the extract, which give a further sense of ← *This <u>links</u> the point with another part of the text.* how erratic his thoughts are. The writer's confusion creates a sense of *This <u>develops</u> the point further.* → unease in the reader, leading them to question their own understanding of the issue.

Would you like to share the joke with the rest of the class?

There are other versions of P.E.E.D., but they all mean similar things — P.E.E.R. (Point, Example, Explain, Relate), P.E.E.C.E. (Point, Example, Explain, Compare, Explore). I just chose P.E.E.D. because it tickles me...

Section One — Exam Basics

Using Examples

This page has some nifty tips about the first 'E' in P.E.E.D. — giving examples to back up your points.

Use details from the text to back up your points

1) Whenever you make a new <u>point</u>, you need to use short pieces of <u>evidence</u> from the text to <u>back it up</u>.

2) You should try to use a <u>mix</u> of different sorts of <u>evidence</u>.

3) If you're using <u>quotes</u>, try to keep them <u>short</u>. It'll really impress the examiner if you <u>embed</u> them in a sentence, like this:

> The writer refers to the situation as "indefensible", suggesting that he is extremely critical of the way it has been handled.

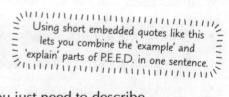
Using short embedded quotes like this lets you combine the 'example' and 'explain' parts of P.E.E.D. in one sentence.

4) <u>Paraphrased details</u> from the text also work well as examples. You just need to describe one of the <u>writer's techniques</u>, or one of the <u>text's features</u>, in your own words, like this:

> The writer begins the paragraph with a rhetorical question that emphasises her feelings of disgust.

5) Here are a couple of <u>examples</u> to show you how to work your evidence into your answer:

PAPER 1

`0 2` How does the writer use language here to describe the fire?

Embedding short quotes will help your answer to flow smoothly.

> The writer uses various linguistic devices to demonstrate how powerful the fire is. At the start of the extract, he paints a vivid picture of the fire as a "pageant" of colour. He then uses a metaphor to equate the destructive power of the fire with that of a beast that is tearing down the workshop and "devouring" it. All of these images make the fire seem impressive and potent.

Your example could just be a description of one of the writer's techniques.

PAPER 2

`0 4` Compare how the two writers convey their different attitudes to international travel.

Try to include a good balance of quotes and references to the text.

> The author of source B has a very negative attitude towards international travel. In her opening paragraph, she uses a long sentence that is packed with negative verbs and adjectives, including "delayed" and "dreary", to convey the hassle of long-distance travelling and to make the reader feel weary. By contrast, the author of source A demonstrates a much more positive attitude, opening her letter with the short but decisive sentence, "The journey was a perfect joy!" which sounds energetic and cheerful.

If you need to use a longer quote, make sure you copy it correctly and use the correct punctuation.

Always make sure I've P.E.E.D. on my work... can I quote you on that?

Backing up your points with evidence from the text is a sure-fire way to impress the examiners. Then, you just need to explain the evidence and develop your point, and you'll be well on your way to P.E.E.D. perfection.

Writing Well

A big chunk of the marks in these exams are for how you write rather than what you write. The next two pages will give you tips on how to write well for the longer reading questions (2-4 on both papers).

Keep your writing formal but interesting

1) For these exams, it's important that you write in Standard English.

2) Standard English is the version of English that most people think is 'correct'. There are a few simple rules that you can follow to make sure you're writing in Standard English:

   - Avoid using informal words and phrases (e.g. putting 'like' after sentences).

   - Avoid using slang or local dialect words that some people might not understand.

   - Avoid using clichés (words and phrases that are so commonly used that they've lost their effect) like 'at the end of the day'.

   - Use correct spelling, punctuation and grammar (have a look at pages 16-17).

3) You should also try to make your writing as engaging as possible by using things like varied sentence lengths and interesting vocabulary. For example, don't overuse the word 'nice' — try to use other adjectives like 'admirable' or 'charming' instead.

Use clear explaining words and phrases

1) You should use explaining words and phrases to make your answers easy to follow.

| This signifies that... | This highlights the fact that... | This image reflects... |

| This is reminiscent of... | Furthermore... | This continues the idea of... |

2) Using words and phrases like these makes your writing sound more professional.

3) They're also really useful when it comes to P.E.E.D. (see page 10). They help you to link the explanation and development parts of your answer to your main point.

4) Here's an example of how to use explaining words and phrases to improve your answer:

PAPER 2

0 4   Compare how the two writers convey their different attitudes to volunteering.

Start your paragraph with a new point, and back it up with evidence from the text. Then, explain how this evidence supports your point.

In source A, the writer suggests that volunteering programmes are beneficial because they educate young people in "the ways of giving and sharing" and encourage young people to do good work for their community. This builds on the idea that young people should do more to help people less fortunate than themselves. Furthermore, it has a persuasive effect on the reader and makes them feel that they should get involved in charity work.

Use explaining words and phrases to show that you've developed your point.

This develops the point by showing its effect on the reader.

Writing Well

Use paragraphs to structure your answer

1) You need to <u>organise</u> your points <u>clearly</u> and <u>link</u> them together
   — to do that you need to write in <u>paragraphs</u>.

2) You can use different paragraph <u>structures</u> to organise your points in different ways. For example:

> - You could write a paragraph for every <u>point</u> you want to make, and each paragraph could have a <u>P.E.E.D.</u> structure (see page 10).
> - You could make two points that <u>contrast</u> or <u>agree</u> with each other within a paragraph — this can be useful when <u>comparing</u> two texts.
> - You could make one point and <u>link</u> together lots of <u>examples</u> with <u>different</u> explanations within a paragraph.

However you structure your paragraphs, make sure you include all the parts of P.E.E.D. in your answer.

3) <u>Linking</u> your paragraphs together <u>smoothly</u> makes your writing sound <u>confident</u> and <u>considered</u>. You could use linking words like these to help you do this:

| However... | In contrast... | On the other hand... | Equally... |

| In the same way... | In addition... | Alternatively... | Conversely... |

4) Take a look at the answer below for an <u>example</u> of how to use <u>paragraphs</u> effectively:

PAPER 1

0 2   How does the writer use language here to create mood?

> *The writer uses a particular range of vocabulary to create a sombre mood in the extract. Adjectives like "dismal" and "bleak", as well as verbs like "creaked" and "yawned" seem to build up and gradually make the reader feel more melancholy and unnerved. They give the sense that something bad is about to happen.*
>
> *Although the narrator's use of particular adjectives and verbs is important, it's not the only way in which the writer uses language to create a tense mood. Later in the extract, the writer also uses personification as a method of creating mood. He focuses specifically on the weather, bringing the rain and fog to life in order to create an eerie atmosphere. The personification of the rain as "stealthy" makes it seem menacing, whilst the image of it "knocking furtively at the door" adds to this mysterious atmosphere and makes the reader feel worried about what is going to happen next.*
>
> *In the same way, the writer also uses onomatopoeia, like the rain's "unsettling pattering" and the hedge's "curious rustling" to reinforce the mood of the piece.*

The beginning of a paragraph needs to show what the paragraph is about. Try to link it to the key words in the question.

This is a new point, so it's in a new paragraph.

Use linking words and phrases to show that you are introducing a comparison or contrast with a previous paragraph.

You could link a new paragraph with a previous paragraph.

This answer fully develops each new point, covering all the different parts of P.E.E.D.

Make sure your answer is a model of structural perfection...

... and I'm not talking about cheekbones. Organise your ideas into paragraphs, and use the phrases on this page to link them together smoothly. A clear structure will show the examiner that you've thought about your answer.

Reading with Insight

To get the top grades, you need to show that you can 'read with insight' — you've got to make it clear that you've worked out what the text is saying beyond the blatantly obvious. Think of it like detective work, my dear Watson...

You need to look beyond what's obvious

Looking beyond what's obvious will help you to make sure you've done the 'D' part of P.E.E.D. — look back at p.10 for more on this.

1) You may understand the <u>facts</u> a writer gives you, but you'll need to write about <u>more</u> than just those facts in your answers.

2) You can show <u>insight</u> if you work out what the writer's <u>intentions</u> are and how they want the reader to <u>feel</u>.

3) Here are a couple of <u>examples</u> of the kinds of things you could write:

> The rhetorical questions make the reader doubt whether homework is a good thing. The writer seems to want to make readers feel guilty.

 Think about the reasons <u>why</u> the writer has included certain features — show you've understood their <u>intended effect</u> on the reader.

> There is a strong sense that the writer is suffering after the loss of his friend. Perhaps the writer felt he needed to make sure the memory of his friend was kept alive.

 You could comment on the writer's <u>attitude</u> and <u>why</u> you think they chose to write the piece.

Show you've thought about the writer's intentions

0 4 A student, having read this section of the text said: "Lilian is essentially an unlikeable character".

To what extent do you agree?

> Dylan glowered across the table at Lilian. She was composed and collected, her pointed, reptilian features gathered into an expression of infuriating complacency; as he watched, a smug smile flickered at the edges of her mouth. She knew she had won.
>
> There hadn't even been a discussion. Lilian had been cool and emotionless, the picture of relaxed indifference. Her cruel blow, calculated to achieve maximum damage with minimum effort, had been delivered with the sniper-like accuracy that Dylan had always known she was capable of. Reeling from the shock of her abrupt revelation, Dylan barely had time to collect himself before the others had arrived.

Always show how your interpretation is based on the text.

Try to offer an alternative interpretation that goes beyond what is obvious in the text.

I agree that Lilian is portrayed as an unlikeable character in this extract. She is depicted as "smug" and she appears to be gloating. However, even though the writer is using the third-person, he is still showing us Lilian from Dylan's perspective. He has clearly been offended by her and so is biased against her. Some readers might side with Dylan against Lilian, finding her arrogant and malicious. Having said that, other readers might suspect that Dylan's pride has been wounded, and he is being overly harsh on Lilian as a result. Personally, I think the writer is using this description of Lilian to influence the reader's opinion of both her and Dylan by demonstrating that they both have flaws.

Try to pick out how the writer has made you feel like this.

Show you've thought about what the writer is trying to achieve beyond the obvious.

Section One — Exam Basics

Reading with Insight

Inference means working things out from clues

Making inferences is especially important for paper 2, which is all about writers' viewpoints and perspectives.

1) Writers don't usually make things obvious — but you can use <u>evidence</u> from the text to make an <u>inference</u> about what the writer <u>really</u> wants us to think.

2) You need to analyse <u>details</u> from the text to show what they <u>reveal</u> about the writer's intentions:

> *The writer uses words like "endless" and "unoriginal", which imply that he did not enjoy the film.*

The writer's <u>language</u> indicates their <u>emotions</u> and <u>attitude</u>.

> *The writer sounds sarcastic when she calls the contestants "the finest brains the country could scrape together".*

The writer will often use <u>tone</u> (see page 31) to <u>imply</u> what they really mean — look out for <u>sarcasm</u> or <u>bias</u>.

3) You could use <u>phrases</u> like these to show that you've made an <u>inference</u>:

| The writer gives a sense of... | The writer appears to be... | This suggests that... |

Try to read between the lines

PAPER 2

0 3 How does the writer use language to show how she feels about the Internet?

> In today's world we are plagued by information. Gone are the days of blissful ignorance; instead we inhabit an era of awareness, where the invention of the Internet has brought the sum total of the world's knowledge to our fingertips. It has reduced us to a collection of walking, talking encyclopaedias. We are gluttons for information, and yet the immediate availability of this information has irrevocably extinguished the dying embers of our curiosity. No longer do we wonder about anything, we simply look it up. I am willing to concede that the Internet might be one of man's greatest inventions, but hey, so was the atomic bomb.

Use words like 'seemingly' to show that you've thought about the meaning of the text beyond the obvious.

Analyse the writer's individual word choices for clues about their attitude (see pages 33-34).

> *The writer makes quite a lot of seemingly positive claims about the Internet: she grandly asserts that it has created "an era of awareness" that has brought all the world's knowledge "to our fingertips". However, the tone of the text suggests that she has a negative attitude towards the Internet. She uses words like "plagued" and "gluttons" to describe the availability of information and seems nostalgic about the "'blissful ignorance"' that existed before its invention. She sounds reluctant to admit that the Internet is "one of man's greatest inventions" and her sarcasm is made plain when she says, "but hey, so was the atomic bomb."*

Your inferences could be based on the general feeling you get from reading the text.

Think about how the tone changes over the course of the text.

Writers will often use sarcasm to imply what they really mean (see page 40).

Make sure you're reading with insight of a cup of tea...

Keep an eye out for any clues that might reveal how the writer has crafted their text to have a particular effect on the reader — they've certainly got a few tricks up their sleeves, these pesky writers.

Spelling, Punctuation and Grammar

A great way to make sure you grab a few easy marks in these exams is to use correct spelling, punctuation and grammar, or SPaG for short. These pages should help you to avoid the most common SPaG errors...

SPaG is especially important for the writing questions

1) It's important that you use correct spelling, punctuation and grammar in all of your answers.

2) However, it's particularly important for the writing questions (question 5 on both papers), as they will test your ability to write accurately and clearly — which includes good SPaG.

3) Here are some tips to help keep your writing as accurate as possible.

Spelling

1) Avoid common spelling mistakes, like 'their', 'they're' and 'there' or 'where', 'were' and 'wear'.

2) Remember that 'affect' is a verb, e.g. 'the simile affects the mood of the text', but 'effect' is a noun, e.g. 'the interruption has a shocking effect on the reader'.

3) Always write words out in full — avoid abbreviations like 'etc.' and 'e.g.', and don't use text speak.

4) Make sure any technical terms, like 'metaphor' or 'onomatopoeia', are spelt correctly.

5) Make sure any information taken from the extract, such as the writer's name, is spelt correctly.

Punctuation

1) Make sure you've used full stops at the end of sentences and question marks at the end of questions.

2) Use commas to separate items in a list or when you've used more than one adjective.

3) Use a comma when you use a joining word like 'and', 'so' or 'but' to link two points together. E.g. 'Jeremy says he isn't bothered by Mandy's behaviour, but his body language suggests otherwise.'

4) You should also use a pair of commas to separate extra information in a sentence. E.g. 'Ranjita, who is much calmer than Ashanti, does not respond to her father's taunting.'

5) Don't confuse colons and semi-colons.

   - Colons can be used to introduce a list or if you want to add a piece of information that explains your sentence.

   - Semi-colons can separate longer phrases in a list, or they can be used to join two sentences together — as long as both sentences are about the same thing and make sense on their own.

Grammar

1) Don't change tenses in your writing by mistake.

2) Don't use double negatives, e.g. 'There wasn't no reason' should be 'There wasn't any reason'.

3) Remember 'it's' (with an apostrophe) is short for 'it is' or 'it has'. 'Its' (without an apostrophe) means 'belonging to it'.

4) Never write 'should of' — it's always 'should have', 'would have', 'could have'.

5) Start a new paragraph for each new point. Show that it's a new paragraph by starting a new line and leaving a gap or indent before you start writing.

Spelling, Punctuation and Grammar

Check over your work when you've finished

1) Try to leave a few minutes at the <u>end</u> of the exams to <u>check</u> your work.

2) There might not be <u>time</u> to check everything thoroughly. Look for the <u>most obvious</u> spelling, punctuation and grammar mistakes.

3) Start by checking your answers to the <u>writing questions</u> (question 5 on both papers), as these are the ones where you get the <u>most marks</u> for accuracy.

4) Here are some tips for <u>correcting</u> any mistakes that you find:

- If you find a <u>spelling mistake</u>, put <u>brackets</u> around the word, <u>cross it out</u> neatly with <u>two lines</u> through it and write the correction <u>above</u>.

- If you've written something which isn't clear, put an <u>asterisk</u> (*) at the end of the sentence. Put another asterisk at the end of your work, and write what you mean beside it.

- If you realise you should have started a <u>new paragraph</u>, put // to show where it <u>starts</u> and write "(para)" in the margin.

- If you find you've <u>missed out</u> a word or two, put a "∧" where the words should go, then write them in <u>above</u> the line.

Make corrections as neatly as possible

PAPER 1

0 5   Write the opening part of a story that takes place in a park on a hot summer day.

The air was stiflingly hot. Monica could feel a dewy coating of sweat materialising on her clammy skin as she ∧(reclined) in the middle of the park. She kept one eye on the romantic novel that she held in her hand, and the other peering through the summer haze at Ollie as he charged around the open space with the other boys. It was difficult to concentrate on anything in this weather; Monica had felt harassed and tormented by the relentless, sweltering heat all week. // Her mind wandered from the novel, and she began to ponder the evening ahead. She had originally planned to wear her comfortable but contemporary denim skirt with her favourite brown boots. This was certainly not an option in this weather though. She would have to think of something else. Perhaps the floral dress that she had worn last summer to Rachel's wedding would work.

Suddenly, her rambling mind was brought back to reality with a start. A loud scream resonated around the park. Monica jumped to her (feet) feet and began running.

Make sure you use semi-colons and colons correctly.

(para)

Commas can be used between two adjectives or before a joining word that is being used to link two points.

Think carefully about how you link your paragraphs.

Accuracy is important, but don't let it put you off using a wide range of vocabulary and sentence structures.

Be careful with your tenses — make sure they're consistent.

Correct any mistakes clearly and neatly.

Follow these simple instructions to produce a SPaG-tastic answer...

Getting your SPaG right is super important, but don't let it put you off using a wide range of vocabulary and sentence types. You need to find a good balance between accuracy and imagination in order to do well.

Information and Ideas

These two pages will help you to deal with assessment objective 1 (see p.2). This page is about picking out information from a text, and the next page is about summarising information from two different texts.

Information and ideas can be explicit or implicit

1) The first thing you need to be able to do in order to <u>analyse</u> a text is to <u>understand</u> the basic things it's <u>telling you</u>.

2) This will help you to pick up some <u>easy marks</u> for <u>paper 1</u>, <u>question 1</u> and <u>paper 2</u>, <u>question 1</u>.

3) The information and ideas you need to pick out will either be <u>explicit</u> or <u>implicit</u>.

4) <u>Explicit</u> information is <u>clearly written</u> in the text.

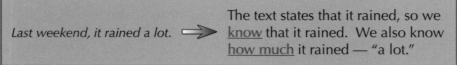

"It rained HOW much?"

> *Last weekend, it rained a lot.* ⟹ The text states that it rained, so we <u>know</u> that it rained. We also know <u>how much</u> it rained — "a lot."

5) <u>Implicit</u> information needs a little more <u>detective work</u> — you'll need to work it out from what is said in the text.

> *The castle was dark, decrepit and freezing cold.* ⟹ In this sentence, it is <u>implied</u> that the author doesn't like the castle very much, but this isn't stated outright.

Underline the relevant facts as you read the text

PAPER 1

| 0 | 1 |

Read again the first part of the source, lines 1 to 9.

List **four** things from this part of the text about Brian's school.

The facts that you use in your answer must come from the part of the text mentioned in the question.

If a question asks you to 'list' something, all you need to do is find the information in the text. You don't need to analyse it at all.

> Brian had hated school. He often thought back to the dreary <u>breezeblock walls</u>, the <u>freezing classrooms</u> and the <u>constant drone</u> of the <u>centuries-old plumbing</u>.
>
> St Mary's had been the closest school to Brian's house, but that was an all-girls school. This meant that every morning Brian had had to withstand the torment of a fifteen-minute bus journey across town to <u>Beeches Hall</u> — the <u>boys' school</u>. This bus journey would have been perfectly tolerable had it not been for the driver: a peculiar, unpleasant man with a severely erratic driving style.

As you read the relevant part of the text, underline the facts that you will use to answer the question.

Make sure your facts are linked to the topic the question asked about.

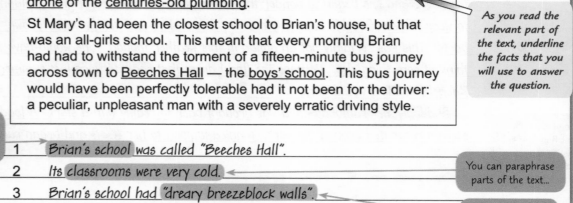

1   Brian's school was called "Beeches Hall".

2   Its classrooms were very cold.

3   Brian's school had "dreary breezeblock walls".

4   The school's plumbing was very old.

You can paraphrase parts of the text...

... or you can quote directly from it.

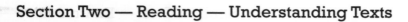

Information and Ideas

You'll also need to summarise information

1) Paper 2, question 2 will ask you to pick out information and ideas on the <u>same topic</u> from two <u>different texts</u>.

2) You'll then need to <u>summarise</u> the <u>similarities</u> or <u>differences</u> in what you've picked out.

3) You'll also need to <u>back up</u> your points with examples from the text.

4) <u>Linking words</u> are essential for writing about similarities and differences, as they show that you've made a <u>comparison</u>.

To show similarities:
- Similarly
- Equally
- Likewise
- Also

To show differences:
- Whereas
- However
- Although
- But

These are a few examples of linking words, but there are plenty more.

Make links between the texts

PAPER 2

0 2   Use details from both sources.
Write a summary of the differences between Andrew and Richard.

Look out for obvious differences between the two texts, e.g. Andrew's and Richard's ages, but don't just limit yourself to explicit details.

Source A — 20th century diary

Friday 21 March 1947
What a truly miserable afternoon. Daddy shouted at me just for being late to school. "You should be more responsible now you're thirteen, Andrew!" he was yelling. He even said he had half a mind to stop wasting his money on my private education. I know he's angry, but I think his outburst was a bit of an overreaction.

Source B — 19th century diary

Saturday 12 September 1868
Today was Richard's 16th birthday party, but it was not such a celebration after all. Richard sat quietly all evening, his hands folded in his lap, as Father ranted about how the party was a waste of the little money we have. Richard only broke his silence to acknowledge Father's tirade with a respectful "Yes, Sir".

Use linking words to show that you've thought about how the texts are similar or different.

Andrew is willing to challenge ideas, as he remarks that his father has overreacted. His defensive tone suggests that he feels he knows better than his father. In contrast, Richard seems much meeker and less cheeky. He sits quietly with "his hands folded in his lap", referring to his father as "Sir", even though he's shouting at him. This is perhaps a result of the fact that their situations are very different: Richard is a nineteenth-century boy from a family with "little money", whereas Andrew is a twentieth-century boy who has had an expensive "private education".

You can make more perceptive observations by commenting on the tone of the texts.

Richard's body language has shown the reader something about his personality.

Use quotes to support the comparisons you make.

It's really no scarier than an elaborate game of spot the difference...

You'll need to sharpen up your observation skills for these kinds of questions — comment on the explicit differences between each text, but don't forget to dig a bit deeper and write about implicit ideas too.

Audience

In the exams, you'll need to think about the audience — the intended readers of the text.

Writers aim their work at general or specific audiences

1) The writer will always have a group of people in mind when they write — this is their audience.

2) The audience of a text can be quite general, e.g. adults, or more specific, e.g. parents with children under the age of 3.

3) Some texts will have more than one audience, e.g. children's books will try to appeal to the kids who read them, but also to the parents who will buy them.

How about this one, Jonny? 'Dictionary' by Colin English. Sounds like a ripping yarn.

Look for clues about the target audience

1) Sometimes you can work out who the target audience is by the text's content (subject matter):

This latest model is a beautiful car. Its impressive engine can send you shooting from 0-60 mph in less than 8 seconds. This text is clearly aimed at someone who's interested in high-performance cars.

2) The vocabulary (choice of words) can tell you about the target audience, e.g. about the age group:

Today, we witnessed a discussion on fox hunting. As one can imagine, this issue, although it has been debated for many years, still managed to elicit mixed emotions from all concerned. The sophisticated vocabulary, like 'elicit', rather than 'bring out', and the complex sentences show that this text is aimed at adults.

Dungeon Killer 3 is the hottest new game of the year! There are 52 awesome levels and 6 cool new characters — don't miss out on the wildest gaming experience of your life! This one uses modern slang and simple sentences, so it's clear that this text is aimed at younger people.

3) The language can also give you clues about the target audience's level of understanding:

The object of a game of football is to get the ball in the opposing team's goal. Sounds easy, but the other team has the same thing in mind. Also, there are eleven players on the other team trying to stop you. The simple, general explanations in this text show that it's written for people who don't know much about football.

The next hole was a par 3 and I hit my tee shot directly onto the green. Sadly, my putting let me down badly, and I ended up getting a bogey. The technical vocabulary here shows that this is for people who know quite a bit about golf.

And now we'll take any questions from the audience...

You need to work out who the intended audience of a text is so that you can discuss the writer's purpose, the techniques they use and how successful they are. Keep the target audience in mind throughout your answer.

Writer's Purpose

Writers rarely write something just for the benefit of their health. Unless it's a letter to their doctor...

There are four common purposes of writing

Pages 22-25 tell you how to spot a text's purpose, and how you can discuss this in the exam.

1) The <u>purpose</u> of a text is the <u>reason</u> that it's been written — what the writer is <u>trying to do</u>.

2) Most texts are written for <u>one</u> of these reasons:

To Argue or Persuade
- They give the writer's <u>opinion</u>.
- They get the reader to <u>agree</u> with them.

To Advise
- They <u>help</u> the reader to <u>do something</u>.
- They give <u>instructions</u> on what to do.

To Inform
- They <u>tell</u> the reader about something.
- They help the reader to increase their <u>understanding</u> of a subject.

To Entertain
- They are <u>enjoyable</u> to read.
- They make the reader <u>feel</u> something.

3) Lots of texts have <u>more than one</u> purpose, though. E.g. a biographical text could be written to both <u>inform</u> and <u>entertain</u> its audience.

4) In the exams, read the texts carefully and make sure that you think about <u>what</u> the writers are trying to <u>achieve</u> (and <u>how</u> they're achieving it).

5) Look out for super helpful exam questions that actually <u>tell you</u> the writer's purpose. E.g. if the question asks you about how the writer uses language to <u>influence</u> the reader, you know it's about <u>persuading</u>.

Purpose is more obvious in non-fiction texts

1) The purpose of most <u>non-fiction</u> texts is usually quite <u>obvious</u>. For example:

> If a speech is trying to <u>argue</u> a particular point of view, the writer might make this very <u>clear</u> to make the argument more <u>powerful</u>.

2) Look out for texts where it might be <u>less obvious</u>, though. For example:

> A <u>magazine article</u> is primarily written to <u>entertain</u> its audience, so it might use a <u>chatty</u> tone to engage the reader. This might make it <u>less obvious</u> that it's also trying to <u>argue</u> a particular point of view.

Barry's porpoise in life had always been to entertain.

3) A piece of fiction's most obvious purpose is to <u>entertain</u>, but writers sometimes use entertainment to achieve <u>another purpose</u>.

> Lots of fiction texts are <u>entertaining</u> stories on the surface, but they can contain <u>another message</u>. The writer might want to <u>argue</u> their own point of view or <u>inform</u> the reader about something.

This page was no accident — I wrote it on purpose...

So purpose can be a little harder to figure out than you'd think. If there's more than one purpose to a text, write about them both. And if you can write about how one purpose is used to achieve another, even better.

Informative Texts

I don't want to blow your mind or anything, but this page about informative texts is *itself* an informative text.

Informative writing tells you something

1) When writing an informative text, the writer's aim is to pass on <u>knowledge</u> to the reader as <u>clearly</u> and <u>effectively</u> as possible.

Have a look back at p.20 for more on audience.

2) They will adapt their <u>language</u> to match their intended <u>audience</u>, e.g. they <u>might</u> need to write for different <u>age groups</u>, or for people with different <u>levels of understanding</u>.

3) Purely informative texts will present information in a <u>balanced</u> and <u>factual</u> way. They will contain lots of <u>facts</u> and <u>figures</u>, but no <u>opinions</u>.

4) Some informative texts might also be <u>arguing</u> a particular viewpoint, though. For example:

> Many newspapers <u>carefully pick</u> information that supports a particular political party. Even though a newspaper article may not say outright what its opinion is, it can still be <u>biased</u>.

Bias is when a piece of writing is influenced by the opinion of its author — see page 42.

Read the passage carefully

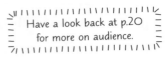

0 1   Choose **four** statements below which are TRUE.

- Shade the boxes of the ones that you think are true
- Choose a maximum of four statements.

Contains facts like dates and statistics.

> The Mini first went on sale in 1959 and is widely regarded as a great icon of British culture. Soon after its release, the Mini became the bestselling car in Europe. Over five million of them were made and many famous people, including The Beatles, bought them.
>
> The Mini is still around today, although it has undergone some major changes. It was originally conceived as an affordable car for the people, but now it is made by BMW and aimed at a different market. Nevertheless, the Mini remains a very popular car to this day.

Uses clear, direct language.

Formal tone makes the information feel reliable.

This is phrased differently in the text, but it's still true.

A	The Mini went on sale in the late 1950s.	■
B	The Mini has sold very well over time.	■
C	The Mini isn't very popular anymore.	☐
D	BMW have always manufactured Minis.	☐
E	Minis have changed over time.	■
F	The Mini was the bestselling car in the world.	☐
G	The Mini is not aimed at the same market as it used to be.	■
H	The Beatles advertised the Mini.	☐

You can only go on what the text says, and it only mentions that the Mini was the 'bestselling car in Europe', so this must be false.

You were promised informative, and you got informative...

Yes indeedio, there's plenty of information here to keep you occupied. You need to be able to recognise informative writing and explain how it's being used. And if the information is biased, be sure to point it out.

Entertaining Texts

After an informative text about informative texts, here's a (hopefully) entertaining text about entertaining texts.

Entertaining writing aims to be enjoyable to read

1) Entertaining writing is the sort of thing you'd read for <u>pleasure</u>, e.g. literary fiction.

2) Unlike informative texts, they contain <u>few facts</u>. Instead, they try to make you <u>feel</u> something, like <u>scared</u>, <u>excited</u>, or <u>amused</u>.

3) Entertaining writing is often very <u>descriptive</u>, and uses <u>narrative techniques</u> to make texts more enjoyable to read (see p.43-44).

4) Writers can also use <u>structural techniques</u> and different <u>sentence forms</u> to create entertaining texts (see p.45-49). E.g. lots of <u>short</u>, <u>punchy</u> sentences can be used to make a text feel more <u>exciting</u>.

Tony's bank statement was lacking in entertaining passages.

> Writers might use entertaining writing to <u>engage</u> a reader when they have <u>another</u> purpose in mind. E.g. travel books are <u>entertaining non-fiction</u>, which are also <u>informative</u>.

Think about what makes the text entertaining

PAPER 1

| 0 | 2 | How does the writer use language here to entertain the reader?

> He could feel the power of the bike humming beneath him as they both hurtled along. They were an elegant couple skimming the dance floor, whirling past plodding onlookers in their graceless automobiles, twisting around sweeping corners with effortless precision and darting along endless straights as they pushed each other on towards the inevitable conclusion. The bike hit the wall with all its hulking force.

Lots of creative vocabulary makes the text more interesting.

The text uses imagery to make the description come to life.

Different sentence lengths vary the pace of the text, making it more interesting.

In order to entertain the reader, the writer uses an extended metaphor that personifies the bike as a dance partner. The bike and the rider become an "elegant couple" whose movements contrast with the "plodding" and "graceless" cars. The writer uses a long sentence to develop this metaphor and build tension. This lengthy second sentence contains several verbs that are related to dancing and speed, such as "whirling" and "darting". The cumulative effect of these verbs makes the reader feel tense. It is as if the sentence is rushing and building towards a conclusion. The writer then disperses this tension with the final short sentence. The phrase "hit the wall" is very blunt, and contrasts to the preceding build-up, adding to the shock and impact of the conclusion.

Use key words from the question to keep your answer focused.

You need to use technical terms.

Try to identify how the writer uses different parts of speech.

You should analyse the language at both word and sentence level.

Write about the writer's intentions and the effects of their language on the reader.

Fortunately, I know a thing or two about entertaining writing...

Entertaining writing really helps to keep readers interested. So even if a writer's main purpose is to inform, argue, persuade or advise, they might still want to make their writing entertaining so the reader enjoys it.

Texts that Argue or Persuade

So many texts are written to argue. If only there was some way we could persuade them all to just get along...

Arguing and persuading are similar

1) When people write to argue, they want to make the reader agree with their opinion. They use clear and forceful language to get their points across, and they might use facts and figures to back up points.

2) Persuasive writing tries to get the reader to do something, such as support a charity. It does this with techniques including emotive language that aims to make the reader sympathise with their cause.

3) When writing to persuade, writers might sometimes be more sneaky about their aims and opinions. For example:

> *It is clear that this is a good school, and that people who attend it do well.* → This writer uses the phrase 'It is clear' to make their opinion sound like fact. This can make the writing sound more informative, when actually it's persuasive.

4) When writing to argue or persuade, writers often use rhetorical devices such as hyperbole, repetition or rhetorical questions (see p.41).

Explain the effects of the writer's choice of language

PAPER 2

| 0 | 3 | How does the writer use language here to influence the reader?

WHY BOTHER WITH BREAKFAST?

David Barowsky, *nutritional analyst*

The writer uses statements to make their point clearly and forcefully.

Eating breakfast improves mental and physical performance. This is a well-known and incontrovertible fact. And yet 20 million of us Britons regularly skip this essential refuelling opportunity. Why is this the case? Are we too busy commuting, getting the kids ready for school, blow-drying our hair? Do you often feel frantic and harassed in the morning? Well, the time has come to change your ways. Allowing your kids to skip breakfast is reckless and irresponsible. You are not providing them with the energy they need to face the day.

Uses rhetorical questions.

Facts and figures are used to back up their argument.

Addresses the reader directly using the pronoun 'you'.

Try to use varied vocabulary to describe the effects of the writer's language on the reader.

> The writer captures the reader's attention by using an alliterative rhetorical question as a title. Barowsky then immediately, and assertively, answers the question in the first line. This makes the writer sound both authoritative and knowledgeable, so readers are more likely to trust him and follow his advice to "bother with breakfast".
> Barowsky also uses the personal pronouns "you" and "we" to establish a connection with the reader, whilst adjectives like "reckless" and "irresponsible" encourage an emotional response. This connection gives the writer a platform from which he can challenge the reader's actions without sounding as if he's attacking them.

Try to use technical terms wherever you can.

Analyse the effects of individual words.

Persuasive texts are great, don't you agree? I knew you would...

If a writer is trying to argue a point or persuade you to do something, they're trying to make you see things from their point of view. It'll be one-sided, with carefully chosen evidence that supports their point of view.

Texts that Advise

Good advice is hard to come by these days, but don't panic — there's no shortage of it here.

Writing to advise sounds clear and calm

1) When writing to <u>advise</u>, writers want their readers to <u>follow their suggestions</u>.

2) The tone will be <u>calm</u> and <u>less emotional</u> than writing that argues or persuades.

3) The advice will usually be <u>clear</u> and <u>direct</u>. For example, it might use:

- <u>Vocabulary</u> that matches the audience's <u>subject knowledge</u>.
- <u>Second person</u> pronouns (e.g. 'you') to make the advice feel <u>personal</u>.
- A <u>logical structure</u> that makes the advice <u>easy to follow</u>.

4) The register (see p.32) may be <u>formal</u>, e.g. in a letter from a solicitor offering legal advice, or <u>informal</u>, e.g. in a magazine advice column.

All Jemima needed was some clear advice from her stylist.

Writing to advise looks like this

PAPER 2

| 0 | 3 | | How does Claire Lohan use language here to guide the reader? |

YOUR MONEY MATTERS

Claire Lohan
independent financial advice

Which is the right pension for me?

Before you buy into a pension, you need to be sure that it's the right one for you — dropping out can mean that you lose a lot of the money you've already paid in.

You should look at the pension company's reputation, past results and penalties for changing schemes.

It might sound scary, but don't worry, you'll find the right one for you.

Uses questions the reader might have.

Addresses the reader directly by using the pronoun' you'.

Friendly warning.

Uses specific details to give practical advice.

Reassures the reader.

The writer uses a friendly tone to communicate her advice in a clear, accessible way. When she says, "you need to be sure", it sounds as if she is talking to a friend. This makes the reader more likely to take the advice, as it seems well-meant and helpful.

The language that the writer uses is specific but uncomplicated. She gives detailed advice, such as "look at the pension company's reputation, past results and penalties". This makes the writer seem well informed and knowledgeable. As a result, the reader is more likely to think that the advice is worthwhile, and act on it.

Remember to explain the effect of the quote.

Explain what sort of impression this type of language creates.

Show that you know what effect it will have on the reader.

Develop the point — say why the writer has chosen this style.

Stay focused on the writer's use of language.

If you want my advice, I'd read through this page a couple of times

Texts that advise can be written for many different audiences, but a lot of the features will stay the same. Pay attention to whether the language is formal or informal — it'll vary depending on the subject and audience.

Writer's Viewpoint and Attitude

Paper 2 is all about writers' viewpoints and attitudes, especially that big ol' question 4...

Viewpoint and attitude are different to purpose

1) A writer's purpose is what they're trying to <u>do</u>, but their <u>viewpoint</u> (or attitude) is what they <u>think</u> about the <u>topics</u> that they're writing about.

2) You can work out what a writer's viewpoint might be by looking for clues in the <u>language</u>, <u>tone</u>, <u>style</u> and <u>content</u> of a text. For example:

> *I urge you to visit this truly unique and hidden valley — you must see such beautiful scenery at least once in your life.*

⟹ This text's <u>purpose</u> is to <u>persuade</u> its audience to visit a place. The <u>author's viewpoint</u> is their <u>belief</u> that the valley is beautiful and that it should be visited. The writer uses <u>emotive adjectives</u> and an <u>upbeat tone</u> to convey their viewpoint.

Use the writers' tone to make inferences about attitude

0 4   Compare how the two writers convey their different attitudes to manners and politeness.

Source A — 19th century etiquette guide

> The way you behave when out in society is paramount. It is essential that you show the highest level of social refinement possible. For example, if someone offers you their hand, take it. Always remove your hat when entering a building. Be punctual to all social events to which you are invited.

Source B — 21st century newspaper article

> Anyone who's ever taken a ride on the London Underground will know that there are some real nuisances out there. All too often, I've seen people refusing to give their seat up to an elderly passenger. I mean, it's just common courtesy, isn't it? Is it really so difficult to just be a little more civil towards other people?

Try to make your observations as perceptive as possible. Examiners will be really impressed if you can pick out subtle differences between the writers' attitudes.

This is a useful phrase to use when you're linking the two texts.

The authors of both sources largely agree that being polite is important. However, there are subtle differences in their attitudes. The author of source A focuses on etiquette in specific situations. They use a confident, assured tone, which is created by the use of imperative verbs such as "take" and "remove". They also give their advice using the pronoun "you", which makes the text sound more like a series of commands than a piece of advice. These things suggest that their ideas about "refinement" are very strict.

By contrast, the author of source B has a more laid-back attitude towards the need for "common courtesy". Rather than telling the reader how to behave as in source A, they use an example and rhetorical questions to make the reader think about why people should be "more civil". This is possibly because source B is from the 21st century, whereas source A was written in the 19th century — a time when etiquette was considered to be much more important.

Looking at the writer's tone is usually a good place to start.

Use technical terms to discuss the different methods both writers use to convey their attitude.

Think about the reasons why their attitudes differ — think about when and why they were written.

These writers are just full of attitude...

Remember, you need to go beyond just <u>what</u> the writer's saying and think about <u>how</u> they're expressing their viewpoint. Even if two writers have the same opinion, one might express it more strongly than the other.

Section Two — Reading — Understanding Texts

Literary Fiction

In paper 1, you'll be given an extract from a piece of literary fiction. So that's a snippet from a nice reading book — shame you won't be able to read it tucked up in bed with a lovely mug of hot chocolate though...

Literary fiction entertains the reader

1) Literary fiction, such as a novel or short story, is written to <u>entertain</u>. It might do this by affecting the reader's <u>emotions</u>, describing the <u>atmosphere</u> of a place, using an intriguing <u>structure</u> or developing the <u>personality</u> of a <u>character</u>.

2) All literary fiction has a <u>narrator</u>. It's most often either a <u>first-person</u> (uses 'I' and 'we') or <u>third-person</u> (uses 'he', 'she' and 'they') narrator.

3) Literary fiction uses lots of <u>descriptive</u> and <u>figurative</u> language (e.g. metaphors, similes, analogy and personification) to capture the reader's <u>imagination</u>.

4) Literary fiction is also <u>structured</u> to interest the reader — texts will often build the <u>tension</u> towards a dramatic climax, or they might use <u>repetition</u> to change the <u>pace</u> of a text.

5) <u>Dialogue</u> is also often used to move the plot along and give insight into the <u>thoughts</u> and <u>feelings</u> of different characters.

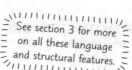

Gary thought he was entertaining, and a character, but no-one wanted to get to know his personality.

© Ljupco/iStockphoto.com

See section 3 for more on all these language and structural features.

Look closely at the language used in a text

PAPER 1

| 0 | 2 | How does the writer use language here to interest the reader? |

These adjectives set the scene as an uninviting place.

The use of very short sentences adds to the feeling of unease and suspense.

The writer uses Dorine's surroundings to tell the reader about her personality.

The narrative is third person, so the reader can see from the perspective of both Edward and Dorine.

Edward hurried down the dark, smog-filled alley. The place had become almost completely unrecognisable: the green fields he remembered from his childhood had long since been drowned in concrete. The alley became darker, and its bends and turns were increasingly disorientating. A creak. A whisper. Every noise put him on edge. But he pressed on.

Eventually, Edward found himself at Dorine's lab. He walked in, stooping to avoid hitting his head on the low door frame. The lab was a large circular room; the walls were lined with hundreds of tattered books, and half-finished research papers lay strewn across the many desks.

The books seemed to whisper to each other, as if disconcerted by the presence of an outsider. Edward felt as though they were watching him.

Dorine was poring over some papers in front of her, and hadn't noticed that Edward had arrived. After a few moments, she looked up from her desk and saw Edward waiting. She could see the flicker of hope glimmering in his eyes — the hope that they might still be able to turn back the clock.

"I'm afraid it's not looking good, Ed," Dorine murmured.

My God, thought Edward. *How could we have let this happen?*

The use of the emotive verb 'drowned' shows that the writer doesn't like that the fields have been covered in concrete.

The fact that Edward carries on even though he is scared makes him seem admirable to the reader.

Personification makes it clear that Edward feels uncomfortable in this lab.

The word 'flicker' implies that there isn't much hope, which creates tension.

This rhetorical question makes the reader want to know what has happened, which creates suspense.

Narrative and descriptive techniques keep the reader interezzz...

There's a lot to learn on this page, but you're <u>always</u> going to have to answer some questions about a piece of literary fiction. That means you're going to need to know all of this stuff really well — best get cracking then...

Literary Non-Fiction

You've had literary fiction, and now it's time for literary non-fiction. Three guesses what the difference is...

Literary non-fiction is entertaining but factual

1) Literary non-fiction texts use <u>literary styles</u> and <u>techniques</u>, but they are based on <u>facts</u> or <u>real events</u>.

2) Non-fiction texts such as <u>biographies</u>, <u>autobiographies</u>, and <u>travel writing</u> will often be written in a similar style to literary fiction.

3) They are written to <u>inform</u> the reader about something, but the writer uses a literary style to make it <u>entertaining</u> too. For example, they might use <u>descriptive</u> language and <u>dialogue</u> to make the information more <u>interesting</u> to the reader.

4) Literary non-fiction is almost always written in the <u>first person</u>, which adds a sense of <u>personality</u> to the text, helping to <u>engage</u> the reader.

Have a look back at the previous page to remind yourself about literary style.

Literary non-fiction tries to engage the reader

PAPER 2

0 3 How does the writer use language to describe their time in Paris?

Directly addresses the reader, making them feel more involved.

Dearest reader — I wish today to impart to you some recollections of my summer spent in Paris, a city which over time has played host to a multitude of great thinkers and artists. A hundred years may have passed since the French Revolution, but Paris remains a shining beacon of revolutionary spirit.

The text uses lots of emotive adjectives to clearly show the writer's viewpoint. Purely informative non-fiction wouldn't use adjectives like these.

Contains facts and refers to real places to inform the reader.

The city of Paris has some spectacular specimens of architecture. One bright evening, I took a particularly enjoyable stroll down the Champs-Élysées, and was quite amazed by the stunning curvature of its Arc de Triomphe. The arch incited within me the strongest feelings of awe and wonderment; it is truly a structure built to inspire.

The writer's viewpoint gives the description a positive tone.

The language used in this text is quite formal, which makes the writer seem more authoritative.

Paris has been ever-popular with the gentleman traveller, but this year the city captures one's imagination more than ever before, as it hosts the annual 'World's Fair'. There I saw many wonderful artefacts, including a magnificent replica of the Bastille, the famous site of the rebellion which began France's Revolution. The replica was incredibly lifelike, from the gloomy outer stonework to the banquet hall within.

This description adds detail, which helps things come to life for the reader.

This sentence creates suspense by not revealing what the 'real star' is right away.

Although the fortress was a thrilling diversion, it was far from the real star of the fair — that honour belonged to the newly-erected 'Eiffel Tower', said to be the largest building on Earth. The new tower amazed fair-goers with its enormous metallic form (although some were not altogether thrilled by its brash modernity). Whether one marvels at this remarkable feat of engineering, or recoils from its audacious magnitude, the new tower is assuredly a sight to behold.

Ends with a strong, memorable statement that will stay in the reader's mind.

We'll always have (a non-fiction text about) Paris...

You probably haven't had much contact with the phrase "literary non-fiction" before, but don't let the jargon fool you — it's just a category that describes any text that is factual, but is written in an entertaining way.

19th-Century Texts

In paper 2, you'll always be given a 19th-century non-fiction text to analyse. Chances are you weren't around much in those days, so this page should have some pretty useful information for you.

19th-century writing is often quite formal

> In the exam, any words in the text that aren't used today will be defined for you in a glossary.

1) 19th-century texts can sound a bit <u>different</u> to more modern texts, but you should still be able to <u>understand</u> what's going on.

2) A lot of the texts will use a more <u>formal register</u> (see p.32) than modern writing, even if the <u>audience</u> is quite <u>familiar</u> (see next page for an example of this).

3) The sentences may be <u>quite long</u> and the <u>word order</u> can sometimes be different to modern texts. Try not to worry about this — just <u>re-read</u> any sentences you can't make sense of at first. Here are a couple of examples:

Then, Albert being gone and we two left alone, Edward enquired as to whether I might accompany him on a stroll in the garden.	This sentence is written using a <u>formal</u> register, e.g. it uses 'enquired' instead of 'asked'. It might seem a bit <u>confusingly phrased</u> too, but 'Albert being gone and we two left alone' is just <u>another way</u> of saying 'Albert had gone and the two of us were left alone.'
I believe it necessary to abandon this foul enterprise.	Sometimes it can seem as if a word has been <u>missed out</u> — modern writers would probably put 'is' after 'it' in this sentence.

19th-century society was different to today

1) Knowing about 19th-century <u>society</u> will help you to <u>understand</u> the text better in the exam.

2) It will also help you to compare the <u>viewpoints</u> and <u>perspectives</u> of writers from different <u>time periods</u> (which you need to do for paper 2, question 4).

Social Class

- Early 19th-century society was <u>divided</u> between the rich <u>upper classes</u> (who owned the land) and the poorer <u>working classes</u>.

- Throughout the 19th century, the <u>Industrial Revolution</u> was creating opportunities for more people to make more <u>money</u>.

- This meant that the <u>middle classes</u> grew in <u>number</u> and <u>influence</u> throughout the century.

Education

- In the <u>early</u> 19th century, <u>few</u> children went to school. Children from poor families often <u>worked</u> to help support their families instead.

- In the <u>late</u> 19th century, <u>education reforms</u> made school <u>compulsory</u> for all young children.

- <u>Rich</u> families often sent their children to <u>boarding school</u>, or they hired a <u>governess</u> to live with the family and teach the children at <u>home</u>.

Women

- After they got married, most women were expected to be in charge of looking after the <u>home</u> and <u>children</u>.

- Women didn't have as many <u>rights</u> as men — they couldn't <u>vote</u> in elections and they often didn't <u>control</u> their own money and property.

Religion

- <u>Christianity</u> had a big influence — most of the <u>middle</u> and <u>upper classes</u> attended <u>church</u> regularly.

- However, <u>science</u> was starting to challenge some religious ideas, e.g. Darwin's theory of <u>evolution</u> questioned the Bible's account of <u>creation</u>.

19th-Century Texts

Have a look at this piece of 19th-century writing

This is a letter written to Princess (later Queen) Victoria of the United Kingdom by her uncle, King Leopold I of Belgium. In it, Leopold describes his new wife, Louise Marie.

Laeken, 31st August 1832.

MY DEAREST LOVE,—You told me you wished to have a description of your new Aunt. I therefore shall both mentally and physically describe her to you.

She is extremely gentle and amiable, her actions are always guided by principles. She is at all times ready and disposed to sacrifice her comfort and inclinations to see others happy. She values goodness, merit, and virtue much more than beauty, riches, and amusements. With all this she is highly informed and very clever; she speaks and writes English, German and Italian; she speaks English very well indeed. In short, my dear Love, you see that I may well recommend her as an example for all young ladies, being Princesses or not.

Now to her appearance. She is about Feodore's* height, her hair very fair, light blue eyes, of a very gentle, intelligent and kind expression. A Bourbon** nose and small mouth. The figure is much like Feodore's but rather less stout. She rides very well, which she proved to my great alarm the other day, by keeping her seat though a horse of mine ran away with her full speed for at least half a mile. What she does particularly well is dancing. Music unfortunately she is not very fond of, though she plays on the harp; I believe there is some idleness in the case. There exists already great confidence and affection between us; she is desirous of doing everything that can contribute to my happiness, and I study whatever can make her happy and contented.

You will see by these descriptions that though my good little wife is not the tallest Queen, she is a very great prize which I highly value and cherish...

Now it is time I should finish my letter. Say everything that is kind to good Lehzen***, and believe me ever, my dearest Love, your faithful Friend and Uncle,

LEOPOLD R.

Glossary

* Feodore — Victoria's half-sister, Princess Feodora

** Bourbon — the Bourbons were the French royal family

*** Lehzen — Princess Victoria's governess, Louise Lehzen

The tone is affectionate but the register is formal — this is common in 19th-century letters.

Being 'virtuous' was an important quality in 19th-century society — it means having strong morals.

Upper class women were considered to be accomplished by their ability in things like riding, dancing, playing music and speaking languages.

19th-century texts often phrase things differently — here, a modern writer might have said "I should end this letter here."

Upper class women were educated in European languages in the 19th century.

This shows the 19th-century viewpoint of what was valued in upper class women.

You might come across a tricky phrase or sentence. Use the context and the rest of the sentence to work out what's going on. Here, Leopold suggests that Louise Marie doesn't try very hard at playing the harp.

Women were often seen as belonging to their husbands.

Superlatives (e.g. 'kindest', 'most gracious' are common in 19th-century writing.

19th-century texts — unlikely to contain any emojis...

It's important to make sure you're comfortable reading and understanding 19th-century texts. This stuff might look a bit like History rather than English, but it'll really help you to improve some of your answers in the exam.

Tone

Tone can be a tricky little thing to put your finger on sometimes, but it comes through in the text's language.

Tone is the general feeling created by the text

1) A writer's tone is the <u>feeling</u> the words are written with, which creates a particular <u>mood</u> and shows what the writer's <u>attitude</u> is. For example, the tone of a text might be:

- happy or sad
- serious or funny
- sombre or light-hearted
- emotional and passionate or cool and logical

> Think of a writer's tone as being like someone's tone of voice when they're talking.

2) The main way to identify a text's tone is by looking at the <u>language</u>. For example, if a writer has used <u>informal</u> language, the tone might be quite <u>personal</u> or <u>familiar</u>, but <u>formal</u> language would suggest a more <u>serious</u> or <u>distant</u> tone.

3) <u>Punctuation</u> can also give you a clue about tone. For example, if there are lots of exclamation marks, that might suggest that the tone is very <u>emotional</u> or <u>passionate</u>.

4) Tone can reflect the <u>purpose</u> of a text (e.g. informative texts usually have a serious tone) or the <u>audience</u> (e.g. a playful tone might suggest a younger audience).

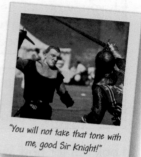

"You will not take that tone with me, good Sir Knight!"

Look closely at language to work out a text's tone

0 4 A student, having read this section of the text, said: "It seems like the character is in a scary place. Reading the text made me feel uneasy."

To what extent do you agree?

PAPER 1

> Phillipa stood on the cold, dark street, peering up at the abandoned hotel. Large wooden boards stood impassively across most of the window frames, sentries to the stillness and silence within, guarding the eerie presence of the dilapidated building.
>
> Despite her misgivings, she pushed gently on the front door, and it crept open with an arthritic creak. As she tiptoed over the threshold, small clouds of dust wheezed out of the carpet where she put her feet.

The sinister tone is gripping for the reader, which keeps the text entertaining.

The adjectives used help to create the foreboding tone.

Don't forget to mention how much you agree or disagree with the statement.

Remember to use technical terms wherever possible.

I strongly agree with the student's statement. The heavily foreboding tone, created by adjectives such as "abandoned", "eerie" and "dilapidated", and reinforced by the personification of the "wooden boards" as silent "sentries", gives the passage a tense atmosphere. The reader shares in the fear and anxiety of the character, as you feel that something shocking could happen at any moment. The imagery of something cold and emotionless watching over the character makes you feel her vulnerability and fear for what might happen next.

Mention the combined effect of different features of the text.

You need to make sure you refer back to the statement for questions like this.

My mum always told me to watch my tone...

Sometimes, the tone will jump right out at you. But watch out for texts that are written with an ironic or sarcastic tone — the words might not mean exactly what they seem to at first (take a look at pages 39-40).

Style and Register

Every text you come across will be written in a particular style, using a particular register...

Style is how the text is written

1) A text's <u>style</u> is the overall way in which it's written, which includes <u>language choices</u>, <u>sentence forms</u> and <u>structure</u>.

2) There are lots of <u>different styles</u> you might encounter. E.g. <u>cinematic</u>, where the text is written as if the reader is watching a film, or <u>journalistic</u> which is a balanced way of writing reported news.

3) <u>Register</u> is the specific language (choice of words) used to match the writing to the <u>social situation</u> that it's for. Different situations require <u>different</u> registers, for example:

> Register can be thought of as a part of style.

> If you wrote a letter to your <u>local MP</u> to ask them to stop the closure of a local leisure centre, you might use a <u>formal register</u> (e.g. 'the closure will have a detrimental effect'). This is because the audience is an <u>authority figure</u> that you <u>don't know</u>.

> If you wrote a letter to your <u>friend</u> to tell them about the leisure centre closure, you might use an <u>informal register</u> (e.g. 'it'll be rubbish when it shuts'). This is because the audience is someone you're <u>familiar</u> and <u>friendly</u> with.

4) Look out for how writers <u>adapt</u> their style and register to suit the <u>purpose</u> and the <u>audience</u> they are writing for.

Write about style and register when analysing language

PAPER 2

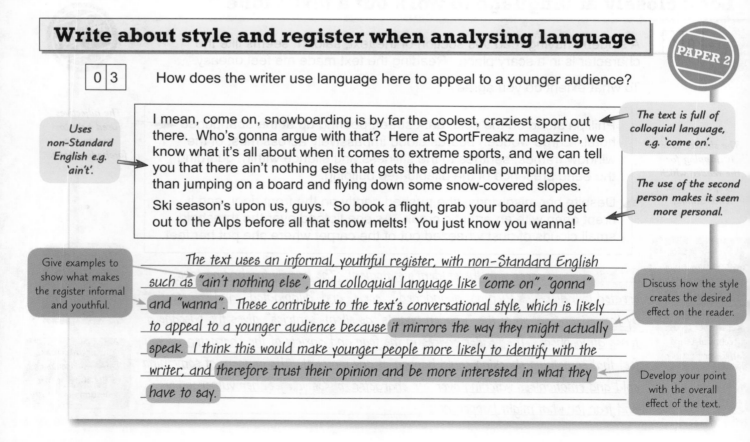

| 0 | 3 |

How does the writer use language here to appeal to a younger audience?

Uses non-Standard English e.g. 'ain't'.

I mean, come on, snowboarding is by far the coolest, craziest sport out there. Who's gonna argue with that? Here at SportFreakz magazine, we know what it's all about when it comes to extreme sports, and we can tell you that there ain't nothing else that gets the adrenaline pumping more than jumping on a board and flying down some snow-covered slopes.

Ski season's upon us, guys. So book a flight, grab your board and get out to the Alps before all that snow melts! You just know you wanna!

The text is full of colloquial language, e.g. 'come on'.

The use of the second person makes it seem more personal.

Give examples to show what makes the register informal and youthful.

The text uses an informal, youthful register, with non-Standard English such as "ain't nothing else", and colloquial language like "come on", "gonna" and "wanna". These contribute to the text's conversational style, which is likely to appeal to a younger audience because it mirrors the way they might actually speak. I think this would make younger people more likely to identify with the writer, and therefore trust their opinion and be more interested in what they have to say.

Discuss how the style creates the desired effect on the reader.

Develop your point with the overall effect of the text.

Yep, if there's one thing I know, it's style...

Style has to do with lots of things — language and vocabulary, structure, tone... so just think about how the style is built up from all these different bits and you'll be laughing in the exam. Well, not too loud, mind...

Words and Phrases

Writers don't just chuck in any old words — they painstakingly select them to produce the desired effect...

Writers use a range of word types

It's important to be able to identify the <u>types</u> of words that a writer is using.
Have a look at the <u>definitions</u> below to remind you:

> <u>Nouns</u> are naming words — they might refer to a person, place, thing or idea, e.g. sister, pen, art.
>
> A <u>pronoun</u> is a word that replaces a noun, e.g. he, she, it, them.
>
> <u>Possessive pronouns</u> are pronouns that show ownership, e.g. his, hers, ours, theirs.
>
> <u>Verbs</u> are action words, e.g. think, run, swim, shout.
>
> <u>Adjectives</u> describe a noun or pronoun, e.g. happy, clever, interesting.
>
> <u>Adverbs</u> give extra information about verbs, e.g. quickly, loudly, accidentally.

Words and phrases can be used to achieve different effects

1) For the <u>reading</u> questions (1-4 on both papers), you need to pay close attention to the reasons <u>why</u> a writer has used particular <u>words</u> or <u>phrases</u>.

   Analysing the connotations of words is a way of 'reading with insight'. There's more on this on pages 14-15.

2) Words can have subtle <u>implications</u> beyond their obvious meaning — these are called '<u>connotations</u>'. For example:

Pedro <u>shut</u> the door. *Pedro <u>slammed</u> the door.*	When the verb 'shut' is used, it <u>doesn't</u> imply anything about Pedro's <u>emotions</u>. The verb 'slammed' has a similar meaning to 'shut', but it gives the impression that Pedro is <u>angry</u> or <u>tense</u>.

I <u>sniggered</u> when I saw Peter's costume. *I <u>chuckled</u> when I saw Peter's costume.*	The verbs 'sniggered' and 'chuckled' both mean the writer <u>laughed</u>, but 'sniggered' has a slightly <u>nastier</u> connotation — as if the writer is making fun of Peter.

3) Words are often chosen to achieve particular <u>effects</u>. For example:

<u>my</u> *dear reader* <u>your</u> *beloved pet*	Phrases that use the <u>possessive determiners</u> 'my', 'your' and 'our' help to establish <u>familiarity</u> between the writer and the reader.

   Determiners are words that help to identify nouns — in this case, they show who the noun belongs to.

a <u>fundamentally</u> flawed proposition *a <u>totally</u> unbelievable situation*	Some phrases use <u>intensifiers</u> to make the text seem more <u>emotive</u> and <u>powerful</u>. Intensifiers are adverbs like 'very', 'really' or 'extremely' that are used <u>alongside</u> strong adjectives to provide <u>emphasis</u>.

Words and Phrases

Words work together to create cumulative effects

1) Writers can use the words from a specific <u>semantic field</u> (the words associated with a particular <u>theme</u> or <u>topic</u>) to convey an idea to the reader. For example:

> *Dessert was simply <u>divine</u>; a <u>cloud-like</u> puff of pastry that was lighter than an <u>angel's wing</u>.*

> Here, the <u>semantic field</u> of <u>heaven</u> is used to make something sound <u>appealing</u>.

2) Keep an eye out for situations where particular <u>types</u> of words are <u>repeated</u>, e.g. sentences with lots of <u>adjectives</u> or paragraphs with lots of <u>verbs</u>.

3) You could comment on the <u>cumulative effect</u> of particular types of words — show you've thought about how the words in the text <u>work together</u> to create <u>tone</u> or <u>affect</u> the reader in some way, e.g.

> *Adjectives like 'electrifying', 'thrilling', 'tense' and 'intriguing' create a cumulative effect of <u>excitement</u>.*

> *The adverbs 'jovially', 'readily' and 'pleasantly' combine to create an impression of <u>enjoyment</u>.*

Archie was keen to understand the cumulative effect of the words.

© Fly_dragonfly/iStockphoto.com

Try to pick out significant words and phrases

 PAPER

0 3 How does the writer use language here to influence the reader?

Adjectives like 'magical', 'beautiful', 'balmy', 'glistening' and 'sumptuous' have an alluring cumulative effect — they create a calming atmosphere.

Watch out for repeated grammatical constructions — they give the text emphasis.

Imperatives like 'sit back' and 'let us' give the text an authoritative tone, whilst the words 'perhaps' and 'maybe' give the impression that the reader has a choice.

A PICTURE-PERFECT PICNIC

Bijoux Birthdays invite you to celebrate your special day in style. Join us for a magical evening of entertainment on the beautiful banks of the River Fairer. Let us help you to relax in the balmy atmosphere of a warm summer's evening, recline next to the glistening waters and indulge in the most sumptuous of picnics.

We can tailor your evening to suit you. We can provide a refreshing feast for your senses. We can transport you to another place and time. Just sit back and let us do all the work. All you need to do is relax.

We have a large selection of menus for you to choose from, as well as a whole host of different entertainment acts — maybe you'd like a string quartet, or perhaps you'd be more interested in a circus act? Whatever your tastes, rest assured that we will be able to accommodate you.

If you're planning a celebration, Bijoux Birthdays really is the only choice.

Phrases that use possessive determiners establish familiarity with the reader and make the text more persuasive.

The list of three verbs — 'relax', 'recline' and 'indulge' — gives the text a convincing tone and makes the offer sound inviting.

Relax, it's just a phrase...

The technical grammar of words and phrases is important, but it's no good just pointing it out — you need to analyse its effects. Think about why certain words and phrases have been used and the impression they create.

Metaphors and Similes

Metaphors and similes are both types of imagery — writers use them to help readers imagine things vividly.

Metaphors and similes are comparisons

1) Metaphors and similes describe one thing by <u>comparing</u> it to something else.

> Metaphors describe something by saying that it <u>is</u> something else. → *His gaze <u>was</u> a laser beam, shooting straight through me.*

> <u>Similes</u> describe something by saying that it's <u>like</u> something else. They usually use the words <u>as</u> or <u>like</u>. → *Walking through the bog was <u>like</u> wading through treacle.*

Similes made Jeremy feel as if the world had been turned upside down.

2) They help writers to make their <u>descriptions</u> more creative and interesting.

3) Metaphors usually create a <u>more powerful image</u> than similes, because they describe something as if it <u>actually were</u> something else.

4) Metaphors and similes are most commonly used in <u>literature</u> and <u>literary non-fiction</u>.

See pages 27-28 for more on literature and literary non-fiction.

You should comment on the effect of metaphors and similes

0 2 How does the writer use language here to describe the situation the soldier is in? **PAPER 1**

Uses 'like' so it's a simile. →

The air clung to me like a warm, wet blanket. It was like living inside a horribly stifling nightmare. I just wanted to wake up, throw the blanket off the bed and breathe some cool, fresh air.

After a while, I couldn't tell what was nightmare and what wasn't. Once I was caught in an ambush, taking fire from three sides. The order came to fall back, and I found myself on my own. I tried to run, but my feet were blocks of concrete. ←

It's a metaphor, as he says his feet actually 'were' blocks of concrete.

Make sure you use the technical terms.

Remember the question — keep referring back to how language has been used to describe the soldier's situation.

The writer uses a simile to describe what the conditions felt like: "the air clung to me like a warm, wet blanket". This image really helps the reader to imagine how unpleasant and sticky it feels, but also helps to create a hostile and suffocating atmosphere.

By using the metaphor "my feet were blocks of concrete", the writer conveys the soldier's panic that, try as he might, he was too scared to flee. I think the use of these images makes the description really effective because it helps the reader to empathise with the soldier.

Develop your points by stating the effect of the language.

I met a phor once — he was a number...

Picking out metaphors and similes will help you to closely analyse the effect of language used in the exam texts. You might need to write about them on paper 1, questions 2 and 4, and paper 2, questions 3 and 4.

Analogy

Analogies are nifty little tricks which writers often use when they're writing to argue or persuade.

Analogies are really fancy comparisons

1) An analogy <u>compares</u> one idea to another to make it easier to <u>understand</u>.

Analogies are like extended similes (see p.35) — they also often use the word 'like'.

2) Analogies provide <u>powerful</u> and <u>memorable</u> images. They can be more <u>familiar</u> or more <u>shocking</u> than the original idea, which makes it easier for the reader to <u>grasp the point</u>. For example:

Deforestation is happening at an incredible speed. An area of rainforest equal to twenty football pitches is lost every minute. → By <u>comparing</u> the area to football pitches, the writer makes it easier to <u>visualise</u> the scale of the problem.

Hoping your exams will go OK without opening your books is like hoping to win the lottery without buying a ticket. → By <u>comparing</u> the chances of success to an impossible situation, the writer <u>emphasises</u> how unlikely it is.

3) Analogies are common in <u>non-fiction</u> texts that are trying to <u>argue</u> a point or <u>persuade</u>, as they can help to get the writer's viewpoint across <u>clearly</u> and <u>forcefully</u>.

Think about why the writer has used an analogy

PAPER 2

0 3 How does the writer use language to try to persuade the reader to agree with her viewpoint?

It's easy to throw facts and figures around, but very few people realise we are releasing almost 30 billion tonnes of greenhouse gases into the atmosphere every year. That's the equivalent of around 150 million blue whales.

The word 'equivalent' shows that this is a comparison.

By pumping these gases into the air, we are choking our planet. This is like starting a fire in your bedroom and slowly letting the room fill with thick, black smoke until you can't breathe.

Uses 'like', so this is another analogy.

It's good to make your point straight away.

The writer uses analogies to help persuade the reader. By comparing the amount of greenhouse gases released annually to "150 million blue whales", the writer helps the reader to understand and visualise the sheer volume of gas being produced. If they can visualise the problem, readers are more likely to be shocked and therefore share the writer's concerns.

It's great to embed quotes into your writing like this.

The analogy which compares polluting the atmosphere to filling your bedroom with "thick, black smoke" makes the threat of climate change seem like a more personal danger to the reader. This might scare the reader and help to persuade them to act on climate change.

Always mention the effect that language has on the reader.

I think I may have developed analogy to this page...

Writers use analogies to make their points clearer and easier to understand. They can also make a piece of writing more interesting — think about how you could use them in the writing section of your exams.

Personification

If it's info on personification you're after, sit back and let this page talk you through it...

Personification is describing a thing as a person

1) Personification describes something as if it's a <u>person</u>. This could be in the way something <u>looks</u>, <u>moves</u>, <u>sounds</u> or some other aspect of it. For example:

Describing an object as if it were alive
The desk groaned under the weight of the books.

Describing an abstract idea as if it were alive
Fear stalked the children with every step they took.

Describing an animal as if it were a person
The cunning fox smiled with a self-satisfied grin.

Try to think of other ways you could use personification in your own writing.

2) Personification makes a description <u>more vivid</u> (so it 'comes to life' for the reader).

3) It can also help to give a sense of the <u>viewpoint</u> or <u>attitude</u> of the <u>writer</u> or <u>character</u>:

Military helicopters prowled the city, their menacing mechanical voices threatening to stamp out the smallest sign of activity. ➞ This shows that the writer feels that the helicopters are an <u>intimidating</u> presence.

Think about how personification improves a description

PAPER 1

0 2   How does the writer use language here to describe the woodlands?

> To Catrin's mind, no pastime could better complement a summer's day than a stroll through the woodlands behind her uncle's house.
>
> As soon as she arrived, before she'd even unpacked, she would feel the forest calling to her. It was never long before she wandered into the cool embrace of the sunlight-dappled shade. The trees would smile as she meandered along the paths, and the friendly chatter of wildlife was always the very best company.

The forest has been given human qualities.

The shade has been personified as it embraces the girl.

The writer personifies the trees by describing how they are "calling" to Catrin. This creates an image of the woodland that is captivating and enticing, which makes the reader want to explore the woods with the character. The smiling trees and the "friendly chatter of wildlife" reinforce this positive image. It shows the reader how happy Catrin feels in her surroundings. This use of personification is effective because it shows that Catrin feels welcomed by the forest.

is is a paraphrase — entioning something m the text without a direct quote.

Examiners love short embedded quotes like this one.

This is good — the point ties into the previous paragraph.

Be clear on the question — mention how the personification adds to the description.

The exam papers cackled as the students filed in...

So personification's a bit of a tricky customer — it's not always as simple to spot as you'd think. When you're writing about personification, concentrate on why the writer's used it and what effect it has on the reader.

Alliteration and Onomatopoeia

Here's heaps hof hinformation hall habout halliteration hand honomatopoeia. Wait a minute...

Alliteration and onomatopoeia are about how words sound

1) Alliteration and onomatopoeia use the <u>sounds</u> of words to create an <u>effect</u>:

> <u>Alliteration</u> is when words that are close together begin with the <u>same sound</u>.
>
> → PM's panic!
> Close call for kids

> <u>Onomatopoeic</u> words <u>sound like</u> the noises they describe.
>
> → thud   crackle
> squish
> hiss   smash

Naina was less than impressed with Chris's attempt to spell 'onomatopoeia'.

2) <u>Alliteration</u> helps a writer to grab a reader's <u>attention</u>.

3) It's often used for <u>emphasis</u> and to make key points more <u>memorable</u>.

4) <u>Onomatopoeia</u> makes descriptions more <u>powerful</u> — it appeals to the reader's sense of <u>hearing</u>, which helps them <u>imagine</u> what the writer is describing.

Alliteration and onomatopoeia keep readers interested

PAPER 2

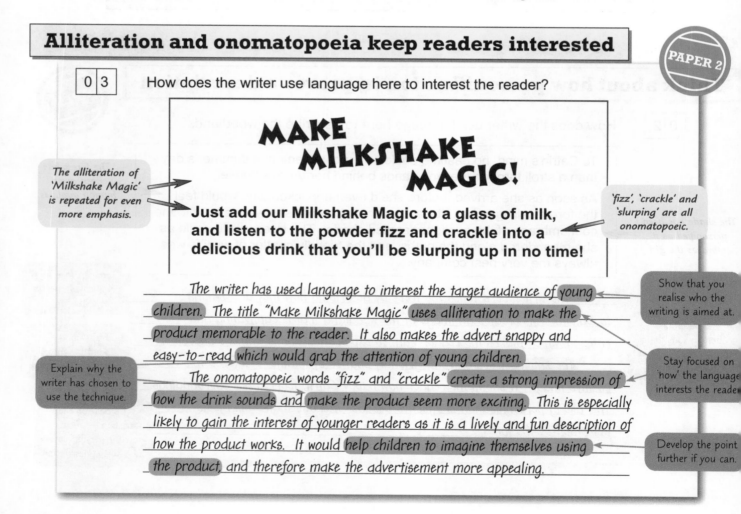

0 3   How does the writer use language here to interest the reader?

MAKE MILKSHAKE MAGIC!

Just add our Milkshake Magic to a glass of milk, and listen to the powder fizz and crackle into a delicious drink that you'll be slurping up in no time!

The alliteration of 'Milkshake Magic' is repeated for even more emphasis.

'fizz', 'crackle' and 'slurping' are all onomatopoeic.

The writer has used language to interest the target audience of young children. The title "Make Milkshake Magic" uses alliteration to make the product memorable to the reader. It also makes the advert snappy and easy-to-read which would grab the attention of young children.
The onomatopoeic words "fizz" and "crackle" create a strong impression of how the drink sounds and make the product seem more exciting. This is especially likely to gain the interest of younger readers as it is a lively and fun description of how the product works. It would help children to imagine themselves using the product, and therefore make the advertisement more appealing.

Show that you realise who the writing is aimed at.

Stay focused on 'how' the language interests the reader.

Explain why the writer has chosen to use the technique.

Develop the point further if you can.

Wait — how many vowels? No, that can't be right...

Yep, the first challenge that this page presents is learning to spell 'onomatopoeia'... But once you've got your head around that, you can enjoy the bloomin' brilliant bang that this page can bring to your writing.

Irony

Irony — nothing to do with clothes or metal, everything to do with the tone of a piece of writing.

Irony is saying the opposite of what you mean

1) Irony is when the <u>literal meaning</u> of a piece of writing is the exact <u>opposite</u> of its <u>intended meaning</u>.

2) The reader can tell the writer is being ironic from the <u>context</u> of the writing.

3) Writers often use irony to express their viewpoint, but it helps to make what they're saying more <u>humorous</u> or <u>light-hearted</u>.

> *It was pouring down with rain — perfect weather for a barbecue.* ⟹ The <u>context</u> (the rainy weather) shows that the writer actually means that it was <u>terrible</u> weather for a barbecue.

Irony can sometimes be a little tricky to spot

0 4 A student, having read this section of the text, said: "The writer makes the character's feelings really clear. It feels as if you really get to know her".

To what extent do you agree?

> Clara sat on her lounger at the edge of the pool, thinking of all the poor souls still trapped in the office. She'd been asked to travel to Spain for work. Stay hunched over her cramped, stuffy desk in London or work in this paradise? A very difficult decision indeed.
>
> As the sun rose higher in the sky and the temperature crept up, she thought of dreary, cloudy London. "It's a tough job" she thought to herself, "but somebody's got to do it".

You can tell she is being ironic because of the context — she describes it as a 'paradise' so it can't have been a 'difficult decision'.

I agree with the first part of this statement, though Clara's feelings are potentially open to misinterpretation. Her comments about a "difficult decision" and a "tough job" are negative if read literally, but the context makes it clear that they should be taken ironically. She clearly prefers being in Spain. Her office in London is "cramped", and the people are "trapped", whereas Spain is a "paradise". The irony emphasises just how happy she is by highlighting this contrast.

I also strongly agree with the second part of the student's statement. Her ironic tone shows that she isn't too serious, but that she is also perhaps quite unsympathetic. The contrast between her situation and that of the "poor souls" in the London office shows that whilst she is "thinking of all" of them, she is most interested in how pleasant her situation is. As a reader, this makes me unsure as to whether I like her character or not.

Don't forget to mention how much you agree or disagree with the statement.

Make sure you clearly explain why the language is ironic.

A further personal response is a good way to develop your answer.

Irony, yeah right, what a great technique...

It might seem confusing that exactly the same words can mean completely opposite things, but the context usually makes it fairly clear when a writer is trying to be ironic — otherwise it wouldn't be very effective.

Sarcasm

The word 'sarcasm' comes from a Greek word that means 'flesh tearing', so you just know it's gonna be fun.

Sarcasm is nastier than irony

1) <u>Sarcasm</u> is language that has a <u>mocking</u> or <u>scornful</u> tone. It's often intended to <u>insult someone</u> or <u>make fun</u> of them, or to show that the writer is <u>angry</u> or <u>annoyed</u> about something.

2) Sarcastic writing usually uses <u>irony</u> — but the tone is more <u>aggressive</u> and <u>unpleasant</u>.

Phil couldn't believe how many people liked his new hat.

> *The food took 90 minutes to arrive, which was just brilliant. I can think of no better way to spend a Saturday evening than waiting around for a plate of mediocre mush.*

→ The writer's used <u>irony</u> and a <u>sarcastic</u> tone to show his <u>frustration</u> and <u>anger</u> — it's meant to <u>insult</u> the restaurant that kept him waiting.

3) <u>Satire</u> is a kind of writing that uses sarcasm to <u>make fun</u> of a particular person or thing — it's often used in <u>journalism</u> and <u>reviews</u>.

Explain how you can tell a comment is sarcastic

PAPER 2

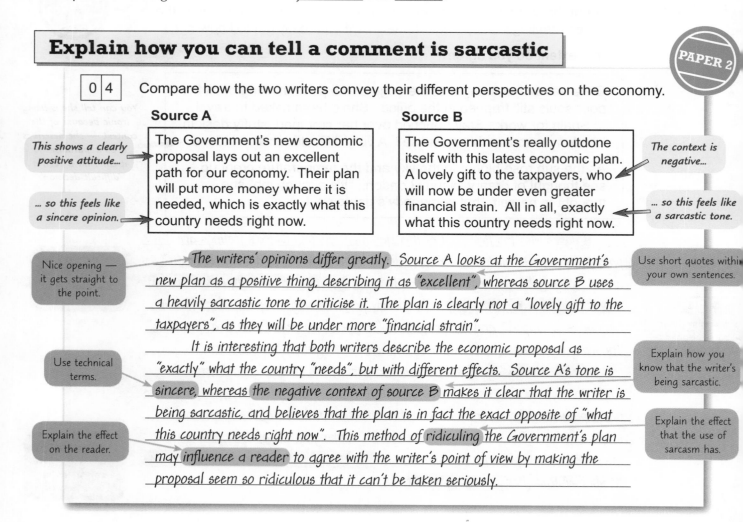

| 0 | 4 | Compare how the two writers convey their different perspectives on the economy.

Source A

This shows a clearly positive attitude...

The Government's new economic proposal lays out an excellent path for our economy. Their plan will put more money where it is needed, which is exactly what this country needs right now.

... so this feels like a sincere opinion.

Source B

The Government's really outdone itself with this latest economic plan. A lovely gift to the taxpayers, who will now be under even greater financial strain. All in all, exactly what this country needs right now.

The context is negative...

... so this feels like a sarcastic tone.

Nice opening — it gets straight to the point.

The writers' opinions differ greatly. Source A looks at the Government's new plan as a positive thing, describing it as "excellent", whereas source B uses a heavily sarcastic tone to criticise it. The plan is clearly not a "lovely gift to the taxpayers", as they will be under more "financial strain".

Use short quotes within your own sentences.

Use technical terms.

It is interesting that both writers describe the economic proposal as "exactly" what the country "needs", but with different effects. Source A's tone is sincere, whereas the negative context of source B makes it clear that the writer is being sarcastic, and believes that the plan is in fact the exact opposite of "what this country needs right now". This method of ridiculing the Government's plan may influence a reader to agree with the writer's point of view by making the proposal seem so ridiculous that it can't be taken seriously.

Explain how you know that the writer's being sarcastic.

Explain the effect that the use of sarcasm has.

Explain the effect on the reader.

Oh great, now sarcasm — even better than irony...

So the Greeks may have been on to something with the whole 'flesh tearing' thing... Sarcasm is often used to ridicule someone or something. Not the nicest thing to do, perhaps, but you can't say it's not effective.

Rhetoric

Rhetorical techniques make language more persuasive — see if this page can persuade you to keep going...

There are lots of rhetorical techniques

Think about how other techniques (e.g. alliteration, sarcasm) could be used as rhetorical devices.

1) Rhetorical questions require no answer — they make readers engage with the text and realise the answer for themselves. This makes the reader feel like they're making up their own mind, when actually the writer is trying to make them think a certain way.

> Is it right that footballers are paid such vast sums of money?

2) Writers often use a list of three words or phrases to emphasise the point they're making. They often repeat three adjectives.

> The cross-country run is painful, pointless and pure evil.

3) Hyperbole is intentional exaggeration. It's used to make a point very powerfully.

> We had to wait forever for the food to arrive.

4) Antithesis is a technique where opposing words or ideas are presented together to show a contrast.

> Just a small donation from you could have huge consequences for others.

5) Parenthesis is when an extra clause or phrase is inserted into a complete sentence. Parenthesis can be used in many ways, such as to add extra information or to directly address the reader.

> This issue, as I'm sure you all agree, is of the highest importance.

Rhetorical devices add impact to an argument

PAPER 2

| 0 | 3 | How does the writer use language to argue their point about homework?

This is a rhetorical question.

The writer repeats 'join me' three times.

This plan to give students across the country more homework is shocking. Can it really be fair to set us even more ridiculous and unnecessary assignments? It's as if they don't think we work every hour God sends already! Join me if you're interested in a better work/life balance. Join me to make our voices heard. Join me in my campaign for less homework!

Here's some hyperbole.

The writer uses 'we' and 'us' to include the reader.

Analysing the effect on the reader develops 'how' the writer has argued their point.

It's good to link your points together wherever possible.

The writer uses a number of rhetorical devices to persuade the reader that students should not be given more homework. The rhetorical question about whether it's fair to set more homework assignments is used to engage the reader. When combined with the forceful adjectives "ridiculous" and "unnecessary", this makes the reader think that it isn't fair, and therefore agree with the writer's point of view. This is immediately followed by the assertion that students are already working "every hour God sends". This hyperbolic statement makes an emphatic point about how hard students work, which generates sympathy from the reader and enhances the argument that more homework would be "shocking".

Opening statement is really focused on 'how' the writer argues their point.

Using the writer's words really backs up your analysis of their viewpoint.

Revision is a fun, exciting, thrilling way to spend a Friday night...

Rhetoric is a powerful tool, but I'm not sure it can convince us to love revision... Remember, there are lots of different types of rhetorical techniques, so keep your eyes peeled. Peeled eyes — now that's disgusting...

Bias

If a text is biased, it doesn't give a balanced view — the writer's opinion affects the writing.

Biased writing is affected by the writer's opinions

1) Biased writers don't usually lie, but they don't give the <u>full picture</u>.

2) Sometimes the writer <u>won't mention</u> something that opposes their viewpoint, or they'll <u>exaggerate</u> something that supports it.

3) Biased writing also often uses <u>generalisations</u> — sweeping statements that aren't necessarily true.

4) Bias isn't always <u>obvious</u>, or even <u>deliberate</u>. Biased writers often <u>seem</u> to be talking in a neutral, factual way — while actually only presenting one point of view.

5) You need to be able to <u>recognise</u> bias, so that you don't mistake opinion for fact.

6) Look out for bias in non-fiction texts like <u>newspaper articles</u> and <u>reviews</u>.

Sylvester's essay on who was boss wasn't the slightest bit biased.

Bias weakens a writer's argument

PAPER 2

| 0 | 4 | Compare how the two writers convey their different viewpoints on *Romeo and Juliet*.

Source A — 19th century review

Biased writers may use hyperbole if they are trying to convince you about something.

> *Romeo and Juliet*, without the slightest shadow of a doubt, is the very greatest work of literature to have ever been penned in the English language.
> It truly is the pinnacle of Shakespeare's momentous talent and will never be matched by any playwright to come.

They often make opinions sound like facts.

Source B — 20th century biography

> *Romeo and Juliet* is one of the most well-known and widely studied works of literature to have ever been penned in the English language.
> It was among the most popular of Shakespeare's plays during his lifetime, and it is still performed to this day.

Try to use more interesting vocabulary to get across your exact meaning.

Source A is written in a very biased way. The hyperbolic statements "without the slightest shadow of a doubt" and "never be matched" emphasise the writer's strength of feeling, but the statements are unjustified: the writer gives no evidence other than their own opinion. This bias presents the reader with an emphatic personal argument for how good the play is, but nothing to back it up. This may convince some readers to watch the play, but others may feel the argument is quite weak.

Develop your point by writing about the writer's purpose and how successful they are

Although source B is also positive about Romeo and Juliet, the writer bases their viewpoint on factual statements, describing the play as "well-known" and "widely studied". The writer of source B is also careful to use phrases like "one of the most" and "among the most", which shows that they are aware that there are other successful and popular plays. Overall, source B presents a more balanced viewpoint towards Romeo and Juliet.

Mention the overall difference between the two texts.

We're too expensive for you — you'll never bias...

A good way to spot bias is when the writer presents their opinion as fact (by saying something confidently), but giving no evidence for it. This weakens their argument, as you can claim all sorts of absurd things this way.

Descriptive Language

Descriptive language pops its head up all over the place — writers just love it. Better get stuck in, then...

Descriptive language makes text interesting

1) Writers use descriptive <u>techniques</u> and <u>vocabulary</u> so that the reader gets a really clear <u>image</u> in their mind of what the writer's describing. It makes the text more <u>interesting</u>, <u>dramatic</u> and <u>convincing</u>.

2) <u>Descriptive techniques</u> include <u>imagery</u> such as metaphors, similes and personification (see p.35-37).

3) Writers often give <u>descriptions</u> based on their five <u>senses</u> (what they can <u>see</u>, <u>smell</u>, <u>hear</u>, <u>touch</u> or <u>taste</u>).

4) Another sign of descriptive language is when the writer uses lots of <u>adjectives</u> — describing words like 'huge' or 'fiery' that give a specific <u>impression</u> of something.

5) Writers might also use interesting <u>verbs</u>, such as 'saunter' instead of 'walk' to make their descriptions really <u>specific</u>.

The sun was setting over the sea. *The view from the beach was incredible.*	This example relies on the reader to picture <u>for themselves</u> what a nice sunset might look like.
The salty sea air whooshed around me as the dark-orange sun melted into the horizon, dyeing the cobalt sky a deep crimson.	This one uses interesting <u>adjectives</u> and <u>verbs</u> to help the reader to picture and even 'feel' what's going on.

6) Writers can also <u>build up</u> the description of something <u>throughout</u> their work. For example, by writing sentences with <u>contrasting</u> descriptions or descriptions that <u>agree</u> with each other.

Talk about the effects of specific words

PAPER 1

0 2   How does the writer use language here to describe how Henry feels?

Describes the smell to add to the description.

The building is personified to emphasise how intimidating it is.

Uses a lot of interesting verbs and adjectives.

Henry crept slowly towards the tall, dark, brooding building, coming to a standstill in its looming shadow. Smoke billowed from its many chimneys, stinging his eyes and filling his nostrils with an overpowering, acrid smell. He watched the other workers scuttling in through the iron gates. With the tall building glowering down at him, he shuddered, forced his right foot out in front of his left, and began to traipse towards the doors.

Mention if language techniques work together to create an effect.

The writer uses descriptive language to make it clear that Henry is feeling very intimidated. The verbs "crept" and "traipse" both carry a negative connotation: they imply walking very slowly and reluctantly, as if the character is unwilling. Henry clearly doesn't want to approach the building. His reluctance is also shown by the use of the cumbersome phrase, "forced his right foot out in front of his left". The verb "forced", coupled with the extra detail of exactly how he moved his feet, shows that it is a considerable effort.

It's great to talk about the effects of specific words.

My dad used descriptive language when I scratched his car...

Descriptive language comes in all shapes and sizes. Look out for it in the literature extract in paper 1 and the literary non-fiction in paper 2, and be prepared to write about the effect the descriptive language has...

Narrative Viewpoint

Literary texts will always have a narrator — a voice that is telling the story.

The narrative viewpoint is usually quite easy to spot

1) A first-person narrator tells the story using words like 'I', 'we' and 'me'. A first-person narrator is often one of the characters, telling the reader directly about their feelings and experiences.

> *I stood on the fringes of the stage, waiting my turn, fear coursing through my veins.* A first-person narrator establishes a stronger, more personal connection with the reader.

2) A second-person narrator tells the story using words like 'you'. A second-person narrator talks as if the reader ('you') is one of the characters.

> *You turn your head to see her walking towards you. Your heart begins to race.* A second-person narrator makes the reader 'feel' what the character is feeling.

3) A third-person narrator is not one of the characters. They tell the story using words like 'he' and 'she' to talk about the characters.

> *Ian's elated expression could mean only one thing: he had got a place at medical school.* A third-person narrator has a more detached viewpoint.

> Some third-person narrators are omniscient — they know what all the characters are thinking. Others are limited — they only know what one character is thinking.

4) When writing about a narrator, think about how reliable they are. You might not be able to trust them fully if they don't know something, or if they're trying to affect the reader in some way.

Think about how the narrator presents the characters

0 4 A student, having read this extract, said: "Alice is clearly a very annoying character."

To what extent do you agree?

> *Uses 'she' and is separate to the characters, so it's a third-person narrator.*

> Polly was walking down the corridor when she noticed that Alice was walking towards her. Polly sighed, rolled her eyes and braced herself.
> "Hi Polly!" chirped Alice, with her typically exhausting optimism, "I hope I'll see you at the party later!"
> Polly's face contorted into an obviously forced smile as she nodded sharply.

> *Think carefully about how the narrator's perspective is being used to affect the reader.*

I agree with the student's evaluation. The writer has used the narrator's perspective to present Alice as unlikeable, despite her actions. Everything she does is positive: she is bright, friendly, optimistic and simply invites Polly to a party. The narrator presents her optimism as "typically exhausting" though, so her actions come across to the reader as tiresome, rather than positive. This is reinforced by the narrator's heavy focus on Polly's expressions, which all betray her personal dislike for Alice: she "rolled" her eyes and had a "forced smile".

> 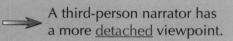 Link your points together to give a really detailed analysis of what the writer has done.

Narrator race — 'I' was first, 'you' were second, 'he' was third...

It can be quite easy to forget about the narrator, because they're often not one of the characters directly involved in the story. But try to think about how they talk, and also if you can trust what they tell you.

Section Three — Reading — Language and Structure

Structure — Whole Texts

Whole text structure is all about the order that writers present events and ideas to the reader.

Structure is important for fiction and non-fiction

1) Structure is the way a writer organises their ideas within a text.

2) In non-fiction texts, writers will use structure to help them achieve their purpose. This might be to:

> - Build their argument to a powerful conclusion.
> - Reinforce the persuasive elements of their text through repetition.
> - Set out an informative text in a clear and balanced way.
> - Order their advice in a logical and easy-to-follow way.

3) In fiction texts, writers will structure their work in a way they think will entertain the reader. For example, story writing could have a linear or non-linear structure:

> Texts with a linear structure are arranged chronologically — events are described in the order in which they happened and the text flows naturally from beginning to middle to end.

> Texts with a non-linear structure are ordered in a way that makes the text interesting, rather than in chronological order. They might include things like flashbacks, changes in perspective or time shifts.

4) Linear texts tend to build towards some form of climax, whilst non-linear texts might begin with a dramatic moment and work backwards from there.

5) Whenever you write about structure, you need to show how the writer has used structure to produce a particular effect on the reader.

Writers use structure to focus the reader's attention

1) One of the easiest ways to write about structure is to think about how the writer is directing your attention as you read. There are lots of ways a writer can do this, for example:

> - The writer might draw the reader in by describing something general, then narrow their focus down to something more specific.
> - The writer could describe things along a journey and make you feel as if you are travelling with them. This might involve moving from the outside to the inside or just from one place to another.
> - A text might start with description and then move on to dialogue. This would shift your focus from setting to characters.
> - Often, a writer will use a new paragraph to start a new topic. This could be a smooth transition or it could have a jarring effect that draws the reader's attention to a particular part of the text.
> - In non-fiction texts, the writer will usually use paragraphs to lead you from their introduction, through their main points and onto their conclusion.

2) Often, descriptive writing will show rather than tell the reader what to focus on. For example, it might move the reader's attention from one place to another, acting like a camera shot does in a film. This type of writing is often called cinematic writing.

Section Three — Reading — Language and Structure

Structure — Whole Texts

The narrative viewpoint will affect the structure

"When you're a grown-up narrator, you can skip about too."

1) The <u>narrator</u> controls what the reader <u>sees</u> and what <u>information</u> they <u>receive</u>.

2) The narrator might <u>withhold</u> some information to create <u>tension</u>, or they could <u>skip</u> over certain parts of a story because they are <u>biased</u>.

3) Different <u>narrators</u> will have different <u>effects</u> on the <u>structure</u> of a text:

> • A <u>third-person</u> narrator (see page 44) will often have an <u>overall</u> view of the story, and so the structure might <u>skip around</u> to cover lots of <u>different</u> events.
>
> • For texts with a <u>first-person</u> narrator, the structure will probably <u>follow</u> that character's experiences quite <u>closely</u>.

4) Look out for texts that have <u>more than one</u> narrator. This might mean that the structure <u>jumps around</u> or alternates between the different <u>perspectives</u>.

5) Some texts use a <u>frame</u> narrative — this is when one story is presented <u>within</u> another. For example, the writer might use one character to <u>narrate</u> a story to <u>another</u> character. This allows the writer to move between <u>multiple settings</u> and sets of <u>characters</u>.

Explain what effect the text's structure has on the reader

PAPER 1

0 3   You now need to think about the **whole** of the **source**.

This text is from the opening of a novel.

How has the writer structured the text to focus the reader's attention?

> *For paper 1, question 3, it will say where in a text the extract is from. Make sure you bear this in mind when writing your answer.*

> The mountain looked a little mysterious in the half-light of the dusky evening. Its snow-capped peak stood alert, bathing in the dying embers of the setting sun. From there, my eye was drawn to the narrow path that wound its way precariously down past the dark woods and craggy outcrops of the mountain face. I traced the weaving path all the way down, until it vanished behind the spire of a magnificent church that loomed over the town nestled at the foot of the mountain.
>
> This was the town of my youth.
>
> This was the town where I had taken my first steps. This was the town where I had been to school, where I had battled through those tough transition years of teenage angst and, finally, where I had first fallen in love. It was permeated with memories of childhood games and, later in my adolescence, secret late-night trysts.
>
> I crossed the road and entered the alley that would take me deeper into the warren of streets that wound their way around the foot of the imposing church. When I finally emerged into the square, I was assaulted by a barrage of sights and smells that instantly took me all the way back to my youth.

> *Think about the overall structure of the text as you read. Try to identify any perspective shifts or other obvious structural features.*

Structure — Whole Texts

Immediately, I was back under the oak tree, crouching silently next to my best friend Sally. We were hiding from James Cotton, and it was matter of grave honour that we preserved our hiding place. Back then, a game of hide and seek was no mere playground triviality, it was a fierce battle of the sexes, a passionately fought war between two equally resolute forces.

Both Sally and I were fascinated with James: he was old for his age, smart and funny. Obviously, at that age, this fascination manifested itself as bitter hatred. The coyness would come later, along with the feelings of claustrophobia and a yearning for the big city. Sally hadn't felt the same longing for the metropolis as I had, but she had discovered the coyness that would replace the naive and innocent feud. She had stayed here and built a life for herself; tomorrow morning I was to attend the wedding at which she would become Mrs Cotton.

The tolling of the church bells brought me back to the present with a start. I needed to hurry if I was to get to my parents' house before dinnertime. With a sigh of nostalgia, I began the final leg of my journey back to my former home.

This text contains time shifts — it has a non-linear structure.

Think about how the writer might have used cinematic techniques to focus the reader's attention.

A perspective shift could involve a shift in time or place or both.

Develop your points by writing about the effects of structural features on the reader.

Always use examples to back up your points — you can use short quotes or descriptions of the text.

The text is structured to control the reader's focus. At the start, it is as if the writer is describing how someone might look at a painting as she draws the reader's attention to the "snow-capped peak" of the mountain and "the dying embers of the setting sun". She then uses the "narrow path" as a device to lead the reader's focus "From there" to the town at the bottom. By narrowing the focus in this way, the writer is able to smoothly shift perspective. She does this using the single sentence paragraph, "This was the town of my youth", which shifts the reader's focus from the landscape to the narrator's account of her youth. This structure enables a transition from the impersonal to the personal without making it obvious to the reader that their attention is being carefully controlled.

The structure includes a time-shift from the present, where the narrator is describing her return to the town, to the past and her memories of childhood. This shift is triggered by a "barrage of sights and smells" and reversed, in the final paragraph, by the "tolling of the church bells" that transports the narrator back to the present. The fact that the narrator's account of the past is framed by her experiences in the present, prevents it from having a jarring effect on the reader. This is also helped by the fact that the town is used as a link between the passages that occur in the past and the passages that occur in the present.

The use of a first-person narrative voice also allows the writer to use structure to control the reader's focus. The reader is taken on the same journey as the narrator, from moving around the town, to moving around her thoughts. This gives the reader a steady trickle of information, as we learn about the setting, then its relation to the character, her youth and finally the complex reason for her return. This gradual supply of information keeps the reader interested and focused on what happens to her.

You need to talk about the text as a whole, but you can also focus on how the writer has used individual paragraphs.

This text has been structured to create a smooth flow of ideas. Other texts might use more obvious perspective shifts to deliberately draw the reader's attention to something.

Recurring themes or ideas (called motifs) can be used to draw together various parts of a text or argument.

Just imagine you're in a film....

That doesn't mean get up and start doing an action sequence in the exam hall. You need to think about how the writer is using structure to direct your attention to certain things. Look out for cinematic techniques.

Sentence Forms

Writing about the effects of different sentence forms will earn you marks in questions about structure and language, so it's well worth reading up on the next two pages. You'll be a sentence pro by the time you're done.

Sentences are made up of clauses

1) A <u>clause</u> is a part of a sentence that has a <u>subject</u> and a <u>verb</u>. A clause will usually <u>make sense</u> on its own.

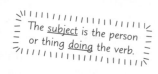
The <u>subject</u> is the person or thing <u>doing</u> the verb.

2) A <u>single clause</u> on its own is called a <u>simple sentence</u>.

> *The sky was grey and sombre.* ⟶ This is a single clause that is also a simple sentence. It has a <u>subject</u> ('The sky') and a <u>verb</u> ('was').

3) Simple sentences can be used to <u>explain</u> something <u>clearly</u> and <u>simply</u>. They are also often used to create a <u>sharp</u> or <u>abrupt</u> tone that keeps the reader <u>engaged</u> or creates <u>tension</u>.

4) A <u>compound sentence</u> has <u>two</u> main clauses, linked by a <u>conjunction</u> like 'but', 'and' or 'so'. <u>Both</u> clauses have to be able to make sense on their own. For example:

> *The sky was grey and sombre, and the rain lashed at our faces.* ⟶ Writers can use compound sentences to do things like <u>expand</u> on their initial statement, creating more <u>detailed</u> and <u>interesting</u> descriptions.

5) <u>Complex sentences</u> have <u>two</u> or more clauses, but only <u>one</u> of them needs to make sense on its own.

> *Above the sleepy town, the sky was grey and sombre.* ⟶ This is a complex sentence — 'Above the sleepy town' wouldn't work as a sentence on its <u>own</u>. This clause could go either <u>before</u> or <u>after</u> the main clause. Writers often <u>create interest</u> by using complex sentences to break up the <u>rhythm</u> of a text.

6) Writers use a variety of <u>sentence forms</u> to achieve different <u>effects</u> and keep the reader <u>interested</u>.

There are four main types of sentence

1) Different <u>types</u> of sentences have different <u>purposes</u>:

- <u>Statements</u> deliver <u>information</u>, e.g. 'The referee made the decision.' They can be found in all texts, but they are particularly common in <u>informative</u> texts like newspaper articles, reports and reviews.

- <u>Questions</u> ask the reader something, e.g. 'What would you do in my situation?' They don't always require an <u>answer</u> — sometimes they are just there to <u>encourage</u> us to <u>think</u> about something.

- <u>Orders</u>, or <u>commands</u>, tell us to <u>do</u> something, e.g. 'Consider the effects of this in the long-term.' They often use <u>imperative</u> verbs (verbs that give an instruction, like 'remember', 'think about' or 'go').

- <u>Exclamations</u> convey <u>strong emotions</u>, e.g. 'This is outrageous!' or 'This cannot be allowed to continue!' They usually end with an <u>exclamation mark</u>, and they're common in <u>persuasive</u> texts.

2) For the <u>reading questions</u>, it's a good idea to think about <u>how</u> and <u>why</u> writers have used particular <u>types</u> of sentence — bear in mind that different sentence types are suited to different <u>purposes</u>.

Sentence Forms

Writers use different sentence forms to interest the reader

1) Varying the <u>length</u> of sentences can create different <u>effects</u>. Here are a couple of <u>examples</u>:

These are just examples — the effects of different sentence lengths will vary from text to text.

> *The sky was growing darker. I couldn't see where I was going. I stumbled.*

Short simple sentences can be used to <u>build tension</u> or to create a <u>worried</u> and <u>confused</u> tone.

> *I waited excitedly at the foot of the stairs, listening to the footsteps above, thinking about the afternoon ahead, pacing the hall and counting down the minutes until we could set off.*

A longer, complex sentence could be used to give the impression of <u>time dragging</u>.

2) The <u>order</u> of words within sentences can also be chosen to create an <u>effect</u>. For example:

> *I had <u>never</u> seen such chaos <u>before</u>.*
>
> <u>*Never before*</u> *had I seen such chaos.*

Writers sometimes use <u>inversion</u> (<u>altering</u> the normal <u>word order</u>) to change the <u>emphasis</u> in a text. Here, inversion helps to emphasise the phrase '<u>Never before</u>'.

3) If you notice something about the way a writer has used sentences, don't just identify it — you need to <u>analyse</u> the <u>effects</u> to show how they <u>influence</u> the reader.

Comment on the effects of different sentence forms

PAPER 1

| 0 | 2 |

How has the writer used language to convey their emotions?

This is a long sentence that leaves the reader breathless by the end. It emphasises the feeling of weariness that the narrator is describing.

The repetition in the sentence beginnings 'My heart began', 'My hands began' and 'My mind began' gives emphasis to the physical effects of the narrator's fear.

> It was late evening by the time I returned home from the shops, tired and weary from barging my way past all the desperate Christmas Eve shoppers. It had been a long day, and I was ready for a relaxing bath and a long sleep. It wasn't until I was halfway up the path that I noticed the front door was ajar. My heart began beating wildly inside my chest as I hesitantly advanced towards the door. My hands began to shake. My mind began conjuring apparitions of the unspeakable horrors that could be lurking inside. On reaching the door, I took a deep breath, collected my senses and stepped across the threshold. Everything was quiet and still. I crossed the hall and put down my shopping. Everything looked normal. Nothing was out of place. Suddenly I heard a noise above me. Someone was upstairs. I gasped. But then a change came over me: my fear had turned to resolute anger. Seldom had I experienced such intense fury in all my life. There was an intruder in my house, and they had no right to be there. I made for the stairs.

Short, simple sentences are used to reinforce the narrator's feelings of dread.

This longer sentence marks a change in tone from fear to anger.

The use of a colon shows that there is going to be some form of explanation. This highlights the move away from unexplained short simple sentences.

This inversion disrupts the usual word order and focuses the reader's attention on the narrator's anger.

Phew, there's a lot to get your clause into on these pages...

This stuff's pretty complex (see what I did there...), but it's worth spending some time on it — it'll really help you in the language questions if you're able to talk about the effects of different sentence forms.

Writing with Purpose

All writing has a purpose — even this introduction, which is here to explain that this page is about purpose.

Structure your writing to suit your purpose

See pages 22-25 for more about writer's purpose.

1) The purpose of your writing might be to <u>inform</u>, <u>advise</u>, <u>argue</u> or <u>persuade</u>, or <u>entertain</u>. It could even be <u>more than one</u> of these.

2) For both papers, question 5 will let you know what the <u>purpose</u> of your writing needs to be.

3) Sometimes it will be <u>obvious</u>, e.g. in paper 2 you might be asked to write a letter to argue or persuade. It can be <u>less obvious</u> though, so sometimes you'll need to <u>work it out</u>, e.g. if you're asked to write a story for paper 1, your purpose would be to entertain.

4) Different purposes will need different <u>structures</u>, so you'll need to think about a <u>structure</u> that will help you achieve your purpose most effectively.

5) You can lay out your structure by writing a <u>plan</u>, so that it stays <u>consistent</u> throughout your answer:

PAPER 2

In this case, your purpose is to argue, so you'll need a structure that sets out your argument effectively.

| 0 | 5 | Write an article for your school newspaper in which you argue that teenagers are portrayed negatively in the media.

PLAN

Stating your point of view clearly at the start of your answer helps to give your article a clear direction.

1) State the problem — negative image of teens in media, changes way teens are perceived, breaks down links between generations.

You could present an opposing argument and explain why it's wrong...

2) Give an example of an unfair news report, explain why it's not fair — not representative of all teens, exaggerates the truth.

... then use a contrasting argument to explain your own viewpoint.

3) Give some positive examples of teenagers to contrast negative examples, explain that they're more accurate / representative.

Choose your tone, style and register to match your purpose

1) In order to get good marks, you also need to show that you can <u>adjust</u> your <u>tone</u>, <u>style</u> and <u>register</u> to suit your purpose.

See p.31-32 for more on tone, style and register.

2) For example, a text written to <u>advise</u> might have an <u>objective</u>, <u>authoritative</u> tone:

> *Upon consultation with local residents, and in light of their strong opposition, this committee recommends that the proposal be withdrawn immediately.*

This text uses a <u>formal</u> register and <u>complex</u> language to make its advice seem <u>reliable</u>.

3) A <u>persuasive</u> text needs to be more <u>subjective</u> (based on personal feelings). It might try to create a <u>personal</u> tone that involves the reader in a text:

See p.41 for some rhetorical techniques that help to achieve this.

> *Like me, you must be weary of the incessant criticism. We're intelligent young citizens who understand the issues threatening our planet. Why are we being ignored?*

This text uses a <u>rhetorical question</u> and the pronouns 'you' and 'we' to <u>involve</u> and <u>persuade</u> its audience.

4) When you adjust your <u>writing</u> to suit your purpose, make sure you're still showing off your ability to use <u>sophisticated vocabulary</u>.

Writing with Purpose

Literary fiction texts are often written to entertain

PAPER 1

0 5 You are entering a creative writing competition.
The winner will have their piece printed in a national newspaper.

Write the opening part of a story suggested by this picture:

> The purpose will always be referred to in the question. In this case, you're writing the opening part of a story, so you're writing to entertain the reader.

> The purpose is to entertain, so this story starts in the middle of the action to grab the reader's interest.

> This uses complex sentences to keep the writing style varied.

> Unusual vocabulary makes your writing more interesting and enjoyable to read.

I'd never in my life needed a break so badly. My airless writing room had begun to feel suffocating; so had the frustration of my unending writer's block. I gave up, threw down my pen, and went out for a walk.
My irritation evaporated almost immediately into the crisp autumn air. Buoyed by the hope of finding inspiration amongst the fiery leaves that surrounded me, I ambled contentedly through the silence of the golden wood.

> Figurative language helps the reader to imagine the writer's feelings.

Non-fiction texts can have a variety of purposes

PAPER 2

0 5 'Cosmetic surgery is a psychologically damaging procedure that increases the pressure to achieve an unrealistic level of perfection. It should be banned.'

Write an article for a broadsheet newspaper in which you explain your point of view on this statement and persuade your readers to agree with you.

> In this task, your purpose is to explain your point of view and persuade your readers.

> If you're writing to persuade, you could structure your answer by stating an opposing opinion and then counteracting it.

Public consensus has long seen cosmetic surgery as a mere vanity project, a procedure dreamed up by the wealthy to aid their endless pursuit of perfection. This seems somewhat unfair on the medical establishment.
In truth, cosmetic surgery sits at the height of medical achievement. Far from being a symptom of a shallow society, cosmetic procedures are a solution: they offer the chance of a new life. Plastic surgery has the power to improve lives, something that has always been an important medical objective.
It is time for a sea-change in attitudes to plastic surgery — it is no longer acceptable for the world to view with scorn those who have chosen to specialise in the improvement of the human form.

> Emotive phrases like this can help to make the audience sympathise with your viewpoint.

> You need to use a confident, assured tone to be persuasive.

This revision guide's purpose is to get you through your exams...

Don't forget that writing can often have more than one purpose — make sure you think about all the reasons that you're writing, so that you can adapt your style and produce a top-quality piece of writing. Easy peasy.

Section Four — Writing — Creative and Non-Fiction

Writing for an Audience

For each writing task, you'll need to bear in mind your audience. Your audience is just anyone who's going to hear or read your writing — it doesn't mean you'll have to perform your work to a room full of strangers...

Work out who your audience is

1) For question 5 on both papers, you'll need to pay attention to the audience you're writing for.

2) In paper 1, the question will usually specify a particular audience:

> PAPER 1

> | 0 | 5 |
> You are going to submit a short story to a magazine. The magazine is aimed at young people aged 14-18.
> Write a short story about somebody who has travelled a long way.

Here's the audience — 'young people aged 14-18'.

3) In paper 2, you might need to work out from the question who your audience is. The form and content will give you some clues:

This statement is about schools, so the audience will be people interested in education, such as parents or teachers.

You're writing a broadsheet newspaper article, so your audience will mostly be well-educated adults.

> PAPER 2

> | 0 | 5 |
> 'Students should attend classes virtually. In today's digital society, it's illogical that students still have to leave the house to go to school.'
> Write a broadsheet newspaper article in which you argue the case for or against this statement.

Choose your tone, style and register to match your audience

1) Once you know who your audience is, you'll need to adapt your tone, style and register so that they're appropriate to the people who will be reading your writing.

See p.31-32 for more on tone, style and register.

2) For example, you might want to consider the age and level of expertise of your audience, as well as your relationship with them.

Age
- If you're addressing a younger audience, you might use a more light-hearted tone, with a colloquial or chatty style.
- A formal, serious register might work better for older audiences. You might also use a more complex style than you would for a younger audience.

Relationship with reader
- If you're writing to a familiar audience, you might use a conversational style and a friendly tone.
- If you're writing to an unknown audience, it might be better to use an impersonal tone and a formal register.

Expertise
- Different audiences will have different levels of expertise in the subject you're writing about.
- For example, if you're writing a report for a panel of experts, your register should be very formal, with a style that uses more specialised language than if you were writing for a general audience.

3) Whoever your audience is, you should always aim to show your writing skills to the examiner by including a range of vocabulary and sentence types.

Writing for an Audience

Literary fiction texts need to engage their audience

0 5 You are entering a creative writing competition. The judges will be a panel of your teachers.

Write the opening part of a story about a character's birthday.

The audience for this question is your teachers.

For this task, your immediate audience is a panel of judges — you need to impress them by writing engagingly. Try surprising them with something unexpected, e.g. addressing the reader directly.

    Amelia's eighteenth birthday had truly been a day like no other. It was the day she first met Jack: a tall, handsome stranger dressed in a naval uniform.
    Don't be fooled by the intrusion of a charming stranger into this narrative. This is not a romance novel, and Amelia was not Cinderella. Jack was her brother — her long-lost brother, who had left to join the Navy before she had been born, and who returned now with the cowed despondence of a disgraced man.
    Amelia could never forget her mother's face as she had opened the door to greet another well-wishing neighbour, only to find her lost son hunched on the doorstep. Her features appeared to melt, losing all definition as they formed themselves into a canvas over which several emotions flashed. At first there was shock, which quickly became anger, then relief, and finally, remorse.

To impress teachers, you will need to use a formal, sophisticated register.

Non-fiction texts can use a personal tone

0 5 'Social media has provided a new way for us to interact with our peers. In turn, this has led to the creation of a new forum for bullying — the Internet.'

Write a speech to be given at your school, advising teenagers on how to cope with the threat of internet bullying.

In this task, you're writing for a teenage audience, so you'll need to adjust your tone, style and register accordingly.

Your tone should be helpful and friendly, but in this case your register should still be quite formal. Don't use any slang or text speak.

    We are a generation that has been raised in the era of social media. Every day, most of us use some form of social media to broadcast our identities. We're telling the world, "This is who I am." That's why cyber bullying can be so upsetting — it can feel like your whole identity is being attacked.
    There are many different ways to deal with online bullying. The first thing you need to do is report it. You can usually do this on the social media site itself, but if you don't feel comfortable doing this, you should talk to someone in person. Suffering in silence will only make things worse.
    If you find you are the victim of persistent bullying, take steps to block the person who is bullying you from contacting you. It's also a good idea to record the bullying in some way — you could take a screenshot, or even just save the messages somewhere. This will make things much easier to report later.

You're writing to advise teenagers. Use words like "we" and "you" to establish a connection and give your advice calmly, without being patronising.

I don't believe it, she's written an essay! And the crowd goes wild!

You'll be pleased to hear that your audience won't actually be there in the exam room — although I suppose it might be nice to have a group of people to applaud you whenever you craft a particularly good sentence...

Writing Stories

Story-writing is a task that might pop up in paper 1, question 5. You might have to write a short story, or focus on writing a particular bit, like the opening or the ending. It's time to sharpen up those storytelling skills...

Grab your reader's attention from the start

1) It's always a good idea to <u>start</u> your stories with an <u>opening sentence</u> that'll make your <u>reader</u> want to <u>carry on</u> reading. For example:

You could start with a <u>direct address</u> to the reader:

> *Everybody has a bad day now and again, don't they? Well, I'm going to tell you about a day that was much, much worse than your worst day ever.*

Grabbing attention had never been a problem for Marvin.

Or you could try a description of a particularly <u>unusual character</u>:

> *Humphrey Ward was, without a shadow of a doubt, the most brilliant (and most cantankerous) banana thief in the country.*

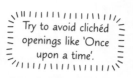

Try to avoid clichéd openings like 'Once upon a time'.

2) If you start your story in the <u>middle of the action</u>, it'll create a <u>fast-paced</u> atmosphere that makes the reader want to find out <u>what happens next</u>:

> *I couldn't believe it. He was gone. "He must be here," I thought to myself as I went through the shed, desperately throwing aside box after box. It was no use. Peter had run away, and it was all my fault.*

3) This example <u>explains</u> some of what's happening after a few sentences, which keeps up the <u>fast pace</u> of the narrative — so the story stays <u>interesting</u>.

4) You could also try <u>prolonging</u> the mystery to create <u>tension</u> in your narrative. Just make sure you <u>reveal</u> what's going on before it gets too <u>confusing</u> for your audience.

5) However you start your writing, you need to make sure it's <u>engaging</u> and <u>entertaining</u> for the reader — so whatever you do, don't <u>waffle</u>.

Try to build the tension from the start

PAPER 1

| 0 | 5 |

Your school is making a creative writing anthology that will be sold to other pupils. You have decided to submit a piece of writing.

Write the opening part of a story about a trip to the beach.

This story starts in the middle of the action — we don't know who the narrator is or why they're shouting.

The waves drowned out my shouts as they crashed against the rocks with thundering force. I had only closed my eyes for a minute, and now I had awoken to find that Amy was nowhere to be seen. I scanned the deserted beach, searching for any sign of my beautiful daughter.

This text solves the mystery of what's going on fairly quick to maintain the pace

Use key words to show as clearly as possible that you're answering the question.

    Amy had been wearing a blue pinafore dress that made her look like Alice in Wonderland. I remembered joking with her about how funny it would be if the Queen of Hearts had suddenly appeared to chase her along the sands. She had merely giggled and returned to the digging project that was taking up all her attention. But where was she now?

Try to keep the tension building as you move on from your opening paragraphs.

Writing Stories

Make your language and narrative viewpoint fit the task

1) Different <u>word choices</u> will have different <u>effects</u>, so you'll need to pick vocabulary that creates the right <u>tone</u> for your story. For example:

> *The door screeched open and I carefully entered the dingy cellar. Shadows cast by my torch leapt up at me through the gloom.*

Words like '<u>screeched</u>', '<u>dingy</u>' and '<u>gloom</u>' make this writing sound <u>spooky</u>.

> *I burst noisily through the thicket of trees and sprinted towards the shore. The men were still chasing me, bellowing threats.*

Words like '<u>burst</u>', '<u>sprinted</u>' and '<u>chasing</u>' make this writing sound <u>exciting</u> and <u>dramatic</u>.

2) You also need to think about what <u>narrative viewpoint</u> you're going to use (see p.44).

3) A <u>first-person narrator</u> uses the pronouns 'I' and 'we', as they're usually one of the <u>characters</u> in the story.

> *I quickly scanned the book for anything that might help. My heart was racing; I knew I needed to work fast.*

The first-person narrative makes things more <u>dramatic</u> by helping the reader to <u>imagine</u> the story is happening to them.

4) A <u>third-person narrator</u> uses words like 'he' and 'she' to talk <u>about</u> the characters from a <u>separate</u> viewpoint.

> *Shamil lit the bonfire carefully, then retreated back a few metres as the feeble fire began to crackle and spit.*

The narrator isn't part of the story. This creates <u>distance</u>, as the narrative voice and the characters are <u>separate</u> from each other.

Use descriptive techniques to make your text engaging

PAPER 1

0 5 Write the opening part of a story suggested by this picture:

Make clear references to the prompt you're given in the question.

Using figurative language, like similes and personification, will help to make your text more engaging.

Use techniques like alliteration and repeating patterns to add rhythm to your text.

Combine visual imagery with other senses to help the reader imagine they are there with the narrator.

This description uses a third-person narrator, so the narrative isn't limited by the rider's perspective.

> The sun dipped low beneath the looming, dusky sky. Its daytime glory was reduced to the fading flicker of a tiny ember that only just protruded above the dark horizon. Down in the valley, the camp hummed with activity: people milled about like ants, erecting tents, cooking meals and lighting fires, the smoke from which crept stealthily up the side of the mound, eventually reaching the rider's nostrils and filling him with the warming aromas of home.
>
> A glance beyond the confines of the camp revealed the open plains beyond, as they bathed in the warmth of the dying light. Come nightfall, these plains would transform from places of refuge into discordant wastelands, answerable only to the laws of nature.

Writing Stories

It's important to write a good ending

1) Whether you're asked to write the <u>end</u> of a story, or a <u>different part</u>, it's still important that you <u>finish it well</u> — you want to leave the examiner with a <u>great impression</u> of your writing abilities.

2) Here are some <u>examples</u> of different ways that you could <u>end</u> a story:

> • You could finish with an unexpected <u>plot twist</u> that will <u>shock</u> the reader.
>
> • You could show the <u>main character</u> coming to some kind of <u>realisation</u>.
>
> • You could create a <u>cliffhanger</u> ending by finishing with a <u>question</u>. This will leave the reader thinking about what will happen <u>next</u>.
>
> • You could have a <u>neat</u>, <u>happy ending</u> that will <u>satisfy</u> the reader.

Buster had come to the realisation that he was going to need a hair cut.

3) If you find you're running out of time, think up a <u>quick ending</u> — make sure you show how the story ends, and finish with a short, <u>punchy</u> line.

4) Under absolutely no circumstances use the ending, "And it was all a <u>dream</u>."

Try to make your ending as powerful as possible

PAPER 1

0 5   Write the ending of a story about somebody who made a bad decision.

> *The narrator has had a realisation, which hints to the reader that the story is about to come to an end.*

I knew I should never have stolen the vase. It had been a moment of madness. I had just seen it sitting there, and it looked so beautiful and elegant. All of my problems stemmed from that decision, that single flash of foolishness.

I spent a long time wondering what to do with the vase. I studied it intently. It was too beautiful to discard, too dazzling to keep concealed any longer. Eventually, I made a decision. I took it to the cliff and threw it over, watching it smash on the rocks below. It was an awful sight, but at least my guilty secret was gone forever.

> *Your final paragraphs should build the tension towards a climax that will resolve the action.*

Late that night, the wind was howling around my tent, and the rain was pelting down on the canvas. Suddenly, there was a huge crash of thunder and a blinding flash of lightning. Terrified, I ran out of the tent, only to be greeted by a strange apparition: there, sitting on top of a tree stump, was the missing vase. It was completely whole. Not a single crack was visible on its smooth, shiny exterior. I whirled around and scoured the field for any sign of an intruder. That was when I saw the old, hunched man walking slowly away.

> *After you've given a satisfying ending, you could go on to add an unexpected twist that leaves the reader with doubt in their mind.*

> *However you end your text, make sure it's exciting and powerful.*

"It was all a dream" — the examiner's nightmare...

Seriously — steer as far away as you can from clichéd endings. All they do is prove to the examiner that you haven't thought very hard about your answer, as well as making your story more boring than double Physics.

Section Four — Writing — Creative and Non-Fiction

Writing Descriptions

For paper 1, question 5 you could be asked to write a description. Your aim is to give your audience a detailed idea about a character or scene, so you'll need to use words to paint a vivid, interesting picture in their mind.

Descriptions are detailed

1) Descriptions use strong <u>visual</u> language to create an <u>impression</u> of a person or place for the reader.

2) You <u>don't</u> need to include as much <u>plot</u> or <u>action</u> — focus mostly on <u>describing</u> the subject.

3) Even though there's no <u>plot</u>, you still need to <u>structure</u> your writing — e.g. you could start with a <u>general</u> description, then go on to describe some more <u>specific</u> details.

4) The purpose of a description is normally to <u>entertain</u> the reader, so you need to adapt your writing <u>style</u> accordingly, and keep your <u>language</u> interesting.

5) Descriptions need <u>detail</u>. For example, a <u>character</u> description might include:

- A character's <u>physical features</u>, e.g. hair colour, clothing.

- A character's <u>personality</u>, e.g. they could be funny, serious, reserved, extroverted.

- Any other particular <u>features</u> that reveal <u>more</u> about them, e.g. any nervous habits.

- Your <u>personal opinion</u>, e.g. what you like or dislike about them.

Alice had nearly forgotten to describe Maria's habit.

Use language to describe a character or scene

PAPER 1

| 0 | 5 | Write a character description about someone who is intimidating.

You can use the character's habits to create an impression of their personality.

> *The woman's fingernails tapped impatiently against the wood of the mantelpiece. She was standing still, but the motion of her perfectly-manicured fingernails, and the impatient huffs of air that were regularly expelled from between her thin lips, made her seem restless and agitated. Somehow she gave off the impression that she never really stopped moving.*

One way to structure your writing is to start with a tiny detail, then expand outwards.

Use figurative language to show off your descriptive skills.

> *She was an angular exclamation mark of a woman, and she stuck out like a sore thumb against our familiar, homely surroundings. She wore her dark hair short; it had been meticulously combed into an unforgiving style that cut into her sharp cheekbones. Her suit was an inky black colour, which only served to emphasise her militantly slender form. When she spoke, her voice was low and commanding, and her expression was set into a permanent frown that was half-angry, half-distracted, and wholly intimidating.*
> *She was the most terrifying person I had ever met.*

Use the five senses to create a really detailed description.

You can write from any narrative viewpoint, as long as it's appropriate to your purpose and audience.

Don't lose your focus — remember that your answer needs to be about somebody intimidating.

How do you contact the Ancient Egyptians? Write to de scribe...

You can really pull out all the weapons in your descriptive arsenal for this one — go to town with metaphors, similes, alliteration, personification, adjectives, the five senses, repetition, onomatopoeia, hyperbole — and lists...

Writing Newspaper Articles

Read all about it... paper 2, question 5 might ask students to write a newspaper article... read all about it.

Newspaper articles report events and offer opinions

1) A newspaper's main purpose is to <u>inform</u> people about <u>current affairs</u> and <u>other topics</u> of interest.

2) Some newspaper articles <u>directly report</u> news. They convey <u>facts</u> about a <u>story</u> or <u>theme</u>, often using an <u>unemotional</u> tone and a <u>sophisticated</u> style to make the information seem <u>accurate</u> and <u>reliable</u>.

3) Other newspaper articles offer the <u>viewpoint</u> of the <u>writer</u> on a news story or theme. These are sometimes called <u>commentaries</u>, <u>columns</u>, <u>editorials</u> or <u>opinion pieces</u>.

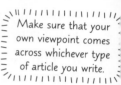
Make sure that your own viewpoint comes across whichever type of article you write.

4) As well as <u>informing</u> the reader, <u>commentaries</u> try to <u>entertain</u> their audience by making readers engage with the <u>personality</u> of the writer.

Commentaries need to engage their audience

1) To grab the audience's <u>interest</u>, a commentary might use a <u>personal</u> tone and a <u>conversational</u> style to help convey the writer's opinions and personality.

It seems to me that this lot all need to take a deep breath and stop whinging. Nobody's going to bulldoze our green spaces any time soon — they'll have to spend 25 years making a planning application first.

This uses <u>colloquial</u> words to create a conversational style and <u>sarcasm</u> to convey the viewpoint of the writer.

2) <u>Rhetorical techniques</u> (see p.41) are commonly used in commentaries to help get the writer's opinions across forcefully and to encourage readers to <u>agree</u> with the writer.

What happened to the good old days, when the presence of a heap of spuds on the table at dinnertime brought delight all round? Has all this 'health food' nonsense made us forget our faithful starchy friend?

This uses <u>rhetorical questions</u> to engage and persuade the reader.

The layout of an article is important

Newspaper articles often use <u>layout features</u> to engage the reader's attention and convey information clearly.

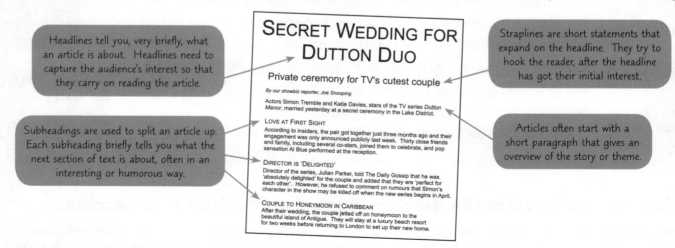

Headlines tell you, very briefly, what an article is about. Headlines need to capture the audience's interest so that they carry on reading the article.

Subheadings are used to split an article up. Each subheading briefly tells you what the next section of text is about, often in an interesting or humorous way.

Straplines are short statements that expand on the headline. They try to hook the reader, after the headline has got their initial interest.

Articles often start with a short paragraph that gives an overview of the story or theme.

SECRET WEDDING FOR DUTTON DUO

Private ceremony for TV's cutest couple

By our showbiz reporter, Joe Snooping

Actors Simon Tremble and Katie Davies, stars of the TV series *Dutton Manor*, married yesterday at a secret ceremony in the Lake District.

LOVE AT FIRST SIGHT
According to insiders, the pair got together just three months ago and their engagement was only announced publicly last week. Thirty close friends and family, including several co-stars, joined them to celebrate, and pop sensation Al Blue performed at the reception.

DIRECTOR IS 'DELIGHTED'
Director of the series, Julian Parker, told The Daily Gossip that he was 'absolutely delighted' for the couple and added that they are 'perfect for each other'. However, he refused to comment on rumours that Simon's character in the show may be killed off when the new series begins in April.

COUPLE TO HONEYMOON IN CARIBBEAN
After their wedding, the couple jetted off on honeymoon to the beautiful island of Antigua. They will stay at a luxury beach resort for two weeks before returning to London to set up their new home.

Writing Newspaper Articles

Newspapers have varying audiences

1) Newspapers are broadly split into two types — <u>tabloids</u> and <u>broadsheets</u>.

2) <u>Tabloids</u> (such as *The Sun* and *The Mirror*) tend to focus on more <u>sensational</u> topics and people, making their news stories accessible and with a wide appeal.

3) <u>Broadsheets</u> (such as *The Telegraph* and *The Guardian*) are thought of as more <u>formal</u>, 'high-brow' journalism — focusing on what are thought to be more sophisticated topics.

> Most newspapers also publish articles on the internet. If you're asked to write a news article for an online audience, think about how your audience might be different (e.g. younger or with a different level of understanding about the subject), and adapt your writing to suit.

4) Question 5 will tell you what <u>form</u> to write in, e.g. 'a broadsheet newspaper article' — make sure you adapt your <u>tone</u>, <u>style</u> and <u>register</u> to the right audience.

Make sure your article gives your opinion

PAPER 2

| 0 | 5 |

'You will never be able to get the real feel of a place by taking a guided tour. The true heart of any country lies off the beaten track.'

Write an article for a broadsheet newspaper in which you explain your point of view on this statement.

> This question is asking you to give your opinion on a topic.

> Your headline needs to be short and punchy to engage the reader.

FORGET THE ROAD LESS TRAVELLED

Guided tours are the best way to experience somewhere new.

> Use a strapline to summarise the article in an interesting way.

> You're giving an opinion, so your tone should be quite personal.

At some point or other, we've all been faced with a travel snob: that particular breed of rough-and-tumble traveller who knows all about where to go, what to see and, most importantly, how to see it. The travel snob thinks that guided tours are for the uncultured bores of this planet. The travel snob believes in travel without a destination. And yet, the travel snob will always find time to tell you about a 'hidden gem' that only they can take you to.

> Use rhetorical devices like repetition to make your writing entertaining and persuasive.

> Make sure you link your answer to the prompt you're given in the question.

You would think someone so worldly-wise would have realised the irony by now — travel snobs are themselves tour guides. The places that they think are 'off the beaten track' are transported, by their recommendation, right onto 'the beaten track'. They are the one beating the track, leading the tourists away from their well-known honeypot attractions and into 'the heart of things'.

> You can use a sarcastic tone to give your writing a sense of personality.

> Opinion articles often combine a conversational style with complex sentences and vocabulary.

In the meantime, guided tours are often run by local people, who will frequently have a real treasure trove of local knowledge. How can a throwaway recommendation from an outsider possibly surpass that? Anybody who wants to see the true heart of a country must be guided by the people who live in it.

"Why do you prefer broad sheets?" "I've got a really wide bed..."

It's worth having a look at some real newspaper articles as part of your revision. You'll soon start to spot some patterns in the vocabulary and structure that they use, which you can use to help you write a top-notch answer.

Writing Leaflets

Leaflets need to give the reader lots of information in a clear, organised way.

Leaflets can have varied audiences and purposes

1) Leaflets can have <u>any</u> purpose, but they're often used to <u>advise</u> (e.g. a leaflet advising the reader to open a savings account) or <u>persuade</u> an audience (e.g. to vote for a particular political party).

2) They can have a <u>general audience</u> (e.g. a leaflet about the importance of healthy eating) or a more <u>specific audience</u> (e.g. a leaflet advertising a particular museum or exhibition).

3) Leaflets need a <u>clear structure</u> to <u>break up</u> information. This could include:

- a clear title
- bullet points
- subheadings
- boxes around extra bits of information

> It's important to break up the information in a leaflet, but don't waste time in the exam trying to make it look pretty or drawing pictures.

4) Leaflets also need to <u>grab the reader's attention</u>, so that they <u>remember</u> all the information they're given. You can use <u>language techniques</u>, such as <u>lists of three</u> or <u>direct address</u>, to achieve this.

Organise your leaflet in a clear and interesting way

PAPER 2

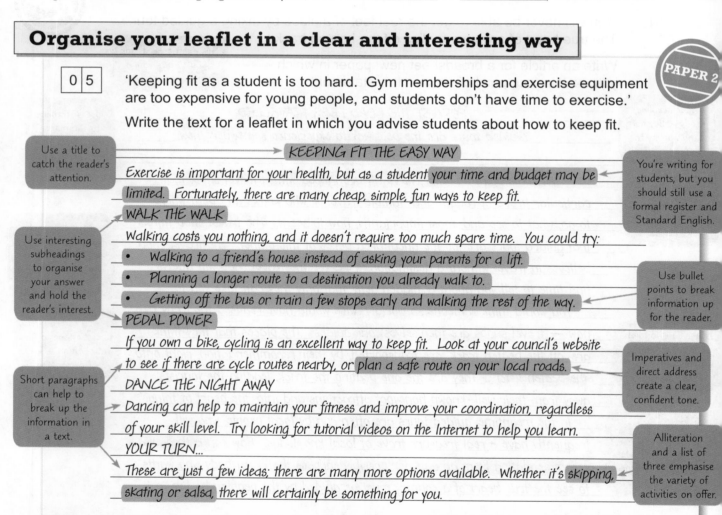

0 5 'Keeping fit as a student is too hard. Gym memberships and exercise equipment are too expensive for young people, and students don't have time to exercise.'

Write the text for a leaflet in which you advise students about how to keep fit.

Use a title to catch the reader's attention.

KEEPING FIT THE EASY WAY

Exercise is important for your health, but as a student your time and budget may be limited. Fortunately, there are many cheap, simple, fun ways to keep fit.

You're writing for students, but you should still use a formal register and Standard English.

WALK THE WALK

Walking costs you nothing, and it doesn't require too much spare time. You could try:
- *Walking to a friend's house instead of asking your parents for a lift.*
- *Planning a longer route to a destination you already walk to.*
- *Getting off the bus or train a few stops early and walking the rest of the way.*

Use interesting subheadings to organise your answer and hold the reader's interest.

Use bullet points to break information up for the reader.

PEDAL POWER

If you own a bike, cycling is an excellent way to keep fit. Look at your council's website to see if there are cycle routes nearby, or plan a safe route on your local roads.

DANCE THE NIGHT AWAY

Dancing can help to maintain your fitness and improve your coordination, regardless of your skill level. Try looking for tutorial videos on the Internet to help you learn.

Short paragraphs can help to break up the information in a text.

Imperatives and direct address create a clear, confident tone.

YOUR TURN...

These are just a few ideas; there are many more options available. Whether it's skipping, skating or salsa, there will certainly be something for you.

Alliteration and a list of three emphasise the variety of activities on offer.

And here I was thinking a leaflet was a baby leaf...

Leaflets can be written for a wide variety of different audiences. Make sure your leaflet is adapted to the audience you're given in the question by choosing a suitable writing style that uses appropriate language.

Travel Writing

Travel writing needs to really convey your feelings about the place you're writing about.

Travel writing is personal and descriptive

1) Travel writing is an <u>account</u> of a writer's travels to a specific <u>place</u>.

2) If you're asked to produce some travel writing for paper 2, you'll need to convey your <u>thoughts</u> and <u>opinions</u> about the place you're writing about, as well as give some <u>information</u> about it.

3) A piece of travel writing can <u>entertain</u> the reader (e.g. if it's in a book or magazine), <u>inform</u> them (e.g. if it's in a travel guide), or <u>persuade</u> them to visit a destination.

4) However, it's usually written for a <u>combination</u> of these purposes, e.g. <u>travel guides</u> are often written to both <u>inform</u> and <u>entertain</u> the reader.

5) Travel writing usually has a <u>personal</u> tone, and it's almost always written in the <u>first person</u>. Try to write in a <u>conversational</u> style, but don't forget to use lots of <u>descriptive techniques</u> too.

The travel brochure had failed to specify exactly what they meant by "transport included".

© Miguel Angelo Silva/iStockphoto.com

Use interesting language to convey your opinions

PAPER 2

0 5 'New York is the city of dreams. There is no greater place on earth.'
Imagine you have just visited New York. Write an article for a travel magazine in which you explain your point of view on this statement.

> This question asks you to write a magazine article. It needs to be entertaining and informative, and could also persuade the reader to agree with your point of view.

An interesting, punchy title and strapline can help to grab your audience's attention.

DISMAYED IN MANHATTAN

Lucy Farthing says "no thanks" to New York.

I've travelled to many cities during my career as a travel writer, and it's fair to say that there are a few I'd rather have avoided. None, however, have quite matched up to the levels of discomfort, disappointment and sheer frustration I experienced in the city of New York.

Use personal pronouns like 'I' to make the tone of your writing more personal.

I suspect my high expectations didn't help. Before embarking on my trip, I'd been regaled with stories from friends and family who'd already visited the place. "It's the city of dreams", I was told; "the best city in the world!"

Link your answer back to the statement.

What I realised instead, somewhere between my fifth cup of overpriced coffee and my fourteenth hour-long queue, was that New York is the city of nightmares. Not only did it feel like the world's busiest city, it felt like the noisiest, too; by the end of my week there I found myself longing for the joys of silence and solitude. Maybe for some, New York is a city where dreams come true, but it was certainly far from the inspiring haven I had hoped to find.

Make your opinion on the statement very clear.

Try to use all five senses to create a sense of the atmosphere of the place.

Use interesting language to make your text more entertaining.

Travel left-ing...   *...Travel right-ing*

You don't necessarily have to sing the praises of the place you're writing about. It's fine to have a negative opinion, as long as you express it clearly and use the appropriate language, tone and style for your audience.

Writing Reports and Essays

Reports and essays use a similar tone and style, but they do have one difference. Read on for the big reveal...

Reports and essays are similar

1) Reports and essays should be <u>impersonal</u> and <u>objective</u> in tone — you'll need to go through the arguments <u>for</u> and <u>against</u> something, then come to a conclusion that demonstrates your <u>own point of view</u>.

2) Reports and essays should follow a <u>logical structure</u>. They need to have:

> • An <u>introduction</u> that sets up the <u>main theme</u>.
>
> • Well-structured <u>paragraphs</u> covering the <u>strengths</u> and <u>weaknesses</u> of the arguments.
>
> • A <u>conclusion</u> that ties things together and offers <u>your own</u> point of view.

3) The purpose of reports and essays is almost always to <u>inform</u>, but they often <u>advise</u> their audience too.

4) You need to make sure you write for the correct <u>audience</u> — <u>essays</u> usually have quite a <u>general</u> audience, but <u>reports</u> are normally written for a <u>particular</u> person or group of people.

Reports should analyse and advise

PAPER 2

0 5   Your school has a certain budget for extra-curricular activities. This year, they have a small amount of money left over, and they are deciding whether to award it to the rock-climbing club or the film society.

Write a report for the board of governors in which you discuss the options and make a recommendation of what you think they should do.

> <u>A Report Into The Possible Uses Of The Extra-Curricular Budget</u>
>
> By: John Coughton
>
> Prepared For: Board of Governors
>
> Date: 21st April 2015
>
> This report has been commissioned by the board of governors to identify the best use of the funds available for extra-curricular activities at St. Swithins Park Secondary School. Two options have been investigated: the rock-climbing club and the film society. After careful consideration of the evidence collected from various interviews and data analysis, the conclusion has been reached that the film club is the most logical recipient of the excess funds.
>
> On the one hand, the rock-climbing club appears to be the most obvious choice as it is the most costly to run: the club organises frequent expeditions involving expensive equipment and high travel costs. Having said that, the club does charge a members' fee, which helps to alleviate some of this financial burden.

At the start, show that you are clearly aware of who your audience is.

You don't need to create any suspense — give your opinion in the introduction.

Phrases like 'on the one hand' show that you have thought about both sides of the argument.

Your language should be very formal and impersonal, but you still need to convey a viewpoint.

In the real answer, you would go on to include several more paragraphs and finish with a conclusion that gives advice.

My school reports certainly covered my weaknesses...

Reports and essays are pretty straightforward when it comes down to it — just make sure that you're being as objective, analytical and formal as possible. It may be a bit boring, but it's a perfect recipe for exam success.

Writing Reviews

Writing a review involves clearly giving your opinion about something. The audience are reading because they're genuinely interested in your opinion, so what you say goes. You have all the power. Mwa ha ha...

Reviews should entertain as well as inform

1) A review is a piece of writing that gives an opinion about how good something is — it might be a book, a piece of music or even an exhibition.

2) Reviews can appear in lots of different publications. If you have to write a review in the exam, the question will usually tell you where it's going to appear.

3) The publication where your review appears will affect what kind of audience you're writing for and how you write. For example, a film review for a teen magazine could be funny and chatty, but a review of a Shakespeare play for a broadsheet newspaper should be serious and informative.

4) You should also pay attention to purpose. Your review could have several different purposes:

- Your review needs to entertain the reader.
- You also need to inform the reader about the thing you're reviewing, based on your own opinion.
- You might also need to advise the reader whether or not to see or do the thing you're reviewing.

5) Don't get too hung up on describing everything in minute detail — it's much more important that you give your opinion. Just keep your review engaging by focusing on the interesting bits and using sophisticated language.

Your review needs to give an evaluation

PAPER 2

| 0 | 5 |

Imagine you have been to a music concert.

Write a review for a broadsheet newspaper that gives your opinion of the concert.

This review is for a broadsheet newspaper, so make sure you adapt your writing appropriately — use a formal register with fairly complex language.

'Music through the Millennium': A Feast for the Ears

Make your opinion clear from the start of the review.

From the moment the audience took their seats, the auditorium was buzzing with excitement, and they were not to be disappointed. This stunning collection of classical and contemporary pieces took the audience on an unforgettable journey through a thousand years of music, from the intense gloom and misery of funeral marches to the pounding excitement of percussion movements, and the intense joy of some truly superb symphonies. This was a sonic experience not to be missed: a congregation of musical heavyweights that each packed a punch strong enough to knock the emotional stuffing out of even the stoniest of hearts. From start to end, 'Music through the Millennium' was a true schooling in the stirring power of music.

Make sure your review is informative as well as entertaining.

Use figurative language to make your review interesting.

I read an article about cheese once — it was a brie-view...

Reviews are quite a nice thing to write — they're all about your opinions, which means you can go to town on saying what you think. You should try to express your thoughts clearly, and in a way that entertains the reader.

Writing Speeches

A speech needs to be powerful and moving. You should aim to have an emotional effect on the people who are listening. See if you can reduce them to tears with your carefully crafted sermon. Go on, I dare you...

Speeches need to be dramatic and engaging

1) <u>Speeches</u> are often written to <u>argue</u> or <u>persuade</u>, so they need to have a <u>dramatic</u>, <u>emotional impact</u> on their audience.

2) One way to make a speech persuasive is to give it an effective <u>structure</u> — arrange your points so that they build <u>tension</u> throughout your answer, then end with an <u>emotive</u> or <u>exciting</u> climax.

3) You can use <u>language techniques</u> to make your writing <u>engaging</u> and <u>persuasive</u>:

> *These accusations are hateful, hurtful and humiliating.*   →   <u>Alliteration</u> and the use of a <u>list</u> of three adjectives make this <u>sound</u> strong and angry.

> Persuasive language techniques like these are known as rhetorical devices — see page 41.

> *Do we truly have no other option? The current situation is a disgrace!*   →   <u>Rhetorical questions</u> and <u>exclamations</u> engage the reader and make your writing sound more like <u>spoken language</u>.

4) Remember that speeches are <u>spoken</u>, not read. Try to use techniques that are effective when they're spoken <u>out loud</u>.

Your speech should make people think

PAPER 2

05 'The practice of keeping animals in zoos cannot be allowed to continue. It is inhumane and encourages the use of animals as mere entertainment.'

Write a speech to be delivered at an animal welfare conference, in which you persuade your audience to agree with your point of view on this statement.

Ladies and gentlemen, I have called you here today to defend the practice of keeping animals in captivity. I believe that zoos represent a positive presence in this country.

The vast majority of modern British zoos are focused on conservation and education. To my mind, these important values are worth preserving. It is essential that we give our youngsters a sense of awareness about the world around them. We must impress upon the youth of today the need to protect endangered species and habitats. Zoos can help us to do this. Modern zoos offer extensive opportunities for these kinds of educational experiences: there are interactive exhibitions, talks from conservationists and live question-and-answer forums that will help to educate our young people.

Zoos can help us inspire a generation with the importance of conservation. Zoos can help us raise awareness of environmental issues. Zoos can help us by providing a space in which we can work together to build a safer, greener and more ecologically friendly world.

Start off by addressing your listeners directly and announcing the reason for your speech — show that you've understood your purpose and audience.

Vary the lengths of your sentences to show pauses and emphasis.

You could use repetition to increase the dramatic impact of your speech.

Try to use lots of personal pronouns like 'I', 'you' and 'we' to engage your audience.

The word 'must' creates a confident tone.

Use rhetorical devices like lists of three to make your argument sound more forceful.

Ladies, gentlemen, and assorted zoo animals...

There are loads of famous speeches throughout history — you could try looking at some of the techniques they use. Luckily for you, your speech doesn't have to impress a huge crowd of people, just a few picky examiners...

Writing Letters

Letters are always addressed to a particular person or group of people. This means that they have very specific audiences, so it's super important that you tailor your letter to suit that audience...

Letters need to start and end correctly

1) If you're asked to write a <u>letter</u>, look at the <u>audience</u> to decide how <u>formal</u> your register should be.

2) If the letter is to someone you <u>don't</u> know well, or to someone in a position of <u>authority</u>, keep it <u>formal</u> with a <u>serious</u> tone. This means you should:

- Use <u>formal greetings</u> (e.g. 'Dear Sir/Madam') and <u>sign-offs</u> (e.g. 'Yours sincerely' if you've used their name, 'Yours faithfully' if you haven't).

- Use <u>Standard English</u> and <u>formal vocabulary</u>, e.g. you could use phrases like 'In my opinion...' or 'I find this state of affairs...'.

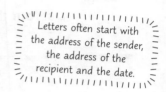
Letters often start with the address of the sender, the address of the recipient and the date.

3) If the letter is to someone you <u>know</u>, or someone who <u>isn't</u> in a position of authority, you might use a more <u>conversational</u> style, although it should still be fairly <u>formal</u>. This means you should:

- Start with your reader's <u>name</u>, e.g. 'Dear Jenny', and <u>sign off</u> with 'best wishes' or 'warm regards'.

- Make sure you still write in <u>Standard English</u> (so no <u>text speak</u> or <u>slang</u>) and show the examiner that you can use interesting <u>vocabulary</u> and <u>sentence structures</u>.

State your viewpoint clearly

PAPER 2

0 5 You have read a newspaper article which states:
'International travel is not worth the cost.'

Write a letter to the newspaper in which you argue for or against this statement.

This letter is for somebody in a position of authority, so it uses a formal greeting and sign-off.

Dear Sir or Madam,

I read with dismay your recent article regarding international travel. As a regular traveller myself, I strongly disagree with your assertion that international travel is not worth the cost. The benefits of international travel far outweigh the expenses incurred: it broadens the mind, adds to your wealth of experience and heightens your awareness of the world around you.

The article claims that UK holidays are cheaper and provide similar benefits. If you are not deterred by the threat of drizzle, perhaps that is true. To me, however, it is worth spending a fraction more to avoid wasting your holidays sheltering from the British rain.

Yours faithfully,
Ms Karen Samuels

Formal language like this helps to set the right tone for your letter and shows that you've understood your audience.

You need to make your viewpoint on the statement clear.

Introducing a counter-argument, then contradicting it, can help to build up your argument.

Your answer would need to be longer than this in the exam, with a few more paragraphs that support your argument.

A love letter has a very specific purpose and audience...

...but you probably won't be asked to write one in the exam. You will need to pay attention to purpose and audience though. Make sure your letter completes the task in the question and is written in an appropriate style.

Sample Exam — Paper 1

These two pages show you some example questions that are like the ones you'll see in paper 1 — the source to go with questions 1-4 is on p.68. First have a good read through the source and the questions, then have a look at the handy graded answer extracts we've provided on pages 69-77.

Question 1 asks you to find some information

| 0 | 1 | Read again lines 12 to 19 of the source. |

List **four** things from this part of the text about the baby.

[4 marks]

Question 2 is about the writer's use of language

| 0 | 2 | Look in detail at lines 1 to 11 of the source. |

How does the writer use language here to describe Mabel's life in Alaska?

You could include the writer's choice of:

- words and phrases
- language features and techniques
- sentence forms.

[8 marks]

Question 3 is about the structure of the whole text

| 0 | 3 | You now need to think about the **whole** of the **source**. |

This text is from the opening of a novel.

How has the writer structured the text to interest you as a reader?

You could write about:

- the time that the writer focuses on at the beginning
- how and why the writer changes the time she is writing about as the extract develops
- any other structural features that interest you.

The attempt at structuring the text to interest the audience hadn't been entirely successful.

[8 marks]

Sample Exam — Paper 1

Question 4 asks for a personal response to the text

| 0 | 4 |

Focus this part of your answer on the last part of the source, **from line 20 to the end**.

A student, having read this section of the text, said: "The writer makes it really clear how Mabel is feeling. It makes me feel the emotions she's feeling too."

To what extent do you agree?

In your response, you could:

- write about your own feelings on reading the passage
- evaluate how the writer created those feelings
- support your opinions with references to the text.

[20 marks]

You have to do some creative writing for question 5

| 0 | 5 |

You are going to enter a creative writing competition.

Your entry will be judged by a panel of people of your own age.

Either:

Write a description suggested by this picture:

© wingmar/iStockphoto.com

Or:

Write the opening part of a story that is set in a cold place in winter.

(24 marks for content and organisation
16 marks for technical accuracy)

[40 marks]

How are you going to find out the writer's purpose? Alaska.

Ha ha ha. Sigh. The good news is that you don't have to answer these questions yourself, because I've done it for you. Read on for some sample answers, which will give you an idea of what you need to write in your exam.

Exam Source

Here's the text to go with the questions on pages 66-67. It's an extract from the opening of *The Snow Child* by Eowyn Ivey, a novel which was published in 2012, but is set in 1920. In the novel, a woman named Mabel and her husband, Jack, have moved to the cold, remote Alaskan wilderness to start a new life.

Wolverine River, Alaska, 1920

Mabel had known there would be silence. That was the point, after all. No infants cooing or wailing. No neighbor children playfully hollering down the lane. No pad of small feet on wooden stairs worn smooth by generations, or clackety-clack of toys along the kitchen floor. All those sounds of her failure and regret would be left behind, and in their place there would be silence.

5   She had imagined that in the Alaska wilderness silence would be peaceful, like snow falling at night, air filled with promise but no sound, but that was not what she found. Instead, when she swept the plank floor, the broom bristles scritched like some sharp-toothed shrew nibbling at her heart. When she washed the dishes, plates and bowls clattered as if they were breaking to pieces. The only sound not of her making was a sudden 'caw, cawww' from outside. Mabel wrung dishwater from a rag and looked out the kitchen

10 window in time to see a raven flapping its way from one leafless birch tree to another. No children chasing each other through autumn leaves, calling each other's names. Not even a solitary child on a swing.

There had been the one. A tiny thing, born still and silent. Ten years past, but even now she found herself returning to the birth to touch Jack's arm, stop him, reach out. She should have. She should have cupped the baby's head in the palm of her hand and snipped a few of its tiny hairs to keep in a locket at her throat.

15 She should have looked into its small face and known if it was a boy or a girl, and then stood beside Jack as he buried it in the Pennsylvania winter ground. She should have marked its grave. She should have allowed herself that grief.

    It was a child, after all, although it looked more like a fairy changeling. Pinched face, tiny jaw, ears that came to narrow points; that much she had seen and wept over because she knew she could have loved it still.

20 Mabel was too long at the window. The raven had since flown away above the treetops. The sun had slipped behind a mountain, and the light had fallen flat. The branches were bare, the grass yellowed gray. Not a single snowflake. It was as if everything fine and glittering had been ground from the world and swept away as dust.

    November was here, and it frightened her because she knew what it brought — cold upon the valley

25 like a coming death, glacial wind through the cracks between the cabin logs. But most of all, darkness. Darkness so complete even the pale-lit hours would be choked.

    She entered last winter blind, not knowing what to expect in this new, hard land. Now she knew. By December, the sun would rise just before noon and skirt the mountaintops for a few hours of twilight before sinking again. Mabel would move in and out of sleep as she sat in a chair beside the woodstove. She

30 would not pick up any of her favorite books; the pages would be lifeless. She would not draw; what would there be to capture in her sketchbook? Dull skies, shadowy corners. It would become harder and harder to leave the warm bed each morning. She would stumble about in a walking sleep, scrape together meals and drape wet laundry around the cabin. Jack would struggle to keep the animals alive. The days would run together, winter's stranglehold tightening.

35   All her life she had believed in something more, in the mystery that shape-shifted at the edge of her senses. It was the flutter of moth wings on glass and the promise of river nymphs in the dappled creek beds. It was the smell of oak trees on the summer evening she fell in love, and the way dawn threw itself across the cow pond and turned the water to light.

    Mabel could not remember the last time she caught such a flicker.

Graded Answers — Question 1

You'll be pleased to hear there are some relatively easy marks on offer for question 1. Get to know the question on p.66, then have a squizz through the stuff on this page — by exam day you'll be ready to go.

Include the right number of facts

1) <u>Question 1</u> asks for <u>four</u> things about the <u>baby</u>, and there are <u>four marks</u> available. That means you get one mark for <u>each</u> thing that you write down about the baby.

2) Careful though — all your facts need to come from <u>lines 12-19</u>.

3) It's also important to <u>check</u> every fact carefully — anything that's <u>inaccurate</u> or not directly about the <u>baby</u> won't get a mark.

4) There's no need to <u>analyse</u> your facts or add any extra information — you just need to show that you can <u>find</u> information from the text.

Here's a grade 4-5 answer

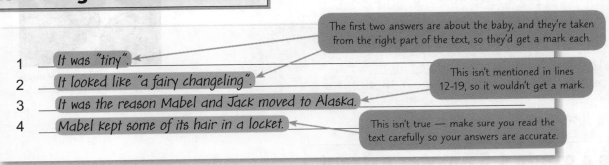

1 It was "tiny".
2 It looked like "a fairy changeling".
3 It was the reason Mabel and Jack moved to Alaska.
4 Mabel kept some of its hair in a locket.

The first two answers are about the baby, and they're taken from the right part of the text, so they'd get a mark each.

This isn't mentioned in lines 12-19, so it wouldn't get a mark.

This isn't true — make sure you read the text carefully so your answers are accurate.

This is a grade 6-7 answer

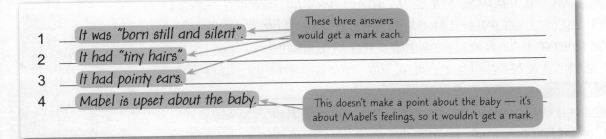

1 It was "born still and silent".
2 It had "tiny hairs".
3 It had pointy ears.
4 Mabel is upset about the baby.

These three answers would get a mark each.

This doesn't make a point about the baby — it's about Mabel's feelings, so it wouldn't get a mark.

And here's a grade 8-9 answer

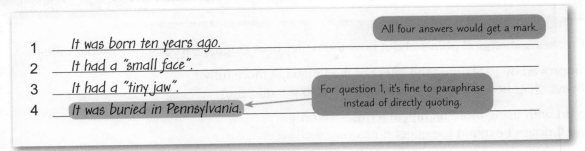

1 It was born ten years ago.
2 It had a "small face".
3 It had a "tiny jaw".
4 It was buried in Pennsylvania.

All four answers would get a mark.

For question 1, it's fine to paraphrase instead of directly quoting.

Section Five — Paper 1 — Sample Exam and Graded Answers

Graded Answers — Question 2

Question 2 (take a look back at p.66) is a tad trickier. Luckily, I've prepared some lovely sample answers...

Pick out key language features and explain their effects

1) <u>Question 2</u> tests how well you can explain the <u>effects</u> of the <u>language</u> used in the extract.

2) The sample question asks you specifically about the language used to describe <u>Mabel's life</u> — so you shouldn't write about the language used to describe <u>anything else</u>.

3) You need to use <u>P.E.E.D.</u> for this question — every point you make should be backed up with an <u>example</u> that's fully <u>explained</u> and <u>developed</u> (see p.10).

4) You also need to use a range of <u>technical terms</u> to describe the writer's techniques.

5) To get top marks, you need to write about <u>all</u> of the <u>bullet points</u> under the question:

- The effect of specific <u>words and phrases</u>, such as how specific verbs are used (see p.33-34).
- <u>Language features and techniques</u>, such as metaphors, similes and onomatopoeia (see p.35-38).
- The effect of different <u>sentence forms</u>, such as short or long sentences (see p.48-49).

Make sure you read each question carefully — this question is only asking about language, not structure.

Grant didn't need P.E.E.D. — he knew he could rely on his friends to back him up.

Here's a grade 4-5 answer extract

The writer says "the broom bristles scritched like some sharp-toothed shrew nibbling at her heart". This shows that Alaska isn't as "peaceful" as Mabel expected. The shrew eating her heart makes it sound like she isn't enjoying her life in Alaska.
    The first sentence in the second paragraph is very long, which shows how significant silence is to Mabel's life in Alaska. The writer compares the silence to "snow" and "air", which makes it feel like her life is empty.
    This emptiness is different to the "clackety-clack" (which is onomatopoeia) and "hollering" of the first paragraph, which makes the silence seem even more like it's an important part of Mabel's life.
    There is a raven "flapping its way from one leafless birch tree to another" too, which makes you feel like something bad is going to happen.

It's great to include quotes, but try to keep them short.

This starts to discuss the effect of the language on the reader.

It's important to mention techniques like this, but you need to write more about the effect they have, too.

This last paragraph doesn't seem relevant to the question — it needs to be clearly linked back to Mabel's life.

1) This answer makes some good points about how the writer uses <u>language</u> to <u>describe</u> Mabel's life.

2) It could be improved by <u>explaining</u> the <u>effect</u> of the language more fully, as it's not always <u>clear</u> how the examples are relevant to the <u>question</u>.

3) It could also do with using more <u>technical terms</u> — it only uses <u>one</u>, and it doesn't explain the <u>effect</u> it has very well.

Graded Answers — Question 2

Here's a grade 6-7 answer extract

The writer uses a short, direct first sentence to introduce the idea that the most prominent thing about Mabel's life in Alaska is how silent it is: "Mabel had known there would be silence."

The language used in this extract implies that Mabel finds this "silence" threatening and uncomfortable. The verb "scritched" sounds like a small animal clawing the "plank floor", which emphasises Mabel's uneasiness. The word is also onomatopoeic, so it interrupts the "silence", but in a way that's painful and upsetting. The writer is emphasising that the "promise" of peace Mabel hoped to find in Alaska has not been fulfilled; instead, she has been left unhappy.

The image of the solitary raven and the "leafless" trees links Mabel's surroundings with the idea of lifelessness. This increases the overall negative tone of the passage, which leaves the reader with a strong impression that Mabel's life is unhappy.

Referring to the writer shows that you understand they chose to use this language for a reason.

Good use of a brief quote to back up a point.

It's really good to focus on the effects of specific words.

It's important to keep linking the answer back to the question.

1) This answer makes some good points about the <u>effects</u> of the language the writer has chosen, which are <u>backed up</u> with appropriate quotations and <u>linked back</u> to the question.

2) It could be improved by mentioning even more <u>language features</u> or <u>techniques</u>.

This is a grade 8-9 answer extract

This extract uses sensory verbs to create images of childhood: verbs such as "wailing" and "hollering" suggest a loud, frenetic atmosphere. This is contrasted sharply with the "silence" of Alaska, which is mentioned twice, at the beginning and end of the first paragraph. This contrast has a jarring effect on the reader, and suggests that Mabel's life in Alaska is characterised by a sense of emptiness and loss.

The writer also uses onomatopoeic verbs such as "scritched" and "clattered" to suggest that the "silence" in Alaska makes any noise seem unnaturally loud and unpleasant, and to bring the reader into the uncomfortable life that Mabel leads. These verbs are used in combination with the vivid simile of a shrew "nibbling" at Mabel's heart, which emphasises her discomfort and suggests that, instead of the peace she had hoped to find, Mabel's life is deeply unhappy.

The writer uses direct speech only once in this extract, when there is "a sudden 'caw, cawww'" from a raven. The intrusiveness of this direct speech is emphasised because of the hard 'C' sound at the beginning of each word. Because the speech feels so out of place, the reader starts to empathise with the intrusion Mabel feels at the noise. This further emphasises the discomfort of her life.

This answer uses a good range of short quotes to back up the points it makes.

It's important to focus on the effect that the language has.

Uses a technical term for a language technique, then fully explains it.

This answer stays focused on the question throughout.

1) This is a <u>really good</u> answer. It makes several points about the writer's <u>choice</u> of language and the <u>effect</u> it has, and then <u>develops</u> each point fully.

2) It also uses complex <u>technical terms</u> correctly and supports each point with relevant <u>quotations</u>.

Graded Answers — Question 3

Question 3 is all about the structure of the text, but don't worry — there will be absolutely no mention of scaffolding or iron girders. We'll just toddle through until we've built up your knowledge... brick by brick...

Think about how the text is put together and the effect this has

1) Question 3 is about the <u>structure</u> of the text — you need to talk about <u>how</u> the writer has used structure to make the text more <u>interesting</u> to read.

2) This question covers the <u>whole text</u>, so make sure you talk about the <u>overall structure</u> of the extract as you're answering the question.

3) However, you should also comment on more specific things, like <u>changes</u> in <u>perspective</u> — aim to comment on a <u>range</u> of structural features.

4) To get top marks, you'll need to write about <u>everything</u> the bullet points mention:

> Question 3 will always be about structure, but it won't necessarily be about why it's interesting — the question will change depending on your exam.

- You need to write about the <u>beginning</u> of the text, and why the writer chooses to start by focusing on Mabel's <u>present-day life</u>.

- You need to comment on the <u>overall structure</u> of the text, by talking about how the writer <u>changes</u> the time she's writing about throughout the extract, and the <u>effect</u> that this has on the reader.

- Any <u>other</u> structural features that interest you — this could include <u>anything else</u> you spot, such as repeated <u>images</u> or places where the text focuses on something <u>specific</u>.

> Don't forget to use P.E.E.D. (see p.10) — every point you make needs to be backed up, explained, and developed.

Here's a grade 4-5 answer extract

> In the first paragraph, the writer tells you that there is "failure and regret" in Mabel's past, but it doesn't tell you why straight away. This keeps you interested to find out more.
>
> The writer next writes about what Mabel thought Alaska would be like before she arrived there, then compares it to what it's actually like now that she lives there. This is interesting because it shows how it is different from how she thought it would be.
>
> It then talks about the past, ten years ago, when she had a baby "born still and silent". It makes you feel sorry for Mabel and helps you understand why she wanted to move away from other people.
>
> Next the writer writes about the future, as Mabel explains what her life will be like over the coming winter. So it goes from present to past to future, which is an interesting structure.

This answer references the question — it talks about why the text is interesting.

A better technical term could be used here, such as 'contrasts'.

This would be better if it made it clear why she wanted to move away from other people.

This sums up the overall structure, but it needs developing further. It also might have been clearer to mention this at the beginning of the answer.

1) This answer describes some <u>structural features</u> of the text and starts to comment on the <u>effect</u> they have.

2) However, it doesn't go into enough <u>detail</u> about how the structure helps to grab the <u>reader's interest</u>, or <u>fully develop</u> why the writer's choice of structure is <u>effective</u>.

Graded Answers — Question 3

Here's a grade 6-7 answer extract

The writer moves from a description of Mabel's present life in Alaska to a recollection of the past, then finally to her fears about the future. This is an unusual structure that helps the reader to understand Mabel, and so engages their interest.

In the first and second paragraphs the focus is on the silence of the present, which emphasises Mabel's sense of "failure and regret". This grabs the reader's interest by making you wonder why Mabel has moved to such a bleak place and what has caused her "regret".

These questions are answered in the third paragraph, in which the writer describes Mabel's memory of having a stillborn baby "Ten years past". The repetition of "She should have" throughout this paragraph brings home the pain and regret of Mabel's past, which increases the reader's sympathy and helps them to identify with Mabel.

The last section of the extract shifts the focus as Mabel begins to think about the winter to come. In lines 29-34, the writer uses repetition again; this time, she repeats the verb "would" to emphasise how sure Mabel is about her future. Mabel's certainty about the winter to come makes the reader want to continue reading to find out if she's right.

This is a strong opening that sums up the overall structure.

This explains an effect of the structure, but could go into more detail about why this would interest the reader.

Good focus on answering the question.

This makes a good point about a smaller-scale structural feature and explains its effect.

This comments on how the focus changes throughout the extract.

This answer could be developed more fully to explain <u>how</u> each element of structure holds the reader's <u>interest</u>.

This is a grade 8-9 answer extract

The passage has a complex non-chronological structure, which seems to follow Mabel's train of thought. This gives the reader an insight into Mabel's mind, which creates interest by building empathy for the character.

The overall structure shifts from present, to past, to future and back to present. However, within this structure the present intrudes time and time again, for example "Now she knew". This constantly brings the focus of the text back to Mabel's current situation, which serves both as a reminder of the monotony of her life, and as a means of highlighting her dread of the winter to come. In this way, the structure simultaneously holds Mabel (and the reader) frozen in time whilst propelling her relentlessly towards the future she fears, creating a narrative tension which interests and engages the reader.

This impression is furthered by the recurrent references to nature that punctuate the narrative. The weather outside is currently "flat" and still, but it promises cold "like a coming death" and "glacial wind". This hint of coming crisis builds the tension in the narrative, which keeps the reader gripped.

High-level vocabulary makes this answer stand out.

This makes an interesting point about the large-scale and smaller-scale structure of the passage...

... and then fully explains its effect.

This explains how the structure helps maintain the reader's interest.

This is a <u>really good</u> answer — it makes several <u>original</u> points about the structure and its effect. The points are <u>fully developed</u> to explain <u>how</u> the structure helps to hold the reader's <u>interest</u>.

Graded Answers — Question 4

Question 4 (see p.67) is worth a whopping 20 marks, so it's worth spending some time figuring out how best to answer it. Handily, that's exactly what these pages are for. It's almost like we planned it...

Write about whether you agree with the statement and why

1) Question 4 is about <u>evaluating</u> how <u>effective</u> the text is.

2) The sample question gives you a <u>statement</u>, which has two parts to it — you need to give <u>your opinion</u> on how the writer shows <u>Mabel's feelings</u>, and how this makes <u>you feel</u>.

3) You also need to state how much you <u>agree</u> or <u>disagree</u> with the statement.

4) Use <u>P.E.E.D.</u> (see p.10) and make sure you include <u>technical terms</u> to get top marks.

5) The bullet points under the question give you guidance about what you <u>need</u> to include in your answer:

Timmy always found enough evidence when evaluating a text.

- You need to write about <u>your own feelings</u> as you read the text.

- You also need to talk about the <u>techniques</u> the writer uses to <u>create</u> these feelings, i.e. the <u>language</u> or <u>structural devices</u> they use.

- The question specifically mentions using <u>quotes</u> in your answer, so you need to include plenty of relevant <u>evidence</u> for every point you make.

Here's a grade 4-5 answer extract

> Overall, I agree with the student. I mostly feel the same emotions Mabel is feeling, and I think the writer makes it really obvious how she's feeling.
>
> Mabel feels frightened of the winter, and especially of the "darkness". The description of the "few hours of twilight" each day makes you imagine what it would be like not to see daylight for months, so you can start to understand Mabel's feelings of fear and anxiety.
>
> The writer also suggests that Mabel is unhappy. She does this by making the Alaskan winter seem very uncomfortable, with the "glacial wind through the cracks" in the walls and "wet laundry" everywhere.
>
> Some of the words rhyme, which sounds really repetitive, so it makes it seem like Mabel's life is monotonous. The way the words sound makes me feel bored and dull too.

This is good — it gives an opinion on the statement.

This starts to address how the text makes the reader feel.

This could be developed by writing about how these phrases help the reader feel what Mabel is feeling.

This is a good point about language and its effect, but it needs a clear example from the text and more explanation.

1) This answer starts to <u>comment</u> on how Mabel <u>feels</u>, and how the text makes the <u>reader</u> feel.

2) However, some of the points in this answer need to be <u>developed</u> further by explaining <u>how</u> the writer's choice of language and structure <u>affects</u> the reader.

3) Every point should also be backed up with a good <u>example</u> from the text.

Graded Answers — Question 4

Here's a grade 6-7 answer extract

I strongly agree with the student that the writer makes you feel how Mabel feels. She uses descriptive techniques to create a very strong sense of the atmosphere of Mabel's life and emotions.

Mabel is "frightened" by winter, and the writer uses vivid language to show and emphasise this feeling. For example, the writer compares the winter to "a coming death" to show the danger Mabel thinks she is facing, then reinforces this impression using violent words such as "choked" and "stranglehold". This use of powerful descriptive vocabulary helps me to imagine myself in Mabel's position and feel her fear.

The writer also suggests that Mabel feels powerless in the face of her fears. The verbs "would stumble" and "would struggle" indicate her hopeless feelings regarding the winter to come. This description of the winter months helps the reader to empathise with Mabel and the inevitable difficulties that her future will bring.

This shows that you've thought about the extent to which you agree with the statement.

This paragraph picks out specific language features and comments on their impact.

This shows that you're thinking about the effect of the text on the reader.

1) This answer clearly focuses on how the writer uses language to create a vivid impression of how Mabel is feeling.

2) It uses a good range of relevant quotes as evidence, and develops the points by relating them to the effect on the reader.

This is a grade 8-9 answer extract

To an extent I agree with the student's statement. The focus of the passage shifts from the dismal external landscape to an oppressive interior of "shadowy corners" and "wet laundry". This highlights to the reader how trapped Mabel feels by the "stranglehold" of the encroaching winter. Her home, which should be a place of safety, has become a place of fear, surrounded by "darkness" and vulnerable to "glacial winds". The writer describes common sensations like darkness and cold, which the reader can easily recognise. This makes Mabel's feelings seem very clear, and helps me to empathise with her plight.

However, it also seems that this bleak depiction of winter is a result of Mabel's attitude, which lessens the extent to which I empathise with her feelings. The repetition of "would not" to describe her lack of activity hints at her negative mindset, which is reinforced by the short, blunt sentence on line 39. By contrasting Mabel's lack of hope with Jack's "struggle", the writer implies that there are more proactive responses to the hardships of winter, and suggests that Mabel's dread is at least partly irrational.

This shows an understanding of how the text's structure affects the reader's response.

This explains how the language used conveys Mabel's feeling and affects the reader.

Keep referring back to the statement to make sure your answer is focused.

The second paragraph makes a well-developed counter-argument.

1) This is a top grade answer — it gives an answer that clearly responds to the statement in an original way.

2) It has a clear structure, and its points are backed up with relevant quotes and examples.

Graded Answers — Question 5

Question 5 is your chance to get creative. You'll have a choice of two tasks — go for whichever one you feel most inspired by, but make sure you don't waste too much time deciding. See p.67 for the full question.

Include lots of description in your answer

1) To write a good answer to this question, you need to match your writing to the form, purpose, and audience in the question.

- The form needs to be either a description or the beginning of a story. Think about the kind of language and writing structures that work well for these forms (see pages 54-57).

- For both tasks, it's a piece of creative writing that's being judged, so the purpose is to entertain the judges. You need to use a range of sophisticated vocabulary and language techniques, and a structure that grabs and holds the judges' interest.

- Your audience is mentioned explicitly in the question — it's a panel of judges who are the same age as you. You need to adapt your language, tone and style so that it's appealing to a teenage audience.

2) There are also loads of marks on offer for spelling, punctuation and grammar in this question, so it's really important to write accurately and clearly (see p.16-17).

Here's a grade 4-5 answer extract

All these extracts are from answers to the second task in question 5 on page 67 — the opening of a story.

> The small house stood on its own, surrounded by fir trees and rocks. Snow had gathered against the walls in deep piles. It did not look very inviting, but to Anneka it was the most welcome sight in the world. She had got lost in the woods and she had been worried that she would have to spend the night outside in the forest, which was freezing cold and as scary as a spider's nest.
>
> Anneka walked towards the door and knocked. To her surprise the door swung open and she could see inside the house. She saw a single room with a fire burning in the fireplace and a table set for two, with hot food piled high on the plates. There was only one thing missing from the scene, there were no people inside.
>
> Anneka walked tentatively into the room and began to warm her hands in front of the fire, wondering where the people who lived in the house had gone. The room looked as if someone had just stepped out, but the only path Anneka had seen was the one she had come along, and she had not passed anyone else. Surely they couldn't have just disappeared?

This sets the scene, but it could do with some more imaginative description.

It's good to use descriptive techniques like similes, but this one isn't very original and it doesn't really create the right tone.

The punctuation in this sentence isn't quite right — a colon would fit better.

This is a good piece of descriptive vocabulary.

This sets up a mystery, which makes the reader want to know what has happened.

1) This answer has a fairly clear structure and gets straight into the story.

2) However, it lacks description, and the vocabulary isn't very varied. It could also be made more exciting or complex for its teenage audience.

Graded Answers — Question 5

Here's a grade 6-7 answer extract

Robin lowered the axe he had been using to chop wood and peered towards the mountains, his eyes squinting in the sharp orange glow of the slowly setting Sun. He was sure he had seen a movement up there, a flash of scarlet against the sparkling white of the snow-capped peaks. But who would be mad enough to venture into the mountains at dusk, in winter, with snow and freezing temperatures forecast that night?

Robin sighed wearily, deciding that it must have been his imagination playing tricks on him, as it so often did out here in the mountains.

A low, ominous rumble echoed down the valley, interrupting his thoughts. Robin froze momentarily, listening intently, then snapped into action, frantically gathering his tools as the sound grew louder and closer.

The avalanche roared destructively and unstoppably towards his isolated home.

This uses the opening sentence of the story to set the scene nicely.

This answer uses interesting language to make the descriptions more vivid and to entertain the audience.

This uses the senses to help the reader to imagine the scene.

The change of pace creates excitement in this story.

1) This has a clear <u>structure</u>, uses good <u>descriptions</u> and builds <u>interest</u> for the reader.

2) It could be improved by using more <u>complex</u> sentence structures and a <u>wider range</u> of punctuation.

This is a grade 8-9 answer extract

I surfaced suddenly from a dreamless sleep, the skin on my forearms tingling with an instinctive awareness that something was wrong. There — that noise again! A skittering, scrabbling, scuffling noise in the far corner of the dimly lit room. I sat up in bed, the quilt clutched to my chest with stone-numb hands, my breath forming foggy billows in the chilly air.

The sun was just rising; its feeble light trickled through the window, fractured into myriad rainbows by the intricate whorls and fingers of ice on the frosty pane. As a brighter beam pierced the gloom, I gasped. There, huddled by the door, a young wolf cub gazed at me with sorrowful, strangely human eyes. His tawny fur was matted with blood, as rich and red as the morning light that now illuminated it fully.

I eased myself out of the wooden bunk, crouched down on the splintered floorboards and held out a trembling hand towards the cub. He gazed at me uncertainly, then slowly, slowly, he stretched forward and snuffled at my fingers, his breath as warm and ticklish as a damp feather duster.

This beginning immediately sets the tone and atmosphere by creating tension.

This uses a first-person narrator to establish a strong connection with the reader.

Vivid description and interesting vocabulary help to set the scene.

Unusual imagery helps to set this answer apart.

1) This has a structure that <u>interests</u> the reader by <u>slowly revealing</u> what's going on.

2) It's also packed with interesting <u>imagery</u> and unusual <u>vocabulary</u> to make it more <u>entertaining</u> to read, which helps it to fit the <u>purpose</u> and <u>audience</u> of the question.

Sample Exam — Paper 2

These two pages show you some example questions that are like the ones you'll see in paper 2 — the sources to go with questions 1-4 are on pages 80-81. First have a good read through the sources and the questions, then have a look at the handy graded answer extracts we've provided on pages 82-91.

Question 1 asks you to identify if statements are true or false

0 1   Read the first part of **source A**, from lines 1 to 17.

Choose **four** statements below which are **TRUE**.

- Shade the boxes of the ones that you think are true
- Choose a maximum of four statements.

A	Lisa made her first batches of soup with her parents.	☐
B	Lisa wasn't initially excited about making and selling soup.	☐
C	Lisa's parents liked the first sample of soup she made them try.	☐
D	Lisa's aunt didn't like throwing food away.	☐
E	Lisa's parents thought the business was a great idea from the start.	☐
F	People were surprised by Lisa working at such a young age.	☐
G	Lisa's dad wasn't very good at negotiating with farmers.	☐
H	Lisa chose working on her business over spending time with friends.	☐

[4 marks]

Question 2 is about summarising information

0 2   You need to refer to **source A** and the **whole of source B** for this question:

Use details from **both** sources. Write a summary of the differences between Lisa Goodwin's parents and the parents of the Victorian street sellers.

[8 marks]

Sooner or later, Lisa was going to realise she needed a smaller spoon.

Sample Exam — Paper 2

Question 3 is about the writer's choice of language

| 0 | 3 |

You now need to refer **only** to **source B**, the interview with the flower seller.

How does the flower seller use language to appeal to the reader's emotions?

[12 marks]

Question 4 asks you to compare writers' viewpoints

| 0 | 4 |

For this question, you need to refer to the **whole of source A** together with **source B**, the interview with the nut seller.

Compare how Lisa Goodwin and the nut seller convey their different attitudes to work and childhood.

In your answer, you could:

- compare their different attitudes
- compare the methods they use to convey their attitudes
- support your ideas with references to both texts.

[16 marks]

You have to explain your viewpoint in Question 5

| 0 | 5 |

"More children should get a job before the age of sixteen. Part-time work would teach children valuable skills that they don't learn in school."

Write an article for a broadsheet newspaper in which you explain your point of view on this statement.

(24 marks for content and organisation
16 marks for technical accuracy)

[40 marks]

GCSE revision — marginally better being a Victorian street seller...

It's a tricky ol' exam and no mistake. Just this time though, we've done it for you. Have a good look through the sources on pages 80-81 and our graded answers that follow, and you'll be more than a match for it.

Exam Source A

Here is exam source A, to go with the questions on pages 78-79. It's an autobiographical article written by a young entrepreneur (a person who starts up a business) for a newspaper in the 1990s.

Setting up SouperStar — From Soup Pan to Soup Stand

Lisa Goodwin recalls how she set up her first business at the age of eight.

When I first told my parents that I wanted to sell soup, I must have been about eight years old — like most sensible parents, they thought I was joking. That weekend, I'd been at my aunt's house helping her harvest vegetables from her garden. It had been a bumper year, and we'd been staggering back and forth, shifting armfuls of all sorts of things into the house. With my aunt, not a single thing could
5   go to waste, so we set about making soup. Gallons of the stuff. We were surrounded by steaming and bubbling pots and pans, and the air was thick with scents of leek and potato, carrot and coriander and spicy butternut squash. Anyway, when my parents didn't take me seriously, I went straight to the fridge to dig out one of the soups my aunt and I had made — it was cream of mushroom, I think — and they absolutely lapped it up. "See!" I said, smiling. So it was then that SouperStar was born.

10 From day one I couldn't wait to get stuck in. My parents would dutifully help me select produce, whizz up batches of soup and drive me here, there and everywhere so that I could set up shop. I would go to school fairs, farmers' markets — anywhere that would have me. Dad was my champion haggler. He'd barter with local farmers to get crates of carrots or potatoes at rock-bottom prices. If he could get anything for free, well, that was even better! I think a lot of people were bemused by the sight of this
15 young kid, buying produce and selling soup, and my parents put up with it because they thought that I would grow out of it at some stage. While other kids my age were glued to the TV or playing in the park, I was peeling vegetables and frying croutons.

I begged and pleaded with my parents to let me be home-schooled, as I wanted to dedicate more time to the business, but they insisted I should have a "normal" childhood, and fill my head with "necessary" stuff
20 like formulae and equations. A few years later, and I was sitting my O levels* — but instead of panicking over revision, I was, of course, dreaming up new recipes. With all my exams passed and done with, I wanted to press on and really dedicate myself to SouperStar. I think at this point my parents genuinely realised how determined I was, and they began to take it a lot more seriously too.

I struck upon the idea of selling soup at our local train station during the winter months — there was a
25 constant stream of customers all in desperate need of something that would warm up their hands and fill their bellies. Before long, I was hiring extra staff in order to open up soup stands in other nearby train stations and Mum was coming up with advertising slogans and snazzy package designs (her years of marketing experience came in pretty handy here). As the business grew and grew, Mum and Dad couldn't keep up with all the support I needed, so it made sense for them to get even more involved.
30 Mum reduced her hours at work and Dad quit his job entirely. Fast-forward to today, and I'm the managing director of one the most successful food companies in the area.

Of course, financially, it's worked out well for us (thanks must go to my parents for the initial investment, not to mention being old enough to buy the wine for my French onion soup!), but for me it was never the dream of becoming a millionaire that got me started or even kept me going. It was the passion for
35 building a great business based on great food — and that remains at the heart of SouperStar today.

Glossary
* O levels — the qualifications that preceded GCSEs, with examinations taken at the age of 16.

Exam Source B

This is exam source B, which consists of two interviews from the 1840s conducted with children who work as street sellers. These articles, alongside many others like them, were published in a newspaper to highlight the plight of the poor in London.

The first interview is with a young girl who sells flowers, and is an orphan.

"Mother has been dead just a year this month; she took cold at the washing and it went to her chest; she was only bad a fortnight; she suffered great pain, and, poor thing, she used to fret dreadful, as she lay ill, about me, for she knew she was going to leave me. She used to plan how I was to do when she was gone. She made me promise to try to get a place and keep from the streets if I could, for she seemed
5   to dread them so much. When she was gone I was left in the world without a friend. I am quite alone, I have no relation at all, not a soul belonging to me. For three months I went about looking for a place, as long as my money lasted, for mother told me to sell our furniture to keep me and get me clothes. I could have got a place, but nobody would have me without a character*, and I knew nobody to give me one. I tried very hard to get one, indeed I did; for I thought of all mother had said to me about going into the
10 streets. At last, when my money was just gone, I met a young woman in the street, and I asked her to tell me where I could get a lodging. She told me to come with her, she would show me a respectable lodging-house for women and girls. I went, and I have been there ever since. The women in the house advised me to take to flower-selling, as I could get nothing else to do. One of the young women took me to market with her, and showed me how to bargain with the salesman for my flowers. At first, when I went out to
15 sell, I felt so ashamed I could not ask anybody to buy of me; and many times went back at night with all my stock, without selling one bunch. The woman at the lodging house is very good to me; when I have a bad day she will let my lodging go until I can pay her. She is very kind, indeed, for she knows I am alone. What I shall do in the winter I don't know. In the cold weather last year, when I could get no flowers, I was forced to live on my clothes, I have none left now but what I have on. What I shall do I don't know — I
20 can't bear to think on it."

The second interview is with a young girl who sells nuts.

"It's in the winter, sir, when things are far worst with us. Father can make very little then — but I don't know what he earns exactly at any time — and though mother has more work then, there's fire and candle to pay for. We were very badly off last winter, and worse, I think, the winter before. Father sometimes came home and had made nothing, and if mother had no work in hand we went to bed to save fire and
25 candle, if it was ever so soon. Father would die afore he would let mother take as much as a loaf from the parish. I was sent out to sell nuts first: 'If it's only 1d.** you make,' mother said, 'it's a good piece of bread.' I didn't mind being sent out. I knew children that sold things in the streets. Perhaps I liked it better than staying at home without a fire and with nothing to do, and if I went out I saw other children busy. No, I wasn't a bit frightened when I first started, not a bit. Some children — but they was such little
30 things — said: 'O, Liz, I wish I was you.' I had twelve ha'porths*** and sold them all. I don't know what it made; 2d. most likely. I didn't crack a single nut myself. I was fond of them then, but I don't care for them now. I could do better if I went into public-houses, but I'm only let go to Mr. Smith's, because he knows father, and Mrs. Smith and him recommends me. I have sold nuts and oranges to soldiers. I was once in a great crowd, and was getting crushed, and there was a very tall soldier close by me, and he lifted me,
35 basket and all, right up to his shoulder, and carried me clean out of the crowd. He had stripes on his arm. 'I shouldn't like you to be in such a trade,' says he, 'if you was my child.' He didn't say why he wouldn't like it. Perhaps because it was beginning to rain. Yes, we are far better off now. Father makes money. I don't go out in bad weather in the summer; in the winter, though, I must. I don't know what I shall be when I grow up. I can read a little. I've been to church five or six times in my life. I should go oftener and
40 so would mother, if we had clothes."

Glossary
* a character — a reference
** d. — pence
*** ha'porths — half-pennys' worth

Graded Answers — Question 1

Not too much to write for question 1... in fact you don't have to write anything at all.
Remind yourself of the question on p.78 then get stuck into this stuff to see how it's done.

You need to pick out the true statements

1) Question 1 gives you <u>eight</u> statements about a part of one of the sources — you have to pick out which statements are <u>true</u>.

2) Only <u>four</u> of the statements are true, and there are <u>four</u> <u>marks</u> available — so you need to shade in <u>four boxes</u>.

3) Always make sure you've shaded in <u>exactly</u> four boxes. If you've shaded in the statements that you're <u>sure</u> about and you still haven't shaded in four, have a <u>guess</u> at the others — you might get them right.

4) This sample question is about <u>lines 1-17</u> of <u>source A</u>, so you only need to look at that part of the text to find the answers.

5) Read the statements <u>carefully</u> as they might be about something that is <u>implicit</u> — something that isn't stated outright, but is <u>implied</u> by what the text says.

Well I'm all out of ideas, lads. I took eight statements from this fella and it looks like only half of them are true.

Here's a grade 4-5 answer

This answer has spotted <u>two</u> of the true statements — <u>D</u> and <u>F</u>.

> This is true — the text says Lisa's aunt believed that "not a single thing could go to waste". This implies that she wouldn't want to throw any food away.

> This is false — the text says "From day one I couldn't wait to get stuck in", so she was excited from the very beginning.

A	Lisa made her first batches of soup with her parents.	☐
B	Lisa wasn't initially excited about making and selling soup.	■
C	Lisa's parents liked the first sample of soup she made them try.	☐
D	Lisa's aunt didn't like throwing food away.	■
E	Lisa's parents thought the business was a great idea from the start.	☐
F	People were surprised by Lisa working at such a young age.	■
G	Lisa's dad wasn't very good at negotiating with farmers.	■
H	Lisa chose working on her business over spending time with friends.	☐

> This is true — the text says "people were bemused" at her working because she was a "young kid". The word "bemused" shows that they were confused and surprised.

> This is false — the text says Lisa's dad was her "champion haggler". This implies he was good at negotiating with farmers.

Graded Answers — Question 1

This is a grade 6-7 answer

This answer has spotted <u>three</u> of the true statements — <u>D</u>, <u>F</u> and <u>H</u>.

A	Lisa made her first batches of soup with her parents.	☐
B	Lisa wasn't initially excited about making and selling soup.	☐
C	Lisa's parents liked the first sample of soup she made them try.	☐
D	Lisa's aunt didn't like throwing food away.	■
E	Lisa's parents thought the business was a great idea from the start.	■
F	People were surprised by Lisa working at such a young age.	■
G	Lisa's dad wasn't very good at negotiating with farmers.	☐
H	Lisa chose working on her business over spending time with friends.	■

> This is false — the text says that her parents initially thought she was "joking".

> This is true — the text says that instead of "playing in the park" as other children did, Lisa was "peeling vegetables". This shows that she was making soup instead of playing with other children.

Sigh... all this playing in the park is OK, I suppose, but I'd really rather be peeling vegetables you know.

And here's a grade 8-9 answer

This answer has spotted all <u>four</u> of the true statements — <u>C</u>, <u>D</u>, <u>F</u> and <u>H</u>.

A	Lisa made her first batches of soup with her parents.	☐
B	Lisa wasn't initially excited about making and selling soup.	☐
C	Lisa's parents liked the first sample of soup she made them try.	■
D	Lisa's aunt didn't like throwing food away.	■
E	Lisa's parents thought the business was a great idea from the start.	☐
F	People were surprised by Lisa working at such a young age.	■
G	Lisa's dad wasn't very good at negotiating with farmers.	☐
H	Lisa chose working on her business over spending time with friends.	■

> This is false — the text says that she made her first batches of soup whilst visiting her aunt's house.

> This is true — the text says that Lisa's parents "absolutely lapped it up". This phrase implies they ate it quickly and with enthusiasm.

Graded Answers — Question 2

It's time for question 2 (take a look back at p.78). Better get your thinking cap on...

Pick out information from both sources

1) Question 2 is testing your ability to pick out information from <u>both</u> sources, then <u>summarise</u> it to show the <u>differences</u> between them.

2) The sample question asks you to pick out information about the <u>parents</u> that feature in the sources — make sure your points focus on the parents, and not <u>anything else</u>.

Use <u>P.E.E.D.</u> (see p.10) and make sure you include <u>technical terms</u> to get top marks.

3) You need to <u>summarise</u> the <u>differences</u> between the parents. This involves making a <u>point</u> about each of the parents, backing it up with good quotations as <u>evidence</u>, then clearly <u>explaining</u> how this shows a difference between them.

It wasn't immediately obvious what was so funny, but Cynthia just went with it.

4) You could then <u>develop</u> your points, e.g. by linking different points together or offering insights into <u>why</u> the parents are different.

5) To get top marks, you need to <u>interpret</u> information from the texts — this means picking out the things that <u>aren't immediately obvious</u> about the parents.

Here's a grade 4-5 answer extract

> The nut seller's parents are poor as they are described as "badly off" and sometimes they have to go to bed early to save money. Lisa Goodwin's parents seem to be well off. This difference means that the nut seller's parents expect their daughter to go out to work rather than go to school. On the other hand, Lisa Goodwin's parents don't expect Lisa to go out to work and even "insisted" that she stay in school.
>
> The flower seller's mother is dead and the text doesn't mention her father. Her mother worried about her a lot as it says she used to "fret dreadful". Both Lisa Goodwin's parents are alive and helped her out a lot with her business.
>
> The nut seller doesn't know what she wants to be when she grows up, whereas Lisa Goodwin wants to "dedicate" herself to her business.

This is a good use of a short quotation to back up the point.

This needs a quote or an example to back up the point.

This is good — it shows that a comparison is being made.

There needs to be an explanation here of how the sets of parents are different.

This final sentence isn't related to the question, so it wouldn't get any marks.

1) This answer gives <u>some differences</u> between the parents in the two sources.

2) It would be better if <u>all</u> the points were backed up with <u>quotes</u> or <u>examples</u> from the text.

3) The points could also be <u>developed more</u>, e.g. by giving thoughtful insights into the reasons <u>why</u> the parents are different.

Graded Answers — Question 2

Here's a grade 6-7 answer extract

> The nut seller's parents are a working-class couple living in 19th-century London, who have been "badly off", though the child feels they are "better off now". However, the child is expected to contribute to the household income, even "if it's only 1d.". The nut seller says she was "sent out", which suggests her parents forced her to work.
>
> This contrasts with Lisa Goodwin's parents, who do not seem to have any financial worries as they were able to provide Lisa with "the initial investment" for her business. Unlike the nut seller's parents, Lisa's parents didn't expect their daughter to work at a young age; in fact they thought she was "joking" when she suggested starting her own business.
>
> Before she died, the flower seller's mother was worried about her daughter being on "the streets", which shows she was concerned for her safety. Lisa Goodwin's parents just wanted her to have a "normal childhood" and go to school. This shows the differences between the time periods the two sets of parents were living in, and their levels of wealth.

Good use of short, relevant quotes to support the points.

This answer makes inferences about the parents — it comments on the thoughts and actions of the parents that aren't directly stated.

This is good — it explains the differences by showing awareness of the context in which the texts were written.

This answer makes several good points, and uses relevant quotes to back everything up.

Here's a grade 8-9 answer extract

> The parents of the nut seller and the parents of Lisa Goodwin have very different attitudes to their own needs and their child's employment. The nut seller's parents are a poor, working-class couple living in 19th-century London. The child recounts how they were "very badly off" in recent winters, but that they are "far better off now". Despite this apparent improvement in their income, the child is still "sent out" to work to contribute to the household income. Lisa Goodwin's parents, by contrast, need no extra support. They dutifully sacrificed their own careers in order to support their daughter's ambitions. Lisa's parents prioritise her ambitions over their own, whereas the nut seller's parents prioritise the need to survive over their child's future prospects. This could be because the concerns of a more affluent family in the 20th century were often different to those of a less wealthy family in the 19th century.
>
> The mother of the flower seller demonstrates a very different attitude to the parents of Lisa Goodwin. She expresses deep concern for her child's safety through her plea that she should "keep from the streets". Lisa Goodwin's parents, however, are concerned at her desire to work so young and perceive her greatest need is to have a "normal childhood". Once again, this demonstrates the very different situations of the sets of parents: the flower seller's mother is destitute and dying, and thinks only of her child's safety. Lisa Goodwin's parents have the luxury of being able to be concerned about the extent of their child's education.

This is great — a point is made straight away.

This is an interesting interpretation of the differences between the parents.

This clearly compares the parents in each source.

Higher level vocabulary and sentence structures help to make this a top level answer.

This answer makes well-developed points, backs them up with good evidence and makes an interesting link to the social and historical context of the texts in order to explore the differences between the parents.

Graded Answers — Question 3

Verily, in thy quest to slay the examination thou hast reached the third question. Journey to page 79 to reacquaint thyself with thine enemy, then unsheathe thy biro and scream "En garde!" at question 3.

Think about the writer's choice of words

1) Question 3 is about <u>how</u> the writer has used <u>language</u> to <u>affect</u> the reader.

2) Make sure you read the question <u>carefully</u> — in this example, you're only supposed to write about the <u>flower seller interview</u> from source B.

3) The sample question is about how the writer uses language to <u>appeal</u> to the reader's emotions — so think about how the language used would make readers <u>feel</u>, and how they might <u>react</u>.

4) To analyse language for this question, you should comment on things like:

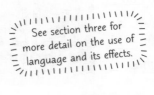
See section three for more detail on the use of language and its effects.

> - The effect of specific <u>words and phrases</u>, such as how certain verbs are used (see p.33-34).
>
> - <u>Language features and techniques</u>, such as rhetorical devices (see p.33-41).
>
> - The effect of different <u>sentence forms</u>, such as short or long sentences (see p.48-49).

No language technique was going to help Dad get Alex off to sleep.

5) Make sure you use a range of <u>technical terms</u> to describe the writer's techniques, and keep your vocabulary <u>varied</u> and <u>interesting</u>.

Here's a grade 4-5 answer extract

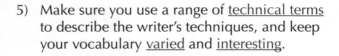

    The flower seller describes all the terrible things that have happened to her in the first person. This helps the reader understand how the girl must be feeling because it is told directly from her point of view.
    The flower seller uses strong, emotional language to describe the death of her mother, for example she says that her mother "suffered great pain". This makes you feel sorry for the mother, as she was in pain, but also for the flower seller as it makes you think about how you would feel in her place.
    The flower seller shows how lonely she feels when she says "I was left in the world without a friend." This is a really effective way of making you feel sorry for her and the situation she's in.

Try to avoid repeating yourself in your answer — even if you want to make a similar point, try to phrase it differently

This paragraph makes a good point, closely related to the question, backed up with an example and with an explanation.

This needs to explain how the language affects the reader.

1) This clearly answers the <u>question</u> — all the points are about how the <u>language</u> might <u>appeal</u> to the <u>reader's emotions</u>.

2) There's room for improvement though — some of the points could do with more <u>examples</u>, and the answer could <u>explain how</u> the language appeals to the reader's emotions more clearly.

Section Six — Paper 2 — Sample Exam and Graded Answers

Graded Answers — Question 3

Here's a grade 6-7 answer extract

> The language the flower seller uses shows that she had to be the one looking after her mother, rather than the other way round. Phrases such as "poor thing" and "fret dreadful" sound more like a mother talking about a child who is ill. This creates sympathy for the flower seller, as readers would feel that she has been denied her childhood.
>
> The repetition in the flower seller's story emphasises how isolated she feels after her mother's death. She uses several similar phrases, such as "left in the world without a friend", "I am quite alone" and "not a soul belonging to me", to reinforce how desolate she is. This makes the reader feel sorry for her, because after the tragedy of her mother's death, the girl has no one to turn to.
>
> The flower seller doesn't say how old she is, but the concern her mother feels for leaving her daughter alone — she "seemed to dread" the thought of her daughter on the streets — suggests that she is too young to look after herself. This makes the flower seller's story seem even more sorrowful.

This is really focused on how the language is used.

This is good — a language technique has been spotted, then the effect of it has been explained and developed.

Making inferences is great — this demonstrates to the examiner that you've read the text carefully and have really thought about its meaning.

This answer makes some <u>interesting inferences</u> about the <u>effects</u> of the language on the reader, but it could be improved by using more <u>technical terms</u> and higher-level <u>vocabulary</u>.

This is a grade 8-9 answer extract

> The interview with the flower seller was one of a number of articles published to highlight the plight of London's poor. As such, the articles chosen would have been those that would have the biggest emotional impact on the reader.
>
> The first-person narrative makes the reader feel they are actually being spoken to by the child, which increases the emotional appeal of her story. The use of her own words allows readers to see the nuances of her feelings; when she repeats how "alone" she is, without "a soul" and "no relation" to help her, the list form of the sentence makes her sorrow clear. This humanises her story, so it resonates more with the readership.
>
> In line 15, the flower seller confesses she was initially too "ashamed" to sell any flowers. This word highlights how young she is, as it emphasises her naivety and inexperience. This makes the readers feel sympathy for the flower seller: she has been put in a position which is beyond her ability to cope with, but she has to in order to survive.
>
> With her final words, the flower seller admits that she "can't bear" to think about the future: she has sold all her possessions and has no one to turn to. This uncertain and desperate ending leaves the reader feeling despondent and helpless, and would perhaps make them feel guilty enough to spur them into helping the poor themselves.

This answer makes an interesting point by looking at how the context of the article relates to the purpose of the text.

Sophisticated vocabulary makes this answer perceptive and detailed.

It's really good to focus on specific words and the effect they have.

This answer comments on the different emotions the text evokes — sympathy, helplessness, guilt. This is much better than repeating the same effect over and over.

This answer makes some interesting and <u>original points</u> about the <u>purpose</u> of the article. Including details like this will really <u>impress</u> the examiner — just make sure that they are <u>relevant</u> to the question.

Section Six — Paper 2 — Sample Exam and Graded Answers

Graded Answers — Question 4

Question 4 is worth a whopping 16 marks. Take a look back at the question on page 79, then have a read through these answers. You might just pick up some tips that will save your life... well, help you out a bit.

Compare the writers' different points of view

1) Question 4 is about what the writers <u>think</u> about work and childhood, as well as <u>how they show</u> what they're thinking.

2) There are some handy bullet points to guide you — make sure you read them <u>carefully</u> and cover what they <u>ask for</u> in your answer.

> - You need to identify what the writers' <u>attitudes</u> to <u>work</u> and <u>childhood</u> are, and clearly <u>compare</u> them.
>
> - You also need to compare <u>how</u> the writers have shown their attitudes to work and childhood, i.e. the <u>words</u>, <u>phrases</u> and <u>language techniques</u> they've used.
>
> - You should back up every point you make with relevant <u>evidence</u> from the text — using <u>short quotations</u> is a great way to do this.

Follow our souper advice for exam success.

3) Make sure you focus on their attitudes to <u>work</u> and <u>childhood</u>, not anything else.

4) The question is also asking you to <u>compare</u>, so make sure you <u>link</u> the two writers' attitudes together using words and phrases such as 'however', 'in contrast' and 'whereas'.

Here's a grade 4-5 answer extract

> Lisa wanted to work during her childhood, as she says that she "couldn't wait to get stuck in." On the other hand, the nut seller doesn't seem bothered about working and says that "Perhaps" it's "better than staying at home".
> Lisa uses 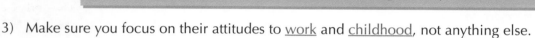 chatty language to talk about her childhood and the work she did, for example she calls herself "this young kid". This shows that she was keen to work when she was young, but she thought it was unusual. The nut seller is different. She "didn't mind" working, and she thinks it's normal for children to be working as she says that she "knew children that sold things in the streets."
> The nut seller does what she's told to do by her parents when it comes to work. She was "sent out to sell nuts". Lisa Goodwin does the opposite. She tries to tell them what to do as 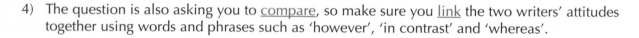 she wanted to stop going to school and start work instead.

This paragraph makes a good, simple comparison, backed up with quotes as evidence.

A better, more technical term to write about informal, conversational language would be "colloquial".

The example doesn't clearly show what the explanation is saying.

This isn't true — she wanted to be home-schooled. Read the text carefully to make sure you understand what it's saying.

1) This answer mentions some different <u>attitudes</u> and starts to comment on how <u>language</u> is used to <u>show</u> the attitudes.

2) However, it could go into more <u>detail</u> by using more <u>examples</u>, and <u>explaining</u> them more clearly and accurately.

Graded Answers — Question 4

Here's a grade 6-7 answer extract

Lisa's enthusiasm for work comes out through her strongly positive, upbeat tone and colloquial language: she describes how even as a child she would work "anywhere that would have" her, and the slang word "whizz" indicates how much she enjoyed making the soup. The attitude she demonstrates to her childhood is that she just wanted to work, rather than have the "normal childhood" that her parents wanted for her. The quotation marks she uses when she talks about "necessary" education show that she is being ironic and doesn't think the education is necessary at all.

The nut seller, however, works because she has to rather than through a personal desire to work, and she seems unenthusiastic about her employment. This is shown by her less positive tone and more reserved style. She says that she "didn't mind" selling nuts and that it is simply "better than staying at home". She shows that, to her, a normal childhood is spent working in the streets like the other children she knew who were all "busy" working.

> Using technical terms correctly will get you marks.

> The answer makes clear comparisons.

> This paragraph consistently covers all the bullet points — what the writers' attitudes are, how they're conveyed and good quotes are used to back up the point.

This answer is good, but to really wow the examiner, try to include some <u>innovative</u> points...

This is a grade 8-9 answer extract

Lisa's passion and positivity about her work are conveyed through her informal style, and colloquialisms such as "whizz up" and "snazzy". This conversational language portrays Lisa as someone who has a confident and easy-going attitude to work. She also uses humour to engage the reader, ending the piece with a joke about needing her parents to "buy the wine". This humour gives the text warmth, and demonstrates Lisa's zeal for work.

Lisa also shows a proud and arrogant attitude to her work and childhood. The bemusement she describes causing as a "young kid" working shows her pride in having worked amongst adults, and her disdain for "necessary" education shows her arrogance. She seems to believe that a "normal childhood" was not right for her, and that her parents insistence upon it was tiresome.

In sharp contrast to Lisa Goodwin, the nut seller "must" work. Her unenthusiastic attitude regarding work itself comes out through her more resigned tone: she says that it "is better than staying at home". However, she does seem to be motivated by a desire to make more money. Her tone becomes more animated when describing her ideas about how she "could do better".

The nut seller shows her naive attitude to working as a child through the device of a story: she recalls her encounter with a soldier who wouldn't like his own child "to be in such a trade", but she thinks that is because it was "beginning to rain". It seems clear that the soldier is concerned for her safety, and that the nut seller doesn't comprehend the danger she is in because of her youth and innocence.

> This answer picks out some of the more subtle attitudes to work and childhood shown by the writers.

> This develops the point by going into more depth about her attitude to work.

> This is a perceptive point — it makes an inference about the situation instead of just taking the writer's words literally.

Graded Answers — Question 5

Question 5 is the Big Daddy of paper 2, so make sure you leave plenty of time to write your answer.
Take a look back at the question on page 79, then enjoy the feast of non-fiction writing before you...

Adapt your writing style to the question

It doesn't matter whether you agree or disagree with the statement as long as your answer is engaging and well-structured.

1) For question 5 you need to respond to the statement, by giving your own perspective on the value of part-time work for children under 16.

2) You need to match your writing to the form, purpose and audience you've been given in the question.

- The form is a broadsheet newspaper article — so you could write in the style of an opinion piece and include layout features such as a headline.

- The purpose is to explain your point of view, but as you're responding to a statement you could do this by making an argument for your viewpoint.

- The audience isn't mentioned specifically, but you can work it out. It's a broadsheet newspaper article about work for teenagers, so it's likely to be read by adults with children who are under 16.

See pages 58-59 for more about writing newspaper articles.

3) It's also important to think about the structure of your writing, especially the opening and ending. You need to link your paragraphs together clearly, too.

4) Don't forget there are 16 marks on offer for spelling, punctuation and grammar for this question — it's really important to write accurately and clearly with a good range of vocabulary (see p.16-17).

Here's a grade 4-5 answer extract

NO PART-TIME JOBS FOR UNDER-SIXTEENS

I think that children under the age of 16 shouldn't get a part-time job. Although some people might argue that having a job teaches children about the value of money, time management and working as a team, I don't think that this is the case.

Firstly, most children already have good time management skills. Schools start at 9 am, and some even earlier than this, so arriving on time to lessons is already second nature to most children. Why should children have a part-time job when they already know how to manage their time? Secondly, most children have been working as a team since primary school. From sports teams in P.E., to group projects in Science, school teaches children how to work together from a very young age. Why should children give up their weekends for a badly paid job when they already have great teamwork skills?

This opening sentence isn't really appropriate for a broadsheet newspaper.

This answer uses a counter argument to strengthen the point it's making.

A new paragraph should start here.

The repetition of rhetorical questions is a nice language feature — it makes the point of view come across more forcefully.

1) This answer makes some good points that are focused on the question.

2) It could be better matched to the form that the question asks for, though — the tone and style aren't really appropriate for a broadsheet newspaper.

3) The language could also be more varied and interesting — including a bit of humour or using more creative vocabulary would gain more marks.

Bradley's part-time job taught him to dress for success.

Graded Answers — Question 5

Here's a grade 6-7 answer extract

> **SAVE THE LEARNING FOR THE CLASSROOM**
>
> Lots of young people have a part-time job, and I am sure that employment teaches them a whole host of valuable skills: communication, time management and independence to name but a few. However, these skills aren't just learnt in the workplace; many young people develop and refine these skills in the classroom.
>
> Take, for instance, communication. Every day in school, pupils communicate with a wide range of people. Pupils learn to talk respectfully to teachers; they learn how to make engaging conversation with their friends; and they learn how to communicate their ideas effectively to their peers during group work. School doesn't just allow pupils to practise their verbal communication — it allows them to develop their written communication too. Essays teach students how to summarise their thoughts, and present their opinions. What part-time job could develop communication more effectively than this?

The answer uses more sophisticated punctuation confidently and correctly.

The tone of this answer is suitable for the form and purpose. It's a bit more chatty than the previous answer, but it still uses good vocabulary.

The ideas are linked together fluently.

1) This answer uses language techniques, a <u>clear structure</u> and <u>creative vocabulary</u> to get its point across.

2) However, if the author's <u>personality</u> came across more strongly, the text would be more <u>compelling</u>.

Here's a grade 8-9 answer extract

A headline and strapline are used to grab the reader's attention.

> **MINIMUM WAGE, MINIMUM GAIN**
>
> Part-time jobs have little value for teenagers under sixteen, argues Charlie Lin.
>
> If someone were to ask me whether I thought under-sixteens should get part-time jobs, my answer, unequivocally, would be "no". As I write this, I can imagine the shocked looks on my readers' faces and the disdainful cries of "but employment teaches children valuable life skills!" To these critics, I say this: there's nothing a part-time job can teach children that they can't learn from other, more rewarding options.
>
> If you don't believe me, then think about the jobs that are actually available to under-sixteens. Paper rounds, waiting tables, shop assistant — essentially an assortment of mundane, badly-paid Saturday jobs. And what 'valuable life skills' might they learn while toiling away for less than minimum wage? "Teamwork!" you might cry triumphantly, "working in a cafe would teach a young person how to work as part of a team." This may certainly be true if you believe being belittled by the chef and bossed around by the manager counts as 'teamwork'. I, however, do not. If that same child was part of a football team, working alongside their peers, practising hard to achieve a common goal (annihilating the rival team), now that would be teamwork.

The writer shows a clear awareness of their audience.

Really interesting and varied vocabulary makes this answer high level.

Lots of rhetorical techniques are used in this paragraph to make the writer's point of view clear and their argument compelling.

A sarcastic tone makes the argument convincingly, but also gives a sense of the writer's personality.

The writer's <u>opinion</u> and <u>personality</u> is clear in this answer, and it's <u>fluently written</u>. The tone is humorous and chatty, but also subtle, which makes the answer <u>engaging</u> and <u>readable</u>.

Glossary

adjective	A word that <u>describes</u> a noun or a pronoun, e.g. heavy, kind, unusual.
adverb	A word that gives <u>extra information</u> about a <u>verb</u>, e.g. carefully, rarely, tightly.
alliteration	When words that are <u>close together</u> start with the <u>same sound</u>. E.g. "the <u>b</u>eat of the <u>b</u>and".
analogy	A <u>comparison</u> to show how one thing is <u>similar</u> to another, which makes it easier to <u>understand</u> or more <u>memorable</u>. E.g. "watching cricket is about as exciting as watching paint dry."
antithesis	A <u>rhetorical technique</u> where <u>opposing</u> words or ideas are presented <u>together</u> to show a contrast.
audience	The <u>person</u> or <u>group of people</u> that read or listen to a text.
biased writing	Gives <u>more support</u> to one point of view than to another, due to the writer's own <u>opinions</u> affecting the way they write.
broadsheet	A more <u>formal</u> type of newspaper, which often focuses on more <u>serious</u> topics. E.g. *The Guardian* or *The Telegraph*.
chronological writing	Presented in <u>time order</u>, from earliest to latest.
cinematic writing	Writing that makes the reader feel like they're watching a <u>film</u>.
clause	Part of a sentence that has a <u>subject</u> and a <u>verb</u>. <u>Main clauses</u> make sense on their own.
colloquial language	<u>Informal</u> language that sounds like ordinary <u>speech</u>.
command	A sentence that <u>tells</u> the reader to do something.
commentary (newspaper article)	A type of newspaper article that expresses the <u>opinions</u> of the writer on a theme or news event. Also called a <u>column</u> or <u>opinion piece</u>.
complex sentence	A sentence that links together <u>two or more clauses</u>.
compound sentence	Two <u>main clauses</u> joined to make one sentence using a <u>conjunction</u> such as 'but', 'and' or 'so'. E.g. "The cat came in, <u>so</u> the dog left the room."
connotations	The <u>suggestions</u> that words can make <u>beyond</u> their obvious meaning. E.g. 'stroll' means 'walk', but it has connotations of moving slowly.
context	The <u>background</u> to something, or the situation <u>surrounding</u> it, which affects the way it's understood. E.g. the context of a text from 1915 would include the First World War.
counter-argument	The <u>opposite</u> point of view to the writer's own view. This is useful when writing to argue or persuade — first give the counter-argument, then explain why you <u>disagree</u> with it.
determiner	A word that goes before a <u>noun</u> to show possession or quantity (e.g. 'his', 'two').
direct address	When a writer talks <u>straight to the reader</u>, e.g. "you might recall..."
double negative	A sentence construction that <u>incorrectly</u> expresses a <u>negative idea</u> by using <u>two</u> negative words or phrases, e.g. "I <u>don't</u> want <u>no</u> trouble."
emotive language	Language that has an <u>emotional</u> effect on the reader.
empathy	The ability to <u>imagine</u> and <u>understand</u> someone else's <u>feelings</u> or <u>experiences</u>.
exclamation	A sentence that conveys strong <u>emotions</u>, usually ending with an <u>exclamation mark</u>.
explicit information	Information that's <u>directly stated</u> in a text.
figurative language	Language that is used in a <u>non-literal</u> way to create an effect, e.g. personification.

Glossary

first person	A narrative viewpoint where the narrator is one of the characters, written using words like 'I', 'me', 'we' and 'our'.
flashback	A writing technique where the scene shifts from the present to an event in the past.
form	The type of text, e.g. a letter, a speech or a newspaper article.
frame narrative	A narrative in which one story is presented within another.
generalisation	A statement that gives an overall impression (sometimes a misleading one), without going into details. E.g. "children today eat too much junk food."
hyperbole	When exaggeration is used to have an effect on the reader.
imagery	A type of figurative language that creates a picture in your mind, e.g. metaphors and similes.
imperative verb	A verb that gives orders or directions, e.g. "run away" or "stop that".
impersonal tone	A tone of writing that doesn't try to directly engage with the reader.
implicit information	Information that's hinted at without being said outright.
inference	A conclusion reached about something, based on evidence. E.g. from the sentence "Yasmin wrinkled her nose at the lasagne", you could infer that Yasmin doesn't like lasagne.
intensifier	A word that is used alongside an adjective to provide emphasis, e.g. "very friendly".
inversion	Altering the normal word order for emphasis, e.g. "On the table sat a hedgehog."
irony	Saying one thing but meaning the opposite. E.g. "What a great idea of mine to go for a nice long walk on the rainiest day of the year."
language	The choice of words and phrases used.
limited narrator	A narrator who only has partial knowledge about the events or characters in a story.
linear structure	A type of narrative structure that tells the events of a story in chronological order.
linguistic devices	Language techniques that are used to have an effect on an audience, e.g. onomatopoeia.
list of three	Using three words (often adjectives) or phrases together to create emphasis.
metaphor	A way of describing something by saying that it is something else, to create a vivid image. E.g. "His eyes were deep blue pools."
motif	A recurring image or idea in a text.
narrative	Writing that tells a story or describes an experience.
narrative viewpoint	The perspective that a text is written from, e.g. first-person point of view.
narrator	The voice or character speaking the words of the narrative.
non-linear structure	A type of narrative structure that tells the events of a story in a non-chronological order.
noun	A naming word that refers to a person, thing, place or idea, e.g. Alex, soup, Germany, freedom.
objective writing	A neutral, unbiased style of writing which contains facts rather than opinions.
omniscient narrator	A narrator who knows the thoughts and feelings of all the characters in a narrative.
onomatopoeia	A word that imitates the sound it describes as you say it, e.g. 'whisper'.

Glossary

Glossary

pace	The speed at which the writer takes the reader through the events in a story.
paraphrase	Describing or rephrasing something in a text without including a direct quote.
parenthesis	A rhetorical technique where an extra clause or phrase is inserted into a complete sentence.
personification	Describing something as if it's a person. E.g. "The sea growled hungrily."
possessive determiner	A determiner such as 'your' or 'my' that tells you who something belongs to.
possessive pronoun	A pronoun such as 'yours' or 'mine' that tells you who something belongs to.
pronoun	A word that can take the place of a noun in a sentence, e.g. 'he', 'she', 'it'.
purpose	The reason someone writes a text. E.g. to persuade, to argue, to advise, to inform.
register	The specific language used to match writing to the social situation that it's for.
repetition	The technique of repeating words for effect.
rhetoric	Using language techniques (e.g. repetition or hyperbole) to achieve a persuasive effect.
rhetorical question	A question that doesn't need an answer. E.g. "Why do we do this to ourselves?"
sarcasm	Language that has a scornful or mocking tone, often using irony.
satire	A style of text that makes fun out of people or situations, often by imitating them and exaggerating their flaws.
second person	A narrative viewpoint that is written as if the reader is one of the characters.
sensory language	Language that appeals to the five senses.
simile	A way of describing something by comparing it to something else, usually by using the words 'like' or 'as'. E.g. "He was as pale as the moon."
simple sentence	A sentence that is only made up of a single main clause.
slang	Words or phrases that are informal, and often specific to one age group or social group.
Standard English	English that is considered to be correct because it uses formal, standardised features of spelling and grammar.
statement	A type of sentence that is used to deliver information.
structure	The order and arrangement of ideas in a text. E.g. how the text begins, develops and ends.
style	The way in which a text is written, e.g. the type of language, sentence forms and structure used.
subject	The person or thing that performs the action described by the verb. E.g. in "Billy ate a sandwich", Billy is the subject.
tabloid	A less formal type of newspaper, which often focuses on more sensational topics.
third person	A narrative viewpoint where the narrator remains outside the events of the story, written using words like 'he' and 'she'.
tone	The mood or feeling of a piece of writing, e.g. happy, sad, serious, light-hearted.
verb	A doing or being word, e.g. dig, breathe, are, is.
viewpoint	The attitude and beliefs that a writer is trying to convey.

Glossary

Index

Index

EN DIREC[T] DE LA FRANCE

French Reading Materials from Authentic Sources

Ray Symons
Head of Modern Languages

Fiona Donaldson
Teacher of Modern Languages

Zina Bowey
Former teacher of Modern Languages

Stanley Thornes (Publishers) Ltd

Interrelation between topics prescribed by examining groups and the chapters of EN DIRECT DE LA FRANCE

The tables show which topics are covered in whole or in part by EN DIRECT DE LA FRANCE

LEAG

No.	Topic	Chapters
1.	Finding one's way	9, 5
2.	Shopping	5
3.	Cafés, restaurants, food and drink	6
4.	Accommodation	10
5.	Public transport	9
6.	Domestic and personal situations	1, 10
7.	Tourist information, banks, and customs	10, 7
8.	Public entertainment, tourist visits	4, 10
9.	Road travel	9
10.	Family and daily routine	1
11.	Leisure activities, sport	4
12.	Yearly routine, festivals, holiday	1, 6, 10
13.	Work and careers	3
14.	Towns, buildings, houses	1, 10
15.	School	2
16.	Communications	7
17.	Health	8
18.	Lost property, possessions	7
19.	People	1, 2, 3, 4
20.	Towns, country, geography and climate	10, 4
21.	Crime and the law	7, 9
22.	History, biography	1, 4

MEG

No.	Topic	Chapters
1.	Personal identification	1
2.	House and home	1, 10
3.	Geographical surroundings	2
4.	School	4
5.	Free time and entertainment	
6.	Travel	9
7.	Holidays	10
8.	Meeting people	1, 2, 3, 4
9.	Shopping	5
10.	Food and drink	6
11.	Weather	10
12.	Accommodation	10
13.	Work and future	3
14.	Emergencies	8
15.	Services	7
16.	Lost property	7

(13. – 16. higher level only)

NEA

No.	Topic	Chapters
1.	Personal identification	1
2.	Family	1
3.	House and home	1, 10
4.	Geographical surroundings and weather	2
5.	Travel and transport	4
6.	Holidays	9
7.	Accommodation	10
8.	Food and drink	10
9.	Shopping	6
10.	Services	5
11.	Health and welfare	7
12.	Free time and entertainment	8
13.	Relationships with others	1, 2, 3, 4
14.	Education and future career	2
15.	Foreign languages	2, 3
16.	Money	7, 5

NISEC

No.	Topic	Chapters
1.	Personal details	1
2.	Education	2
3.	House, home and lodging	1
4.	Geographical environment, plants/animals, climate/weather	1, 10
5.	Journeys and travel	9, 7
6.	Holidays/Accommodation	10
7.	Shopping and shops	5
8.	Public and private services	7, 9
9.	Hygiene and health	8
10.	Profession/job/occupation	3
11.	Leisure/sports/entertainment	4
12.	Relationships with others	1, 2, 3, 4
13.	Food and drink	6

SEG

No.	Topic	Chapters
1.	Personal details, daily routine, home and family	1
2.	School/college/work routine and future plans	2, 3
3.	Relationships with others	1, 2, 3, 4
4.	Free time/leisure interests/entertainments	4
5.	Local and foreign environment	1, 10
6.	Shopping	5
7.	Food and drink	6
8.	Money matters	8
9.	Public services	7, 5
10.	Health and welfare	7
11.	Holidays/accommodation	8
12.	Travel and transport	10
13.	Weather	9
15.	Pets*	1
16.	Money*	5, 7
17.	Time, dates and weather*	9, 10

* For oral work only

WJEC

No.	Topic	Chapters
1.	Self, family and friends	1
2.	Home and daily routines	1
3.	Time, weather, dates and numbers	10, 9
4.	Finding one's way	7
5.	Transport and travel	9, 5
6.	Food and drink	9
7.	Accommodation	6
8.	Shopping	10
9.	Services	5
10.	Language	7
11.	Leisure	4
12.	Town and region	1, 3
13.	School routine and education	4, 9
14.	Communications and the media	10
15.	Emergencies	7, 8
16.	Health and welfare	8

(14. – 16. higher level only)

SCE STANDARD GRADE

No.	Topic	Chapters
1.	People and personal relationships	1, 2, 3, 4
2.	Home	1
3.	Family and daily routine	1
4.	School	2
5.	Work	3
6.	Leisure	4
7.	Holidays and travel	9, 10
8.	Environment, places, facilities	4, 10
9.	Food and drink	6
10.	Goods and services	5, 7
11.	Accidents and emergencies	7, 8
12.	Events, concerns and ideas of adolescent and general interest	9, 10
13.	Self*	6
14.	Clothes and fashion*	5

* For oral work only

Contents

Notes for Teachers

En direct de la France aims to prepare students for the reading comprehension papers set in the GCSE examinations at basic and higher levels, and for the equivalent elements of SCE Standard Grade. It contains a selection of authentic materials, with questions in English, marked **E** for examination-type questions that test various reading skills (such as skimming, scanning, extracting relevant information and identifying points and themes). Each item has been selected to appeal to the interests and experiences of young people and also because of its intrinsic worth and insight into the French way of life.

The book is divided into ten chapters that encompass all the topic areas defined by the GCSE and SCE syllabuses. The two final chapters contain mock GCSE type tests – one at basic level, one at higher level. The thematical classification permits easy adaptation of the materials to graded test schemes, to TVEI/modular courses and to individual assignments as well as to the GCSE.

Though primarily a reading comprehension book, each chapter can be used as a springboard for communicative activities in French. Questions marked **P** for *pratique orale* are designed for oral work in French. Other items could lend themselves to the production of written work, if desired.

The materials in the book aim to form the basis of an essential classroom resource, enabling pupils to practise strategies to cope with authentic texts and GCSE or SCE type questions. Teachers might wish at a later date to supplement the chapters with their own selection of materials.

The Authors

Ray Symons is currently Head of Modern Languages at Newquay Tretherras School, Cornwall.

Fiona Donaldson now teaches modern languages at Culford School, Suffolk.

Zina Bowey is teaching English as a foreign language for the British Council in Peking.

All three were working at Mullion School, Cornwall, during the preparation of this book.

Chapter 1
La vie personnelle, publique et à la maison

Cette section consiste en quelques annonces et articles sur la vie personnelle, publique et à la maison.

A Les détails personnels

A French friend shows you her identity papers.

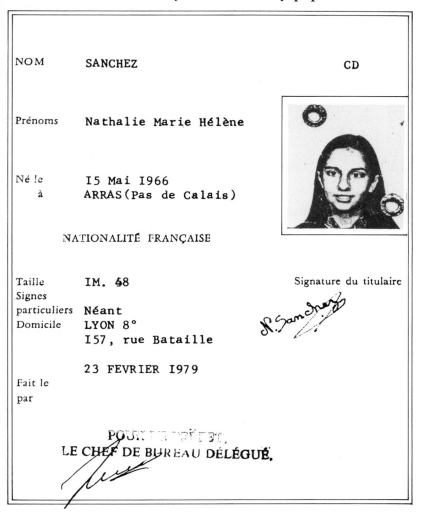

E1

Here is an identity card. Everyone in France has to carry one.

1 What information about Nathalie Sanchez can be obtained from her card?

2 How often should it be renewed?

P

a) Quels sont les avantages d'un système de cartes d'identité?

b) Aimeriez-vous voir arriver ce système en Angleterre?

E2

1 What sort of document is this?

2 Where could you return it to?

3 Where and when was this person born?

E3

When would you use this card?

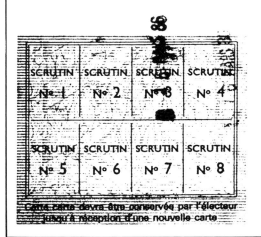

RECOMMANDATIONS IMPORTANTES

L'électeur ne sera admis à voter qu'après être passé par l'isoloir où il doit placer son bulletin dans l'enveloppe réglementaire mise à sa disposition à l'entrée de la salle de vote.

Quiconque aura voté, soit en vertu d'une inscription frauduleuse, soit en prenant faussement les nom et qualité d'un électeur inscrit, sera puni d'un emprisonnement de six mois à deux ans et d'une amende de 720 F à 20 000 F.

Sera puni de la même peine tout citoyen qui aura profité d'une inscription multiple pour voter plus d'une fois.

| SCRUTIN N° 1 | SCRUTIN N° 2 | SCRUTIN N° 3 | SCRUTIN N° 4 |
| SCRUTIN N° 5 | SCRUTIN N° 6 | SCRUTIN N° 7 | SCRUTIN N° 8 |

Cette carte devra être conservée par l'électeur jusqu'à réception d'une nouvelle carte

RÉPUBLIQUE FRANÇAISE

LIBERTÉ · ÉGALITÉ · FRATERNITÉ

CARTE D'ÉLECTEUR

La présente carte remplace la carte précédemment délivrée qui devra être détruite

« Voter est un droit c'est aussi un devoir civique »

MINISTÈRE DE L'INTÉRIEUR ET DE LA DÉCENTRALISATION

CRÉDIT AGRICOLE

LIBRE SERVICE BANCAIRE

SANCHEZ ANGELE   02

CRCAM DE LA LOZERE

| BUREAU | LOT | N° DE COMPTE | EXPIRE FIN |
| 00003 | 555 | 65711113900 | 12 88 |

E4

Copy out and fill in as many details as you can about this bank card.

Name of Bank: _____

Account Holder: Mr/Mrs/Miss: _____

Account Number: _____

Expiry Date: _____

E5

Here are three 'birth announcement' cards. Can you understand them?

Bruno et Nicolas ont la joie d'accueillir leur petit frère

Benoit

né le 17 Avril 1982

Odile et Rémy Julien

1, rue des Engoulevents
76130 Mont Saint Aignan

Clinique Jeanne d'Arc

Rue Saint Maur
76000 Rouen

Marie
est née le 18 Novembre 1980
à la grande joie de Kristell
et de ses parents

M. et Mme Michel Durose
13 C, rue des Capucins
Landerneau

Claire et Julien Dauguet

ont la joie de vous annoncer la naissance

de

Guillaume

le 17 Novembre 1981

M' et M'' E. DAUGUET
10, rue Debordeaux
02200 SOISSONS

1 Which baby do you know was born in a hospital?

2 Who was born in November?

3 Who has two brothers?

4 Which family now has two daughters?

P

a) Quand êtes-vous né(e)? Où?

b) Avez-vous des frères, des soeurs, des tantes, des oncles?

c) Décrivez un membre de votre famille.

E6

Mme Moreau has had a problem with her son's English pen-friend, Philip, who is staying in France on an exchange visit. She has left the following message for the English teacher accompanying the group.

1 What date will Philip leave hospital?

2 When and how will he return to England?

à Mr *SIMON*
Mme *MOREAU*

a téléphoné ☒   est passé ☐

le *30/07*   à *21* h.

le rappeler au n° ....

rappellera ....

◆ ◆ ◆ ◆ ◆ ◆ ◆ ◆ ◆ ◆ ◆

a laissé le message suivant :

Nous sortons Philippe de l'hôpital demain en début d'après Midi –

Nous le ramenons à Morlaix Samedi Après Midi

Il va prendre le bateau dimanche avec les autres –

E7

– Je suis votre petite voisine... et je suis toujours libre pour garder les bébés.

Why do you think the little girl's offer may be refused on this occasion?

Je suis née le 13.09.72.
J'aime la nature, les animaux et la moto. Je suis en classe de 3ème et j'ai 3h d'anglais et 2h d'espagnol.
Mon père est conducteur de travaux publiques dans la région. Ma mère ne travaille pas. J'ai 2 frères : Thierry 21 ans et Olivier 10 ans. J'ai 2 chiens, 2 chattes, des poissons rouges et un petit lapin blanc qui s'appelle "Choupette."

E8

Your French teacher at school has received a request for pen-friends. Above is the first paragraph of the letter that you are offered to reply to.

1 Name three of the writer's main interests.

2 What two things does she say she studies?

3 What does she say about her family?

4 What pets does she have?

P

Est-ce que vous avez les mêmes goûts que cette jeune fille française ?

Sian

Salut, je suis ta correspondante Française, je suis contente d'avoir une nouvelle correspondante anglaise car celle avec qui je devais aller ne peut pas venir chez moi. J'habite à la campagne à 7 km de Morlaix où je vais à l'école en car, et toi comment vas-tu à l'école? Mes chanteurs préférés sont Den Harrow, et sting, ma chanteuse est madonna, je la trouve super. A la maison tu auras ta chambre pour toi toute seule J'espère qu'elle te plaira car elle n'est pas tout à fait terminée, il manque la tapisserie.

J'espère que la France te plairas si tu n'y est jammais allée.

Sylvie

E9

Sian is a friend in your class at school who is not very good at French. She thinks she has understood the letter from her new pen-friend, Sylvie, but asks you to check for her.

Which of Sian's statements below are true about Sylvie's letter?

1 Sylvie's previous pen-friend could not visit her in France.

2 Sylvie lives in the centre of Morlaix.

3 Sylvie goes to school by car.

4 Sylvie's pen-friend will be able to have a bedroom to herself.

5 There is no carpet in the room.

6 The spare room is not yet built.

7 There is a spelling mistake in the letter.

P

a) Décrivez les traits de votre caractère.

b) Décrivez ceux d'un de vos amis.

c) Pourquoi êtes-vous des amis?

d) Votre famille, où habite-t-elle actuellement?

e) Ça vous plaît, l'endroit où vous habitez?

f) Fournissez une description de votre maison.

g) Décrivez votre chambre idéale.

E10

You enjoy reading the problem pages in teenage magazines.

1 What are the readers of this magazine asked to do?

2 What does Claudine say about her relationships with boys at the age of 16?

3 What is different about her relationship with Xavier?

4 How long has she been going out with him?

5 What happened when the school holidays ended?

6 What has her mother now forbidden her to do?

7 What is Claudine's worry?

8 What suggestion did Claudine make to her mother?

9 Why does Claudine think that her mother has this attitude towards Xavier?

P

a) Avez-vous un problème pareil à celui de Claudine?

b) Avez-vous un ami spécial? Vos parents, que pensent-ils de vos amis?

La main tendue

Vous pouvez les aider

Comme vous, ce sont des lectrices de notre journal. Elles ont un problème et demandent du réconfort. Nous publions ici leur courrier en préservant leur anonymat. Mais si vous pensez pouvoir les aider, écrivez-leur par notre intermédiaire. Nous leur ferons parvenir toutes vos lettres. Et si, comme elles, vous en éprouvez le besoin, écrivez-nous.

Ma mère ne veut plus me laisser sortir

A seize ans, je suis déjà sortie avec un certain nombre de garçons. Mais cela n'allait jamais très loin, cela ne durait jamais très longtemps et, jusqu'à maintenant, mes parents n'y trouvaient absolument rien à redire.

> **Je ne peux plus voir celui que j'aime**

Et puis, un jour, j'ai rencontré Xavier. Il a vingt ans et avec lui, ce n'était pas la même chose. Peu à peu, j'ai senti que j'éprouvais un sentiment plus fort qu'avec ceux que j'avais connus avant lui. Nous sortons ensemble depuis plusieurs mois et on s'aime à la folie. Pendant les dernières vacances, on s'est vus tous les jours. Hélas, à la rentrée, on s'est rencontrés moins souvent. Bien sûr, je vais au lycée et, le soir, j'ai des devoirs à faire. J'ai donc moins de temps libre. C'était normal et on supportait quand même de se voir moins.

Mais maintenant, les choses ont changé. Ma mère ne veut plus que je rencontre Xavier. Elle m'interdit en effet de sortir quand il fait nuit. Et, à cette saison, la nuit tombe vite. Elle ne veut même pas que je sorte sur le seuil de la porte, devant la maison, pour discuter un moment avec Xavier. Elle dit que je le vois suffisamment pendant le week-end. Mais ce n'est pas vrai, car elle ne me permet de sortir qu'un week-end par mois. Les trois autres, il doit sortir sans moi et j'ai peur qu'il se lasse ou qu'il trouve une autre fille. J'ai proposé à ma mère de m'autoriser à recevoir Xavier à la maison. Mais elle m'a dit qu'elle ne voulait pas. Je ne comprends pas pourquoi. Peut-être qu'elle n'aime pas ce garçon, qui est pourtant très bien et très gentil. Peut-être a-t-elle peur que les choses deviennent trop sérieuses entre nous? Je suis malheureuse et je ne sais que faire. Bien entendu, je ne veux pas causer de peine à ma mère, mais je la trouve injuste. Croyez-vous que je doive lui céder et accepter de ne voir mon ami qu'une heure ou deux par semaine et un week-end sur quatre? Seulement, je l'aime, il m'aime, et il est normal que nous ayons envie de nous voir. Pourquoi ma mère refuse-t-elle de le comprendre? Que faire? Dites-moi ce que vous en pensez.

Claudine.
Réf. 68.01

Je déteste mon père...

Anne, quinze ans, est désespérée parce que son père n'arrête pas de la critiquer à tout propos : vêtements, maquillage, copains, résultats scolaires. Elle dit qu'elle le déteste, mais s'enferme dans sa chambre pour ne pas le voir. Anne rêve d'un père compréhensif.
Réf. 58.03

■ J'ai le même âge que toi et je vis une situation presque identique à la tienne, mis à part que mon père me battait. Il est dépressif. J'ai fait plusieurs fugues. Depuis, ses violences ont cessé, mais ses remarques acerbes continuent. Et ça fait très mal. Alors, Anne, pour te sortir de cette situation sans faire de bêtises, dialogue avec ton père. Ce sera dur de l'approcher la première fois, de lui dire « écoute, papa... je souffre... alors... ». Car il souffre, lui aussi. Ce n'est pas sans raison, ces remarques... Il a peur de te voir lui échapper. Il t'a connue petite fille obéissante et te retrouve adolescente qui s'affirme. Il cache ses sentiments sous un comportement qui, fatalement, te fait mal. Il ne comprend plus... Alors, dialogue. Au fur et à mesure, tu réapprendras à l'apprécier, à l'aimer. Car lui t'aime. Patiente, Anne. La haine se détruit quand l'amour s'apprend. Je t'embrasse.
Magdalena

■ Je connais votre cas. Mais je suis de l'autre côté. Du côté des parents critiqueurs. J'ai une fille de dix-huit ans, et un fils de seize ans. J'avoue que nous les critiquons beaucoup, trop peut-être. Nous sommes différents de caractère, de personnalité, donc nous ne voyons pas les choses de la même façon. Nous, les parents, voudrions leur transmettre notre expérience dans la tête, avec un entonnoir. Ils ne se laissent pas faire. Et nous avons peur pour eux. Au lieu de prendre le chemin que nous leur indiquons parce que, l'ayant pris, nous en connaissons les embûches, ils veulent en prendre un autre. Nous avons souvent l'impression que nous aurions pu leur éviter ce piège. Réaction : nous critiquons. Vêtements, maquillage, copains, tout ! On voit bien que vous ne détestez pas votre père. Vous détestez que votre père vous critique. C'est différent. Alors, que faire ? Prendre les choses avec le plus d'humour possible, ne pas se fâcher, faire des concessions, en obtenir. Soyez gentille, affectueuse : l'angoisse de n'être plus aimé par sa fille le rend encore plus critique. Je vous assure que votre lettre dit : « Je déteste mon père », mais qu'elle n'est qu'un cri d'amour. Prenez l'habitude de dire « je t'aime » quand vous aimez et ne simulez pas la haine pour provoquer l'amour. Gros bisous.
Andrée

E11

Anne has a problem and Magdalena and Andrée have written to the magazine to give her advice.

1 What does Anne's father criticise her about?

2 How does Anne try to avoid him?

3 Name the quality which Anne's father seems to lack most.

4 What does Magdalena advise Anne to do?

5 How old are Andrée's children?

6 Why does Andrée criticise them?

7 How does she advise Anne to tackle the problem?

8 Why does Andrée think Anne's father is becoming more and more critical?

9 What does Andrée advise Anne not to do?

P

a) Avez-vous jamais vécu une situation pareille à celle d'Anne?

b) Connaissez-vous quelqu'un dans cette situation?

c) Discutez avec un partenaire le problème des parents critiques.

d) Les réponses à la lettre d'Anne, qu'en pensez-vous? A-t-on trouvé la solution?

Mariages Rencontres

A

"Mieux que jolie", IN-FIRMIÈRE cél., 23 a., 1,65 m, mince, Mlle Joëlle Dubois, 64 av. de la République, 69470 Lyon.

B

PINCE-SANS-RIRE, 28 ans, 1,65 m, souhaite rencontrer jeune femme heureuse, pour partager vie commune, 6.000 F/mens, et grande maison dans Sud-Finistère. Ecr. M. Thierry Julien, 1, bd. de la Croix Rousse, Quimper.

C

DIRECTEUR entreprise, quarantaine, veuf, 2 jeunes enfants, désire refaire sa vie avec compagne, 30–40 ans sympa, équilibrée, gaie, sincère, enfant accepté. M. Georges Dumontet, 104 rue Sully, 69500 Bron.

D

M. SOIXANTAINE, propriété, agréable, renc. F. cinquantaine, mélomane, aimant vie à la campagne. Ecr. avec photo, M. Frédéric Cuminal, 54, chemin des châtaigniers, 48562 Mende.

E12

You are reading the personal advertisements of a newspaper with your pen-friend and she decides to make up a few replies!

Can you match the replies below to the advertisements?

1 *Je suis veuve, j'ai 49 ans et je déteste le bruit et les foules.*

2 *Divorcée avec un fils (9 ans), je cherche homme d'affaires pour partager sa vie.*

3 *Je suis jeune, j'ai 22 ans. Je suis beau, j'aime les sports et les sciences.*

4 *Je suis jeune fille cherchant propriété et amitié.*

E13

Here is an advertisement for a dating agency. Answer the following questions from the choice of 'lonely hearts'.

1 Which person has an interesting job and earns quite a lot?

2 How many people are widows or widowers?

3 Who has blue eyes and is shy, sentimental and affectionate?

4 Who is good looking, plays sport and a musical instrument?

5 Who is slim and has green eyes?

6 Who is sober and understanding?

7 Describe Jean Louis.

UNIONS C.R.M.
12, place Maurice - Gillet
(St-Martin) - **BREST**
Tél. 44.86.06

MARIE 25 ANS, cél., sans charge, très jolie JF. svelte aux yeux verts, grande, féminine, soignée, sentimentale, calme, franche, aime musique, lecture, danse, cinéma, souh. renc. JH. 25/30, sérieux.

LINDA 33 ANS, jolie veuve aux yeux bleus, sent., affec., un peu timide, propriétaire, voiture, bcp. de gentillesse et de patience, dés. renc. M. sincère, sérieux, aimant les enfants.

ANNICK 46 ANS, veuve, jolie F. sentimentale, affec., gaie, bonne maîtresse de maison, aimant promenades, musique, cinéma, vie de famille, dés. renc. M. 45/55, sit. indif., enf. bienvenus.

ANNE 53 ANS, sans charges, très bonne situation, grande, élancée, très féminine, soignée, senti., gaie, propriétaire, voiture, aimant musique, lecture, promenades, renc. M. franc, sobre, aimant les voyages.

Gabrielle 60 ANS, veuve, sans charges, retraitée, de jolis yeux verts, affec., sensible, patiente, franche, aimant le jardinage, les promenades, souh. renc. M. 60/65, sobre, compréhensif.

PATRICK 24 ANS, militaire, beau garçon, sportif, gai, ayant le sens de l'humour, dynamique, enthousiaste, musicien, aimant le cinéma, la danse, désire renc. JF. 20/25, sit. indif., enf. bienvenu.

JACQUES 27 ANS, cél., prof. libérale, grand, sportif (tennis, voile), très bons revenus, sens., calme, volontaire, ayant le sens des responsabilités, aimant la musique, souh. vie heureuse avec JF. naturelle.

YVES 33 ANS, cél., grand, les yeux bleus, beau garçon, un métier intéressant, bons revenus, propriétaire, sensible, prévenant, dynamique, sens des responsabilités, renc. dame aimant vie de famille, sit. indif.

Chef d'entreprise **42 ANS,** excellents rev., propr., prévenant, sensible, soigné, gai, ayant sens de l'humour, aimant campagne, cinéma, danse, bateau, renc. D. simple, naturelle, sit. indif., enfts. acceptés.

JEAN-LOUIS 54 ANS, veuf, propriétaire, exc. revenus, sens., réservé, dyn., un métier de création, aimant les arts (peinture, sculpture), le sport, les responsabilités, dés. renc. D. 45/55, naturelle, aimant vie de famille.

Nom	Prénom	Age
Profession	Veuf (ve)	Célib.	Div.
Adress		Tél.

Désire renseignements sur personnes entourées ou soulignées.

P

a) Faites une comparaison entre tous les candidats et choisissez-en un copain/une copine idéal(e) pour votre partenaire dans la classe. Justifiez votre choix!

b) Quel candidat choisiriez-vous pour vous-même? Pourquoi?

c) Essayez de décrire votre femme/homme idéal(e)!

If you are interested in astrology this advertisement will appeal to you.

Read the advertisement carefully and answer the questions below.

1 Which astrological study offers you predictions for the next twelve months, A, B or C?

2 Which study claims to enable you to act appropriately at all times?

3 How much would a character study cost you?

4 List all the details which you would have to supply on the request slip about your date and place of birth.

POISSONS
20 février/20 mars

Vie professionnelle : Allez, un peu d'optimisme. Cette période de transition vous semble difficile à vivre, mais ce n'est pas une raison pour vous enfermer dans une boîte de sardines ! Evitez les associations, les crises de nerfs et les dépenses compensations dont votre portefeuille ne saurait se relever...

Amour : Evidemment, ce n'est pas le Pérou... ! D'une histoire simple vous faites un casse-tête que même un Chinois ne saurait pas démêler. Si vous êtes célibataire, acceptez la précarité des rencontres sans lendemain qui vous dépayseront.

Forme : Vous frisez le crash nerveux. Buvez de la verveine...

BIBA plus : Prenez cette période comme une remise en cause positive.

BELIER
21 mars/20 avril

Vie professionnelle : Vous devez vous attendre à quelques changements inattendus qui peuvent déstabiliser un temps vos affaires. Vos idées et vos relations vous mettent en valeur.

Amour : Le règne de l'illusion ! Ne perdez pas la tête, et dites-vous que vous vivez un superbe film, mais que le mot « fin » apparaîtra fatalement. Mais par pitié, ne prenez pas un vulgaire figurant pour le grand rôle masculin...

Forme : Stoppez les excitants, vous êtes assez énervée !

BIBA plus : Tablez beaucoup sur votre entourage amical.

TAUREAU
21 avril/20 mai

Vie professionnelle : Attention : ce mois peut être l'un des plus importants de votre vie. Ce que vous en ferez engagera votre avenir et sous les plus heureux auspices. C'est une chance fabuleuse qui vous sort des sentiers battus et qui peut vous permettre de réaliser vos rêves.

Amour : Mais qu'est-ce qui vous prend ? Vous vous prenez pour une aventurière des cœurs, la mèche ravageuse et l'œil langoureux... Attention au réveil ! Vous avez trop besoin de sécurité pour le jeter à la poubelle sur un coup de tête.

Forme : Du calme. Buvez beaucoup d'eau.

BIBA plus : Bravo pour les affaires, mais gare à votre vie privée.

You look at the horoscopes in a magazine so you can tell your friends what will happen to them in the coming month.

Joanna's sign is Pisces.

Sandra's sign is Aries.

Peter's sign is Taurus.

1 Who will experience changes at work?

2 Who will worry unnecessarily about their love-life?

3 Whose health might be bordering on nervous collapse?

4 For whom is this month vitally important in terms of work?

5 Which one needs to be optimistic?

6 Which one needs to lean on friends for moral support?

7 Which one should drink plenty of water?

Psycho-test

Êtes-vous une « intello » ?

Entre celles qui marchent uniquement à l'instinct, et celles qui n'aiment que jongler avec les idées, où avez-vous tendance à vous situer ?

● **Donnez une définition de l'intelligence :**
- [I] c'est une griffe qui se brise en égratignant
- [N] elle commence au moment où elle se fait oublier
- [T] c'est 4/5 de culture et 1/5 d'hérédité

● **Vous aimez l'homme de votre vie parce que :**
- [N] il est beau et sent bon le sable chaud
- [T] c'est plus fort que vous
- [I] il vous aime et sait vous comprendre

● **Ce qui retient aujourd'hui le plus votre attention :**
- [T] les Législatives
- [N] la situation en Afrique du Sud
- [I] l'arrivée de nouvelles chaînes de télévision

● **Vous avez aimé ou vous aimeriez voir :**
- [I] Jules César, mis en scène par Robert Hossein
- [N] les Misérables, avec Lino Ventura
- [T] Amadeus, ou la vie de Mozart

● **Votre chanteuse préférée :**
- [I] Marie-Paule Belle
- [T] Sylvie Vartan
- [N] Nana Mouskouri

● **Vous préférez :**
- [I] le Scrabble
- [N] le jeu des chiffres et des lettres
- [T] les dominos

● **Vous ne croyez guère :**
- [I] aux jeux de hasard
- [N] aux sondages
- [T] aux bruits de couloir

● **Vous compléteriez la phrase : « ... est en train de devenir un art », par :**
- [I] la publicité
- [T] l'informatique
- [N] la gymnastique

● **Laquelle de ces affirmations approuvez-vous le plus ?**
- [N] science sans conscience n'est que ruine de l'âme
- [T] il n'y a pas de mauvais élèves, que des mauvais maîtres
- [I] plus on en sait, plus on se rend compte que l'on ne sait rien

● **Un(e) intellectuel(le) doit aussi avoir :**
- [N] de l'intuition
- [I] du cœur
- [T] de la créativité

Calculez votre score : I = 2 points ; N = 1 point ; T = 0.

E16

You see this personality test in a magazine. You decide to try it out.

1 Add up your score and put the figure on your answer paper. Then check your result with the information on the right.

2 According to your score name one positive and one negative trait of your character.

■ **De 0 à 6 points**
Vous êtes certes tout à fait capable d'analyser une situation, un spectacle, un livre, mais ce n'est pas votre tendance naturelle. Vous, vous fonctionnez surtout à l'instinct, vos réactions étant plus affectives que raisonnées, les intellos, vous les trouvez très forts dans les universités mais sur le terrain ils vous déçoivent souvent... quand ils ne vous ennuient pas ! Votre bon sens et votre débrouillardise, vous permettent de réaliser plus d'économies que n'importe quelle étude de marché sur la meilleure façon de consommer ou de produire. C'est grâce à cela que tous vos proches se sentent tellement en sécurité avec vous.

■ **De 7 à 13 points**
La polyvalence est votre qualité principale. Vous pouvez tout aussi bien éplucher le mode d'emploi de votre machine à laver et construire vous-même vos étagères que trouver votre bonheur dans la lecture de Jean-Paul Sartre. Vous avez besoin de diversifier vos centres d'intérêt, de faire alterner activités intellectuelles et activités sportives ou manuelles. Vous « pigez » vite ce qui est essentiel et vous vous impatientez devant les analyses qui n'en finissent pas. Quant aux loisirs, ce sont vraiment des loisirs : lorsque vous allez au cinéma, ce n'est certainement pas pour vous plonger dans des problèmes métaphysiques. Saine attitude !

■ **De 14 à 20 points**
Intellectuelle, oui, on peut dire que vous l'êtes. Les constructions de l'esprit, le jeu des idées, les mots vous fascinent et vous pouvez vous montrer très brillante. L'intelligence est le propre de l'homme et c'est la seule supériorité que vous lui reconnaissez vraiment. Vous n'admettez rien sans avoir réfléchi, vous aimez disséquer les causes et analyser les effets. Attention, votre image, auprès de votre entourage, risque de manquer de chaleur. A moins que vous n'ayez ces indispensables compléments à votre puissance intellectuelle : les qualités de cœur et l'humour.

Stéphanie en Amérique :
« gare à mon gorille ! »

Pauvre Stéphanie. Venue passer une soirée au « Lime-light », une boîte new-yorkaise, en compagnie d'un beau brun, la princesse a eu quelques déboires. Alors qu'elle s'était absentée quelques instants, son chevalier servant en profitait pour inviter une autre fille à danser. De retour à sa table, Stéphanie s'est assise, a retiré calmement la bouteille de champagne du seau à glace et commencé à bombarder l'inconnue avec des glaçons. Mais, imperturbable, la rivale a continué sa danse... Stéphanie de Monaco, hors d'elle, a appelé son garde du corps qui s'est chargé d'éjecter l'intruse. Scène classique, a confié une amie de la princesse : « *Stéphanie a horreur de perdre, même s'il ne s'agit que d'un petit flirt* ». Ah, si tout le monde avait un gorille... ■

Madonna recherche Sean, désespérément

Elle possède une superbe propriété à Malibu (Californie) et voudrait bien filer un amour tranquille avec son mari Sean Penn (le fils d'Arthur) épousé en août dernier. Mais Madonna, qui a fait un tabac dans *Recherche Susan désespérément*, ne s'en tirera pas comme cela. La pop star est souvent sollicitée par les metteurs en scène. Pour ne pas quitter son homme, elle a envie de refuser une offre pourtant intéressante des studios Walt Disney (pas pour jouer Blanche Neige, mais pour incarner une bourgeoise de Beverly Hills kidnappée...). ■

According to the articles above which of the following statements are true?

1 Princess Stéphanie was drinking champagne at a New York night-club.

2 Princess Stéphanie threw ice-cubes at her companion.

3 Princess Stéphanie's escort stormed out of the night-club.

4 Madonna lives in Beverly Hills.

5 Madonna apparently wants a quiet life now she is married.

6 Madonna has just been offered a part by Walt Disney Studios.

P

a) Aimez-vous suivre la vie des vedettes?

b) Essayez de décrire, ou de présenter comme pour une émission à la télévision, une petite histoire de votre vedette préféré(e).

c) Comparez les deux articles. Croyez-vous qu'ils présentent bien les vedettes? A votre avis, est-ce que l'un est mieux écrit que l'autre?
Justifiez vos réponses.

E18

LES FORBANS

6 jeunes garçons qui font du rock-and-roll comme dans les années 60

Du rythme, beaucoup d'humour et plusieurs succès, c'est le cocktail FORBANS sur le GRAND PODIUM EUROPE 1

Who would be attracted to *Les Forbans*?

B   Les maisons

E19

You come across these three advertisements in an estate agents' window.

A VENDRE

A MORLAIX ""La Boissière''

BELLE PROPRIETE bourgeoise
Tout confort
Jardin 3000 m²
Libre.

_____

Ref: M 20

A VENDRE

A MORLAIX (Près de Pont-Bellec)

MAISON sur cave en sous-sol
R.D.C: Cuisine, salle à manger,
garage, salle d'eau: W.C. et étage
de 2 chambres, salle d'eau et
grenier au-dessus. Jardin.

_____

Ref: M 32

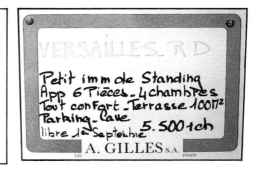

VERSAILLES_RD

Petit imm de Standing
App 6 Pièces - 4 chambres
Tout confort - Terrasse 100m²
Parking - Cave
libre 1er Septembre   5.500 +ch

A. GILLES S.A.

Which property would you seek further information on if you:

1 hated gardening?

2 wanted a garden and a cellar?

3 would like to occupy it in early September?

Cahors centre, part. vd maison indivi. comp. 2 garages + gde pièce + cave, à l'étage, séjour, cuisine, 2 ch., s.d.b., chauff. central, jardinet, vue imprenable sur le Lot. 450.000 F. Tél. 16.1.48.27.99.90

Lot 30 km de Cahors, 20 km de Gourdon, vds petite habitation tout en pierre + garage ds très beau site, 5.000 m² terr. Prix 380.000 F. Tél. 65.22.57.85 ap. 18h.

Figeac-Nayrac, vends cause décés. pavillon F4, libre, sous-sol en garage, chauffage central au fuel, très bon état, terrain 430 m². Tél. 65.31.11.60 H.R. 65.34.04.78 H.B.

A vendre village Lot maison meublée, 3 pièces, b.e. conf., pour couple ou retraité, ni jardin, ni garage 13 U. à débattre. Tél. 65.32.48.60 H.R.

Vds terrain exposition plein sud, Regourd, combe du Paysan, (Cahors Nord) 1 lot 1000 m², 2 lots de 1000 m² Tél. 65.31.26.25 H.R.

Vds Vers (Lot) maison de village en pierre, 3 niveaux, 140 m² habitables, potager 100 m². Tél. 91.73.21.32

Urgent vds cause mutation maison neuve F6 Cahors Le Failhal, très grand confort, calme, point de vue. Tél. 65.35.50.30 H.R.

Vds Cahors centre ville appt T4 entièrement rénové. Prix 45 U. à débattre. Tél. 65.35.17.45 H.B. ou 65.30.05.76 H.R.

Vds maison pierres à 12 mn de Cahors, état neuf superficie 235 m², terrain 1 400 m². arboré et clôturé. Tél. H.B. 65.30.13.09

Pour votre Publicité

PUBLI-LOT

ALLO : 65.30.14.11

CAHORS

Vds terrain à bâtir 1000 m² à Puy-L'Evêque belle exposition prix intéressant. Tél. 65.30.81.83 H.R.

A vdre sur Figeac immeuble ensoleillé, centre ville, local commercial (rapport annuel 18.000F) + 3 pièces. Prix à débattre. S'adre. M. Yves Sagnes Labastide l'Eveque 12200 Villefranche de Rouergue

Cause mutation vends pavillon T4, cuisine équipée. Tél. 65.35.71.16 Les Escales Labéraudie

Urgent cause départ étranger vds villa Puy-L'Evêque, F3, garage, jardin, prix intéressant. Tél. 65.35.67.42 le soir

Vds maison camp restaurée vallée du Lot, 46 Bouzies, 300 000 F. Tél. 75.43.63.79 (Dols, 5 rue Bach 26 Valence)

Vds bâtiment neuf 250 m² contigu à logement à finir de 135 m², conviendrait tous usages, région St-Céré. Tél. 65.38.07.20 Saint-Céré

Part. vend Cahors charmant grenier, séjour, 2 ch., cuisine. s.de.b.. tout confort. Tél. H.R. 65.35.48.80

Part. vd Caillac Pavillon 5 pièces, s/sol total, const. 1982. Séjour en L, cheminée, cuisine aménagée, 2 s.d.b., terrasses, jardin 1200 m² Paysagé, fruitier, droits mutation réduits. Tél. 65.20.02.34 ou 68.21.38.83

A vendre plein centre Cahors F4 état neuf tout confort ou échange contre villa ou maison jardin dans Cahors. Tél. 65.35.14.40 H.R.

8 km au Sud de Cahors, cause mutation **vends maison 130 m² habitables + 30 m² de garage.** 3 chambres, 2 bains, salon séjour 40 m² avec mezzanine et cheminée, cuisine intégrée, sur 1 400 m² de terrain, école avec maternelle + ramassage scolaire, environnement agréable 550 000,00 F. Tél. H.R. 65.21.01.10

E20

A number of your friends in France are trying to move house. You take a look at the small advertisements in this paper.

The families requirements are listed below.

1 Modern house, large cellar, open fire, well landscaped garden, with fruit trees if possible.

2 House with cellar and garage, oil fired central heating, in good condition.

3 A renovated flat in town centre.

4 A stone-built house not far from town, with large garden and land with trees.

Which phone numbers do you think each family would ring?

P

a) Voyez-vous une maison/un appartement où vous aimeriez habiter? Pourquoi ou pourquoi pas?

b) Avez-vous jamais déménagé? Comment était l'ancienne maison? Comment est la nouvelle?

E21

Here are three firms that you could contact if you wanted things for your home.

Which could you go to if you wanted the following?

1 A cooker
2 A new fitted kitchen
3 Wallpaper
4 A fitted shower
5 Roof repairs

E22

Cody is a French DIY store.

Which department would you find these goods under?

1 A lawn mower
2 A spanner
3 House paint
4 Wallpaper
5 Light bulbs
6 A sink plunger
7 Wood for shelves
8 Nails
9 Torch batteries
10 A spade

E23

This extract is from a magazine article about kitchen renovations.

If you wanted a new kitchen, but were on a fixed budget and were not very good at DIY, which system (1, 2 or 3) would you choose?

Quelle formule choisir ?

Selon votre budget, vos goûts et vos dons pour le bricolage, vous avez le choix entre trois formules pour acheter votre cuisine.

1 La cuisine intégrée : sur vos indications, un cuisiniste encastre les meubles et appareils ménagers que vous choisissez et les adapte parfaitement à votre pièce, quels que soient son état, sa forme et ses caractéristiques. Une fois installée, votre cuisine présente un plan de travail continu, et des meubles « en ligne » sans raccord. *Avantages.* L'implantation est toujours rationnelle, les moindres recoins utilisés, le nettoyage simplifié. *Inconvénients.* Pour « coller » précisément aux dimensions de votre cuisine, l'installateur peut faire ap-

pel à une main-d'œuvre importante (carreleur, plombier, électricien...). Cette formule est garantie mais souvent onéreuse.

2 Les meubles prêts à poser : vous dressez vous-même le plan de votre aménagement et achetez les meubles dont vous avez besoin. Ceux-ci sont vendus montés. Il ne vous reste plus qu'à les placer ou bien encore à les fixer en les juxtaposant. *Avantages.* Cette formule souple et moins chère que la précédente vous permet d'acquérir, petit à petit, la cuisine de vos rêves. *Inconvénients.* Les dimensions de votre cuisine s'adaptent rarement au centimètre près à celles des meubles standardisés. Il en résulte des « coins per-

dus ». Par ailleurs, entre les meubles et les appareils subsistent des séparations qui nécessitent de fréquents nettoyages.

3 Les meubles en kit : vous achetez les meubles qui correspondent à vos plans. Le plus souvent vous les transportez vous-même, avant de les assembler et de les poser. *Avantages.* C'est à la fois la formule la plus souple et la meilleure marché (40% environ) à qualité égale. *Inconvénients.* S'il est facile de monter des meubles vendus en kit, certains éléments de cuisine (meuble évier...) demandent des connaissances approfondies en bricolage (plomberie, électricité) et parfois pour plus de sécurité, l'appel à un spécialiste...

E24

'Maison & Travaux' is a popular French magazine that contains articles on homes, gardens, and DIY.

This edition has a page giving details of back issues.

1 Choose any three back issues to send for, and list briefly, in English, the contents.

2 How much would it cost, including postage, to have these three issues sent to England?

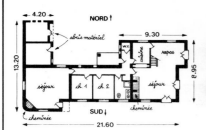

A la place des vignes

Reportage Annick Stein
Photos Jean Verdier.

1964 : la construction à son premier stade.
Les murs sont montés en parpaings.

1968 : la première étape est terminée.
La maison n'est pas encore pourvue de son
deuxième séjour et des ateliers (voir plan).
L'enduit des murs a été réalisé à la truelle,
« au jeté », par un artisan maçon, dans la tradition de la région aixoise. Il présente un grain
et une souplesse qui lui sont conférés à la fois
par la qualité du sable de carrière dont la partie
la plus fine a été éliminée, et le dosage du mor-
tier, assez liquide.

1981 : la végétation a poussé. Au fil des
années, tout s'est mis en place : le saule pleu-
reur, la piscine côté sud qui se fait discrète,
dans la prairie, les murets qui retiennent
des jardins de rocaille et des massifs de fleurs,
où viennent butiner les abeilles des onze ruches !

▲ *La terrasse sous les chênes rouvres est une
extension de la salle à manger. De ce point
d'observation, on voit arriver le visiteur dans le
sentier et on jette un œil attentif sur les enfants
qui jouent dans la piscine en contrebas.*

Le point de départ de cette maison
de week-end et de vacances a été,
dans les années 1965, un petit caba-
non avec bergerie, construit dans les
vignes. Mais ce n'est plus qu'un
souvenir dont il ne reste que les
belles pierres récupérées pour faire
des murets.

Après dix-sept ans de travail, le
propriétaire qui l'a conçue et construite presque entièrement par lui-
même et avec l'aide d'amis, consi-
dère qu'elle sera « bientôt finie ».

C'est un long corps de bâtiment
bas, couvert de tuiles canal dans le
style provençal. D'où vient son
charme particulier ? Simplement de
son air champêtre sous les chênes-
rouvres, de son décor clair et dé-
contracté. C'est une maison que l'on
sent vivante, sans contraintes. La
famille s'y réunit volontiers pour
les fêtes et les anniversaires. Son plan
semble extensible au fur et à mesure
des besoins : deux séjours, trois
chambres, des ateliers pour bricoler…
de quoi accueillir plusieurs géné-
rations aux préoccupations et goûts
différents. La piscine en pleins
champs est la dernière touche qui lui
donne un petit air de luxe.

E25

This article concerns the conversion of a simple dwelling into a beautiful residence.

1 What, according to the article, is the attraction of the residence?

2 Is the house used as a main residence, or occasionally?

3 What is the one luxurious feature to be found there?

4 How do we know that the conversion was 'a labour of love'?

5 What was added to the simple dwelling after 1968?

La maison de l'an 2000 est arrivée

En l'an 2000, notre maison fonctionnera "toute seule" grâce aux ordinateurs. C'est ce que nous promettent les spécialistes. Délivrés des tâches ménagères, nous pourrons travailler et nous divertir à domicile. C'est magique et... un peu effrayant.

Huit heures du matin. Madame Martin s'étire dans son lit. Deux fois déjà, le réveil à la voix synthétique lui a intimé l'ordre de se lever. Comme elle n'obtempère pas, le plafonnier s'allume tandis que le store se relève, laissant entrer à flots le soleil. La voix de stentor de son professeur de gym électronique envahit la chambre : *"On s'étire bien. Recommencez...".* Lorsque l'odeur du café et des toasts grillés lui chatouille les narines, Mme Martin abdique enfin : allons, cette fois-ci il faut se lever... La même voix synthétique lui rappelle les rendez-vous de la journée : *"dentiste, conseil des parents d'élèves".* D'habitude elle communique avec les autres parents par claviers et écrans interposés, mais aujourd'hui elle a envie d'avoir une "vraie discussion". Passage dans la "salle de corps" (autrefois, salle de bains). Là, un appareil enregistre au jour le jour poids, tension, rythme cardiaque etc.

Une maison modulable

Il est relié au cabinet d'un médecin qui, à distance, peut établir des "télé-diagnostics". Rien à signaler. Mme Martin, rassurée sur son état de santé gagne son bureau... pas de transport, elle travaille de son living. Elle s'installe devant l'ordinateur : un terminal multi-fonctions avec console, écran de contrôle, clavier. Grâce à lui, Mme Martin qui est expert-comptable, peut accéder à tous ses dossiers, demander des suppléments d'information à telle ou telle banque de données etc. Un télécopieur ou une imprimante reliée à l'ordinateur lui permet en outre d'échan-

ger documents et photos... à plus de 150 000 km/h !
La vie de Mme Martin n'est pas un scénario de science fiction. Cette maison du futur entièrement informatisée et automatisée existe déjà... A l'état de prototype. Notamment aux USA où une vingtaine de sociétés de travaux publics, de spécialistes de l'isolation et de l'informatique se sont associées pour la construire, à Ahwatukee, en Arizona. Mieux, les industriels, comme l'Américain General Electric et le Japonais Mitsubishi ont, dès à présent, des systèmes d'automatisation domestique. *"C'est à Bruxelles en*

1979 qu'est sortie de terre la toute première maison de l'an 2000 construite par un scientifique américain de la NASA" explique Bruno de Latour, président de l'association pour les maisons du futur (APMF). Pour Bruno de Latour, c'est la révélation. Il crée l'APMF et part en croisade pour les "maisons de demain". *"A moins de quinze ans de l'An 2000, explique-t-il avec fièvre, il est urgent de préparer avec soin l'avenir de l'homme dans son logement. Les nouvelles technologies vont en transformer les données."* Cette maison, le plus souvent en bois, sera démontable car

en l'an 2000, on n'hésitera plus à changer de région pour trouver un emploi. Elle sera économique et saura utiliser toutes les formes d'énergies (solaire, éolienne). *"Ce qui est certain, c'est que la dernière décennie sera marquée par l'éclosion de la "domotique" (du latin domus : maison, et tique : pour informatique) explique Bruno de Latour. Toute notre vie et celle de la maison vont reposer sur la capacité des micro-processeurs. En clair, cela veut dire que l'ordinateur, programmé selon les besoins de chacun, va prendre en charge la gestion et la sécurité de la maison.*

Le robot qui sert le petit déjeuner au lit : le rêve ! mais la maison de demain, c'est avant tout une maison totalement programmée et reliée avec le monde entier. Un seul risque : ne plus avoir besoin d'en sortir... L'enjeu consistera encore à ne pas se laisser piéger par le progrès.

D. GOLDBERG/SYGMA

E26

Here is an article about the house of the future.

Have you understood the main points?

1 Describe the new style alarm clock.

2 What other things are done automatically in order to induce Mme Martin to get up?

3 What does the machine in the bathroom measure?

4 Where does Mme Martin work? How is this possible?

5 Does this type of house exist solely in someone's imagination?

6 Where and when did the first 'House of the Year 2000' appear? Who built it?

7 What will be important aspects of the house of the future? Why?

> # P
> Que pensez-vous d'une vie ainsi organisée?

C   Les animaux

E27

If you wanted to buy a pet, which one would you choose?
Here is an article on the matter.

1 What pets are mentioned?

2 Which ones are popular with young people?

3 What should one bear in mind when choosing a dog?

4 When should one choose a parrot?

5 According to the article, is it true that male parrots
prefer female owners, and vice versa.

P

Avez-vous des animaux domestiques chez vous?
Faites-en une description!

Les animaux à la maison

Le nombre de chiens, en France, augmente selon une progression continue dans les foyers familiaux et, de manière parallèle, les expositions canines attirent des foules de plus en plus denses, dont les éléments jeunes s'apprêtent à assurer une relève élargie.

Un chien dans un appartement est toujours d'une agréable compagnie. Bien sûr, certains de taille très importante, préfèrent les maisons avec un coin-jardin.

Les chats sont également très appréciés. Et pas seulement par les grands-mères et les petits enfants...

Que dire des oiseaux? Certains spécialistes en parleraient pendant des heures.

Alors ne parlont que des perroquets. Eux au moins ont obtenu le « droit de réponse ».

Il y a longtemps que les amateurs d'oiseaux essaient d'apprivoiser les perroquets. Une encyclopédie de 1784 indiquait déjà : « Les perroquets que les sauvages ne dénichent pas, mais qu'ils prennent en adultes déjà grands, sont très sauvages et ils mordent cruellement ; ils les adoucissent en fort peu de temps par le moyen de la fumée de tabac qu'ils leur soufflent par petites bouffées, ce qu'on appele donner des camouflets de tabac; la vapeur les étourdit; pendant la stupeur qu'elle cause, on les manie sans risque et lorsque l'effet en est passé, leur première violence est déjà apaisée et leur humeur adoucie; on recommence au besoin et les perroquets finissent par être plus ou moins traitables... ».

Un psychologue analyse même : « tous les propriétaires de perroquets ont pu remarquer que leur compagnon a une préférence pour telle ou telle personne de son entourage. On a même constaté que les mâles préféraient les dames et les femelles les messieurs. Mais, reconnaît-il, pour vérifier cette règle, il faut être sûr du sexe, difficile à déterminer avec certitude chez grand nombre de perroquets, en particulier le Gris du Gabon... ».

Pour n'importe quel oiseau, il est préférable de choisir un sujet jeune car il est certain que celui-ci deviendra plus facilement familier...

Quant aux poissons à accueillir en aquarium d'appartement, ils sont nombreux et votre commerçant spécialiste pourra vous en présenter quelques espèces.

A Lyon, les toutous sont les rois

Sur l'immense affiche, un fox-terrier à poils lisses interpelle le passant : « Merci Caninet. » C'est en découvrant ces placards publicitaires que les Lyonnais ont, du même coup, appris l'existence des vespasiennes pour chiens.

Au premier abord, le (la ?) caninet(te ?) ressemble à une tombe : un rectangle de terre noire encadré de béton, une stèle à l'arrière et un mince liseré d'arbres pour masquer le tout. En s'approchant, la chose prend des allures de juke-box primitif avec des voyants lumineux sur le côté. Mais ce n'est qu'en appuyant sur le bouton « Nettoyage, hors toute présence » que l'on comprend enfin : la terre, dans un ronron sourd de moteur électrique se déroule jusqu'à ce que la litière soit entièrement renouvelée. La stèle est en fait un réservoir de terre qu'emplit chaque matin un employé de la voirie.

Déjà troublés par les motos vertes et blanches qui pétaradent à l'affut du moindre canin négligeant, les toutous lyonnais auraient-ils du mal à s'acclimater à ces nouvelles techniques ?

Jusqu'à présent, en tout cas, ces "petits coins" disséminés dans la ville restent désespérément vierges. ∎

E28

Your pen-friend knows that England is a nation of dog lovers. He therefore shows you this report. Is it a joke?

> Vocabulaire: toutous = chiens

1 Where is this report based?

2 The caninet is said to look like:

   a) a row of trees.

   b) a tree.

   c) a grave.

   d) a primitive juke-box.

3 How is the caninet powered?

4 What does the caninet aim to do?

5 What success is it having?

P

Les «caninets» qu'en pensez-vous? Croyez-vous qu'on devra développer un tel service en Grande-Bretagne? Pourquoi ou pourquoi pas?

Chapter 2
La vie au collège

Vous participez à un échange scolaire et après la visite de votre correspondant(e) vous vous trouvez dans son collège. Vous remarquez qu'il y a beaucoup de différences entre les deux systèmes. Pour vous expliquer un peu il/elle vous montre des documents scolaires qu'il/elle a reçus pendant sa carrière.

A   L'entrée en sixième

E1

Here is the list of subjects your pen-friend's younger brother studies.

Compare his subjects with the list below. Which subjects does your pen-friend's brother study?

1 Music

2 A foreign language

3 Maths

4 Geography

5 Religious Education

6 PE

7 Latin

8 General Studies

notez ici
le nom des professeurs

souligner le nom du professeur principal.
_____

français
_____
mathématiques
_____
langue vivante
_____
histoire et géographie
_____
sciences expérimentales
_____
éducation artistique
_____
éducation manuelle
_____
éducation physique

3 - *Exécution et contrôle du travail scolaire*

Chaque élève possède un cahier de textes sur lequel il reporte l'emploi du temps de sa classe et consigne le travail à faire à la maison : devoirs, exercices, leçons, enquêtes et travaux divers.
Il est fortement conseillé aux Parents de consulter régulièrement ce cahier afin de mieux suivre le travail de leurs enfants.
A tout moment, les élèves peuvent se documenter sur la nature exacte du travail à faire à la maison en consultant le cahier de textes de la classe (bureau des Surveillants).

Un carnet de liaison est remis à l'élève en début d'année. Il doit être soigneusement complété par l'élève avec son Professeur Principal d'une part, et les Parents d'autre part. Sur ce carnet, l'élève reporte ses notes (notation 0 à 20 en pratique dans l'établissement, un zéro doit précéder toute note inférieure à 10) et le carnet doit être visé par la famille tous les mois. Une grande partie du carnet de liaison est consacrée à la correspondance établissement-parents.

E2

This is an extract from a letter sent to all new pupils by the headteacher.

Briefly summarise the purpose of:
1 *un cahier de textes.*
2 *un carnet de liaison.*

These following extracts explain some subjects that a pupil will study in his/her first year at a French secondary school.

3 heures

mathématiques :

Leur étude a un double but :

- doter l'élève d'un bagage de connaissances pratiques et techniques utilisables dans la vie courante.
- développer sa pensée logique et son goût de la rigueur.

2 heures

éducation artistique :

Par un certain nombre d'activités à caractère esthétique, on s'efforce :

- de sensibiliser les enfants à des formes d'expression multiples :
  arts plastiques,
  architecture,
  artisanat d'art,
  musique,
  danse,
  art dramatique,
  poésie,
  cinéma ;
- de favoriser leur désir de création.

3 heures

sciences expérimentales :

Par cet enseignement on cherche à donner aux enfants une véritable initiation scientifique, afin de les préparer à la connaissance et au respect de la vie sous toutes ses formes.

Les sciences expérimentales comportent l'étude :

- des sciences physiques :
  propriétés physiques des solides, des liquides, des gaz,
  compréhension concrète du circuit électrique,
  compréhension des combustions,
- des sciences naturelles :
  êtres vivants et végétaux

3 heures

éducation physique et sportive :

A travers cet enseignement on cherche :

- à aider les jeunes à acquérir une bonne maîtrise de leur corps,
- à contribuer à la formation de leur personnalité, à leur épanouissement physique, intellectuel et moral.

Here is some advice given to parents.

A

votre rôle :

- fournir à l'enfant des instruments pour qu'il puisse se livrer à celles de ces activités qui l'attirent le plus.
- voir s'il existe des ateliers, des clubs, des chorales ou des orchestres. L'encourager à participer à leurs activités.
- l'emmener visiter des musées, des expositions.

B

votre rôle :

- lui donner le goût de vaincre certaines de ses difficultés.
- l'encourager là où il réussit le mieux.
- favoriser ses activités de plein air.

C

votre rôle :

Peut être vous êtes-vous senti « dépassé » dans ce domaine... Acceptez le... mais vous pouvez toujours vérifier que les leçons sont bien sues, les devoirs faits complètement.

Donnez à votre enfant le goût des calculs, le sens des formes. Certains jeux y contribuent.

D

votre rôle :

Profiter des vacances, des promenades pour lui faire observer les plantes, les animaux, développer son esprit de curiosité.

Can you match up the advice to parents (**A, B, C, D**) with the relevant subject area?

E4

1 Name two facilities in a secondary school which are probably not found in a primary school.

2 What worries could a new pupil have?

P

Décrivez votre première journée au collège.

---

les régimes scolaires

l'externat :

L'élève externe revient à la maison pour les repas de midi. Attention à la longueur du trajet entre le domicile et le collège.

la demi-pension :

L'élève demi-pensionnaire prend ses repas de midi dans l'établissement. Cette solution s'impose si le domicile est trop éloigné du collège, ou si les parents n'ont pas la possibilité de s'occuper de l'enfant à ce moment-là.

Après le repas les élèves peuvent participer aux activités qui existent dans le collège : au foyer socio-éducatif (voir ci-contre), au C.D.I. (voir page 11) ou bien ils se rendent en permanence.

Les frais de demi-pension varient suivant les établissements. Ils sont payables au début de chaque trimestre scolaire.

l'internat :

Il n'existe que très rarement dans les collèges. L'élève interne réside complètement dans l'établissement pendant la semaine scolaire.

Lorsque les circonstances imposent cette solution, il faut tout faire pour éviter que l'enfant se sente isolé, coupé de son milieu familial.

Il faut lui écrire souvent, le faire sortir régulièrement, prévoir pour lui un correspondant, même si le règlement intérieur de l'établissement ne l'exige pas.

Les frais d'internat varient suivant les établissements. Ils sont payables au début de chaque trimestre scolaire.

---

depuis la rentrée votre enfant découvre :

un nouvel établissement et une nouvelle manière de vivre :

Le collège est souvent beaucoup plus grand que ne l'était son école : davantage d'élèves, davantage de classes, peut-être une bibliothèque, un centre de documentation et d'information (1), une infirmerie... L'élève devra aller d'une classe à l'autre entre les cours... A l'école tout le monde se connaît, mais au collège il rencontrera surtout beaucoup de nouveaux visages.

En CM2, il était parmi les « grands » de son école. Au collège, il se trouve parmi les « petits », et les petits sont souvent « bousculés » par les grands...

Il quitte un établissement situé tout près de la maison, il pouvait s'y rendre à pied, tout seul. Pour aller au collège il va parfois être contraint d'utiliser l'autobus ou le métro, ou de prendre un car de ramassage. Enfin peut-être votre enfant est-il demi-pensionnaire, ou même interne... encore quelques nouvelles habitudes à prendre...

E5

The leaflet contains some details about three different types of pupil.

1 What does a day pupil do at lunch time?

2 Why might a pupil decide to become a *demi-pensionnaire*?

3 How are school dinners costed and paid for?

4 Where does an *interne* stay during the school week?

5 What problem might he/she encounter?

6 What steps can be taken to remedy this?

P

a) Êtes-vous «interne»?
   Si non, comment arrivez-vous au collège le matin?

b) Où mangez-vous le déjeuner?

B Les règlements

EXTRAITS DU RÈGLEMENT INTÉRIEUR

HORAIRE DE L'ETABLISSEMENT :

Les cours se dérouleront selon l'horaire suivant :

Matin :
8 h. 05 -	9 h.
9 h. -	9 h. 55
Récréation de 9 h. 55 à 10 h. 10	
10 h. 10 - 11 h. 05	
11 h. 05 - 12 h.	

Après-midi :
14 h. -	14 h. 55
14 h. 55 - 15 h. 50	
Récréation de 15 h. 50 à 16 h. 05	
16 h. 05 - 17 h.	

Les élèves ne doivent entrer dans le Collège que 10 minutes avant le début du premier cours de la demi-journée.

PRESENCE DANS L'ETABLISSEMENT :

Les externes n'ayant jamais cours de 11 h. à 12 h. et de 16 h. à 17 h. seront rendus à leurs familles à 11 h. et 16 h.

En revanche, les demi-pensionnaires ne seront autorisés à quitter l'établissement qu'en fin de journée scolaire (voir l'emploi du temps de la classe).

E6

Here are some of the rules of your pen-friend's school.

Consult this timetable:

1 When is the first lesson of the day?

2 What happens between 9.55 a.m. and 10.10 a.m.?

3 What happens between 12 and 2 p.m.?

4 When should pupils assemble before morning and afternoon school?

5 Your pen-friend goes home to lunch. In what circumstances can he/she go home early?

P

Décrivez votre emploi du temps.

E7

Read this extract concerning pupil absences.

1 What does it say parents should do if they know their child will be absent from school?

2 Your pen-friend has been ill for two days, should he/she send in a medical certificate?

3 How would your pen-friend's parents be informed if their child were truanting?

4 After an absence, what must a pupil do before returning to class?

ABSENCES ET RETARDS :

Toute absence prévue par la famille doit être signalée à l'avance et par écrit à Monsieur le Sous-Directeur.

En cas d'absence imprévue, la famille préviendra immédiatement le Secrétariat du Collège par téléphone (si possible), par lettre ou de vive voix.

Si l'absence dure plus de trois jours, il sera produit un certificat médical.

Toute absence non justifiée sera signalée aux parents au moyen d'une carte postale ad hoc. Les parents sont tenus de la renvoyer, en indiquant le motif de l'absence.

Il est interdit de rentrer en classe après une absence ou un retard sans avoir obtenu de la Surveillance un bulletin de rentrée. Les retards et absences seront relevés.

TENUE DES ELEVES :

Une tenue correcte et décente est exigée et les parents doivent y veiller.

Tous les vêtements qui ne sont pas portés constamment dans la journée doivent être marqués solidement au nom de l'élève.

Une tenue de sport est obligatoire pour l'éducation physique (short et chaussures).

Le port apparent de tout insigne à caractère politique ou religieux est interdit.

Il est interdit aux élèves de fumer dans l'établissement.

La mauvaise tenue dans les cars de ramassage peut entraîner la perte du bénéfice de ce service.

E8

Which of the following sentences are true?

1 There is a school uniform.

2 Special clothing is required for sport.

3 All clothing worn at school must be named.

4 The wearing of a religious badge is not allowed.

5 No smoking is allowed at school.

6 Bad behaviour on the school buses can lead to expulsion.

E9

Which of the following punishments apply in French schools?

1 Detention on Thursday morning.

2 Caning.

3 Extra work to be done at home.

4 Pupils sent out of class have to do extra work supervised by ancillary staff.

5 Temporary expulsion.

SANCTIONS :

En cas de nécessité, les punitions suivantes pourront être infligées :
— devoir supplémentaire à faire à la maison ;
— renvoi en permanence avec devoir supplémentaire contrôlé par les surveillants ;
— retenue le mercredi matin ;
— avertissement du chef d'établissement à la famille ;
— exclusion temporaire prononcée par le chef d'établissement.

En cas de faute grave commise par un élève, le Conseil de Discipline sera convoqué dans les dix jours qui suivent l'infraction.

P

a) Comment vous comportez-vous au collège?

b) Votre directeur/directrice, est-il/elle sévère?

c) Quelles sont les sanctions dans votre collège?

C Les professeurs

Mieux vivre

Vos enfants et vous

Comment discuter avec les profs?

Les relations entre parents et enseignants ne sont pas simples. Il y va pourtant de l'intérêt de l'enfant. Alors, abordez le dialogue dans de bonnes conditions...

De l'école primaire à la terminale, les récriminations des élèves envers les enseignants sont nombreuses. *« La maîtresse m'a encore puni et c'était pas de ma faute ». « Le prof de maths est mauvais, on n'y comprend rien... »* Du côté des parents, les positions manquent le plus souvent de nuances. Il y a ceux pour qui les profs sont toujours en vacances, toujours en grève, voire toujours absents.

Eviter les malentendus

Il y a aussi ceux pour qui *« aucun effort n'est fait pour comprendre les enfants »* (et le leur en particulier). Pour d'autres, au contraire, l'enseignant a toujours raison. Mais bien que descendu de son piédestal, le professeur reste redouté. Les rapports parents-enseignants pâtissent d'une absence de simplicité. Un problème en classe ? On critiquera le professeur, mais on n'osera pas aller le voir, de peur qu'il ne se « venge » sur l'enfant. Comme si certains parents n'arrivaient pas, face aux professeurs, à être tout à fait des adultes et restaient les enfants soumis ou chahuteurs qu'ils étaient... De leur côté, les enseignants qui se sentent systématique-

ment critiqués, ont souvent la sensibilité à fleur de peau. Ils estiment que les difficultés de leur métier sont méconnues. Et certains prennent la moindre demande d'explication pour une agression. Mais ils sont nombreux aussi à regretter de n'avoir pas plus de contacts avec les parents de leurs élèves. Ils déplorent tous qu'ils soient si rares s'y vont aux réunions qu'ils organisent. *« Une bonne discussion permet d'éviter bien des malentendus »*, explique un instituteur. Alors, bien sûr, il faut venir discuter avec les enseignants, mais il faut aussi savoir s'y prendre... D'abord ne pas les considérer systématiquement comme des ennemis qui s'acharnent gratuitement sur votre enfant. Lorsqu'il y a un problème, écoutez, bien sûr, la version de votre enfant, mais n'oubliez pas qu'elle peut être déformée. Réservez donc votre jugement jusqu'à votre entretien avec le professeur. Même si certains enseignants manquent de pédagogie, en général leur expérience des enfants est réelle. Et leur perception du vôtre mérite d'être entendue. Plutôt que l'affrontement, envisagez la collaboration. L'en-

Même si vous ne partagez pas l'avis du professeur, essayez d'établir le dialogue avec lui : Il ne demande que ça.

E10

This extract deals with the times that the staff are available to meet parents.

Your pen-friends parents want to discuss their son's/daughter's progress with:

a) the head teacher.

b) the science teacher.

How and when can they do this?

E11

You have been talking about teachers with your pen-friend. Here is an article about relations between parents and teachers.

1 Give two typical complaints made by pupils about the teachers.

2 Give five opinions commonly expressed by parents about their children's teachers.

3 Why do parents hesitate to see teachers when there is a problem in class?

4 What does a majority of teachers think about meetings with parents?

E12

This is another extract from the same article.

1 If your pen-friend was having problems, whom could his parents see about his work? He is 15.

2 In what circumstances would the parents of an eight-year-old child approach the head teacher?

Qui aller voir ?

● **A l'école primaire,** l'interlocuteur privilégié est, bien sûr, l'instituteur de votre enfant. N'hésitez pas à aller le voir au moindre problème, même si vous pensez qu'il a tort. Une discussion sans animosité vaut mieux que des ressentiments ressassés.
En cas de conflit plus important, le directeur (ou la directrice) peut s'avérer un médiateur utile. Mais attention : les enseignants apprécient peu qu'on passe par dessus leur tête.
● **Au collège,** c'est avant tout le professeur principal qu'il faut voir. Il centralise, pour chaque classe, les remarques de ses collègues, et peut leur faire part des vôtres. Mais, si vous le pouvez, allez voir, ne serait-ce qu'une fois dans l'année, tous les professeurs : un prof de gym ou de musique peut vous apprendre beaucoup sur votre enfant. En cas de problème avec un professeur précis, c'est celui-ci qu'il faut rencontrer.

P

a) Que pensez-vous de votre collège? Et vos parents, qu'en pensent-ils?

b) Avez-vous un(e) professeur préféré?

c) Qu'est-ce qu'il/elle vous enseigne? Depuis quand? Comment est-il/elle?

d) Décrivez le système d'enseignement secondaire dans votre région.

D   Les responsabilités

Your pen-friend has just been elected as class representative and gives you this information about the post.

DES DROITS

1 les délégués et le conseil de classe

Le conseil de classe se réunit au moins une fois par trimestre.

Deux délégués des élèves élus par la classe participent à ces réunions au cours desquelles sont examinées les questions pédagogiques.

Le conseil de classe constitue un organisme d'information réciproque, de dialogue, de coordination et d'animation. C'est également le conseil de classe qui arrête les propositions relatives au déroulement de la scolarité de chaque élève et notamment les propositions d'orientation.

2 les délégués et le chef d'établissement

Dans chaque collège ou lycée, le chef d'établissement réunit l'ensemble des délégués d'élèves, éventuellement par niveau, pour un dialogue sur les conditions de vie scolaire. Cette réunion a lieu au moins une fois par trimestre ou lorsque la moitié des délégués en fait la demande.

Copyright: *Centre régional de documentation pédagogique de Grenoble* reproduced by kind permission.

Consider carefully this information about class representatives (*délégués*) and their rights (*les droits*).

1 A *conseil de classe* is a meeting where the general progress of pupils is discussed. How often does it meet?

2 How many class representatives are there at this meeting?

3 Apart from the headteacher, who can call a meeting to discuss matters relating to school life?

P

Est-ce qu'un tel processus existe en Angleterre? Aimeriez-vous y participer?

This extract is from a school handbook outlining arrangements for participating in sports at the school.

VIII - ASSOCIATION SPORTIVE (U.N.S.S.)

Avec l'accord de leurs parents, les élèves qui désirent faire du sport peuvent s'inscrire à l'Association Sportive du collège. Les entraînements peuvent avoir lieu, soit le mercredi, soit après les cours. Les déplacements vers les lieux d'entraînement se font sous la responsabilité des familles.

1 Are sports lessons compulsory?
2 When do practices take place?
3 Whose responsibility is it to get to the practices?

E   Les bulletins

E15

A French friend shows you two of her old school reports for you to compare. Here is the first.

1 How often were these reports issued?

2 How old was Nathalie when this report was issued?

3 What comments did her French teacher make?

4 What foreign languages did she study?

5 What was the overall comment?

<table>
<tr><td colspan="3">COLLÈGE VICTOR GRIGNARD
177, Avenue Paul Santy
69008 LYON
Tél. : 74.30.45</td><td>NOM SANCHEZ
Prénom Nathalie
Date de naissance 15.05.66</td><td>1er TRIMESTRE 1979 1980
CLASSE 4°3 Redoub. ☐ Boursier ☐</td></tr>
</table>

DISCIPLINES		Types d'exercices	Notes sur 20	APPRÉCIATIONS ET RECOMMANDATIONS DES PROFESSEURS
FRANÇAIS	Comp. fran.		12,5	Bien Doit faire des efforts de participation orale .
	Grammaire	}	12	
	Orthographe			
	Lect. expliq.	}	13	
M	Récitation			
LATIN M				
HISTOIRE GÉOGRAPHIE M AGNIEL			12	A. Bien dans l'ensemble . Travail sérieux
ÉDUCATION CIVIQUE M				
LANGUE VIVANTE I Écrit Anglais M Pouillat Oral			12	Assez bons résultats à l'écrit . Participation active à l'oral —
LANGUE VIVANTE II Écrit Espagnol Mlle DUBUS Oral			11,5	Assez bien à l'oral - Nathalie est en progrès -
MATHÉMATIQUE M Armain			10	Résultats en dents de scie, il faut travailler régulièrement Ensemble trop moyen
TECHNOLOGIE M				
SCIENCES NATURELLES M			14	Travail sérieux —
SCIENCES PHYSIQUES M			13	Assez bien
ÉDUCATION ARTISTIQUE	MUSIQUE M	13,5	11	A Bien
	DESSIN Callamard		16	Satisfaisant
ÉDUCATION MANUELLE ET TECHNIQUE Mme BONNEL			13,5	Bon ensemble
ÉDUCATION PHYSIQUE M				

COMPORTEMENT

Appréciations globales et recommandations (conseil de classe)

du chef d'établissement

Assez bon travail

P

a) Quelles étaient les matières que vous avez étudiées en sixième?

b) Quelles sont les matières que vous étudiez en ce moment? Laquelle préférez-vous? Pourquoi?

c) Combien d'élèves et de professeurs y-a-t-il dans votre collège actuel?

Here is one of Nathalie's later reports.

6 How old was Nathalie when this report was issued?

7 What additional subjects was she taking and what subjects had she dropped?

8 What comments did her PE teacher make?

LYCÉE D'ÉTAT A. et L. LUMIERE 50, boulevard des États-Unis 69008 LYON	NOM _SANCHEZ_ Prénom _Nathalie_ Né le _15 - 5 - 66_ Classe de _T A2/_ REDOUBLE ☐ NON REDOUBLANT ☐	ANNÉE SCOLAIRE 19 _83_ 19 _84_ 1er TRIMESTRE

DISCIPLINES	NIVEAU ET NOTE	APPRÉCIATIONS ET RECOMMANDATIONS DES PROFESSEURS	Signature des Professeurs
Mathématiques	12,25	A Bien —	
Sc. physiques			
Sc. naturelles			
Philosophie	11	Travail sérieux - Résultats convenables - Continuez -	
Histoire Géographie	H = 6 G = 11	Un "accident" en Histoire - des progrès sont possibles	C.Z.
Sc. économiques			
Français			
Latin			
L. V. I	13	Travail sérieux En progrès	
L. V. II esp	11.5	Notes Bonne élève —	
italien Grec ou L. V. III	écrit. 08,5 participation orale: 10	Doit améliorer la correction de la langue - Mais le travail et l'attention sont soutenus → pas de découragement !	
Dactylographie			
Ed. musicale			
Dessin			
Tr. manuels			
E. P. S.	Gym Athlé Nat.	De la bonne volonté mais le niveau reste moyen.	

ABSENCES	APPRÉCIATIONS GLOBALES ET RECOMMANDATIONS DU CONSEIL DE CLASSE
	Bon trimestre Doit progresser en Histoire
	Le Chef d'Établissement

ATTENTION IL NE SERA PAS DÉLIVRÉ DE DUPLICATA

P

a) Existe-t-il des bulletins scolaires pareils dans votre collège? Si non, en quoi diffèrent-ils?

b) Avez-vous reçu de bonnes notes en français cette année? En quelles matières avez-vous bien réussi cette année?

F   Les cours particuliers

DIPLOMES DE LANGUES
pour la vie professionnelle
anglais, allemand, espagnol, italien, russe

Quels que soient votre âge, les études que vous faites (ou vous avez faites), votre profession actuelle, vous pouvez préparer facilement, à distance, donc chez vous, un diplôme d'une Chambre de Commerce Etrangère ou de l'Université de Cambridge, le BTS, Traducteur Commercial, etc. Ts niveaux (même débutant). Cours oraux complém. Formation continue. Doc grat. à LANGUES et AFFAIRES, service 2008, 35, rue Collange, 92203 Paris-Levallois. Tél. : 270-81-88 (Ets Privé).

E16
In France, it is considered very important to speak a foreign language. This is an advertisement for a language school.

1 Which languages are offered here?

2 Is there an age limit?

3 Is prior knowledge needed?

4 Where does one study?

E17
Here is a list of private tutors offering their services.

Which phone number would your pen-friend ring if he/she wanted the following tuition?

1 Chemistry taught by a fully qualified teacher.

2 Spanish conversation with a native speaker.

3 Arabic lessons at home.

4 Classes in silk screen painting.

5 Greek during the Easter holidays.

COURS PARTICULIERS

MATHS - PHYSIQUE - CHIMIE Cours ts niveaux par élèves de l'Ecole Nat. Sup. des MINES de Paris. Tél. 325-28-03.

ANGLAIS - ALLEMAND - ARABE - RUSSE et CHINOIS, particulier et entreprises. Tél. 721-06-70.

Français, latin, grec, cours tous niveaux. Préparation aux examens. Tél. 805-42-26.

ESPAGNOL, ts niveaux. Professeur Argentine. Tél. 8 à 14 et 16 à 18 h (pas après) 567-19-17.

Professeur donne cours d'arabe littéraire, chez lui ou à domicile. Tél. 238-16-32 - 280-49-17.

American student giving english conversation, lessons Paris Area. Tél. 576-11-65.

Prép. bac MATHS PHYSIQUE, Vac. Pâques par élèves MINES de Paris. Tél. 907-65-11.

Cours toutes matières, tous niveaux par diplômés grandes écoles. Tél. 224-17-95 et 97.

FRANÇAIS - LATIN - GREC 3e à terminal. Vacances Pâques et 3e trimestre par professeur agrégé docteur ès lettres. Tél. 346-99-57.

AMERICAIN avec professeur américain qualifiée Paris 15e. Tél. 250-39-45.

CHINOIS. Cours particuliers, conversation, peintures ts niveaux. Tél. 828-04-34.

RESTAURATION DE TABLEAUX. Cours ts niveaux par spécialiste. Tél. 278-60-59.

MATHS - PHYSIQUE - CHIMIE. Révisions intensives. Vacances Pâques et 3e trimestre par prof. agrégé. Tél. 347-14-70.

TAPISSERIE HAUTE LICE par ancienne élève Gobelins. Tél. 586-04-01.

LE MEILLEUR des cours de **PEINTURE SUR SOIE.** Prix stables jusqu'à fin avril. Mlle Renouard, 29, Bd Edgar-Quinet, 75014 Paris. Tél. 322-45-67.

LANGUES
« Phonelab », école d'enseignement des langues par téléphone, propose des cours sur mesure, notamment techniques : informatique en anglais, commerce en japonais, chimie en allemand, etc. (Le professeur vous téléphone à l'heure de votre choix. Chaque cours dure vingt-cinq minutes).
« Phonelab » prépare également à l'examen des Chambres de commerce britannique et américaine. Le cours pour la préparation à l'examen de la Chambre de commerce britannique dure trente-cinq heures, sans compter le travail personnel. Prix forfaitaire : 6 800 F hors taxe (Phonelab accorde des facilités de paiement). Cette formation peut être prise en charge par votre entreprise.
Renseignements : Phonelab, 11, boulevard Malesherbes, 75008 Paris. 42.65.48.84.

EVALLIER

E18
This article catches your eye in a magazine.

1 What kind of institution is Phonelab?

2 How is teaching done?

3 Name three courses currently on offer?

4 How long does each lesson last?

5 Where are lessons held?

6 What help can employees apply for?

P
a) Comment apprenez-vous les langues étrangères à l'école?

b) Quels sont les avantages et les inconvénients du système Phonelab?

Chapter 3
Les carrières et le travail

Cette section concerne le monde du travail et les études professionnelles. Après la troisième année on peut entrer au lycée, au LEP (Lycée d'enseignement professionnel), une école spécialisée ou bien faire un stage de formation professionnelle. On a l'embarras de choix. Après avoir étudié les extraits suivants vous connaîtrez mieux cette riche variété.

A   L'orientation professionnelle

E1

In France, pupils are advised to write for career information to *ONISEP*.

Here is the application form they need to obtain such information.

Motif de non-distribution

☐ adresse insuffisante

☐ n'habite pas à l'adresse indiquée

☐ refusé

ONISEP
75225 PARIS CEDEX 05

Nom et adresse: _____

_____

_____

_____

PAQUET POSTE

Nom _____

Adresse _____

_____

Nom et adresse à écrire deux fois

Mode de paiement (ni timbre, ni espèces) à joindre impérativement à la commande.

Chèque bancaire ☐ Chèque postal ☐ Mandat ☐ à l'ordre de l'Agent Comptable de l'ONISEP date _____ Signature _____

Titres commandés	Références	Prix franco
_____	⊔⊔⊔⊔⊔⊔⊔	_____
_____	⊔⊔⊔⊔⊔⊔⊔	_____
_____	⊔⊔⊔⊔⊔⊔⊔	_____
_____	⊔⊔⊔⊔⊔⊔⊔	_____
_____	⊔⊔⊔⊔⊔⊔⊔	_____
_____	⊔⊔⊔⊔⊔⊔⊔	_____

Total à reporter sur le chèque ou le mandat

BON DE COMMANDE A ENVOYER A: ONISEP DIFFUSION 75225 PARIS CEDEX 05

You decide to complete the form for *ONISEP*.

1 How many times do you need to write your name and address?

2 Name two possible methods of paying for an order.

3 What method of payment is not allowed?

4 Give two reasons why your order might not be received from *ONISEP*.

E2

This article mentions the people you can turn to for career advice.

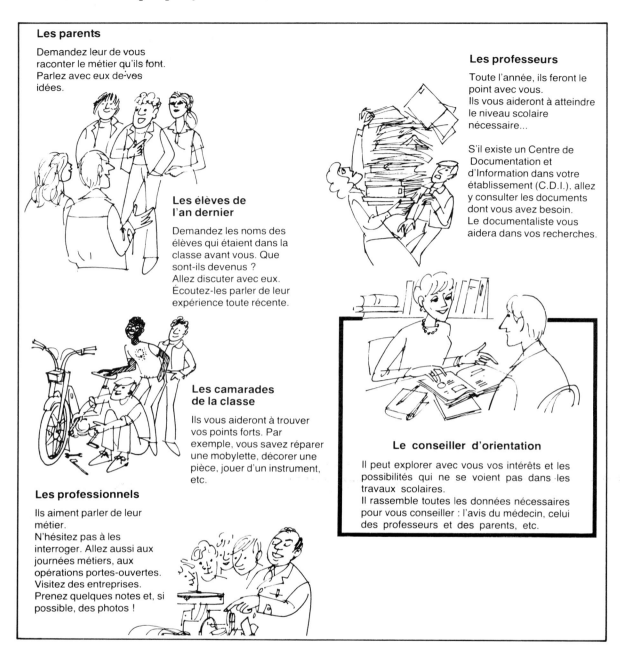

Les parents

Demandez leur de vous raconter le métier qu'ils font. Parlez avec eux de vos idées.

Les élèves de l'an dernier

Demandez les noms des élèves qui étaient dans la classe avant vous. Que sont-ils devenus ? Allez discuter avec eux. Écoutez-les parler de leur expérience toute récente.

Les camarades de la classe

Ils vous aideront à trouver vos points forts. Par exemple, vous savez réparer une mobylette, décorer une pièce, jouer d'un instrument, etc.

Les professionnels

Ils aiment parler de leur métier. N'hésitez pas à les interroger. Allez aussi aux journées métiers, aux opérations portes-ouvertes. Visitez des entreprises. Prenez quelques notes et, si possible, des photos !

Les professeurs

Toute l'année, ils feront le point avec vous. Ils vous aideront à atteindre le niveau scolaire nécessaire...

S'il existe un Centre de Documentation et d'Information dans votre établissement (C.D.I.), allez y consulter les documents dont vous avez besoin. Le documentaliste vous aidera dans vos recherches.

Le conseiller d'orientation

Il peut explorer avec vous vos intérêts et les possibilités qui ne se voient pas dans les travaux scolaires. Il rassemble toutes les données nécessaires pour vous conseiller : l'avis du médecin, celui des professeurs et des parents, etc.

1 According to the above advice, whom should you contact to:

  a) talk about recent job experience.

  b) be told about your strong and weak points.

2 What should you try to do when you visit firms?

3 What is the teacher's role?

4 What is the main role of the careers' officer?

P

a) Que ferez-vous l'année prochaine? Où?

b) Avec qui vous êtes-vous entretenu(e) pour vous informer sur votre futur métier? À votre avis, avez-vous reçu de bons conseils?

c) Si, par hasard, vous n'avez pas encore choisi un métier, pourquoi pas? Comment remédier à cette situation?

E3

This extract comes from one of *ONISEP's* documents called *Orientation après la troisième*.

1 What two things should you bear in mind when choosing a career?

2 List those personal qualities below which are not mentioned in the extract.

a) Enterprising	*f)* Good-looking
b) Honest	*g)* Energetic
c) Diligent	*h)* Independent
d) Shy	*i)* Creative
e) Caring	*j)* Courteous

The article continues . . .

Bien choisir votre orientation, c'est prendre la voie qui vous conviendra le mieux...
A cela, deux conditions nécessaires : être informé et bien vous connaître... Cette brochure vous donne un début de réponse à la première condition : l'information. Pour la seconde, c'est à vous de jouer !

Savoir qui vous êtes, ce qui vous intéresse, quels sont vos goûts, vos possibilités, c'est important pour choisir... même s'il est vrai que vous allez évoluer, que vos goûts vont se préciser et votre personnalité s'affirmer. Etes-vous direct, entreprenant ou timide, consciencieux et persévérant, actif, imaginatif ? aimez-vous commander, être seul, vous occuper des autres ? Avez-vous besoin de vous dépenser physiquement, de prendre des responsabilités, d'organiser ?... Les questions peuvent être multiples, les réponses nombreuses. Chacun d'entre vous est différent.

Et en classe, comment vous situez-vous ? Où réussissez-vous le mieux, où rencontrez-vous des difficultés ? Quelles sont les matières que vous préférez ? Travaillez-vous peu ou beaucoup, vite ou lentement ? Avez-vous la plume facile ? Préférez-vous les raisonnements rigoureux ? Etes-vous curieux d'histoire, d'actualité, de technique ?

---

3 Which other elements do you need to consider when weighing up your future career?

a) Where you sit in class.	*d)* Whether you travel a lot.
b) Which subjects you find difficult.	*e)* Whether you write well.
c) Which subjects you prefer.	*f)* Whether you keep up with current affairs.

E4

This extract lists certain qualities required for certain jobs.

Into which of the groups (**1–10**) would the following jobs be classified?

a) Businessman	*f)* Photographer
b) Secretary	*g)* Train driver
c) Accountant	*h)* Builder
d) Dairy farmer	*i)* Lifeguard
e) Policeman	*j)* Chemist

P

a) Quelles sont vos qualités personnelles? Analysez-les et aussi celles de votre partenaire.

b) Quel métier vous convient le plus? Pourquoi?
Comparez votre choix avec celui de votre partenaire.

UN MÉTIER SELON VOS GOÛTS

Vous aimeriez...	Cela demande...
Faire du commerce **1**	Un sens des contacts humains avec les clients par la discussion, le conseil, la persuasion.
Travailler en contact avec la nature ou vous occuper d'animaux **2**	Un goût très net pour la vie au grand air, qu'il vente, qu'il pleuve... Une bonne santé physique, une tendance à aimer le calme et la solitude.
Travailler au dehors **3**	Goût pour le travail en plein air, même par mauvais temps. Robustesse, bonne santé.
Travailler dans un bureau **4**	Goût pour un travail sédentaire. Ordre et méthode, sociabilité.
Manier les chiffres **5**	Ordre et méthode, précision. Raisonnement mathématique et logique.
Travailler en laboratoire **6**	Précision, calme, rigueur, patience, méthode, soin et ordre.
Exercer un métier artistique **7**	Esprit de création, imagination, vouloir ou accepter souvent d'avoir une vie non conventionnelle, aimer souvent travailler seul.
Exercer une activité sportive et physique **8**	Goût pour le sport et résistance physique, mais aussi goût des contacts.
Surveiller et défendre **9**	Discipline, goût de la hiérarchie, sens de la décision rapide.
Vous déplacer souvent **10**	Aimer bouger. Sens de l'initiative, des responsabilités, bon équilibre physique et nerveux, parfois goût du risque, respect des consignes de sécurité.

B La formation professionnelle

E5

This is an advertisement for correspondence courses.

1 When is one urged to start learning a new trade?

2 How long does it take to study to become:
  a) a nurse?
  b) a courier?
  c) an interior decorator?

3 Name three courses that require no formal entry qualifications.

P

Quels sont les métiers de vos parents?
Depuis quand?

E6

Your pen-friend shows you several job descriptions.

7 Un métier de l'habillement

Mécanicienne en confection

Le tissu a été découpé suivant le patron et les différents morceaux s'entassent dans de grands paniers.
Il faut assembler ces morceaux les uns avec les autres pour qu'ils deviennent un blouson, une robe ou un blue-jean.

La mécanicienne coud une partie du vêtement sur sa machine à coudre.

1 Where are the cut pieces of cloth kept?

2 What three things are these made into?

Il est 8 heures.

Christophe, l'apprenti, André, l'ancien de l'équipe, et Mathieu écoutent les ordres de M. Melois, le patron.
— « Sur la "1501" de M. Nutel les vitesses passent mal. Va la chercher et répare la boîte », dit-il à André.
— « Christophe, après avoir réparé ce pneu et fait la vidange de la R5 bleue, tu aideras André à démonter le moteur. »
— « Matheiu, la 605 a un problème de transmissions, tu regardes et tu feras au mieux pour réparer. »
Pendant ce temps, le patron essaiera la 2 CV dont il'a réparé le système d'allumage, la veille. Des mises au point seront peut-être nécessaires.
Voilà, c'est parti pour la journée. Les portes sont grandes ouvertes. Il y a des courants d'air. On y attrape facilement un rhume. Cela fait partie de nos conditions de travail.

E7

1 What is the matter with M. Nutel's car?

2 Name two things Christophe has to do to the *Renault 5*.

3 What work has already been carried out on the *2 CV*?

4 What is said about working conditions?

5 Having read this short description, do you think you would enjoy working in a similar establishment? Try to justify your answer.

LA CAISSIERE

Elle rend la monnaie et vérifie les chèques de centaines de clients. Dans les grandes surfaces, en moyenne, elle tape 40 tickets de 100 F par heure. A la fin de son service, elle fait ses comptes. Elles ne doit pas avoir fait d'erreur Pour avoir une idée de l'argent manipulé par une caissière qui a fait un service de 5 heures, **faites les multiplications suivantes :**

100 F × 40 × 5 = ...

E8

Name one important qualification for a cashier.

Les grandes surfaces

Il y a plus de possibilités d'emploi. Les horaires sont réguliers. Le vendeur doit parfois travailler le soir quand il y a des nocturnes.

Les petits commerces

Le vendeur fait un peu tout (vente, caisse, nettoyage du magasin, rangement). Les salaires sont souvent plus élevés que dans les grands magasins mais les horaires sont plus lourds.

E9

1 Name two advantages of working in a large store, and in a small business.

2 Name one disadvantage of each.

P

Racontez l'histoire d'une journée dans la vie d'un(e) professeur, d'un(e) infirmièr(e), d'un pêcheur, et d'une secrétaire.

E10

Here is an extract which relates the experiences of three young workers.

Eric 17 ans

Quand mon frère s'est acheté une moto, il m'a donné sa mobylette. Mon copain apprenti boucher m'a dit que son patron cherchait un livreur. Il m'a pris à cause de ma mob. Maintenant, je connais bien toutes les rues de la ville, j'ai quelquefois des pourboires. Je fabrique mon mélange moi-même parce que ça revient moins cher. Les pannes, j'en répare beaucoup. L'hiver c'est moins drôle, mais le printemps revient !

Eric

Which of the following statements are true?

1 Eric was given his moped by his brother.

2 Eric saw an advertisement for his job.

3 Eric's boss liked his personality.

4 Eric knew the locality well.

5 Eric sometimes receives tips.

6 Eric sometimes delivers bread.

7 Eric doesn't like winter.

Nathalie 17 ans

Le jour de mes 16 ans, j'ai quitté le LEP. J'avais fait un an de vente-comptabilité-commerce et je commençais la 2e année. Mais je ne voulais plus aller à l'école tous les jours. Personne n'a voulu de moi pour travailler dans un bureau. Alors je mets sous plastique du linge de toilette qu'on expédie à travers toute la France. Il faut aller vite et c'est toujours la même chose. Mes parents sont contents de me voir gagner 90 % du SMIC et je peux discuter avec les copines de l'usine !

Bernard 16 ans 1/2

A 16 ans, à la fin de l'obligation scolaire, j'ai trouvé une place de garçon-chariot dans un magasin grande surface. Toute la journée je remets à l'entrée les chariots que les clients abandonnent près du coffre de leur voiture. De temps en temps, je m'occupe du verre cassé et des poubelles. Je ne reste pas sans bouger, je gagne 80 % du SMIC, je vois beaucoup de monde !

Nathalie

8 When did Nathalie leave school?

9 Where did Nathalie not want to work?

10 What two things does she say of her present job?

Bernard

11 Where do customers normally leave their trolleys?

12 List three activities he does.

P

a) Que pensez-vous qu' Eric, Bernard et Nathalie feront à 25 ans?

b) Lesquels des trois emplois préféreriez-vous, et pourquoi? Discutez avec votre partenaire.

E11
Your French pen-friend is reading an article about the experiences of an apprentice.

1. Je suis apprenti menuisier chez Delorme. J'ai signé un contrat d'apprentissage voilà trois mois. J'ai débuté par des travaux simples à la main. Je commence à me débrouiller. Les machines, c'est pour bientôt. Mon employeur a demandé l'autorisation à l'Inspecteur du travail.

2. Je vais quelquefois en déplacements. J'aime bien ça. Sur les chantiers, chez les clients, j'aide Robert et Lucien à poser des portes, des fenêtres, des placards. Là, au moins, on peut voir le résultat de ce qu'on fait ! Mais il faut être costaud pour faire ce travail.

3. Vite et bien, c'est le slogan de la maison. Mais il faut garder la qualité : des assemblages qui tiennent et des finitions impeccables. Quand les commandes pressent, il faut quelquefois faire des heures supplémentaires.

4. Une semaine sur quatre, je vais au CFA (Centre de formation d'apprentis). Je me perfectionne en technologie, en français, en calcul. Je fais aussi un peu d'atelier.
Au CFA, il y a des apprentis de presque tous les métiers.

1 How long has this young man been an apprentice?

2 What work has he been given to do?

3 Name three things he has helped to install.

4 When are there opportunities for overtime?

5 How often does he attend technical college?

5. Chez Delorme, le travail commence à huit heures. Comme j'ai une heure de trajet, je me lève de bonne heure. Pas autant que Patrick qui est apprenti boulanger; lui, il commence à six heures, mais il dort l'après-midi. Il travaille le samedi comme Héléna qui est apprentie coiffeuse.
Pour les vacances, j'aurai droit à trente jours de congés par an.

6. Pour l'instant, je ne gagne pas beaucoup, mais ce n'est qu'un début. Les compagnons gagnent plus, mais eux ils connaissent le méteir. Ils m'appellent quelquefois pour leur donner un coup de main. Ils sont sympas et déjà ils me considèrent un peu comme un copain.

7. On dit que Roger est le meilleur ouvrier de l'atelier. C'est avec lui que je travaille. Il est dans le métier depuis 15 ans et il pense s'installer à son compte. Peut-être que je pourrai en faire autant un jour... Mais pour l'instant il faut que j'aie mon CAP. Et si je peux avoir aussi le Brevet professionnel, ce serait encore mieux.

6 What time does he leave home?

7 Patrick and Helena work on Saturdays. What do they do?

8 How much holiday will he get?

9 How do the other workers get on with him?

10 What is his ultimate ambition?

11 Do you think this report creates a good impression of an apprentice's working life? Give a reason for your answer.

C   Les demandes d'emploi

PETITES ANNONCES ✕ RALLYE

cherche jeune fille pour
surveiller devoirs (classes 6eme et CM1)
de 17h30 à 19h, 3-4 jours par semaine

NOM _____   Tél. 62.04.69
Adresse _____   (le matin)
                            Date 25 juillet 86

Demandes d'emplois

A J.H. 18 ans, 3 ans LEP, poss. écrit, ch. EMPLOI-FORMATION MÉTALLIER, pour complété CAP. J.-P. Robert H.L.M. A5 Cité Aulne, Châteaulin.

B J.H. 32 ans, déclarant en douane, bonnes connaiss: anglais, ch. emploi IMPORT–EXPORT. Ecrire au "Télégramme" Brest, n° 36.271, qui transmettra.

C J.H. 16 a. ch. place APPRENTI COIFFEUR. Tél. (98) 02.03.79.

D J.F. 18 ans, ÇAP NETTOYAGE-APPRÊTAGE EN TEINTURERIE, ch. emploi région 29, 22, 35. Libre de suite. Tél. (16.48) 61.25.14.

E J.F. 22 ans CAP IND. HABILLEMENT, ch. emploi COUTURIÈRE–RETOUCHEUSE ou contrat emploi-formation, vente en confection, à partir du 1.9. Tél. (98) 49.06.87.

F J.F. ayant travaillé 6 a. comme secrétaire-assistante dentaire + 1'année prép. école infirmière, ch. emploi comme SECRÉTAIRE, ASSISTANTE ou autre. Ecrire "Télégramme" Brest, n° 10.755, qui transmettra.

G DAME GARDERAIT ENFANT après-midi. Ecrire "Télégramme" Brest, n° 10.755, qui transmettra.

P

Choisissez une de ces publicités et jouez le rôle d'interviewer avec votre partenaire.

E12

This advertisement attracts your attention in a supermarket.

1 What is the person required to do?

2 How long is the working day?

3 How does one apply?

P

a) Avez-vous un emploi à mi-temps?

b) Gagnez-vous de l'argent? Recevez-vous de l'argent de poche?

c) Comment avez-vous dépensé cette somme la semaine dernière?

E13

This is an extract from a newspaper in which young French people are looking for work.

Study these requests for work (**A–G**). Whom would you contact if you wanted someone:

1 to work in a dry-cleaners?

2 to work as a dental assistant?

3 to look after children?

4 who can speak English?

P

Avez-vous jamais travaillé pendant les grandes vacances?
Vous avez gagné combien?

E14

You consult this page of a newspaper because you want to earn some extra cash in France.

1 Which advertisements would you use as a model if you wanted to offer:
   a) babysitting?
   b) English lessons?
   c) to do the cleaning for someone?
   d) to work for someone in your own home?

2 Whom would you contact if you wanted the following services?
   a) A haircut
   b) A letter typed
   c) Extra French lessons

CHERCHE étudiant (e) capable de donner cours angais à-dulte débutant.prendre contact. Tél: .23.09.60

CHERCHE pour CHATEAU-THIERRY heures ménage, vendeuse car expérience commerce ou autre écrire WYPART.F 3 rue P.Doucet CHATEAU THIERRY

BANLIEUE OUEST PARIS jeune ménage 3 enfants cherche employée de maison débutante acceptée si très sérieuse logée nourrie Tél (1)608.56.56. (4)420 27.46.

DAME 50 ans cherche à garder personne âgée ou malade ou handicapée 4/5 nuits par semaine Tél:53.37.76 références.

COIFFEUSE dames cherche emploi Tél: 59.64.70 ap.19H.

Très urgent cherche emploi vendeur ou autre assur. s'abstenit MARECHAL.D 24 Place des Vergers appt.27 VENIZEL.

CHERCHE emploi dessinateur métreur libéré OM 1 1/2 an expérience CHATELAIN.D 40 bd Poincaré SOISSONS

DAME cherche enfant à garder quartier ST Crépin Tél:59.40.92.

JEUNE FEMME cherche enfant à garder 19 rue Pasteur BEL LEU.

CHERCHE travail à domicile Tél: 80.91.29.

DAME 60 ans cherche place emploi maison ou dame de compagnie préférence chez personnes âgées ou handicapée logée nourrie Tél: 80.12.42. Les Lilas.

DAME DACTYLO expérimentée possédant machine cherche travaux à domicile Ecrire TUB: E.7178.

DAME cherche enfant ou bébé à garder 4 rue Dr.Roy 64 Tél: 53.45.30.

JEUNE FILLE cherche à dactylographier menus mariages, communions 1,20f pièce. Images 1f pièce. Tél: 59.57.92.

ENSEIGNANTE donnerait cours particuliers anglais français prix intéressant Tél: 53.27. 73.

CHERCHE personne sérieuse proximité quartier Presles SOISSONS pour garder enfant 2 ans à la journée. Tél:59.56.53 Ap.19h

D   Le monde du travail

Le métier de la semaine
L'interprète, elle contribue au dialogue

Le développement des échanges internationaux a multiplié les emplois dans ce secteur. Au rang de ceux-ci, l'interprétariat.

Anne-Marie Chave, trente-six ans, est interprète indépendante depuis douze ans. Dès sa sortie de l'école, elle trouve des engagements. Les honoraires sont modestes, mais elle accomplit ses premiers pas dans la vie professionnelle. *« Il faut faire ses preuves dès le premier contact. Ensuite, le sérieux, les qualités de la personne se transmettent de bouche à oreille »*, explique Anne-Marie, qui est de ces interprètes que l'on demande. *« Attention, nous ne traduisons pas des conversations mondaines. L'interprétariat n'est pas un travail d'amateur »*, précise-t-elle. Elle a raison. La multiplication des échanges internationaux sur le plan scientifique, technique, industriel et commercial voire politique, exige la connaissance d'une ou plusieurs langues. Chacun ne maîtrise pas obligatoirement une langue étrangère. D'où l'importance de l'interprète. Elle contribue au dialogue, à une meilleure compréhension entre plusieurs personnes ne s'exprimant pas dans la même langue. Ce n'est pas aussi simple qu'il y paraît. Ecoutons Anne-Marie : *« Qu'il s'agisse d'un congrès de médecins ou d'ingénieurs, il me faut à chaque fois effectuer un très important travail : il me faut apprendre le vocabulaire technique et me documenter. Les interprètes sont en quelque sorte les « caméléons » de la communication. »*

Les interprètes ne sont pas seulement "douées" pour les langues : elles doivent maîtriser des vocabulaires techniques.

MONIQUE MANCEAU

E15
Here is a magazine article about interpreting as a career.

1 How old was Anne-Marie Chave when she first became a freelance interpreter?

2 Which areas have expanded to create a demand for interpreters?

3 What must an interpreter do before undertaking an assignment?

4 Would you have chosen another title for this report? Think of one you could use instead.

E16
Florence Doré was the founder of a very special company.

1 How many girls did she start with?

2 How many languages did they speak altogether?

3 Where was her office?

4 Describe the present uniform of the girls.

5 What distinguishes her male interpreters?

6 How many people apply to her for work?

7 How many people are taken on?

8 What type of student does she recruit?

9 How does the writer feel towards Florence Doré?

LE CHARME, ÇA S'APPREND

DIRECTRICE DE CHARME D'UNE AGENCE D'HOTESSES BCBG – AVEC POUR MOTS D'ORDRE : CLASSE ET COMPETENCE – FLORENCE DORE, CONVAINCUE DE L'IMPORTANCE DU « LOOK », VEUT APPRENDRE AUX FEMMES A SE METTRE EN VALEUR.

Etre sans diplôme n'est pas toujours un handicap. Florence Doré, complètement autodidacte, dirige aujourd'hui une florissante agence d'hôtesses et d'hôtes interprètes qui porte son nom : 600 filles et 180 garçons. Signes particuliers : leur classe et leur parfaite connaissance d'une langue étrangère. Le haut de gamme : un bataillon de charme efficace qu'elle déploie dans les manifestations de prestige.
Sept années en Sicile « à ne rien faire », sinon pratiquer l'italien, ont orienté la carrière de Florence Doré qui, de retour en France, a commencé par travailler comme interprète-hôtesse d'italien, grâce à des relations. « Comme j'ai tendance à beaucoup parler, cela m'a apporté des affaires. »

Une sélection très rigoureuse

Première bonne idée : en juillet 1972, elle décide de réunir autour d'elle une douzaine de jeunes femmes parlant des langues étrangères différentes pour augmenter les chances de chacune de trouver du travail. Elle débute chez elle, sans bureau. Seuls frais : l'achat d'uniformes turquoise – la couleur alors à la mode – pour se personnaliser. Aujourd'hui « ses filles » sont en noir « parce que je suis une femme classique » dit-elle. En 74 elle engage des garçons, les habille en costume sombre et cravate rouge, une première : « Difficiles à caser au début, ils sont maintenant de plus en plus sollicités. »
Florence Doré recrute elle-même : des personnes qui viennent parce qu'elles ont entendu parler de l'agence : « J'en vois une cinquantaine par semaine, mais je n'en prends pas plus de quatre par an. » Une sélection draconienne qui fait la force et la réputation de sa maison.
« Une fille très bien physiquement doit aussi parler parfaitement une langue étrangère, sinon elle ne travaillera qu'à 40 %. » Ces oiseaux rares doivent avoir entre 22 et 26 ans et pratiquer une langue étrangère dès le berceau. Si elle engage des étudiants, en général de Sciences Po ou des grandes écoles de commerce, elle évite les étudiantes : « Cela représente trop de travail administratif.

Chapter 4
Les sports et les loisirs

Quand vous passerez du temps en France, soit chez des amis français, soit avec la famille en vacances, vous aurez du temps libre. Il vous sera utile de savoir lire les panneaux, les annonces et les affiches. Vous consulterez aussi les articles sur le sport et les spectacles.

A   La mer, la pêche, la natation et le canotage

E1

The symbols on the left were used in a guide book of a coastal resort in Brittany to introduce details of various activities in the region.

Match the drawings with this list of activities. Write the number and letter only.

a) *Football*
b) *Tennis de table*
c) *Voile*
d) *Natation*
e) *Tennis*
f) *Aviation*
g) *Golf*
h) *Culture physique*
i) *Plongée sous marine*
j) *Pétanque*
k) *Equitation*
l) *Bridge*
m) *Planche à voile*

E2

Whilst you are on holiday in Brittany you see details of a competition organised by a local newspaper.

Gagnez une planche à voile

avec **Le Télégramme**

Remplissez le bon ci-dessous et déposez-le dans l'urne prévue à cet effet sur le stand du **Télégramme** durant le Salon de Carantec. Un tirage au sort effectué le dimanche 18, à 18 h, désignera le gagnant.

Nom .... **Prénom** ....
Adresse ....

1 What do you have to do to enter the competition?

2 What prize could you win?

3 When is the draw being made?

Here are some signs you might see at the seaside.

A

B

E3

If you wished to go swimming, near which of these two signs would you go? Give reasons for your answer.

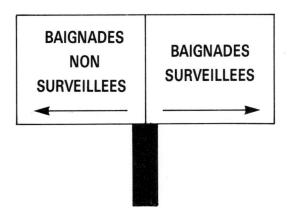

E4

Should you go right or left if you are not a strong swimmer?

E5

What is prohibited here?

E6

Can you visit these islands on a Sunday afternoon in July?

E7

You will be in Morlaix on the 27 and 28 July. What will be happening in the evening?

DIEPPE

PROMENADES
EN MER

RAYDITH

EXCURSIONS en Rade de Dieppe

PÊCHE EN MER

PRIX SPÉCIAUX POUR GROUPES ET COLONIES

SE RENSEIGNER

Syndicat d'Initiative, Bd de la Libération, DIEPPE, Tél 84 11 77, à l'Embarcadère
ou au Siège Social R LETESSIER, 10, Route de Pourville, Tél. 84.11.57

E8

1 Name two activities that this poster advertises.

2 What does it say about group bookings?

HORAIRES DES MAREES
des Côtes du Nord
JUILLET

Jours	PLEINES MERS				BASSES MERS			
	matin		soir		matin		soir	
	heure	haut	heure	haut	heure	haut	heure	haut
L 1	3 30	92	16 02	95	9 58	34	22 31	31
M 2	4 30	94	16 55	99	10 59	31	23 26	28
M 3	5 19	97	17 41	102	11 51	28	— —	—
J 4	6 02	100	18 21	105	0 15	25	12 36	26
V 5	6 39	102	18 56	106	0 57	22	13 16	24
S 6	7 13	102	19 29	107	1 35	21	13 53	23
D 7	7 45	102	20 01	106	2 10	21	14 26	24
L 8	8 16	101	20 30	104	2 40	22	14 53	25
M 9	8 45	98	21 00	101	3 05	24	15 18	27
M 10	9 15	96	21 30	97	3 32	27	15 47	30
J 11	9 48	92	22 06	93	4 02	30	16 19	33
V 12	10 26	89	22 49	89	4 36	34	16 56	37
S 13	11 15	86	23 48	86	5 18	38	17 46	39
D 14	— —	—	12 25	85	6 19	40	18 56	40
L 15	1 06	86	13 47	88	7 35	39	20 15	37
M 16	2 26	89	15 03	94	8 55	35	21 33	31
M 17	3 39	95	16 11	102	10 09	29	22 42	23
J 18	4 41	103	17 10	110	11 13	21	23 44	16
V 19	5 37	110	18 03	116	— —	—	12 12	15
S 20	6 28	114	18 51	120	0 40	10	13 07	10
D 21	7 15	117	19 37	121	1 33	05	13 57	07
L 22	7 58	117	20 18	120	2 20	04	14 40	08
M 23	8 38	114	20 57	116	2 58	07	15 15	12
M 24	9 16	109	21 35	109	3 32	12	15 50	17
J 25	9 55	102	22 18	101	4 08	20	16 27	25
V 26	10 40	94	23 07	92	4 48	28	17 11	33
S 27	11 40	87	— —	—	5 38	37	18 11	40
D 28	0 19	85	13 03	83	6 51	42	19 33	42
L 29	1 47	82	14 30	85	8 17	43	21 00	41
M 30	3 09	84	15 44	89	9 39	41	22 13	36
M 31	4 15	89	16 41	95	10 43	36	23 11	31

E9

While you are on holiday in Brittany you would like to take out a small boat. You look at the tide tables to find out the best time between the 20 and 30 July.

1 Which day could you leave early in the morning on a high tide and return on a high tide at around 9 p.m.?

2 On which dates would it be impossible to leave on a high tide after breakfast?

3 On which days does the tide rise highest and go out lowest?

LA MAISON DE LA RIVIÈRE, DE L'EAU ET DE LA PÊCHE présente :

● **Des aquariums :** saumons adultes, truites de mer évoluent dans un bassin de 15 m³, en prise directe sur la rivière ...

● **Une exposition permanente :** 45 panneaux répartis sur 300 m² détaillant cinq thèmes :
○ La vie des poissons dans les rivières bretonnes, mais aussi à travers le monde ...
○ L'eau en Bretagne, son importance dans notre vie quotidienne, le bilan de santé des rivières.
○ La richesse et la diversité de la flore et de la faune de nos vallées.
○ Les activités économiques régionales ; leur dépendance avec la qualité des eaux.
○ Le renouveau des rivières d'Armorique depuis 15 ans. Quel avenir pour l'ensemble de ces cours d'eau ?

● **Des maquettes :** vallée de l'Élorn 2,50 m x 4 m, station de production d'eau potable ...

● **Du matériel de pêche ;** évolution depuis près d'un siècle (cannes, moulinets). La réalisation des mouches artificielles pour la pêche à la truite et au saumon.

● **Des films** sur les rivières, les salmonidés et leur pêche, les actions de remise en valeur des cours d'eau.

● **Une salle de documentation** à la disposition du public (hebdomadaires, mensuels, rapports et études scientifiques, articles de presse).

● **Des circuits.** Sur demande possibilités de visites guidées :
○ Circuits courts à proximité de la Maison de la Rivière.
○ Circuits organisés de découverte de la vallée de l'Élorn : stations d'épuration, parcours aménagés, salmoniculture, trappes de comptage, observations de remontées de saumons à certaines périodes de l'année, rencontres avec des scientifiques, des responsables d'associations.

● **Interventions possibles en milieu scolaire.**

E10

Above are details of a tourist centre in Brittany. Name five attractions of *La maison de la rivière, de l'eau et de la pêche.*

VILLE DE COMPIEGNE

Tél. 440.05.41   *BASSIN D'ÉTÉ*   2, Cours Guynemer

Ouvert tous les jours de JUIN à AOUT
de 9 h. 30 à 20 h. sans arrêt (Semaine et Dimanche)

Terrain de Jeux pour les Enfants

au Bar : Casse-Croute, Boissons, Glaces au bord de l'Oise

Entrées et Leçons: mêmes tarifs qu'à la piscine d'hiver

E11

You would like to go swimming in the French town where you are staying and you see this poster.

1 Could you go to this swimming pool on a Monday?

2 What other facility is offered for children?

3 Name two things you could buy at the bar?

VILLE DE COMPIEGNE
PISCINE MUNICIPALE D'HIVER

Tél. 420.46.06   15, Avenue de HUY

HEURES D'OUVERTURE AU PUBLIC :   TARIFS :

LUNDI	12 h à 14 h	17 h à 19 h	ADULTES	6 F 00
MARDI		17 h à 21 h	Carnet de 13 tickets	60 F 00
MERCREDI	9 h 30 à 12 h	15 h à 19 h	ENFANTS	
JEUDI		17 h à 22 h	moins de 5 ans accompagnés	**gratuit**
VENDREDI		17 h à 19 h	de 5 à 16 ans	3 F 00
SAMEDI	12 h à 13 h 30	14 h 30 à 19 h	Carnet de 13 tickets	30 F 00
DIMANCHE	9 h 30 à 13 h	14 h à 17 h	SPECTATEURS	2F,00

Demi-Tarif le Dimanche Après-midi

LEÇONS DE NATATION : 12 F 00   la leçon
(sur rendez-vous)   100 F 00 le forfait de **10** leçons

Même horaire, sauf mercredi et samedi où les leçons ne débutent qu'à 17 heures

Pas de leçons le DIMANCHE.

E12

The town has a second swimming pool and you consult the opening times above.

1 Could you go on a Wednesday at 11 a.m.?

2 Could you go on a Sunday at 1.30 p.m.?

3 Could you go on a Tuesday at 8 p.m.?

4 How much would it cost your friend, who is 15, to go?

5 What is special about Sunday afternoons?

6 How much are swimming lessons?

P

a) Savez-vous nager? Quand avez-vous appris à nager?

b) Allez-vous à la piscine ou à la mer? Laquelle préférez-vous?

E13

You are staying with a friend at the *Camping Echo du Malpas* in Argentat. On 9 August you decide to hire a canoe for two days to travel to a campsite at Vitrac.

TARIFS LOCATION 1987 (AU 1/05/87)

	canoë ou k2* 2 pers.	kayak*	vélo 1 pers.	planche à voile	tente	bidon
Heure (sur plan d'eau)	31	21		35		
Journée	130	95		100		8
Semaine	650	450	250	520	160	50
Quinzaine	1170	810	490	830	260	80

*Ces prix comprennent la fourniture des pagaies et des gilets.

● Assurance dommages (1) canoë ou kayak : 4 F par heure -12 F par jour.
● Participation remontée des personnes : 12 F par personne et par étape (entre deux bases).
● Transport des bagages : 12 F par personne et par jour.
● Descentes accompagnées : 12 F pour groupes sur demande.

(1) L'assurance dommages couvre la casse, la perte ou le vol du canoë ou du kayak, à l'exclusion des accessoires.

Copy out the *bulletin d'inscription* and complete it with the required information.

BULLETIN D'INSCRIPTION
(Voir nos conditions générales)

NOM : _____ Prénom : _____

Adresse : _____ Tél. : _____

Je désire louer le matériel ci-dessous aux conditions de votre tarif

pour la période du _____ au _____ inclus.

Point de départ : _____ Point d'arrivée : _____

	NOMBRE	DUREE			PRIX
		journée	semaine	quinzaine	
canoës					
kayaks bi.					
kayaks					
tentes - vélos pl. à voile					
			Assurance-dommages canoë ou kayak		
			TOTAL		

Ci-joint un acompte de 30 %, soit la somme de _____
(Crédit Agricole Prayssac n° 01073971000)

On the right are details of the campsite. Briefly describe the situation and attractions of *Camping «Borie de Bar»*.

120 km   en Canoë-Kayak

ARGENTAT	— Plan d'eau - Initiation Camping GIBANEL****
	— Départs circuits : Camping ECHO DU MALPAS Tél. : 55 28 80 70
	21 km
BEAULIEU	Base nautique - Piscine Tél. : 55 91 21 83
	Étape intermédiaire possible à la Ginguette à Puybrun. Nuit au Camping "La Sole"***
	23 km
SAINT-DENIS MARTEL	Base SAFARAID (au pont) Tél. : 65 32 52 72
	Étape pour la nuit au Camping Les Granges ***
	15 km
SAINT-SOZY	Camping MONTAZEL (au pont) Tél. : 65 32 25 03
	17 km
SOUILLAC	Camping de LANZAC (au pont) Tél. : 65 32 72 00
	14 km
ST-JULIEN-L.	Camping Municipal (au pont) Tél. : 53 29 82 84
	16 km
VITRAC PLAGE	Base SAFARAID (plage) Tél. : 53 28 22 19
	14 km
BEYNAC	Arrivée Sous le pont de chemin de fer de VEZAC, rive droite

Sur la Commune de VITRAC,
Entre SARLAT et la DORDOGNE,

CAMPING A LA FERME
"Borie de Bar"
VITRAC - 24200 SARLAT
Tel : 53 59 17 57

Ses emplacements en terrasse, dans un joli sous-bois, vous offriront tranquilité et détente.

Nombreuses activités très proches (dans un rayon de 5 km) Baignade, Canoë, tennis, équitation, randonnée pédestre ......

B   Le tennis, le cyclisme, le hippisme et le ski

E14
You want to improve your tennis whilst in France and you see these details of a club.

Tennis-Club de Coat-Congar

4 COURTS EXTÉRIEURS
2 COURTS COUVERTS

Abonnement à l'année
Location horaire

ÉCOLE DE TENNIS
Jeunes : mercredi - samedi
LEÇONS PARTICULIÈRES
COURS COLLECTIFS - STAGES

Tél. 62.07.31

1 Can you play tennis at this club when it rains?

2 When are young people specifically catered for?

3 Can you have private coaching?

CULTURE PHYSIQUE — Dans les clubs de plage au nombre de quatre, répartis sur les trois plages, ainsi que diverses activités (volley-ball, hockey, jeux pour enfants, natation).

NATATION — Piscines d'apprentissage, de perfectionnement. Piscine d'eau de mer chauffée à l'Institut de Cure Marine.

TENNIS — Perros-Guirec dispose de cinq courts en terre battue sur la plage de Trestraou, 2 courts à Ploumanach, 2 à Kervoilan. Tournoi International début août.

TENNIS DE TABLE — Se pratique toute l'année à la salle du T.T.C.G., rue des Fr. le Montréer. Des tournois hebdomadaires ont lieu au cours de la saison.

E15
You have selected your favourite four sports from the local tourist brochure.

1 Where can you play volley-ball?

2 What sort of water is in one of the swimming pools?

3 When does the international tennis tournament take place?

4 When can you play table tennis?

5 Given the list of activities in this area, which of the above four sports do you think is best provided for?

P
a) Pratiquez-vous un sport en particulier? Lequel? En quelle saison?

b) Pourquoi aimez-vous (ou détestez-vous) le sport?

E16
This article is about cycling.

1 When did Laurent Fignon fracture his collarbone?

2 How did the accident occur?

3 According to the reporter, what problems will he have to face?

4 His great cycling rival is Bernard Hinault. How much older is Hinault than Fignon?

CYCLISME

Laurent Fignon : le coup dur

Début de saison compromis pour Laurent Fignon, qui a été victime d'une chute aux Six Jours de Madrid : fracture de la clavicule.

Laurent Fignon a abandonné les Six Jours cyclistes de Madrid, victime d'une fracture de la clavicule droite. Laurent Fignon a chuté vers midi à l'issue d'une course-poursuite entre lui et Navarro, remportée par le Français. Alors que Navarro attendait Fignon pour lui lever le bras en signe de victoire, le Français a perdu l'équilibre. Dans la chute, il a en outre cassé ses lunettes et s'est coupé à une arcade sourcilière.

Fignon, qui faisait équipe avec son compatriote Alain Bondue, doit rentrer aujourd'hui en France.

Réadaptation

C'est un coup dur pour le vainqueur du tour 1984, qui reprenait progressivement une activité de haut niveau, après une opération de la cheville en avril, par les soins du docteur Saillant. Bien sûr, pareille opération doit en général réussir, et les possibilités d'échecs sont minces. Mais un champion sait aussi que, pour reprendre sa place dans l'élite, il lui faut un « plus » qu'il n'est jamais certain de retrouver tout à fait. Fignon n'était-il pas resté 258 jours sans aucune activité physique réelle?

La longue rééadaptation de son grand rival Bernard Hinault après une opération au genou, également pour des douleurs tendineuses, était déjà là pour démontrer combien la reprise de contact est difficile. Même si Fignon a quelque six ans de moins que son aîné et ex-coéquipier chez Renault, il savait bien que la passe serait difficile à franchir.

Il n'y aurait rien eu de dramatique, en temps ordinaire, à une fracture de la clavicule chez un champion en pleine forme physique. Mais dans le cas de Fignon cette chute va retarder sa réadaptation lente au rythme de la haute compétition. Elle va l'empêcher de paraître dans les classiques de printemps, et l'on peut craindre qu'elle n'hypothèque le rôle qu'il espérait tenir dans les grands tours de la mi-saison.

La malchance s'acharne donc sur un surdoué. C'est dorénavant donc sur son caractère qui va être mis à l'épreuve, plus que son talent naturel. Plus que jamais le voilà condamné à faire aussi bien... que Bernard Hinault !

ÉQUIPEMENT DES CENTRES HIPPIQUES

Raison Sociale	Localité	Boxes	Stalles	Manèges	Nombre de chevaux à la disposition du Club	Activités	Carrière	Encadrement
Centre équestre d'EPOURDON	BERTANCOURT-EPOURDON	37		23 x 12,5 35 x 13	15	Stages, instruction compétitions, promenades	100 x 80	Instructeur diplômé
Equitation du Soissonnais	BELLEU	25	10	40 x 20	35	Instruction, stages, promenades, compétitions	60 x 20	Moniteur diplômé
Ecole d'équitation de la forêt de Retz	DAMPLEUX	25			20	Instruction, randonnées, stages	Une	Moniteur diplômé
L'Eperon de RIBEMONT	RIBEMONT	16	10	30 x 15	10	Randonnées, promenades, tourisme équestre 1 semaine, week-end, randonnées	20 x 40	Accompagnateur ANTE
Ranch YY (Ker-Equestre)	VILLIERS-ST-DENIS	16	4	15 x 30	12	Location de chevaux pour promenades	120 x 30	Accompagnateur Moniteur diplômé temps partiel

E17

You love horse riding and your pen-friend suggests you go for a ride in the area one day.

1 Which centre has the most horses?

2 You particularly wanted to go on a riding holiday for one week. Which centre offers this facility?

P

a) Avez-vous jamais fait des promenades à cheval?

b) Aimeriez-vous posséder un cheval? Comment serait-il?

Profession : JOCKEY

Par Christian Fabre

Parmi cette génération, il est rare de trouver un apprenti de la trempe de celui que je vais vous présenter. Frédéric GRENET est né le 4 avril 1967 et comme beaucoup de jeunes garçons, c'est en regardant le tiercé à la télévision qu'il a décidé un beau jour de devenir jockey. Dès l'âge de 13 ans, il se présente au foyer des apprentis-jockeys à Maisons—Laffitte. Evidemment, il est déjà très passionné et il s'applique à apprendre son métier chez un expert en la matière en la personne d'Henri Gleizes. Ce maître d'apprentissage a formé de nombreux professionnels. Son école est réputée comme difficile et éprouvante pour ces adolescents. Pourtant, à la fin de cet apprentissage, chacun est fier d'être devenu un homme. Frédéric s'est accroché et dès l'âge de 16 ans il sortait du lot de tous les prétendants apprentis en même temps que lui chez son patron.

IL lui fallu une dérogation pour monter sa première course car sa licence n'était pas encore arrivée. C'était en 1983 à Saint—Cloud, associé à ALIDAD. Frédéric ne se mit en selle que deux fois l'année de ses débuts mais, dès la saison suivante, il fut largement sollicité.

En 1984 et 1985, il participa à une centaine de courses en plat pour sept gagnants et une cinquantaine de montes en obstacles pour deux gagnants.

FREDERIC GRENET

Il est assez exceptionnel de rencontrer un apprenti qui exerce ses talents aussi bien et avec autant de réussites en plat que sur les obstacles. Frédéric GRENET est un de ces rares garçons à être apprécié par de nombreux entraîneurs dans les deux spécialités. Malheureusement, Frédéric a décidé cette année d'abandonner Auteuil et Enghien pour se consacrer uniquement aux parcours moins dangereux que constituent les courses plates. Evidemment, il est tombé une dizaine de fois mais ce n'est pas la peur ou le risque qui lui ont fait changer d'avis mais tout simplement un raisonnement logique. Frédéric ne connait pas pour l'instant de problème de poids et il a plus à gagner pour l'instant dans la plus prestigieuse des spécialités. Aussi bizarre que cela puisse paraître son plus mauvais souvenir réside dans une chute en plat. Il y a quelques semaines, en raison d'un tassement dans le peloton, Frédéric a chuté. Il s'est relevé avec un saignement de l'oreille et une lésion du rocher. Arrêté une quinzaine de jours, il n'a au contraire rien perdu de sa fougue comme un véritable passionné et professionnel qu'il est. Un cheval restera à jamais gravé dans sa mémoire c'est le brave NATURE qui lui a offert sa plus belle victoire aussi bien en plat ou il devançait deux chevaux de valeur tels que GREEN monté par Saint—Martin et SOUTHGALE monté par Guignard. NATURE a donné également à Frédéric sa plus belle victoire à Auteuil. Au plus profond de lui même Frédéric éprouve plus de sensations dans un parcours sur la Butte Mortemart qu'à Longchamp. Il exerce au mieux son métier et nous espérons avoir le grand plaisir de le revoir vaincre dans un tiercé aussi bien sur l'hippodrome du Bois de Boulogne qu'à Auteuil. Ce garçon sérieux est digne du nom de jockey.

E18

This article is about a young jockey, Frédéric Grenet.

1 What inspired Frédéric Grenet to become a jockey?

2 What role did Henri Gleizes play?

3 When did Grenet become a really popular jockey?

4 What sort of racing has Grenet become expert in?

You know that skiing is a dangerous sport. This article catches your attention in the newspaper.

1 What, briefly, is the article about?

2 Why were so few people injured?

3 Whom did the reporter speak to about the cause of the accident?

4 In what condition was Mme Lehenaff-Prigent?

Chute d'une télécabine à La Plagne
Six blessés, dont deux Brestoises

SIX PERSONNES – trois femmes et trois enfants – ont été blessées vendredi, à la suite de la chute de plusieurs mètres d'une télécabine de la station de La Plagne (Savoie).

« La télécabine s'est détachée à la sortie de la station La Plagen-Belle-Cote alors qu'elle se dirigeait vers la Belle-Plagne et elle est tombée sur les pistes de ski où elle s'est écrasée », a expliqué une responsable de la station.

Selon la gendarmerie, la télécabine a fait une chute de 8 m alors qu'à la direction de la station on affirme que celle-ci n'est tombée que d'une hauteur de 4 m.

L'accident s'est produit vendredi, vers 1 h du matin, peu avant l'arrêt nocturne des télécabines qui assurent la jonction entre les 10 villages disposés en étage qui constituent la station de La Plagne. Selon les gendarmes, c'est la rupture du filtrage de tension

d'un galet porteur qui est à l'origine de l'accident.

Mme Alice Lehenaff-Prigent, 61 ans, demeurant à Brest, a été gravement blessée, elle souffre de plusieurs fractures. Les autres blessés sont : Mireille et Roselyne Lehenaff, âgées de 30 et 34 ans, demeurant respectivement à Brest et Malakoff (Hautes-de-Seine), ainsi que Mathieu et Dorothée Ruellan, 8 et 4 ans, de Malakoff, et Laurence Trognon, âgée de 13 ans, et domiciliée à Saint-Cyr-l'Ecole (Yvelines).

Vos enfants et vous
Les centres de loisirs

Toutes les communes de France ont leur centre de loisirs, ouvert aux enfants du primaire le mercredi et pour les « petites vacances ». Mais êtes-vous sûre de bien le connaître ? Lui aussi évolue...

La cocotte en papier bat de l'aile et l'enfilage des perles file un mauvais coton ! Plus question maintenant pour les municipalités de faire vieux jeu dans les centres de loisirs. *« Sur Paris, nous proposons aux 16 000 enfants qui fréquentent nos centres une palette complète d'activités : ils peuvent pratiquer le tir à l'arc, l'informatique, le karaté, la vidéo, la photo, l'escrime... Ils peuvent s'inscrire dans des ateliers de pâtisserie, de mime, de fer forgé, travailler le cuir ou le bois, aller au cirque, au musée, ou au cinéma... »*

P
a) Les centres de loisirs français – qu'en pensez-vous?

b) Quelles sont les différences entre un centre de loisirs et «a leisure centre» en Angleterre?

Centres de loisirs, mode d'emploi

● **Renseignements et inscriptions :** à la mairie de votre commune ou de votre arrondissement, au bureau des centres aérés ou à la caisse des écoles.

● **Quel prix ?** Le prix de la journée en centre est fixé en fonction de vos ressources familiales (salaire plus allocations familiales moins loyer, le tout divisé par le nombre de personnes à charge). Concrètement, la fourchette s'étend de la gratuité totale à un maximum de 60 francs. Ce prix comprend toujours le repas du midi en cantine, le goûter et les activités. Parfois, pour les plus petits, une distribution de lait est organisée le matin.

● **A quel âge ?** Les centres maternels accueillent les enfants de quatre à six ans. Les centres primaires, eux, de sept à douze ans. Certains, toutefois, accueillent les enfants dès l'âge de deux ans.

● **Y-a-t-il une réglementation ?** Oui. Chaque centre a son propre règlement, mais tous sont soumis à la réglementation de la Jeunesse et des Sports qui fixe, entre autres, le nombre d'animateurs nécessaires : un animateur pour 12 enfants en centre primaire, un pour huit enfants en centre maternel.

● **Pouvez-vous choisir le centre où inscrire votre enfant ?** Normalement non. Le centre de loisirs étant financé par vos impôts locaux, on refuse à quelqu'un qui n'est pas contribuable de la commune de profiter de ses avantages sociaux. Si vous êtes jaloux du centre de loisirs de la ville voisine, à vous de convaincre vos élus de rattraper le retard.

Your French pen-friend has mentioned to you that his young brother attends a *centre de loisirs* in his town on Wednesdays. You cannot understand why you are not allowed to go along as well. His parents show you this article.

1 Where can you find these leisure centres?

2 How many children use leisure centres in Paris?

3 Which of the activities listed below are provided in the centres?
a) Swimming   d) Mime
b) Photography   e) Films
c) Aerobics   f) Woodwork

4 Read the points raised on the left. Make one list of positive and one list of negative aspects of French leisure centres.

C La photographie, la lecture, la télévision et le cinéma

CONSEIL GÉNÉRAL D'INDRE-ET-LOIRE

Grand concours photo départemental

Jusqu'au 30 mai 1986

THEME 1986

PORTES, PORCHES et PORTAILS de Touraine

TROIS CATÉGORIES :
- Plus de 16 ans
- 16 ans et moins
- Etablissements scolaires, mouvements et organismes de jeunes

10 450 F de PRIX

ÉPREUVES NOIR ET BLANC OU COULEURS
format : mini 13 × 18 maxi 18 × 24

BIEN PRÉCISER

nom, adresse, date de naissance ou organisme, date, légende et lieu de la prise de vue AU DOS DE LA PHOTO.

RENSEIGNEZ - VOUS - DEMANDEZ LE RÉGLEMENT

CONSEIL GÉNÉRAL D'INDRE-ET-LOIRE
CONCOURS PHOTO - B.P. 3217 - 37032 TOURS CEDEX
☎ 47.61.61.23

IMPRIMERIE DÉPARTEMENTALE

E21

A friend who knows that you like photography shows you this advertisement for a competition.

1 What are the themes of the competition?

2 Under which categories are entries allowed for the competition?

3 How much prize money is to be made available?

4 Do the photographs have to be in colour?

5 Name five things that must be written on the back of the photograph.

P

a) Est-ce que vous aimez faire de la photographie?

b) Avez-vous un appareil-photo?

c) Quand prenez-vous des photos?

d) Quelle est la meilleure photo que vous ayez jamais prise? Faites-en une description.

E22

Your pen-friend enjoys reading books, and is considering joining a book club. What do you understand of the special offers?

1 How much do you pay for the first three books you choose?

2 When can you obtain a free book?

3 What obligation is there to purchase a book regularly?

4 What additional gift do you receive if you join straight away?

Alain AUBRY, Président :
"Voici les grands avantages que vous offre le Service International du Grand Livre du Mois..."

■ Tout de suite, 3 livres au choix pour le prix d'un seul !
Choisissez vite vos 3 livres préférés parmi tous les grands succès de l'édition présentés à gauche (pages 1 et 2). Ces 3 livres vous sont offerts en édition **intégrale**, spécialement **reliée** et agrémentée d'une jaquette en couleurs, pour seulement 80 FF les trois (+ frais d'envoi).

■ Gratuitement, un lien permanent avec l'actualité littéraire.
Vous allez recevoir par avion, **gratuitement**, la passionnante Revue Littéraire du Grand Livre du Mois. Elle vous présente, sur une trentaine de pages, les **nouveautés** de l'édition : romans, documents, histoire, biographies, guides pratiques...

■ L'opinion de grands écrivains et critiques français
Toutes les nouveautés présentées dans la Revue sont décrites et commentées pour vous par de grands écrivains et chroniqueurs littéraires français. Ils vous parlent du sujet et de l'auteur, vous donnent leur opinion.

■ Les livres qui vous plaisent, dès leur sortie à Paris.
Lorsque vous aurez envie d'un livre, il vous suffira de le commander directement au Grand Livre du Mois. Quel

plaisir pour vous de pouvoir lire les œuvres qui viennent de paraître à Paris... aux meilleurs prix ! Et quelle facilité !

■ Des livres reliés au prix de l'édition brochée.
De plus, ces livres sont l'édition originale **reliée**, plus **luxueuse** et plus durable, au prix d'une édition brochée ordinaire. C'est un avantage bien agréable !

■ Des livres gratuits.
Enfin, pour toute commande d'au moins 4 livres, vous pourrez en choisir un 5e, **à titre gratuit**, plus d'autres cadeaux ! Soit des économies supplémentaires !

■ Une légère obligation d'achat
La seule chose que nous vous demandons pour bénéficier de tous les avantages du Club et du cadeau de bienvenue, c'est d'acheter 4 livres au rythme que vous souhaitez.

EN CADEAU SUPPLÉMENTAIRE
si vous renvoyez ce Bon tout de suite
un jeu de cartes exclusif
(Voyez vite au verso)

P

Lisez-vous les revues, les bandes dessinées ou les journaux? Lesquels préférez-vous? Pourquoi? Racontez votre histoire favorite.

21.45 Multifoot
Magazine du service des sports.
Présenté par Thierry Roland.
A l'heure où nous imprimions ce numéro de « Télé Star », les sujets « magazine » et l'invité de ce soir ne nous avaient pas été communiqués.
« Multifoot » présente des extraits de quatre matches, choisis parmi les dix rencontres qui devraient se dérouler ce soir pour la 36e journée de championnat : Marseille/Bordeaux, Auxerre/Lille, Nice/Toulouse, Brest/Bastia, Nancy/Metz, Paris-St-Germain/Monaco, Lens/Strasbourg, Sochaux/Toulon, Rennes/Nantes, Le Havre/Laval.

23.30 Journal
23.45 TSF
Télévision sans frontières.
Spécial Kassav. Concert enregistré en Angola.
(0.45 : fin)

Jean Tigana, le milieu de terrain bordelais.

E23

You pick up a TV magazine to find out why your pen-friend particularly wants to see a programme at 9.45 p.m.

What sort of programme does your pen-friend intend to watch?

JEUDI 28 AOUT

TF. 1

10.45 ANTIOPE 1
11.15 CROQUE-VACANCES
11.45 LA UNE CHEZ VOUS
12.00 TOURNEZ MANÈGE
13.00 LE JOURNAL DE LA UNE
13.50 DALLAS. Feuilleton américain.
14.40 BOÎTE A MOTS. Jeu. Suite à 17.00.
14.45 SCOOP A LA UNE. Jeu.
Avec Christophe LAMBERT.
15.35 QUARTÉ A VINCENNES
15.45 CROQUE-VACANCES
17.25 HISTOIRES INSOLITES. Série fantastique française. « Une invitation à la chasse », de Claude CHABROL.
18.25 DANSE AVEC MOI. Feuilleton brésilien.
19.10 LA VIE DES BOTES
19.40 LE MASQUE ET LES PLUMES.
Avec Charlélie COUTURE.
20.00 LE JOURNAL DE LA UNE
20.30 L'HOMME A POIGNE. Feuilleton allemand de Wolfgang STAUDTE (6e épisode).
● Gustav Hackendahl, « l'homme à poigne », est ruiné. Eva et Erich, ses enfants, sont tombés dans la déchéance. Sophie, devenue infirmière, lui propose un emploi qu'il refuse...
21.30 ÉTAT DE GUERRE NICARAGUA. Reportage de Sylvie BLUM et Carmen CASTILLO.
22.25 HOMMAGE AU CHORÉGRAPHE ANTHONY TUDOR. Spectacle du Théâtre national de l'Opéra de Paris.
23.05 UNE DERNIÈRE

ANTENNE 2

6.45 TÉLÉMATIN
8.30 FORTUNATA ET JACINTA. Dernier épisode.
9.15 ANTIOPE VIDÉO
12.00 RÉCRÉ A. 2
12.45 A. 2 MIDI
13.30 LA CONQUÊTE DE L'OUEST.
Feuilleton western.
14.20 L'ART AU QUOTIDIEN.
« Petits échos de la mode ».
15.15 SPORTS ÉTÉ.
Athlétisme : Championnat d'Europe.
18.50 DES CHIFFRES ET DES LETTRES
19.15 ACTUALITÉS RÉGIONALES
19.40 AFFAIRE SUIVANTE...
20.00 LE JOURNAL
20.35 MÉLODIE EN SOUS-SOL. Film français.
Voir sélection.
22.35 ATHLÉTISME. Championnat d'Europe.
23.30 ÉDITION DE LA NUIT

FR. 3

17.30 CHEVAL MON AMI
18.00 GAUGUIN. Feuilleton français.
19.00 19/20. Actualités régionales.
19.55 LES ENTRECHATS. Dessin animé.
20.05 LES NOUVEAUX JEUX DE 20 HEURES
20.35 L'AMOUR EN FUITE. Film français de François TRUFFAUT (1978).
C'est le cinquième et dernier épisode de la série consacrée à Antoine Doinel.
● Après avoir divorcé de Christine, Antoine cherche sa voie...
■ Avec Jean-Pierre LÉAUD, Marie-France PISIER, DOROTHÉE, Claude JADE...
22.05 SOIR 3
22.30 CONTES D'ITALIE. « Hiver de malade ».
23.30 PRÉLUDE A LA NUIT. Robert Schumann.

E24

One evening you and your pen-friend decide to watch television. You wonder how the programmes compare with those broadcast in Britain.

The above list shows a typical selection of programmes on British television. Which of these could you watch on French television on Thursday 28 August?

1 Regional News	**4** Films	**7** Talk shows	**10** Cartoons
2 American series	**5** Game shows	**8** Interviews	
3 Sports programmes	**6** Documentaries	**9** Plays	

E25

You switch on the television and find you are part-way through an episode of the series *Commissaire Moulin*. You remember that the TV guide contains a resumé of the programme.

Having read the résumé, which of the following statements are true?

1 Moulin is trying to break up a drugs network based in Marseille.

2 He tries to pose as a member of the gang involved in this.

3 Moulin is seduced by a beautiful dancer in a night-club.

4 Moulin demands money from Fragoni, the young lady's protector.

5 Moulin reveals his true identity to Fragoni.

6 Fragoni decides that Moulin will have to be silenced.

P

a) Regardez-vous souvent la télé?

b) Quelles sortes d'émissions aimez-vous regarder?

c) Quelle est votre émission favorite? Pourquoi?

C·I·N·E·M·O

SEMAINE du 25 au 31 JUILLET

RIALTO 1
Tous les jours : 20 h. — 22 h.
Sauf Mardi : 20 h. 30
Dimanche : 14 h. 30 — 17 h. — 20 h. — 22 h.

PINOT, Simple Flic

Un film réalisé et interprété par Gérard JUGNOT avec J.-Cl. BRIALY, Pierre MONDY, Fanny BASTIEN

RIALTO 2
Tous les jours : 19 h. 45 — 22 h.
Sauf Mardi : 20 h. 30
Dimanche : 14 h. 30 - 17 h. - 19 h. 45 - 22 h.

NOTRE HISTOIRE

Avec Alain DELON, Nathalie BAYE

COMMISSAIRE MOULIN

Eve Harling, Yves Rénier

La Bavure

SCÉNARIO DE PAUL ANDRÉOTA
RÉALISATION DE CLAUDE GRINBERG

Le commissaire Moulin **Yves Rénier**
Neubauer . . . . . . **Raymond Pellegrin**
La chanteuse . . . . **Eve Harling**
L'inspecteur . . . . **Clément Michu**
Fragoni . . . . **Albert Médina**
Lorca . . . . **Grégoire Aslan**
Alain Forget . . . . . **Michel Albertoni**

SI VOUS AVEZ MANQUÉ LE DÉBUT

Décidé à démanteler un réseau de trafiquants d'origine marseillaise, le commissaire Moulin cherche à se faire passer pour un truand auprès des membres du gang. Pour y parvenir, il doit être officiellement déchu de sa fonction pour corruption, effectuer un hold-up et abattre l'un de ses collègues. Tout cela est évidemment truqué et il agit avec l'accord de ses chefs hiérarchiques. Dans un night-club, Moulin est séduit par une ravissante chanteuse. En la raccompagnant chez elle, il est victime d'un guet-apens. Fragoni, le protecteur de la jeune femme, prenant Moulin pour un riche industriel, veut lui extorquer, sous la menace, une grosse somme d'argent. Mais le commissaire révèle sa qualité de policier pour maîtriser Fragoni. Ce dernier cherche alors à acheter le silence de Moulin...

E26

You want to go to the cinema and see a film.

1 Can you see the film *Pinot, simple flic* at 8 p.m. on a Friday?

2 You are free all evening on Tuesday. Can you choose to see either film?

3 If you wish to see *Notre histoire* on a Sunday evening, what time do you have to be at the cinema?

LES FILMS

BON PASSABLE MAUVAIS

MOURIR D'AIMER
(Lundi, 20 h 25, La 5)

● On n'a pas oublié l'affaire Gabrielle Russier, cette femme professeur de lettres qui, s'étant éprise d'un de ses élèves, avait fini par se suicider, abandonnant ainsi la partie désespérée qu'elle jouait contre la société. C'est Annie Girardot, coupante, brusque et poignante, qui évoque ce personnage dans l'adaptation qu'André Cayatte et Pierre Dumayet nous proposent de cette histoire vraie. On y frise souvent le mélodrame, certains effets y sont faciles, mais l'émotion qui se dégage de ce film généreux laissera place, peut-être, à la réflexion.

> *Ce soir, ce sont les téléspectateurs de M6 qui décideront, par leurs appels téléphoniques à la chaîne, lequel de ces deux films ils souhaitent voir :*

GAROU-GAROU LE PASSE MURAILLE
(Lundi, 20 h 30, M6)

● D'après la très fameuse nouvelle de Marcel Aymé, une petite mise en images, mais une grande interprétation d'un comédien irremplaçable. Tendre et lunaire, Bourvil fait merveille dans le rôle d'un petit employé falot qui se découvre le don de transpercer les murs. L'humour et la poésie qu'il porte en lui sauvent de l'ennui un film qui, sinon, aurait bien du mal à... passer l'écran.

LES GAULOISES BLEUES
(Lundi, 20 h 30, M6)

● Michel Cournot, critique sévère et emporté du *Nouvel Observateur*, réalisait son premier film en cette année 1968. Intelligent et sensible, le film manque hélas

d'unité et son scénario de rigueur. Annie Girardot évolue avec Bruno Cremer dans une ambiance très « nouvelle vague attardée » et le tout dégage une petite impression d'ennui.

LE TOURNANT DE LA VIE
(Mardi, 20 h 30, A2)

● Un superbe affrontement entre Shirley McLaine et Anne Bancroft, tourné par l'ancien chorégraphe Herbert Ross : c'est justement dans le milieu de la danse que se situe ce beau drame psychologique. Un « décor » passionnant et riche en tensions dramatiques ! En prime pour les amateurs : la présence du grand danseur Mikhail Baryshnikov, qui se révélait à cette occasion être aussi un véritable comédien.

RIO CONCHOS
(Mardi, 20 h 35, FR3)

● Du beau, du très beau western pour commencer cette *Dernière séance* d'été ! Tout y est : splendides paysages, méchants Indiens, bons, brutes et truands ! La réalisation musclée de Gordon Douglas ne laisse aucune minute sans action et le duo Richard Boone-Tony Franciosa est efficace à 100 %. Distraction assurée.

ALLEZ FRANCE
(Lundi, 20 h 30, FR3)

● Signée Robert Dhéry, voici une authentique comédie branquignolesque ! Les malheurs des supporters de l'équipe de France de rugby, en visite à Londres, ont fait éclater de rire les spectateurs de l'époque. N'hésitez pas à retrouver votre esprit de potache pour commencer cette semaine dans la joie, sans redouter que l'humour de Dhéry et ses acolytes ait pu vieillir : les grands enfants restent éternellement jeunes.

DRACULA, PRINCE DES TENEBRES
(Mardi, 23 h 10, FR3)

● Programme éclectique ce soir sur FR3 : quittez le territoire des Apaches pour celui du comte Dracula, au beau milieu des Carpathes. Cette version de Terence Fisher, le maître du renouveau de l'épouvante en Grande-Bretagne (vous avez pu revoir récemment son *Chien des Baskerville*, marque la dernière apparition de Christopher Lee dans le rôle du vampire : pour des raisons techniques et financières, ses apparitions y sont déjà chichement comptées. Qu'importe : le baroque des décors, le classicisme des situations, la qualité de certains effets spéciaux font de ce film une excellente introduction à une nuit agitée.

KARATEKA CONNECTION
(Mercredi 22 h 25, M6)

● Six fois champion du monde de karaté, Chuck Norris, le nouveau baroudeur du cinéma américain, sait faire des effets de manchette ! Vous pourrez le vérifier ce soir si vous êtes amateur de ces films très particuliers : tous les ingrédients du genre inventé à Hong Kong et repris ici par Hollywood sont au rendez-vous. A noter que ce film est sorti en France en 1979 sous son titre original de *Force One*. A noter aussi : la présence apaisante de la belle Jennifer O'Neill, l'héroïne d'*Un été 42*.

N. A PRIS LES DES
(Mercredi 23 h 00, FR3)

● Une curiosité, ce film produit par l'ORTF en 1971 qui est un remontage des séquences de *L'eden et après*. Le titre de l'un est d'ailleurs l'anagramme de celui de l'autre, et Alain Robbe-Grillet, pape du nouveau roman et passionné de jeu narratif, s'est essayé au récit aléatoire, l'ordre des séquences n'étant dicté que par des jets de dés. Très intellectuel, ce petit jeu-là.

E27

Here is a list of films currently being shown on television. Which film would you consider watching if you liked the following different types?

1 Westerns
2 Comedies
3 Horror films
4 Martial arts
5 Films based on true stories
6 Sports

P

a) Fréquentez-vous souvent le cinéma?

b) Vous vous intéressez le plus à quel genre de film?

c) Décrivez un film que vous avez vu récemment.

D   Le théâtre, la musique et les spectacles

THÉÂTRE ET CULTURE

THÉÂTRE EDOUARD VII
8, Place Edouard VII - Paris-9e
Métro : Opéra, Madeleine, Havre-Caumartin

NOVEMBRE - Mercredi 29   –   Samedi 25
DÉCEMBRE - Mercredis 6, 13   –   Samedis 2, 9, 16
JANVIER - Mercredi 10   –   Samedi 13

LES FEMMES SAVANTES
de MOLIÈRE

14 h 30   Mise en scène de Marcelle TASSENCOURT

avec **Dora DOLL**

suivi d'un débat

BILLET SPÉCIAL - Avec ce billet il sera perçu 11,50 F (orchestre et corbeille)
valable pour deux places   par place   8,50 F (balcon)
4,00 F (galerie)

Ce billet n'étant valable que dans la limite des places disponibles, il est recommandé de louer d'avance : 6 jours avant la date choisie

Location : à notre bureau Théâtre et Culture, 25, rue Caumartin, Paris-9e et à 073-43-41
tous les jours de 11 h à 13 h 30 et de 16 h à 19 h, sauf dimanche et lundi

E28

Above are details of a performance of a play by the French dramatist Molière.

1 How many seats do you receive with the special ticket?

2 How much does it cost in the stalls?

3 Where can you buy this ticket?

4 Could you buy a ticket on a Monday?

5 Could you see this play performed on a Tuesday in January?

RAINER WETTLER
"L'HOMME-OISEAU"

"Pourquoi l'homme en vol devient forcément un chasseur-bombardier ?". R. W.

Un homme grand, maigre et inquiétant, habillé de sombre et illuminé par la ferveur d'un prophète nous persuade que nous sommes tous, au fond de nous mêmes, des oiseaux.

C'est RAINER WETTLER, l'homme-oiseau, à la fois mime, jongleur, clown et... philosophe. Son spectacle nous entraîne dans un univers où le burlesque se mêle à l'étrange et au baroque.

L'humour de l'HOMME-OISEAU et ses gags, son rire et ses larmes, la morale de cette histoire hautement loufoque nous illustrent tout le talent de RAINER WETTLER.

E29

Leafing through a theatre prospectus you come across this picture.

1 What sort of act does Rainer Wettler perform?

2 What is the reviewer's opinion of him?

LES TRAINS DU SPECTACLE

vous proposent

Concert "MADONNA"

LE SAMEDI 29 AOUT 1987

PARC DE SCEAUX A PARIS

RC PARIS 5520 49447 B

FORMULE PLUS

LES TRAINS DU SPECTACLE

CONCERT "MADONNA"

PRIX AU DEPART DE :

-MAYENNE	390F
-ILLE ET VILAINE	420F
-COTES DU NORD	470F
-MORBIHAN	480F
-FINISTERE	510F

Le prix comprend :
-Le transport aller et retour en 2ème classe
-Les transferts aller et retour par autocar spécial au Parc de Sceaux (départ de PARIS-MONTPARNASSE à 16 H)
-L'entrée au concert
-Les services d'un accompagnateur
-Les assurances assistance/annulation

DATE LIMITE D'INSCRIPTION : 25 AOUT 1987

RENSEIGNEMENTS ET RESERVATIONS DANS VOTRE GARE OU AGENCE DE VOYAGES

NOMBRE DE PLACES LIMITE

E30

At the beginning of August you are staying in Finistère, Brittany and are delighted to see details of a Madonna concert. Your pen-friend is also a fan.

1 Where is the concert to be held?

2 How much does a ticket cost with this special offer?

3 What does this price include?

4 Why must you decide quickly if you wish to go?

5 Where could you book this special offer?

Lyon, le 2 mai 1987

Chère Sandra,

Merci pour ta lettre. Je suis contente de savoir que tes vacances se sont bien passées. Pour moi, tout s'est bien passé.

Je t'écris pour te raconter ma soirée d'hier qui a été l'une des meilleures que j'aie jamais passées.

Je suis allée voir Sade en concert avec deux amies. Déjà, au départ, nous avions eu des problèmes pour obtenir des places ; nous avions été obligées de prendre les moins chères, donc les moins bien placées. Une fois sur place, nous nous sommes débrouillées pour être mieux placées.

Le concert a été génial. Quel choc ! Quelle joie quelle voix et quelle présence sur scène ! Je ne regrette vraiment pas du tout d'y être allée. Le disque n'est rien à côté de sa prestation sur scène. Si jamais Sade passe dans ta région, va la voir. Cela vaut vraiment le déplacement.

Amitiés,

A Bientôt !

Nathalie —

E31

Here is a letter describing a concert.

1 When did the concert take place?

2 What did Nathalie think of the concert?

3 Who went with her?

4 Why did she move seats?

5 How does Sade's live performance compare with her records?

SPAGNA "Easy lady"

Spagnia, comme son nom ne l'indique pas, est née à Vérone en Italie (la ville de Roméo et Juliette !). Son père jouait du piano, son frère compose et joue de la basse, il était donc assez logique qu'elle se laisse, elle aussi, attirer par la musique. Au départ, elle faisait cela plutôt par jeu, participant même à quelques petits groupes. « *Je chantais pour moi*, se souvient-elle, *mais je n'imaginais jamais que je me retrouverais seule sur une scène.* » Manquant peut-être d'assurance auparavant, elle a écrit pendant trois ans des chansons pour les autres et puis, finalement, elle s'est laissée convaincre par son entourage et a enregistré « Easy lady », son premier disque, en solo. Grand bien lui en a pris puisqu'aujourd'hui, elle déclare fiévreuse : « *La musique c'est plus qu'une passion, c'est toute ma vie.* » Quand elle ne travaille pas, Spagnia aime passer du temps avec ses chats ou bien peindre des portraits de ses amis. Elle dit ne pas avoir étudié particulièrement son look (bien qu'il soit spécial). « *Aujourd'hui, je suis comme ça, demain, je peux être autrement, l'important c'est que je sois bien dans ma peau.* » Elle se définit comme étant déterminée, passionnée, aimant la sincérité. « *Même*, avoue-t-elle, *si pour les petits détails, je ne le suis pas toujours moi-même.* » Superstitieuse, elle ne quitte pas une petite croix qu'elle a autour du cou. « *J'ai beaucoup de chance* », conclut-elle quand on lui parle de son succès.

E32

You come across this article in a teenage magazine.

1 What is Spagna's musical background?

2 How did she start her career?

3 What does the title refer to?

4 What are Spagna's pastimes?

5 What qualities does she recognise in herself?

PLOUGASNOU

Vendredi 27 juillet au port de PRIMEL

Vieux-Gréements
Goélette de la marine nationale

17 h - Arrivée des bateaux de pêche et Vieux Gréements

19 h - Buffet

20 h - Chants de Marins avec le groupe CABESTAN

A partir de 22 h - JAZZ et FEST-NOZ

avec les groupes
- HOT GAZ BAND
- TASSILI

aujourd'hui dans votre ville LE CIRQUE ZAVATTA FILS

PRESENTE

8 h - Arrivée de la caravane et montage du

SUPER CHAPITEAU JAUNE et BLEU

11 h - PARADE et SPECTACLE GRATUIT sur le
car podium géant

18 h - JEUX ET SPECTACLE GRATUITS sur le CAR PODIUM

21 h - sous le CHAPITEAU
SUPER GALA SPECTACLE

E33

Whilst on holiday with your family, you catch sight of this poster as you are driving along. Your parents ask you to tell them what is happening.

1 Where is the event taking place?

2 What could you do if you arrived at 5 p.m., and left at 9 p.m.?

E34

Your younger brother is excited when he sees the above poster.

He asks the following questions.

1 When is the circus coming to town?

2 What colour is the big top?

3 When does the show begin?

Can you answer him?

E35

You decide that you would particularly like to visit a *son et lumière* event.

1 You are with a group of five adults. How much will it cost you altogether?

2 You wish to go on Friday 15 August. What time must you be there to ensure a good view?

Spectacle Son & Lumière

dans la cour intérieure du FORT de SALSES

Des Romains à nos jours, ou les tribulations d'un site

Un spectacle haut en couleur dans un cadre unique

en Juillet : les mardi et vendredi, ouverture des portes à 22 h. Début du spectacle à 22 h. 30 précises.

en Août : les mardi et vendredi, ouverture des portes à 21 h. 30 Début du spectacle à *22 h.* précises.

Adultes : 30 Frs Enfants : 15 Frs Groupes de 30 : 25 Frs

Les groupes doivent obligatoirement réserver la veille au plus tard : ☎ 68 35 08 46 : répondeur

Spectacle préparé et réalisé par l'AEPR 15, rue du Bastion Saint-François, PERPIGNAN
avec la participation de l'Office Régional de la Culture

E36

You are on holiday with your ten-year-old brother and parents and you are interested in attending various events.

	PRIX DES ENTRÉES		

Date	Heure		Prix du billet
20	21 h 00	Concert de chorales	30 F
22	21 h 00	Soirée Triskell	40 F
23	21 h 00	Théâtre en breton	25 F
	21 h 00	Fest-noz et jeux bretons	15 F
24	18 h 00	Présentation de costumes bretons	15 F
	21 h 00	Concert à la cathédrale	40 F
	21 h 00	Théâtre : Le Festin des Gueux	25 F
25	16 h 00 18 h 00	Conteurs - Ouïr Dire - Bretagne	20 F
	21 h 00	Soirée Folk - Wolfe Tones	45 F
26	14 h 00	Exposition culturelle	50 F
	15 h 00	Concert-exposition-vente artisans luthiers	10 F
	15 h 30	Marionnettes	20 F
	19 h 00	Animations éclatées	20 F
27	10 h 30 14 h 00	Concours d'instruments bretons	10 F
	14 h 30	Danses bretonnes et concert de bagadou	25 F
	16 h 00	Concert harpes et vielles	20 F
	21 h 00	Ballet chinois de X'ian	50 F
28	10 h 30	Grand défilé des ''guises'' bretonnes	15 F
	14 h 30	Abadenn-Veur	45 F
	21 h 00	Soirée musique et danses de Bretagne	25

Tous les autres spectacles, conférences, animations sont gratuits.

Possibilité de vente de billets par correspondance. A partir du début juillet, adresser chèque correspondant au nombre de places désirées.

Places assises au départ du défilé, Place de la Résistance, sans majoration.

	RÉDUCTIONS	

FORFAIT AU CHOIX :	A) Concerts des mercredi et jeudi	. . . . . .	75 F
	B) Samedi - toute la journée	. . . .	75 F
	C) Dimanche - toute la journée	. . . .	75 F
GROUPES	: A) Samedi soir	. . . .	30-40 F
	B) Dimanche (billet jumelé défilé et Abadenn-Veur)	. . . .	50 F
	Réservation pour le spectacle du dimanche après-midi.		
COLONIES DE VACANCES	: Samedi soir	. . . .	10 F
	Défilé gratuit		
	Dimanche après-midi	. . . .	10 F
ENFANTS	: Gratuit jusqu'à 12 ans, sauf spectacles de marionnettes et de conteurs.		

Imp. Le Berre - Quimper

1 How much will it cost for all of you to see the following shows?

  a) A concert in the cathedral.

  b) A puppet show.

  c) An evening of Breton music and dance.

2 If your parents wanted to go to all the events on Saturday 27, how much would they save altogether if they bought two special day tickets?

RENSEIGNEMENTS PRATIQUES

Musée de la Résistance Bretonne

Ouvert toute l'année :

de 10 h à 19 h, du 1ᵉʳ juin au 30 septembre

de 10 h à 12 h - 14 h à 18 h, du 1ᵉʳ octobre au 31 mai

ENTRÉE :
14 F pour adultes
 9 F pour les groupes (20 personnes minimum)
 8 F pour les enfants de 12 à 18 ans
gratuit pour enfants en-dessous de 12 ans

STATIONNEMENT :
à 150 mètres pour les voitures
Approche pour les cars

Documentation : dans les trois langues :
Français, Anglais, Allemand

Restaurant au bourg : 100 couverts.

A PROXIMITÉ :
MALESTROIT : charmante petite ville de caractère.
Renseignements touristiques au syndicat d'initiative,
téléphone : 75.14.57
LIZIO : Village vacances
ROCHEFORT EN TERRE : une des plus jolies cité
bretonne.
VANNES : golf du Morbihan
ST CYR COETQUIDAN : musée du souvenir.

E37
In Brittany you see details of this museum.

1 What sort of museum is it?

2 You would like to go in; it is midday on Sunday 29 July. Can you?

3 How much would your brother who is ten years old, pay to enter?

4 Where can you leave the car?

5 Your parents do not understand French, will they be able to understand anything?

P

a) Est-ce que vous avez une fête dans votre ville/village?
   Qu'est-ce qui s'y passe?
   Quand a-t-elle lieu?

b) Expliquez la fête de Saint-Valentin et Mardi gras.

c) Quelle est la date de ces fêtes?
   Le jour de l'An
   La fête nationale
   La fête de l'Assomption.

d) Qu'est-ce que c'est la Toussaint?

E38
Your parents decide to spend August in this town, and they ask you to describe the various events they could see. Which of the following could your parents attend?

1 Circus
2 Dances
3 Cabaret
4 Theatre
5 Church music
6 Swimming contest
7 Guitar concert
8 Art Exhibition
9 Organ and trumpet concert
10 Flower show
11 Poetry evening
12 Windsurfing regatta
13 Old postcard exhibition
14 Procession

AOÛT :

1ᵉʳ août - Soirée cabaret au blochaus

3 août - A l'église : Festival de musique sacrée, art et culture en Finistère, concert Deller Consort.

5 et 6 août - Helistar : baptême de l'air (terrain de football)

6 et 7 août - Escale du Belem

7 août - A l'église : concert orgues et trompettes, direction PH. Boringer

8 août - Place du phare, spectacle de funambules

9 août - Soirée cabaret

10 août - A la salle de basket, soirée dansante du tennis de table

11 août - Kermesse des dockers au port en eau profonde

12 août - Soirée poésie

13 août - A l'église : quator vocal du Léon

14 août - Soirée dansante (bal S.N.S.M. et Muco)

15 août - Inauguration des Orgues de l'Eglise, messe : 9 h30 et 17 h par l'organiste Gaston Litaize

15 août - Nouveau cirque Jean Richard

15 août - Régates de planches à voile

18 août - Exposition de vieilles cartes postales, salle de basket

19 août - Spectacle de danses ''compagnie les Algues''

20 août - Cirque

21 août - A l'église Trio Robert Devisé, flûtes, luthe théorbe et viole de Gambe

22 août - Soirée cabaret

25 août - Régates ''tour de l'Ile de Batz'' en planche à voile

28 août - A l'église, concert d'orgues P. Ch. Figuiere

du 1ᵉʳ au 30 août - ''Habitat de la Mer'', exposition sur le Port

Chapter 5
Faire des courses

Il n'y a pas de doute que faire des courses constitue une activité principale lorsqu' on visite un pays étranger soit en famille, soit en groupe scolaire, soit à titre individuel.

Il faut donc vous habituer à la publicité et aux annonces commerciales qui attirent votre attention.

A   Dans la rue

Here are some of the shop signs you will see in the street.

A    B    C

D    E    F

G    H

I    J

E1
Write the letter of the shop(s) that you would go to if you wanted the following articles or services.

1 A cake

2 A leather handbag

3 Some stamps

4 To have some dry cleaning done

5 To get your hair cut

6 A pair of earrings

7 A saucepan

8 A tap washer

9 A newspaper

10 Some fish

P

a) Comment s'appelle la personne qui travaille: dans une bijouterie? dans une boulangerie? dans une plomberie? dans un café? dans une école?

b) Qu'est-ce qu'on peut acheter dans une quincaillerie? Et dans une pharmacie? Que fait-on dans l'enterprise Lebrun?

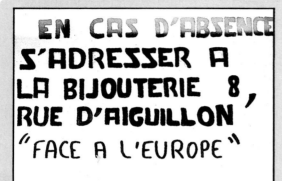

BOUCHERIE
ALIMENTATION COOP
BOULANGERIE PATISSERIE
CRÊPERIE

E2

1 Which of the following statements are true, according to this sign?
a) This way to the library.
b) This way to the jewellers.
c) This way to the butchers.
d) This way to the auction.

2 Can you eat in any of the places indicated?

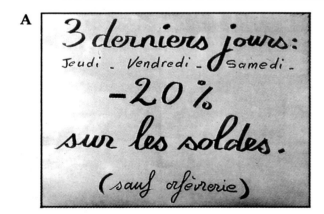

A

EN CAS D'ABSENCE
S'ADRESSER A
LA BIJOUTERIE 8,
RUE D'AIGUILLON
"FACE A L'EUROPE"

B

HEURES D'OUVERTURE DE L'AGENCE

DU MARDI AU VENDREDI

8H - 12 H ET 14 H - 18 H 30

LE SAMEDI   FERMETURE A   17 H 30

FERMEE LE LUNDI

E3

These signs are to be seen on the door of two different businesses.

1 Which sign (**A** or **B**) tells you what to do when the business is closed?

2 Look at sign **B**:
a) What day is the shop closed earlier than usual?
b) When is it always closed?
c) Is it open at 1 p.m. on a Tuesday?

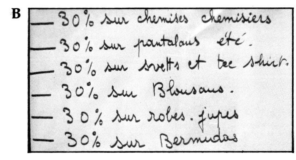

A

3 derniers jours:
Jeudi - Vendredi - Samedi -
-20%
sur les soldes.
(sauf orfèvrerie)

B

— 30% sur chemises chemisiers
— 30% sur pantalons été.
— 30% sur svetts et tee shirt.
— 30% sur Blousons.
— 30% sur robes. jupes
— 30% sur Bermudas

E4

Some special signs are shown above.

1 What are both these signs advertising?

2 In photo **A** what days are mentioned?

3 What sort of shop is shown in photo **B**?

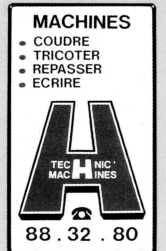

MACHINES
• COUDRE
• TRICOTER
• REPASSER
• ECRIRE

TEC**H**NIC'
MAC **H** INES
88.32.80

E5

This sign advertises a firm that sells and repairs machines. Which types of machine? Name them!

P

Qu'est-ce que c'est, un aspirateur? Un frigo? Un cassettophone? Un appareil-photo? Un magnétoscope?

E6

You see the following information in an advertisement for a shopping centre near you.

PRESLES PRESSING

ouvert du mardi
au samedi
8h-12h15 et 14h-19h15

Tél. 59.59.60

Carte de fidélité

des pantalons, mais aussi des pulls, chemises, jupes et robes...

Retouches gratuites. Carte bleue
Avenue Robert Schumann

**TABAC
CADEAUX
JOURNAUX
PAPETERIE**

LOTO

M. DUFIEF

53.59.05

**librairie
du boulevard**

librairie-papeterie
disques - jeux - cadeaux

ani disc'

SNC DUBAELE et Cie
4 bd de Presles - Tél. 59.59.14

carte de fidélité

au pêcheur matinal

6 bd Presles Tél. 59.25.92

TOUS MATÉRIELS
TOUS APPÂTS
ET AMORCES

MICHEL PARANT
un pêcheur expérimenté
au service de tous
les pêcheurs

You decide to go to the shopping centre on a Monday afternoon with several items on your shopping list. Which ones can you accomplish?

1 Take your trousers to the dry cleaners.
2 Buy the current "number one" record.
3 Take a library book back.
4 Buy a French newspaper.
5 Buy a pack of cards.
6 Buy fishing bait.
7 Buy stamps for postcards.

E7
Can you get a late night drink here?

**CAFÉ - BAR
P.M.U.**

Le Presles

Mme MAGNE

Tél. 53.64.55

Ouvert de 6h30 à 21h

SUPREL

alimentation

*le spécialiste
des produits frais*

**Ouvert le dimanche matin
et le lundi après-midi**

Tél. 53.26.50

E8
What sort of shop is Suprel?

P

a) Faites-vous les achats pour votre famille? Où allez-vous? Quand?

b) Est-ce qu'il y a un supermarché ou de petits magasins près de chez vous? Racontez ce qui s'est passé la dernière fois que vous êtes allé(e) en ville.

c) Quelles sont les heures d'ouverture de votre supermarché local?

d) Est-ce qu'il y a des magasins ouverts le dimanche près de chez vous? Lesquels?

e) Préférez-vous qu'ils soient ouverts ou fermés le dimanche? Pourquoi?

B Dans les journaux

Here is a selection of adverts for various kinds of shops.

HORLOGERIE BIJOUTERIE ORFÈVRERIE

BÔNE
L. ROBINE gendre et succ.
60, GRANDE-RUE
TÉL.: 84.24.08

TOUTES RÉPARATIONS SOIGNÉES ET GARANTIES

E9

1 Can you buy bracelets here?

2 Can you get your watch repaired here?

ROSE FRANCE
85, Grande-Rue
FLEURISTE

LA SERRE
LIBRE SERVICE PLANTES
83, Grande-Rue
Entrée Libre
Tél. : 84.21.26 - 84.38.45

DINER'S-CLUB
—
INTERFLORA

E10

Is it true that you can help yourself to whatever is on sale?

LES PARFUMEURS DE PARIS
18, Grande-Rue - DIEPPE

EXCLUSIVITÉ
REVLON
RUBINSTEIN
STENDHAL

Elisabeth ARDEN, AYER, LANCOME, ORLANE, PAYOT, ROCHAS, CARON, CARVEN, ACADEMIE, Max FACTOR, PATOU, REVILLON, etc...

- TOUS ACCESSOIRES DE TOILETTE ET D'HYGIÈNE -

E11

1 Could you buy a sponge bag here?

2 Could you buy a film for your camera here?

RADIO TÉLÉVISION ÉLECTRICITÉ
A. SERGENT
3, grande-rue du Pollet (à côté du terrain de camping)

E12

Where exactly is this establishment?

CENTRALE PEINTURE

"La Maison de la Peinture"

67, Rue de la Barre - DIEPPE
Téléphone : 84.15.41

TOUT pour la DÉCORATION de votre INTÉRIEUR

PEINTURES - REVÊTEMENTS MURAUX
PAPIER ET MOQUETTE

PAPIERS PEINTS

Dépositaire NOBILIS - INALTERA - P. DUMAS - ZUBER
LEROY - Société FRANÇAISE - Papiers peints de NANCY

E13

Can you buy a picture here to take home as a present?

Les **DISQUES** *toutes marques*
Les Téléviseurs-Electrophones-Transistors-Magnétophones
PATHÉ - MARCONI
"LA VOIX DE SON MAITRE"
aux Ets ANGOT *"Tout pour la Musique"*
à DIEPPE - Tél. 84.18.07 - 13-15, rue Lemoyne
Les Machines à laver et Réfrigérateurs
CONORD
CANDY
Atelier de réparation
Service après vente

E14

1 Apart from records, what other six items can you buy here?

2 Name one other service advertised.

P

Choisissez quatre de ces magasins ci-dessus. Jouez un scène avec votre partenaire et prenez les rôles de l'employé(e) et du (de la) client(e).

E15

It will shortly be your brother's birthday. You look at this advertisement because you may buy him a present in this shop.

You have 130 F to spend and he already has a radio. What could you get for him?

P

Quel était le dernier disque que vous avez acheté?

E16

This advertisement is for a shop near a campsite. List those of the following statements that are true.

1 You can hire rooms here.

2 This shop sells both sleeping bags and camp-beds.

3 You can pitch a tent here.

4 You can hire tents here.

5 You can buy rucksacks here.

6 This shop sells boats.

7 You can buy waterproof clothing here.

8 You can get your bottles of camping gas refilled here.

E17

Name four items of clothing for young people sold here.

E18

Look at the advertisements **A, B, C** and **D**.

1 Which shop is open on a Sunday morning?

2 Which one is a shoe shop only?

3 Where could you buy knitwear?

4 Where could you buy a silk tie?

5 Where could you buy Wellington boots?

P

a) Est-ce que vous êtes obligé de porter un uniforme scolaire? Comment est-il? Qu'en pensez-vous?

b) Que porteriez-vous si vous étiez invité à une discothèque?

E19

You need to do some washing and dry cleaning – what service does this establishment offer?

1 What could an average four kg dry cleaning load consist of?

2 How long would it take to wash an ordinary four and a half kg load? If it then took 15 minutes to dry, what would be the total cost?

3 Could you use this service at 5 p.m. on a Sunday?

ESSAYEZ .... *VOUS SEREZ ETONNES !*

LAVOMATIQUE

4 ,Rue des Lavoirs   MORLAIX CENTRE
Face Place des Viarmes Parking

PRESSING AU POIDS SELF SERVICE
40 F

Exemple 4 kg Vêtements	1 costume 2 pantalons 2 jupes 2 pulls

= 45 mn

Vêtements , couvertures , couvre-lits , tentures , rideaux..

LAVERIE SELF - SERVICE
Lavage 4,5 kg de linge   **30mn 15 F**
Lavage 10kg   **45m 30 F**
(couettes , duvets,grosses couvertures)

Séchage 7,5mn   **2 F**

OUVERT TOUS LES JOURS DE 8H A 20H SANS INTERRUPTION
ARTS ET LOISIRS 98.88.25.51

E20

If you had a holiday home in France, these advertisements might interest you.

Meubles LELION
Grand choix d'ensemble pour tous vos intérieurs
13, Rue Jeanne-d'Arc — CLERMONT-FERRAND
Téléphone : 42.67
Conditions spéciales aux Mutualistes et facilités de paiement

Aux Galeries de Jaude
CLERMONT - FERRAND

LE MAGASIN LE PLUS IMPORTANT DE LA REGION

Nouveautés - Meubles   Articles Ménagers
Articles   de   Paris -   Alimentation

39, Rue de la Barre
DIEPPE
TÉLÉPHONE
84 · 36 · 42
(2 lignes groupées)

LE GRAND MAGASIN DE DIEPPE
3000 m² pour vous offrir
**ses TISSUS
ses VÊTEMENTS
ses MEUBLES
sa LITERIE**
tellement mieux qu'ailleurs et bien moins cher
LIVRAISON GRATUITE A DOMICILE
LARGES FACILITÉS DE PAIEMENT

1 What do all three establishments sell?

2 Which one offers home deliveries?

3 Which one sells food?

4 Which ones offer credit facilities?

5 Only one sells clothes- which one?

P

Décrivez les meubles qui se trouvent actuellement dans votre salle à manger.

E21

Here are two very different specialist firms.

COUVRE-PIEDS – COURTEPOINTES – ÉDREDONS
TISSUS D'AMEUBLEMENT – DESSUS DE LIT
DOUBLE-RIDEAUX – LITERIE – TAPISSERIE

Maison Aubertot

7, Rue Saint-Jacques - DIEPPE

CONFECTION —— RÉFECTION

Teinturerie - Nettoyages - Stoppage

Maison BRUNET

47, Grande-Rue-DIEPPE

Livraisons Rapides Travail soigné et garanti

Make out a grid like the one below in your exercise book. List what each establishment offers in the appropriate column.

1 Upholstery cloth
2 Quick deliveries
3 Duvets
4 Dry cleaning
5 Bedspreads
6 Darning
7 Curtain making
8 Hem repairs
9 Carpeting
10 Bed linen

Maison Aubertot	Maison Brunet

CHAUFFAGE CENTRAL
BRULEURS MAZOUT
PLOMBERIE - ZINGUERIE - SANITAIRE
COUVERTURES TUILES ET ARDOISES

E^TS^ CHAMBONNET Père & Fils

15, Rue Massillon
CLERMONT - FERRAND
Téléphone : 92.61.39

CHARBONS

POUR CHAUFFAGE ET CUISINE

Thoumyre-Graigola

DIEPPE

Bureau de Détail : Rue de la Barre, 64
Téléphone : 84.29.31

CHAUFFAGE CENTRAL
INSTALLATION : MAZOUT-GAZ
TRANSFORMATION : MAZOUT
Crédit 3 à 5 ans

Bruleurs FRANCIA

SANITAIRE
Salles de Bains
couleurs

COUVERTURE
— RÉPARATIONS —
RAPIDES —

REMY LEBAS

TÉL. 84.37.78
14, RUE DE LA RADE
DIEPPE

E22

These are businesses that you might need to contact in winter.

1 What do all three of these businesses deal in?
2 Which of these shops is a family owned firm?
3 Which shop advertises easy credit terms?
4 Which one advertises a quick roofing repair service?
5 Where could you buy coal?

Here are three notices concerning hairdressers.

La Coifferie

Tél 67 - 30 - 28

INSTITUT KARINA

SOINS ESTHÉTIQUES
SUR RENDEZ – VOUS

Place du Général Leclerc
29228 PLOUGASNOU

TARIF TVA ET SERVICE 15% COMPRIS	
COUPES	
STYLISEE	60
COLORATION	
COLORATION	65
DECOLORATION	54
PERMANENTE DIRECT	91
MISE EN PLIS	44
	54
BRUSHING	44
LONG	60
SHAMPOOINGS	
BAINS TRAITANTS	27
SPECIFIQUES	21

NELSON

E23
If you wanted to have a manicure, what do you need to do?

E24
What is the special offer?

CORINNE COIFFURE

PRIX CHOC
SHAMPOING _ MIS en PLIS
15,00
SALON CLIMATISE TEL.33.71.18

E25
How much would it cost to have your hair tinted here?

Il y a les cheveux gras, les cheveux secs, les cheveux qui tombent, ceux qui sont fatigués, abîmés, ceux qu'il faut préserver, et puis ...il y a les plantes.
C'est à la fois une façon nouvelle d'aimer vos cheveux et une recette de grand-mère que je vous propose. Avec cette gamme de produits naturels, à base de plantes et d'herbes plus ou moins rares, j'ai voulu retrouver ce temps où les cheveux vivaient sainement. Alors, pour eux, choisissez soigneusement la formule qui leur convient pour vivre longtemps. Rapidement vos cheveux sentiront bon la campagne et vous surprendront par leur brillant et leur qualité.

Martine Mahé

UNE FAÇON
NATURELLE
D'AIMER VOS CHEVEUX

Martine Mahé
La coiffure
par les plantes

La coiffure par les Plantes
26, rue Vignon
Paris 75009
Tél.(1) 42. 65. 71.54

E26
You see this advertisement for a range of hair-care products.

1 What different types of hair condition does Martine Mahé mention?

2 What is the base for her products?

C Les offres spéciales

You are on holiday with your family in Brittany. You park the car in the town of La Baule and when you return to it you find the following leaflet attached to the windscreen.

TOUJOURS du SENSATIONNEL à LA BAULE...

A partir du 17 AOUT et jours suivants

Grande VENTE LIQUIDATION
du Stock

Loi du 30-12-1906   Autorisation Municipale

PLACE NETTE... TOUT DOIT DISPARAITRE

MISE EN VENTE IMMÉDIATE de MILLIERS DE VÊTEMENTS DE QUALITÉ

RABAIS CONSIDERABLES
DEMARQUES MASSIVES

CHAQUE ÉTIQUETTE PORTERA EN ROUGE LE PRIX DÉMARQUÉ

Quantité limitée

--- aperçu de quelques prix ---

Pour Hommes	ANCIEN PRIX	PRIX VENDU	Pour Hommes	ANCIEN PRIX	PRIX VENDU	Pour Dames	ANCIEN PRIX	PRIX VENDU
PANTALONS tergal léger	79	49	COSTUMES divers été	319	219	PANTALONS depuis	109	69
PANTALONS tergal divers	109	89	COSTUMES divers mode	459	379	BLOUSONS divers	159	119
PANTALONS tergal mode	139	109	COSTUMES luxe	569	479	CIRÉS fantaisie	79	59
PANTALONS tergal luxe	159	129	COSTUMES velours divers	439	349	IMPERS polyuréthane	229	179
VESTONS divers	169	89	COSTUMES velours luxe	559	479	IMPERS » luxe	299	269
VESTONS laine mélangée	289	229	INPERS tergal	239	179	IMPERS tergal	269	189
VESTONS mode	339	309	IMPERS tergal luxe	309	279	IMPERS tergal luxe	339	279
BLAZERS divers	239	169	IMPERS fourrés démont.	319	259	GABARDINES diverses	319	259
BLAZERS luxe	329	279	TROIS-QUARTS fourrés	389	339	GABARDINES » luxe	349	309
BLOUSONS tergal	139	99	CANADIENNES toile four.	239	159	MANTEAUX divers	319	249
BLOUSONS tergal fourrés	269	229	PARKAS divers	289	229	MANTEAUX loden	439	379
BLOUSONS imitation peau	219	159	CABANS divers	279	229	ENSEMBLES PANTALONS	448	379
VESTES TRICOTS SUÉDINE	269	219	CABANS luxe	389	339	VESTES diverses	219	149
ENSEMBLES SPORT	269	219	PARDESSUS	459	389	BLAZERS depuis	319	249
						KABIGS luxe depuis	339	309

GRAND CHOIX PULLS - CHEMISERIE - SPORT-VEAR - RAYON GARÇONNETS
et **10** % sur le RAYON PEAUSSERIE hommes - dames : MANTEAUX, VESTES, BLOUSONS agneau
Quantité limitée - Spécialité grandes tailles

vêtements P.K.
230, avenue de-Lattre-de-Tassigny - LA BAULE

OUVERT TOUS LES JOURS de 8 H. 30 à 19 H. 30 et DIMANCHE MATIN
ENTREE LIBRE

R. C. SAINT-NAZAIRE 56 A 371   ÉDITIONS LA BAULE

Your parents ask you to explain it.

1 What sort of event does it advertise?

2 Do you know how many days it will last?

3 What is the reduction on men's overcoats?

4 Are all the women's trousers for sale at 69 F? Give reasons for your answer.

Pour vos photos couleurs
- **Prix avantageux**
- **Qualité soignée**
- **Rapidité**

NOUVEAU!
Vous pouvez choisir maintenant
simple tirage ou double tirage

Nous développons aussi
le nouveau **disc** Kodak

Affranchir
au tarif
paquet-poste
en vigueur.

NASHUA PHOTO FRANCE
FILMPOST
B.P. 60
60500 CHANTILLY FRANCE

E28

You want to develop the photos you have taken whilst in France. You find this envelope in a magazine.

1 What three claims are made about this photo processing company?

2 What special facility is offered to customers?

BON DE COMMANDE			
Développement et **tirage simple** (1 photo par négatif)	Prix	Nb Films	Total
12 poses	34 F		
15 poses uniquement DISC	40 F		
20 poses	50 F		
24 poses	56 F		
36 poses	75 F		
	SOUS-TOTAL 1		
Développement et **double tirage** (2 photos par négatif)			
12 poses x 2	51 F		
15 poses x 2 uniquement DISC	64 F		
20 poses x 2	77 F		
24 poses x 2	90 F		
36 poses x 2	126 F		
	SOUS-TOTAL 2		
Participation port et emballage - France Métropolitaine + 5 F. - Départements d'Outre Mer réexpédition avion + 10 F.			
TOTAL GENERAL (sous-total 1 + 2 + frais de port)			

Ci-joint mon règlement par :
☐ chèque bancaire ☐ chèque postal 3 volets ☐ mandat lettre.
Ne pas envoyer de timbres ni d'espèces. Merci.

Un service assuré par
NASHUA PHOTO FRANCE
R.C.B. 308.819.994.40036.8706

3 How much does it cost to develop a 135 mm × 36 print film?

4 How much extra do you pay to have an extra copy made of the same film?

5 What else do you have to pay for?

6 What is not accepted as a means of payment?

POUR ENVOYER VOS PELLICULES COULEUR DANS CETTE ENVELOPPE, C'EST TRES SIMPLE

1 - Inscrivez très lisiblement vos nom et adresse sur l'étiquette ci-dessous.
2 - Complétez le bon de commande.
3 - Glissez pellicules et paiement dans cette enveloppe.
4 - Fermez l'enveloppe, affranchissez-là et postez-là.

FP7068
Mr. Mme, Mlle
Prénom
Rés. Bât. Esc. (etc...)
N° Rue
Lieu dit ou hameau
Code postal Ville

N'envoyez pas de pellicules noir et blanc, ni de diapositives. Merci!
Si possible, inscrivez votre nom sur chacune de vos pellicules, **Merci!**
Toutes les marques de pellicules sont acceptées.

7 To complete your order you will need to:
  a) enclose films and payment.
  b) seal, stamp and post envelope.
  c) fill in order form.
  d) complete name and address for return label.
  Which number of the French instructions 1–4 corresponds with the English instructions a), b), c), d)?

8 Before you seal the envelope, you remember you've finished off a black and white film as well. Can you use this company?

D Aux supermarchés et aux hypermarchés

Here is a list of items available at the local supermarket.

EPICERIE SPECIAL VACANCES

Dénomination de l'article (Contenance et Prix)		Prix au kilo et au litre	Prix compara-ratifs
Café Dégustation moulu, Stentor Le paquet de 250 g.	11,30	45,20	......
Café Expresso en grains ou moulu, Maison du Café Le paquet de 250 g.	12,70	50,80	......
Le Grand Café pur Arabica, moulu, Maison du Café Le paquet de 250 g.	13,30	53,20	......
Croissants Le sachet de 10 (400 g.) ...	5,90	14,75	......
Pains aux raisins Le sachet de 6 (240 g.)	6,50	27,08	......
Chaussons aux pommes La barquette de 4 (400 g.) .	9,90	24,75	......
Galettes de Pleyben La boîte 1/4 (850 g.)	23,50	27,65	......
Galettes des Monts d'Arrée Le sachet de 700 g.	12,80	18,28	......
Palets des Monts d'Arrée Le sachet de 550 g.	12,80	23,27	......
Boudoirs Delos La boîte de 18 (85 g.)	3,50	41,17	......
Assortiment de biscuits Menuet La boîte de 200 g.	6,70	33,50	......
La boîte de 400 g.	13,10	32,75	......
Cornets glace assortis La boîte de 165 g.	11,50	69,69	......
Chocolat ménage lait Le lot de 5 tablettes de 100 g.	9,90	19,80	......
Chocolat noisettes Milka Suchard La tablette de 100 g.	3,70	37,00	......
Chocolat au riz Milka Suchard La tablette de 100 g.	4,20	42,00	......
Chocolat noir extra supérieur Lindt La tablette de 100 g.	3,20	32,00	......
Bonbons menthe claire, Pie-qui-Chante Le sachet de 216 g. + 20 % gratuit	3,95	18,29	......
Le sachet de 485 g.	7,50	15,46	......

CREMERIE SPECIAL VACANCES

Dénomination de l'article (Contenance et Prix)		Prix au kilo et au litre	Prix compara-ratifs
Camembert Marcillat 45 % M.G. La boîte de 240 g.	4,95	20,62	......
Edam tendre 40 % M.G. Le kilo	27,50	27,50	......
Mimolette tendre 40 % M.G. Le kilo	28,90	28,90	......
Gouda tendre 48 % M.G. Le kilo	29,50	29,50	......
Tartare ail et fines herbes 70 % M.G. La boîte de 80 g.	4,20	52,50	......
St-Nectaire Auvergnat 45 % M.G. Le kilo	29,90	29,90	......
Bleu d'Auvergne Auvergnat 50 % M.G. Le kilo	29,00	29,00	......
La portion de 120 g.	4,80	40,00	......
Reblochon Reybier 60 % M.G. Le kilo	37,70	37,70	......

SURGELES CREMES GLACEES SPECIAL VACANCES

Dénomination de l'article (Contenance et Prix)		Prix au kilo et au litre	Prix compara-ratifs
Pimlico Miko La boîte de 8 (480 ml.)	9,90	20,62	......
Café ou chocolat Liégeois Miko La boîte de 4 (500 ml.)	12,00	24,00	......
Poires Belle-Hélène Miko La boîte de 4 (500 ml.)	12,00	24,00	......
Pâte feuilletée Vivagel Les 400 g.	5,60	14,00	......
Pizza Bellissima Vivagel 450 g.	13,90	30,89	......
Tranches pânées de merlu Vivagel La boîte de 8 (400 g.)	10,80	27,00	......
Filets de merlan Vivagel La boîte de 400 g.	13,50	33,75	......
Coquilles St-Jacques Mikogel Le sachet de 500 g.	49,90	99,80	......
Cuisses de grenouille Green Le sachet de 500 g.	18,60	37,20	......
Cailles Mikogel prêtes à cuire La barquette de 6 (780 g.) .	33,80	43,33	......

LIQUIDES SPECIAL VACANCES

Dénomination de l'article (Contenance et Prix)		Prix au kilo et au litre	Prix compara-ratifs
Whisky 12 ans d'âge Produit Blanc, 40° La bouteille de 70 cl.	55,80	79,71	......
Porto Sandeman Ruby 19,5° La bouteille de 75 cl.	36,90	49,20	......
Vin Côtes du Rhône Pierre Vincent La bouteille de 75 cl.	7,50	10,00	......
Gros Plant La bouteille de 73 cl.	5,20	7,12	......
Pelure d'oignon La bouteille de 73 cl.	4,95	6,78	......
Muscat d'Alsace 1982 La bouteille de 70 cl.	13,50	19,28	......
Bordeaux rouge Fonset Lacour 1982 La bouteille de 75 cl.	11,95	15,93	......
Gamay de Touraine rouge 1983 La bouteille de 75 cl.	9,95	13,26	......
Sauvignon de Touraine blanc La bouteille de 75 cl.	10,90	14,53	......
Vin rosé de Loire Cellier La bouteille de 75 cl.	9,80	13,06	......
Vin rouge d'Anjou Cellier La bouteille de 75 cl.	9,80	13,06	......
Vin blanc Layon Cellier La bouteille de 75 cl.	11,50	15,33	......
Bière Kanterbrau Le pack de 10 bouteilles de 25 cl.	15,37	6,15	......
Bière Kanterbrau Le pack de 6 boîtes de 33 cl.	12,50	6,31	......
Bière Panach' Le pack de 10 bouteilles de 25 cl.	15,95	6,38	......
Bière Force 4 Le pack de 10 bouteilles de 25 cl.	16,50	6,60	......
Cidre brut ou doux La Cidraie Le pack de 4 bouteilles de 25 cl.	7,50	7,50	......
Boisson à l'orange Oasis Le magnum de 2 litres	7,90	3,95	......
Orangina Le pack de 6 bouteilles de 20 cl.	7,95	6,62	......
Boisson Cola Produit Blanc La bouteille de 1,5 L	4,50	3,00	......

You are doing the shopping for your French family today. Copy out the list below and write down the price beside each article if it is available and put a circle around it if it cannot be bought at this store.

1 Coffee beans

2 Ice cream cornets

3 Apple turnovers

4 Soft cream cheese with garlic and herbs

5 Yoghurt

6 Frogs' legs

7 Onions

8 Bottle of champagne

9 Pack of ten beers – the cheapest sort!

10 Lemonade – two bottles

E30

You have heard a lot about hypermarkets in France and as you are travelling along the motorway you see this sign.

EUROMARCHÉ St Brieuc
UN GEANT AU BORD DE L'AUTOROUTE

Will you have to make a long detour to go to this hypermarket?

SAINT-BRIEUC
Route de Rennes - Langueux
Ouvert tous les jours
de 9 h à 22 h.
Fermé le dimanche.

E31

Here are the opening times of the hypermarket.

Is the hypermarket open at 8 p.m. on a Monday? If so, how long will you have before it closes?

E32

When you arrive in the car-park you see this sign.

What should be done with the shopping trolleys after use?

Why?

chariots

pour éviter tout accident
replacer ici les chariots
après utilisation. merci

(23) **alim. enfants**
biscottes

parfumerie (25)

liquides (27)

E33

You are in a hurry and need to read the signs to save a lot of time.

Which aisle (23, 25 or 27) would you go along if you wanted to buy some biscuits?

LAIT

lait écrémé /VERT		1 l.	2.85
lait entier /ROUGE		1 l.	3.65
lait demi-écrémé		1 l.	2.78
lait demi-écrémé		6 l.	16.68

E34

This sign shows the types of milk on sale.

1 What colour carton do you look for to buy full cream milk?
2 What type of milk can be bought in six litre containers?

E35

You want some frying steak.

Would you look here?

Give reasons for your answer.

PORC			AGNEAU		
COTE 1ER		35,30	GIGOT		59,00
– FILET		38,20	–	RAC	65,00
– ECHINE		30,90	–	MILIEU	66,00
ROTI	A/OS	30,90	–	TRANCHE	80,00
PALETTE	A/OS	25,80	SELLE		41,00
POINTE	A/OS	20,60	COTE		60,00
–	S-OS	25,70	– FILET		61,00
ROTI FILET	S/OS	47,70	EPAULE	A/OS	44,80
FILET MIGNON		58,00	–	S-OS	49,60
POITRINE		19,90	POITRINE		26,00
ROGNON		19,90	COLLIER		39,80
COEUR		17,80	ROGNON		40,00
CERVELLE		3,45			

A

B

C

E36

You have bought your biscuits, milk and steak. Which exit do you use? (**A**, **B** or **C**).

P

a) Quelle est la différence entre un hypermarché et un supermarché?

b) Faites avec votre partenaire une liste des rayons dans un hypermarché, et puis une liste de ce qu'il y a à vendre à chaque rayon.

EUROMARCHE SERVICES

CORDONNERIE EXPRESS
TALON - MINUTE

REPRODUCTION IMMEDIATE DE TOUTES VOS CLES,
VOITURE, VERROU, SURETE, STYLE, etc...

PLASTIFICATION DE VOS PIECES D'IDENTITES

QUALITE. RAPIDITE. SERVICE.

E37

You are handed this advertisement as you leave the hypermarket. You wonder what services are available since you've run into a few problems!

You need to:

1 get your shoe stitched.

2 get your watch mended.

3 have a passport photograph taken.

4 buy a toy car for your younger brother.

5 get a key cut.

Which tasks can be accomplished here?

E38

You come across a very long article about shopping in *les grandes surfaces* – that is, large superstores. The article puts forward the advantages and the dangers. Here are the article's main points.

> **P**OINT de rencontre privilégiée de la grande majorité des consommateurs : les grandes surfaces. Que l'on aille dans un super ou un hyper, on n'y trouve que des avantages. Le choix est énorme, les prix sont sans commune mesure avec l'épicier du coin. Bref, c'est le nec le plus ultra de la société de consommation.

1 Can you list the attractions of superstore shopping?

2 Can you say how one should get the best from visits to these shops?

3 Do you think that the original article in full was for or against superstores?

Comment éviter les pièges

IL n'existe bien entendu pas de recette miracle pour éviter de tomber dans ces pièges. Mais on peut tout de même être un peu plus attentif :

- En premier lieu, il faut prendre soin de venir avec une liste des courses que l'on veut faire.

Cela évitera ainsi de se laisser tenter par des produits attirants, mais pas vraiment indispensables.

- Ensuite, et dans la mesure du possible, il est préférable de venir sans les enfants. Leur enthousiasme devant les belles vitrines, et aussi leur inexpérience en font des cibles privilégiées pour les annonceurs.

- N'hésitez pas non plus à faire jouer la concurrence. Malgré le nouveau système de code-barres, les prix doi-vent obligatoirement être affichés.

- Evitez, là aussi quand c'est possible, de venir aux heures de grosse affluence. En étant plus au calme, et sans la crainte de faire la queue aux caisses, vous aurez plus le temps de faire attention à ce que vous mettrez dans votre caddie.

- Dernier point, et malgré la généralisation de ce système, ne venez pas avec des cartes de crédits ou, éventuellement, un chéquier. Avec de l'argent liquide, on «concrétise» mieux ce que l'on dépense.

E   Les achats automatisés

Shopping is undergoing a revolution, according to the two articles that follow.

PROFIT

Les chemises et les jeans se vendent comme des bonbons...

Le prêt-à-porter se met à l'heure du prêt-à-distribuer : au PLM St-Jacques, il suffit de choisir une chemise dans un distributeur automatique puis de payer avec une carte bancaire. En octobre, il en sera de même pour les jeans, dans le métro parisien.

Une nouveauté pour les consommateurs : se payer un Jean ou une chemise dans un distributeur tout comme n'importe quelle friandise. Le produit est présenté dans la vitrine de la machine, on choisit sa taille et son modèle, on paie avec une carte bancaire et on l'emporte immédiatement.

Le distributeur de jeans Levi's installé à la station de métro Aùber à Paris (voir *Libération* du 02/07) a disparu. Il est actuellement à la foire de Cologne en Allemagne. Mais que se rassurent tous ceux qui n'ont pu en profiter, six machines identiques seront installées dans le métro parisien début octobre. La BMP, société créée par les inventeurs du distributeur de jeans, projette également d'en diffuser une centaine dans les grandes villes françaises ainsi qu'au Canada et en Grande-Bretagne. En attendant, il n'y a plus qu'une machine à la disposition des adeptes de ce système : le distributeur mis en place par la firme Centmil Chemises à l'hôtel PLM St-Jacques, à Paris.

Cette nouvelle forme de vente en est à ses tout premiers pas mais, aux dires des fabricants, il s'agirait d'un marché en pleine expansion. Les résultats des tests préliminaires ont été concluants : une moyenne de 8,6 pièces par jour pour les jeans et de 2 par jour pour les chemises, ce qui permet d'amortir rapidement le coût de la machine (100 000 francs pour Centmil Chemises et 160 000 francs pour la BMP).

Les avantages de ce type de distribution sont nombreux. Pour le consommateur, c'est la possibilité d'acheter vite, à toute heure et à un moindre prix que dans le commerce (5 à 15 % moins cher) : les chemises sont vendues 290 francs, les Levi's 319 francs. Les appareils sont suffisamment au point pour qu'il ne puisse pas y avoir erreur sur la marchandise. Le principal problème est que le choix est encore très limité.

A la BMP, on estime que la vente par distributeur ne vaut que pour des produits connus. Il faut en effet sélectionner le produit avec soin. Un jean ou une chemise classique sont des valeurs sûres. Plus délicat est de s'attaquer aux vêtements féminins si on veut toucher une vaste clientèle. Pour la société qui gère le distributeur, ce système de vente entraîne peu de frais : pas de fond de commerce, un personnel très réduit (entretien et réassortiment de la machine), une rentabilité très vite atteinte sont des atouts précieux.

Le PLM St-Jacques a gracieusement prêté un espace à Centmil Chemises, estimant qu'il bénéficierait indirectement d'une bonne publicité. Mais la société envisage, à terme, de vendre son appareil à divers hôtels. Pour ce qui est des jeans Levi's, le produit est destiné à une plus large diffusion, il se vend d'ailleurs plus facilement.

La société Prométro, mandatée par la RATP se charge de trouver les emplacements adéquats dans le métro parisien. Pour cette société il s'agit de rendre service aux usagers et de rendre les lieux plus attrayants avec cette condition : ne pas gêner le trafic. La BMP loue ces espaces au même titre que n'importe quelle boutique déjà installée dans les couloirs du métro.

Les projets sont de multiplier les distributeurs, affirme-t-on chez les fabricants, et pas seulement dans le domaine vestimentaire. Dans nombre de pays, on connaît déjà les distributeurs de journaux et de cigarettes, pour lesquels la France ne donne pas les accords nécessaires. Les études sont en cours, c'est déjà un pas vers une autre forme de consommation.

Laure PANERAI   *La vente automatique, un marché en pleine expansion*

1 If you wanted to buy a shirt urgently how could you do so at PLM St. Jacques?

2 What else is to be sold in this way?

3 Is this method of selling a one-off experiment? Give reasons for your answer.

4 List the advantages *a)* to the customer *b)* to the company.

5 What is the main drawback of the system?

6 Is the article above generally sympathetic to this innovation?

P

Que pensez-vous de ce système de vente?

...et l'essence s'achète à la carte et sans pompiste

Les stations-service se modernisent. Finies les attentes interminables, adieu aux pompistes : Mobil, Shell, Total lancent de nouvelles stations où le client se sert lui-même, paie avec sa carte de crédit automatiquement et sans passer à la caisse.

De notre rédaction lyonnaise.

Un grand panneau bleu et blanc à l'entrée de la pompe à essence explique au client le nouveau système de règlement : «*paiement automatique par carte bancaire jour et nuit*». Cette station-service Mobil de Lyon, automatisée depuis deux mois, fait partie des quelques stations expérimentales lancées par les compagnies pétrolières pour tester les réactions du public.

Total en a ouvert une la semaine dernière en Dordogne, Elf inaugurera sa première station dans deux mois sur l'autoroute A26 dans la région de Saint-Quentin, tandis que Shell teste depuis bientôt un an deux Shellmatics à Villeurbanne et Rillieux-le-Pape près de Lyon.

Si les premiers tests sont positifs, ces stations automatisées – pour un surcoût de 250 à 300 000 francs – copiées sur les modèles belges et allemands, pourraient se multiplier sur le territoire français. Total envisage déjà d'ouvrir 50 à 60 stations munies de bornes automatiques d'ici à la fin de l'année, 150 à 200 en 1987. Shell, de son côté, prévoit d'installer à la mi-1987 une dizaine de stations entièrement automatisées et une vingtaine associant paiement traditionnel et automatique.

Mais avant de généraliser le système, encore faut-il convaincre le client de son utilité. *A priori*, rien de plus simple. «*C'est comme pour retirer de l'argent aux guichets automatiques des banques*», explique René Pradier, le patron de la station Mobil, transformé pour l'heure en démonstrateur de service. Le client introduit sa carte bleue dans l'automate, il pianote son numéro de code confidentiel puis se sert directement à la pompe. Plus d'interventions du pompiste, finis les attentes interminables à la caisse, la pompe fonctionne 24 heures sur 24. Un gain de temps allié à plus de sécurité pour le pompiste : le risque de braquage disparaît.

L'automate de Mobil est programmé pour donner un plein en 3 minutes. Au-delà de ce temps, il s'arrête. «*S'il n'y avait pas de limite*, explique René Pradier, *l'automobiliste suivant pourrait tenter de profiter gratuitement de la carte du premier.*» Sécurité incendie aussi : si le feu prend, l'automate couvre client, pompe et voiture de mousse. Et puis, fin du fin, «*je n'ai plus de contestation sur les prix*, s'extasie René Pradier, *c'est comme les boîtes noires des avions, j'ai un journal de caisse ininflammable installé à l'intérieur de l'automate qui recense toutes les factures.*» L'automate surveille aussi les clients en ne leur accordant qu'une minute pour composer leur code confidentiel. Au-delà de cette limite, il décide que la carte doit être volée et... la mange.

Caroline TALBOT

E40

1 How would you know that you were entering a new style service-station?

2 In which countries have these already been operating?

3 What procedure should one follow to operate the pumps?

4 What are the advantages of this system?

5 What precautions are built into the system:
   a) In the case of fire?
   b) in case of fraudulent use?

E41

Study this set of instructions.

1 Where would you be sitting if you were operating this machine?

2 What precautions are you advised to take when using this facility?

P

Comment imaginez-vous la societé de consommation en 2001?

Chapter 6
Manger et boire

Pour les Français l'art de bien manger et de bien boire est peut-être l'art le plus important de la vie. Sans doute connaissez-vous bien les plats français, ou bien peut-être le vin français! A votre avis est-ce que la gastronomie est aussi importante pour les Anglais?

A Les provisions

In France you will find yourself constantly surrounded by tempting signs and advertisements about food.

E1
What two things could you buy here?

E2
What can you buy here apart from ice-creams?

E4
Apart from pancakes containing jam and liqueurs, what other fillings are there?

PRIX	
PARISIENNE	4·00
CROISSANT	3·20
PAIN AU CHOCOLAT	3·40
CROISSANT AUX AMANDES	4·80
POMME	4·40
CHAUSSON	4·80
FAR BRETON	5·80
GRANDES BRIOCHES 9·90 &	19·80
KOUIGN AMANN	7·20
ORANAIS	5·20
FEUILLETÉ RAISINS	3·40
BRIOCHE	3·40
TOUT BEURRE	

CRÊPES FROMENT

Beurre - sucre	5.00
Compote pommes	5.00
Chocolat	7,50
Confiture abricot	6.00
fraises	7,00
myrtilles	8,00
Au miel	
Citron orange (fruits pressés)	9,00
Chocolat chantilly	12,00
Cointreau, cusenier orange	14,00
Grand marnier - rhum	13,00
Sibérienne	16,00

E3
What ingredient is in all these cakes?

P

a) Nommez quelques sortes de pains français.

b) Nommez quelques sortes de pâtisseries françaises.

You are on a self-catering holiday and you see this promotion on certain items of food at your local supermarket.

Here is part of your shopping list:

jar of apricot jam   tin of peaches   1 kg coffee beans

20 eggs   6 coffee eclairs   500 g butter.

How much would these purchases cost you?

P

Avec un ami, décidez ce que vous allez acheter pour faire un pique-nique. Vous n'avez pas beaucoup d'argent à dépenser mais vous avez des préférences individuelles.

Le choix du vin ne doit pas être une aventure ! une idée de cadeau ?

LA CAVE DU CHÂTEAU

51, rue du Château
BREST
TÉL. 98.80.40.24
Ouvert le dimanche
Nous livrons toute la France à domicile

E7

You see this advertisement in a newspaper.

1 What is the advertisement about?

2 Why could this firm be of use to you, even though you are holidaying in Morlaix?

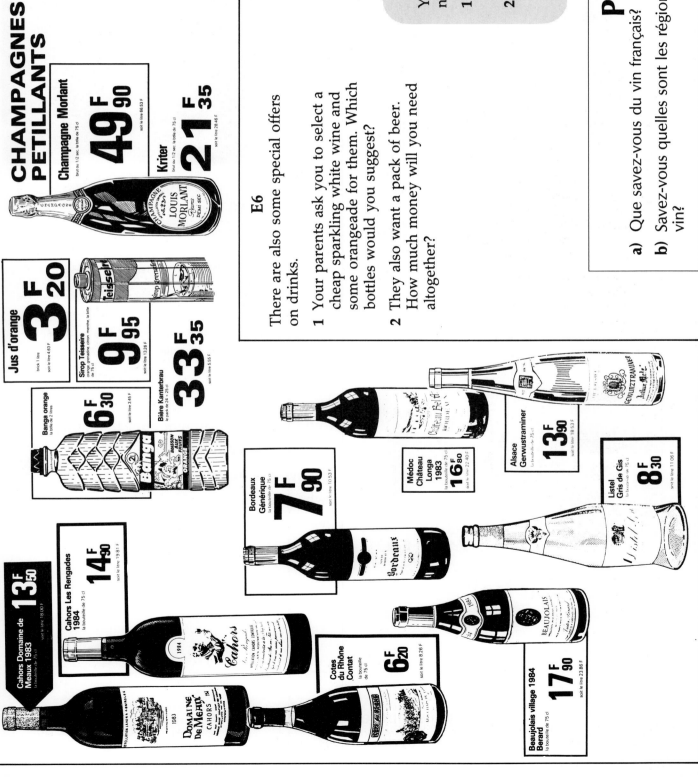

E6

There are also some special offers on drinks.

1 Your parents ask you to select a cheap sparkling white wine and some orangeade for them. Which bottles would you suggest?

2 They also want a pack of beer. How much money will you need altogether?

P

a) Que savez-vous du vin français?

b) Savez-vous quelles sont les régions de la France d'où vient le bon vin?

B   Les cafés-restaurants: les publicités

Here is a selection of advertisements for places to eat.

E8
Why would this establishment appeal to you if you were considering celebrating a special occasion with a large group of friends?

E9
Why should you go here if you were on a tight budget?

Cafeteria du Royallieu

RUE ALEXIS CARREL   ☎ 420.40.54

nos installations

▲

— BAR

— SELF SERVICE
  Pratique, rapide, économique

— RESTAURANT (au 1er étage) - 2 menus + 1 carte

Salle pour groupes jusqu'à 300 personnes.

6 menus au choix, prix net boisson comprise.

Service traditionnel par personnel qualifié.

Réservation au moins 72 heures à l'avance.

HOTEL du MARCHÉ
Son RESTAURANT ★★
La Bouillabaisse
Spécialités
Langoustes Bouillabaisse Poissons fins
PLACE Victor Hugo   St RAPHAËL (VAR)
Téléphone : 95.03.57

E10
Would this establishment appeal to someone:

1 looking for accommodation?

2 fancying a steak?

3 who is a vegetarian?

Give reasons for your answers.

P

a) Qu'est-ce que c'est, le plat qui s'appelle «fruits de mer»?

b) Que fait un pêcheur? Que fait un poissonnier?

E11

List the sentences which are true about this restaurant.

1 This restaurant has a set menu.

2 This restaurant can serve buffet meals.

3 This restaurant serves only lamb and mutton.

4 This restaurant can cater for wedding receptions.

5 This restaurant does not deal with business functions.

6 You could eat trout here.

7 You could eat lunch here on a Wednesday.

8 You could not eat here on a Tuesday evening.

E12

You are staying in the Aisne region. Compare these two restaurant advertisements. Which establishment will you choose if you wanted the following?

1 You wish to eat very late at night.

2 You want to eat on a Tuesday evening.

3 You wish to arrange a business lunch.

4 You just want a light meal.

5 You want to eat lobster.

E13

This extract comes from a guide book to Brittany.

LESNEVEN `45`

HÔTEL DE FRANCE*
RESTAURANT

Dans une maison de Maître du XVIIᵉ siècle
Le propriétaire, Chef de Cuisine : Jean-Claude PETIBON
vous propose une cuisine légère et raffinée avec
quelques spécialités :
St-Jacques au Pernod - Saumon braisé au champagne
Steak de lotte aux petits légumes - Sole François 1ᵉʳ

Chambres à prix modérés, menu étape pour VRP
et pour la sécurité de nos clients nous mettons gratuitement à leur disposition notre PARKING PRIVÉ - (5 boxes
+ 10 places) Clos le soir

LOGONNA-DAOULAS `46`

LA GRIGNOTIÈRE
RESTAURANT

Monsieur et Madame R. JAOUEN

Spécialités de Fruits de Mer et Poissons

à 2 5 km de Brest par voie EXPRESS

3 salles particulières pour mariages et banquets
(piste de danse) - 3ᵉ Âge
29224 LOGONNA DAOULAS
TÉL. 98.20.64.36

MORLAIX `47`

LA CIGALE
RESTAURANT

Françoise et Yannick

Menus à 39 et 50 F + carte variée

Fermé le mardi

3, PLACE DE VIARMES - 29210 MORLAIX
TÉL. 98.88.00.49

PLOUGUERNEAU `48`

AUBERGE DU CORREJOU
Club vidéo - Discothèque
Ouvert toute l'année

RESTAURANT
Vue imprenable sur la mer
Ouvert toute l'année

Mariages - Séminaires - Baptêmes
Sortie 3ᵉ âge (prix très spéciaux)

Spécialité de homard à l'Armoricaine
Spécialités de fruits de mer et poissons

CORREJOU à PLOUGUERNEAU - TÉL. 98.04.70.98

From the information in the advertisements above, where would you go if you wanted the following?

1 A meal and a dance afterwards.

2 Fresh, local shellfish.

3 To eat in historic surroundings.

4 A restaurant with a view of the sea.

P

a) Avez-vous jamais mangé dans un restaurant français?

b) Quelle sorte de cuisine préférez-vous–
la cuisine française, anglaise, chinoise ou italienne? Pourquoi?

A

HÔTEL RESTAURANT ST MÉLAINE
Pierre PAUMARD

MENUS A 36 F et 42 F
Le plaisir de la cuisine traditionnelle dans une ambiance sympathique !

Ouvert tous les jours midi et soir
sauf dimanche midi
75, 77 rue Ange de Guernisac
MORLAIX
Tél. 88.08.79

B

TOUT NOUVEAU A MORLAIX
MENU A 36 F
Prix net vin compris

● Hors d'œuvre à volonté
● Brochettes
● Fromage - Dessert

RESTAURANT LA BAGATELLE
19, rue Ange de Guernisac
MORLAIX - Tél. (98) 88.10.98

C

Restaurant *"La Marée Bleue"*
M. et Mme. COQUART
Spécialités de fruits de mer, poissons
et viandes. Cuisine traditionnelle,

Carte et menus carte - Ouvert midi et soir
tous les jours sauf samedi midi et lundi
Réservations de 10 h à 14 h et à partir de 18 h
3, rampe St-Melaine - MORLAIX
Tél. 63.24.21

D

RESTAURANT LA TAVERNE
Prise de commande de 19 h30 à 23 heures
à midi : **PLATS A EMPORTER**
Bd. Sainte Barbe - ROSCOFF
Tél. 69.77.63

E

Service jusqu'à minuit

Dans une typique maison bretonne du xvi siècle
Auberge de la
"Pomme d'Api"
spécialités régionales et produits de la mer
49 RUE VERDEREL ST-POL-DE-LÉON tel. 69.04.36

F

RESTAURANT PÉKIN
spécialités Chinoises et Vietnamiennes
Plats à emporter
ouvert tous les jours de
12 h à 14 h et 19 h à 23 h
sauf mardi midi et mercredi midi
4, Venelle au Son - MORLAIX
Tél. (98) 62.18.03

E14

You are on holiday with a group of friends who all have different ideas about eating out. Here are all your suggestions!

1 Takeaway food.

2 Kebabs.

3 A pleasant atmosphere.

4 Sea food.

5 Chinese food.

6 A set menu with wine for less than 40 F.

7 A meal at 11.30 p.m.

8 A meal in a typical Breton building.

Which establishment (A–F) corresponds to which suggestion (1–8)?

C   Les cafés-restaurants: les menus

E15

One day on holiday you see a restaurant displaying a set menu.

Restaurant
de la
Reine Anne
45, Rue du Mur
29210 MORLAIX
Tél. 98 88 08 29

```
M E N U

                    Prix Net
                    74,00 F

          Boissons non comprises

Terrine de Canard ou
6 Escargots Petits gris ou
Crudités ou
Crevettes Roses ou
Soupe de poisson ou
Jambon de Bayonne ou
6 Huitres creuses
          _____
Coquille de poisson gratinée ou
Truite Meunière ou
Charcuterie
          _____
Steak Grillé Me d'Hôtel ou
Escalope de Dinde à la Crême ou
Côte de Porc aux Champignons ou
Caille sur Canapé ou
Côtes d'Agneau grillée
          _____
Fromages ou Fruits ou
Glaces ou Monaco ou Mystère ou
Orange ou citron Givré
```

RESTAURANT
de la REINE ANNE
45, rue du Mur · 29210 MORLAIX
Tél 83.08.29

Your mother hates fish, game and lamb and your father loves ham, trout and mushrooms.
Suggest what they should order from this menu using a grid as below.

Course	Mother	Father
First		
Second		
Third		
Dessert	They love them all!	

P

a) Qu'est-ce que c'est la volaille? Et le gibier?

b) Avez-vous jamais goûté d'un plat régional français?
    Savez-vous le faire cuire?

N° 3 - MENU A 44 F

> HORS-D'ŒUVRES VARIÉS
> CARRÉ DE PORC ROTI AUX HERBES
> PRINTANIÈRE DE LÉGUMES
> FROMAGE
> GATEAU TUTTI FRUTTI AU KIRSCH

BOISSON : 1 Vin cuit, 1/3 bouteille de Vin de Pays, 1/4 eau minérale, 1 café.

N° 4 - MENU A 50 F

> QUICHE LORRAINE
> PINTADE ROTIE GRAND-MÈRE
> FROMAGE
> POIRE BELLE HÉLÈNE

BOISSON : 1 Muscat, 1/3 bouteille de Beaujolais AC, 1/4 eau minérale, 1 café.

N° 5 - MENU A 65 F

> ASSIETTE CRUDITÉS RICHES
>
> (Asperge, cœur de palmier, cœur d'artichaut, maïs, tomate, œuf, salade)
> COQUILLE DE POISSON DIEPPOISE
> PIECE DE BŒUF ROTIE NIÇOISE
> TOMATE, HARICOTS VERTS, FRITES
> FROMAGE
> PLATEAU DE DESSERT AU CHOIX

BOISSON : 1 Vin cuit, 1/6 bouteille de Sauvignon, 1/3 bouteille de Beaujolais, 1/4 eau minérale, 1 café.

N° 6 - MENU A 80 F

> COQUILLE DE COLIN A LA PARISIENNE
> BRIOCHE A LA REINE
> ROTI DE VEAU PORTE MAILLOT
> SALADE DE SAISON
> PLATEAU DE FROMAGES
> PECHE MELBA

BOISSON : 1 Apéritif de marque, 1/6 bouteille de Sauvignon, 1/3 bouteille de Beaujolais, 1 café, 1/4 eau minérale, 1 digestif.

Ces repas sont servis à table.
Toutes consommations ou supplément, qui ne feront pas l'objet d'accord préalable avec les organisateurs, seront perçus directement.

PARKING : 200 places.

E16

Your pen-friend asks you out for an evening meal. Here are the menus.

1 What is the least you could pay for a meal?

2 Name three drinks offered with the 80 F meal.

3 You do not want to be restricted in your choice of dessert. Which menu offers you a choice?

4 You would like to eat roast beef and chips and your friend would like to eat veal. Which menus do you choose?

P

Quel est votre menu préféré de la liste à gauche? En quoi consiste-il?

E17

Here is a newspaper article about eating out in Paris.

1 What is the main attraction of this restaurant?

2 How long has the owner been offering this fixed-price menu?

3 What is a typical menu offered?

4 What else is included in the price?

5 How many people can eat in this restaurant?

6 Who used to help her run the restaurant?

7 Why does the owner not put her prices up?

8 Where does Maria live?

P

Si vous étiez étudiant(e) à Paris, choisiriez-vous ce restaurant? Pourquoi?

Un menu complet à 5 F en plein Paris !

A LA « CASA MIGUEL », 48, rue Saint-Georges, dans le 9ᵉ arrondissement de Paris, l'inflation, on ne connaît pas... Maria Codina, 76 ans, affiche depuis cinq ans un menu à 5 F !

Voici, par exemple, le menu du jeudi 25 juillet :

Entrée : tranche de melon, salade de tomates ou haricots blancs.

Plat garni : couscous ou ragoût aux pâtes.

Dessert : demi-banane, demi-pamplemousse ou portion de fromage.

(Vin, pain et service compris.)

Depuis le 17 juillet, la vitrine de ce petit restaurant de 32 places affiche un diplôme du *Guiness book* des records qui fait de la « Casa Miguel » l'établissement « **le moins cher du monde... occidental** ».

Pendant 37 ans (« on a ouvert le **15 mars 1949** »), Maria a travaillé avec son époux. Depuis sa mort, en 1981, elle fait tout toute seule. « **Je pourrais augmenter les tarifs, bien sûr, mais quand je vois la misère, je me dis que tant que je le puis, c'est bien de garder les prix comme ils sont, c'est mieux.** » Bien entendu, pas de bénéfices. « Ce n'est vraiment pas le problème, explique la vieille dame, et puis, d'ailleurs, heureusement pour moi, j'ai une fille, elle s'appelle Rose, travaille comme secrétaire à Marie-Claire, elle m'aide et j'habite chez elle près de la gare de Nord. »

Commentaire d'un étudiant : « **C'est bien meilleur qu'au R.U. et presque deux fois moins cher...** »

D Les cafés-restaurants: les additions

E18

Bills can act as proof of past events! See if you are a good detective and answer the questions below.

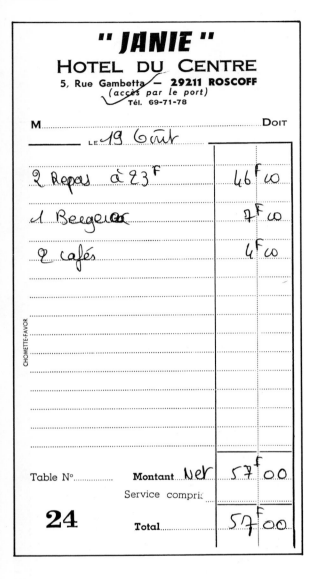

1 How many people ate in each restaurant?
2 Which restaurant is near the harbour?
3 In which one did the customers not drink coffee after the meal?
4 In which one did the customers drink rosé wine?
5 Which restaurant does Yves Cariou work for?

P

L'autre jour, vous êtes allé(e) avec deux amis à un hôtel-restaurant. Le patron s'appelait M. Fawlty. Il y avait beaucoup de problèmes avec le service et les plats. Qu'est-ce qui s'est passé?

E   Les fêtes

This is an extract from an old letter from your pen-friend.

Sais-tu que je viens d'avoir douze ans? Cela a été un grand jour. Pour l'occasion, mes parents ont tenu à m'emmener au restaurant. Nous y sommes donc arrivés vers 20 heures. Il y avait maman, papa, Lija (ma soeur) et moi. J'étais très intimidée car c'était la première fois que j'allais dans un restaurant .... Papa a demandé au maître d'hôtel de nous apporter la carte et les menus. Après avoir longuement réfléchi, nous nous sommes enfin décidés et nous avons pris le menu à soixante francs. Il y avait: des hors-d'oeuvres variés (tomates en salade, choux-fleur, pomme de terre, céleris, artichauts et bien d'autres choses encore), puis du poulet rôti avec des frites, puis du fromage et enfin une pâtisserie maison. J'ai choisi une tarte aux pommes. Enfin, pour tout te dire, c'était délicieux.

1 What special occasion was celebrated by a meal?

2 Why did she feel nervous?

3 How much was the set menu they chose?

4 What was there for starters?

5 How was the chicken cooked?

6 Name two things they chose after the main course.

P

a) Racontez comment vous avez passé votre dernière anniversaire.

b) Comment allez-vous célébrer la fin de vos examens scolaires?

KRITER BRUT DE BRUT

Le Club Kriter Brut de Brut en direct sur Europe I, avec Christian Barbier, André Boisseaux et Paul-Loup Sulitzer.

Le Château de Meursault, magnifique domaine de plus de cinquante hectares où s'est déroulé le baptême de la Cuvée Château de Meursault 1986.

Présentation du trimaran Kriter Brut de Brut avec le skipper Philippe Monnet, Paul-Loup Sulitzer, M. et Mme André Boisseaux, Jean-Paul Saubesty. Ci-dessous, le baptême de la Cuvée Château de Meursault 1986, avec Alexandra Stewart, Daniel Ceccaldi et Marie Dubois.

La fête qui réunit à Beaune, en novembre de chaque année, au cœur de la Bourgogne en liesse, sportifs, comédiens, comédiennes, personnalités des arts autour de la Maison Patriarche Père et Fils, de Kriter Brut de Brut et du Château de Meursault, est de plus en plus belle, de plus en plus réussie. Et celle de 1986, les samedi 15 et dimanche 16 novembre, a été placée sous le signe de la chance et du bonheur. De la générosité aussi, comme toujours.

Depuis 1964, c'est une tradition ; André Boisseaux, président de Kriter Brut de Brut et Patriarche Père et Fils, remet le Bouchon d'or Kriter... en or 18 carats, aux grandes vedettes sportives désignées par le jury de "L'Équipe". Cette année, Jean-Marc Boivin pour l'alpinisme, Eric Berthon pour le ski acrobatique, Thierry Marie pour le cyclisme, Bruno Carabetta pour le judo, et Patrick Edlinger, "le grimpeur aux mains nues", étaient à l'honneur et ont reçu cette haute distinction sportive en présence de nombreuses autorités et de Noël Couëdel, rédacteur en chef de "L'Équipe".

Ils ont également emporté leur poids en bouteilles de Kriter Brut de Brut et ont dû, pour cela, sacrifier à l'amusante et sympathique tradition de la pesée. Toujours dans la tradition, la journée de samedi s'est clôturée par un magnifique dîner servi dans les anciennes cuveries du Château de Meursault. 290 invités privilégiés ont pu admirer cette demeure exceptionnelle, située au milieu d'un domaine viticole de plus de cinquante hectares, répartis sur cinq grands crus en Côte de Beaune : Meursault, Volnay, Pommard, Beaune et Savigny. Une demeure historique puisqu'elle fut édifiée au XVIe siècle par les seigneurs de Meursault, en remplacement de la forteresse construite en 1377 par Robert de Grancey, seigneur du lieu. Les vastes caves où sont logés les vins en fûts et en bouteilles des récoltes du domaine du Château de Meursault s'étendent sous le château proprement dit et sous ses dépendances. Certaines furent creusées par les moines de Cîteaux qui exploitèrent à partir du XIIe siècle des vignobles en Bourgogne. Une référence ! Au cours de ce dîner aux chandelles absolument prestigieux, on procéda solennellement au baptême de la Cuvée "Château de Meursault" 1986, à l'arôme fleuri et fruité avec beaucoup de finesse et d'élégance, au dire de Jean-Luc Pouteau, meilleur sommelier du monde, appelé à donner le premier son avis sur cette nouvelle cuvée.

E20

This extract reports an event concerning Kriter.

1 What sort of product is Kriter?

2 How often is the celebration held at Beaune?

3 Who are honoured at the event?

4 What will each winner take away?

5 What does the writer think of the *Château de Meursault*?

F   Les recettes

E21
You fancy making French style curried rice!

1 How long does this recipe take to prepare?
2 How long does it take to cook?
3 Which ingredients do you need apart from stock, pepper and curry powder?
4 What should you fry in butter first of all?
5 At what point should you add the rice?
6 What should you mix in at the last minute?

P

a) Est-ce que vos parents consacrent beaucoup de temps à faire la cuisine?
b) Préparez-vous les repas quelquefois?
c) Quel plat vous offre le plus de plaisir à préparer?
d) Décrivez à votre partenaire comment vous préparez votre plat favori.

C'est facile!

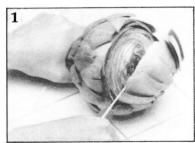

a TOURNEZ. Tournez un demi-tour le cône des feuilles centrales avec les doigts pour l'enlever, puis retirez le foin.

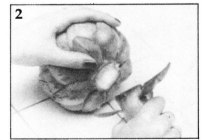

b LAVEZ-COUPEZ. Après avoir lavé votre "Prince de Bretagne" dans une eau vinaigrée, coupez le tiers supérieur des feuilles avec un couteau scie, en le maintenant fermement par la tige.

c VERSEZ à l'intérieur l'accompagnement de votre choix. Votre artichaut à la coque est prêt! Pour le déguster utilisez les feuilles comme mouillettes.

d CASSEZ LA TIGE PUIS CUISEZ. Mettez dans votre autocuiseur et laissez cuire 15 mm environ. Egouttez et laissez refroidir.

E22
You are staying in Brittany where artichokes are very popular. Your mother asks you how to cook them from this French recipe. Unfortunately the printer has made an error and mixed up the photos and instructions.

1 Read the recipe opposite with care.
   Try to match up the instructions **a, b, c, d** to their picture. The pictures are in the correct order (1–4).
2 Can you suggest any suitable fillings for artichokes?
3 What part of the artichoke do you dip into the filling?

G   Les bons conseils

TOURISTES

Les Organisations Agricoles et plus spécialement la Chambre d'Agriculture et le C.D.J.A. sont heureux de vous accueillir en HAUTE-SAVOIE. A cette occasion, ils vous présentent les délicieux produits du terroir, avec leur implantation géographique. N'hésitez-pas, là où vous serez, à prendre contact avec les Producteurs ; vous serez aimablement reçus. Nous vous souhaitons de bonnes vacances et un heureux séjour dans nos montagnes.

LES FROMAGES

L'Emmental : ce fromage à pâte cuite, savoureuse, avec un certain nombre d'ouvertures franches et de la grosseur d'une noix, fait partie de la famille des Gruyère, où l'on trouve avec lui le Comté et le Beaufort. Il se présente sous la forme de meules de 70 à 80 Kg fabriqué avec 900 à 1.000 litres de lait. La production haut-savoyarde de 12.000 tonnes par an provient de quelque 250 fromageries, coopératives, appelées fruitières. C'est un fromage de gourmets, spécialement recommandé pour la fondue savoyarde.

Le Reblochon : ce fromage de montagne à pâte molle se fabrique presque exclusivement pour le fermier, dans le pays de THONES, la CLUSAZ et les ARAVIS. Trois semaines sont nécessaires pour transformer cinq litres de lait de montagne en Reblochon de 500 grammes de forme cylindrique. Sa qualité et sa finesse en font un des meilleurs fromages français.

La Tomme de Haute-Savoie est le plus ancien fromage du pays. Il se présente sous la forme d'une petite meule cylindrique de 1 à 2 Kg dont la croûte est moisie. Il dose de 40 à 50 % de matière grasse.

> Que vous soyez en famille ou au restaurant,
> ne terminez jamais votre repas
> sans le plateau de fromages haut-savoyards.

LES VINS

En parcourant ce département, découvrez les "Vins du Pays". Vous apprécierez d'excellents produits de cru avec :

— les "ROUSSETTES" des coteaux de Frangy et Seyssel,

— les "CREPY" de la Région de Douvaine,

— le "Vin d'AYZE", pétillant, produit exceptionnel de la Vallée de l'Arve,

— des spécialités telles que le "RIPAILLE" et le "MARIN", vins fruités des vignobles de la région de Thonon,

— des vins rouges "MONDEUSE" et "GAMAY", qui s'associent parfaitement aux fromages de nos montagnes.

> Un bon vin de Savoie sur votre table
> c'est la joie pour vos Vacances.

FRUITS — Faites confiance à cette marque :

"Les VERGERS de HAUTE-SAVOIE".

De son terroir d'altitude la Savoie vous offre des produits de santé et de goût parfait. Nos arbres poussent dans un sol et sous un climat de montagne qui leur sont spécialement favorables.

LES JUS DE FRUITS DE SAVOIE

Vous avez peut-être eu l'occasion d'apprécier la qualité des Fruits de Savoie, alors consommez des jus de Fruits de Savoie.

Parmi la gamme de ses produits, la SICA "VERGERS de SAVOIE" vous recommande tout particulièrement ses jus élaborés exclusivement à partir des fruits de Savoie à la saveur si franche, si vraie, qui vous permettra de retrouver tout l'arôme des fruits de montagne : pommes, framboises, fraises etc....

• • • •
• •

E23

Whilst on holiday with your family in the French Alps, you are given this leaflet. Your parents can only recognise the words cheese, wine and fruit!

1 You all want to make a fondue, which cheese should you buy?

2 Which local wines would be particularly suitable for this meal?

3 What fruits are grown locally?

E24

You visit a hypermarket near the town you are staying in and you pick up a consumers' advice leaflet.

SERVIR LE PAIN

- Ne pas couper le pain plus de 10 min avant de servir.
- Ne pas griller du pain frais.
- Ne pas griller le pain de seigle.
- Proposer plusieurs sortes de pains.
- Le ranger à l'abri de l'humidité, de préférence dans une boîte en bois.

- Si le pain est entamé, placer la face tranchée contre le bois.

- Ne jamais conserver du pain dans un sac plastique : il se ramollit et s'affadit.

Which of the instructions below are true about how to serve bread?

1 Never toast fresh bread.

2 Do not cut bread more than half an hour before serving.

3 Keep bread in a plastic bag.

4 Keep bread in a wooden box in a dry place.

5 Put the sliced end of the bread against a wooden surface. '

6 Always serve several different kinds of bread.

E25

There is a large variety of bread in France to choose from. Which sort of bread would you buy if you wanted one which:

1 has a slightly sweet flavour?

2 keeps well?

3 would be nice if eaten with shellfish?

4 is made with white flour?

5 contains lots of fibre?

6 contains whole wheat grains?

LES DIFFÉRENTS PAINS

Pain blanc	Baguettes (250 g), pain (400 g), petits pains (60 g).
Pain de campagne	Composé de blé et pétri avec un levain sauvage qui lui donne sa saveur et lui assure une meilleure conservation.
Pain de son	Un pain très diététique à forte proportion de son de froment qui facilite la régulation du transit intestinal.
Pain complet	A base, comme son nom l'indique, de grains de blé moulus entiers.
Pain de seigle	Fabriqué avec de la farine de seigle. Parfait pour accompagner les huîtres, praires et autres coquillages.
Pain viennois	Un pain fantaisie très agréable. A la farine de froment, à la levure, au sel et à l'eau sont ajoutés du beurre et un peu de sucre.

P

a) Que signifie l'expression «être au régime»?

b) Enumérez ce que vous avez mangé hier pour le petit déjeuner, le déjeuner et le dîner.

c) Devriez-vous manger plus de pain, de légumes, de fruits?

QUAND LES ACHETER

	FRUITS	LÉGUMES
JANVIER	Pommes, oranges, bananes, poires	Salades, carottes, navets, radis, poireaux, salsifis
FÉVRIER	Les mêmes	Les mêmes
MARS	Pommes, oranges, bananes	Choux-fleurs, carottes, pommes de terre, épinards
AVRIL	Les mêmes	Les mêmes
MAI	Fraises, pommes, cerises, bananes	Asperges, carottes, artichauts, choux-fleurs, épinards
JUIN	Abricots, cerises, fraises, pommes,	Petits pois, artichauts
JUILLET	Pêches, prunes, abricots, melons	Aubergines, haricots verts, tomates
AOÛT	Pêches, prunes, poires, raisins, melons	Aubergines, haricots verts, tomates, carottes, haricots blancs
SEPTEMBRE	Pommes, poires, prunes, raisins, melons	Les mêmes
OCTOBRE	Pommes, poires, raisins, bananes	Poireaux, carottes, choux-fleurs, haricots blancs
NOVEMBRE	Pommes, poires, bananes	Les mêmes
DÉCEMBRE	Pommes, oranges, poires, bananes	Choux-fleurs, salades, poireaux, carottes, salsifis, radis, navets

LA FRAICHEUR ÇA A BON GOUT

Un impératif pour choisir fruits et légumes : la fraîcheur. C'est d'elle dont dépend principalement le goût des produits que vous choisirez. Choisir un fruit ou un légume est uniquement une question de coup d'œil ou d'habitude.
Un beau produit, ferme, aux couleurs bien nettes, à l'air appétissant, sera toujours préféré à un produit terne et ramolli.

RALLYE

E26

You also pick up this fact sheet on fruit and vegetables.

1 It is August. What fruit and vegetables are in season and good to buy?

2 Are the same fruit and vegetables recommended for March? If not, which ones are recommended?

3 How many different types of *a*) fruit *b*) vegetables are mentioned in this leaflet?

4 Name three characteristics of 'good produce'.

Poisson Et Diététique

Les qualités nutritives du poisson sont reconnues par tous les diététiciens, nutritionnistes et hygiénistes. La valeur protéique de 100 g de poisson est la même que pour 100 g de viande.

Et si, tout comme la viande, la chair de poisson apporte de nombreuses vitamines, elle est nettement plus riche que la viande en phosphore, en calcium, en oligo-éléments. Enfin le poisson maigre convient à tous les régimes puisqu'une portion de 200 g de poisson fournit seulement 70 calories contre 200 pour 100 g de viande.

Bien Choisir Le Poisson

La première qualité du poisson sur l'étal du poissonnier doit être sa fraîcheur. Un poisson est frais quand :

1. Son corps est ferme, sa peau saine et de belle couleur, ses écailles fermement attachées.
2. Il ne dégage pas d'odeur trop prononcée de poisson.
3. Son œil, ni enfoncé, ni vitreux, est vif et brillant.
4. Ses branchies (faciles à observer en soulevant les ouïes) sont rouges ou rose vif, jamais grisâtres.

Conserver Le Poisson

Un poisson doit être, en principe, consommé le jour de l'achat. On peut cependant le conserver un jour ou deux à condition de le vider - ou de le faire vider - de saler légèrement l'intérieur et de le conserver au réfrigérateur dans une boîte hermétiquement close.

Principaux Noms Régionaux Des Principaux Poissons

Un même poisson peut avoir selon la région où on le trouve plusieurs noms. Voici les principaux :

Bar : loup, loubine.

Cabillaud : C'est la morue fraîche. On le confond souvent avec l'églefin, le lieu jaune, le lieu noir, le merlu ou colin, la julienne. Tous font partie de la même famille et sont différemment appréciés au plan gastronomique. Toutes les recettes applicables à l'un sont cependant généralement applicables aux autres.

Carrelet : Plie, brette.

Lotte : Baudroie, diable de mer.

Dorade (ou daurade) : La dorade forme une grande famille aux espèces assez différenciées qui peuvent s'accommoder selon les mêmes recettes. Voici les principales : griset, brème, pageau, denté, pagre, castagnole, hirondelle.

Merlan : Tacaud, caplan, poutassou, motelle.

Roussette : Chien de mer, émissole.

Thon : germon thon blanc, bonite thon rosé.

E27

Here is another leaflet for consumers – this time on fish.

1 Briefly summarise the advantages of eating fish.

2 What is the quickest way to tell that the fish is fresh?

3 When should you eat the fish?

4 What is a recommended way of cooking mackerel?

5 Name four other ways of cooking fish.

P

a) Vous aimez mieux le poisson ou la viande? Pourquoi?

b) Notre plat national c'est le poisson frites! Savez-vous le faire cuire?

Cuire Le Poisson

Il existe une infinité de recettes de poissons qui peuvent cependant se regrouper en sept principaux modes de cuisson.

Pocher

Le poisson immergé dans un liquide qui le recouvre tout juste cuit à petit bouillon. Le court-bouillon est la préparation type pour pocher un poisson. C'est une préparation d'eau aromatisée avec sel, poivre, thym, laurier, oignon, carottes, vin ou vinaigre ou cidre, épices, etc... Un bon court-bouillon doit avoir bouilli une bonne demi-heure puis refroidi avant d'y plonger le poisson. Il faut alors faire à nouveau bouillir la préparation et compter 10 min de cuisson par livre à l'eau frémissante à partir de l'ébullition.

Mariner

Huile, vin ou jus de citron aromatisés en marinades entrent dans la composition de nombreuses recettes de darnes ou filets de poissons.

Frire

Les poissons frits entiers, en darnes ou en filets doivent auparavant être soit farinés, soit trempés dans une pâte (genre beignet), soit panés. Pour le reste (choix de la matière grasse, mode de cuisson, égouttage) ils se préparent comme les frites.

Sauter - Poêler

Il s'agit de saisir à la poêle ou à la sauteuse un poisson dans une matière grasse (huile, beurre) très chaude et de l'y faire cuire rapidement. C'est la cuisson à la "meunière" idéale pour les poissons plats ou peu épais. C'est aussi le premier stade de préparation des poissons en matelote.

Griller

Tous les poissons peuvent être grillés et surtout les poissons gras tels que sardines, maquereaux, harengs... Grill et poissons doivent être enduits d'huile avant la cuisson et le grill préalablement chauffé. On peut inciser au couteau les poissons épais avant de les cuire et envelopper les poissons fragiles dans des papillottes de papier aluminium.

Rôtir

Ce mode de cuisson n'est pas réservé à la viande et les beaux poissons entiers ou farcis gagnent à être préparés ainsi exactement comme un rôti : four préchauffé, plat creux ovale et épais, arrosage fréquent en cours de cuisson avec le jus.

Mijoter

Les poissons coupés en tranches et farinés sont préalablement sautés puis cuisent à petit feu dans une cocotte couverte. Ce sont les matelotes, équivalent pour le poisson des ragoûts.

Fumet De Poisson

C'est un court-bouillon dans lequel on fait cuire à l'eau frémissante pendant 30 min à 1 heure, têtes, peaux, arêtes, parures de poissons. Le fumet entre dans la composition de nombreuses sauces.

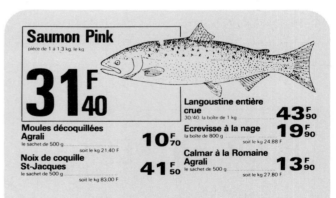

Saumon Pink
pièce de 1 à 1,3 kg, le kg

31 F 40

Moules décoquillées Agrali
le sachet de 500 g
soit le kg 21.40 F
10 F 70

Noix de coquille St-Jacques
le sachet de 500 g
soit le kg 83.00 F
41 F 50

Langoustine entière crue
30/40 la boîte de 1 kg
43 F 90

Ecrevisse à la nage
la boîte de 800 g
soit le kg 24.88 F
19 F 90

Calmar à la Romaine Agrali
le sachet de 500 g
soit le kg 27.80 F
13 F 90

E28

Name three different types of seafood or fish on sale here.

Chapter 7
Les services publics

On ne peut pas éviter les services publics à l'étranger, soit quand on passe à la douane, soit quand on veut téléphoner ou envoyer des cartes postales, soit quand on veut toucher un chèque de voyages. Cette section vous aidera à vous débrouiller!

A   Les services en général

Here are some signs concerning public services in France.

La Poste
Théâtre
Sécurité Sociale
Recette des Finances
Gendarmerie
S.N.C.F.

Syndicat d'Initiative	60m
Commissariat	600m
Sous-Préfecture	
Hôtel des Arcades à 250m	
Autres hôtels	

E1
Would you take the road to the left or to the right if you wanted to go to:

1 the railway station?

2 the tourist office?

3 the social security office?

4 the post office?

E2
If you had a cash card for this bank, why would this sign be of use to you?

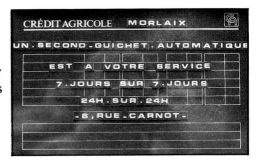

POUR ENTRER

1– SONNER

2– ATTENDRE DECLIC

3– TIRER–ENTRER

E3
How do you get into this bank?

TOILETTES

pour entrer :

le voyant libre est allumé

• introduire une pièce de 1 franc

• la porte s'ouvre et se referme automatiquement

• ces toilettes chauffées sont nettoyées à chaque utilisation

E4
How do you operate this public service? What is special about it?

E5
If you wanted to see the town hall and go to the post office, which direction would you take?

SYNDICAT D'INITIATIVE
TOURIST AGENCY
TAPISSERIE
MUSÉE
CATHÉDRALE
HÔTEL DE VILLE
POSTE
POLICE
GARE

E6

You see this local radio sticker on a car.

1 Why would this station be useful to you if you wanted to go fishing at sea?

2 Between what times could you tune in to this radio station?

RADIO CORSAIRE
96.3 Mhz

MÉTÉO MARINE et HORAIRES DES MARÉES

STEREO

Tous les jours
9 h - 18 h

☏ (98) 63.43.21

96.3Mhz
Z.I.de Kérivin St.Martin-des-Champs

E7

The local newspaper publishes a list of phone numbers for various services.

LISTE DES SERVICES

Syndicat d'Initiative, Allées de la République	65.41.06.40
Mairie, ouverture 9 h à 12 h et 13 h à 17 h 30	65.41.05.37
Sous-préfecture	65.41.00.08
Gendarmerie	65.41.00.17
Pompiers	65.41.00.18
Hôpital, Avenue Pasteur	65.41.01.04
SNCF, gare	65.41.02.19
Météorologie, station	65.41.00.14
Avertissements agricoles	65.41.14.34
P.T.T., Place du Général-de-Gaulle	65.41.00.24
E.D.F., 42, bd Galiot-de-Genouillac	65.41.01.06
Grottes de Caugnac	65.41.18.02
Presbytère, 4, rue Cardinal-Farimé	65.41.12.90
Crédit Lyonnais, Place de la Libération	65.41.04.26
Bibliothèque au Syndicat d'Initiative	65.41.06.40

Which number would you dial to:

1 find out about local weather conditions?

2 report a fire?

3 ask for further information on the town?

4 report a stolen article?

5 find out about train times?

P

a) Une station de météorologie, à quoi sert-elle?

b) A quoi sert un hôpital? Une station de pompiers?

c) Connaissez-vous bien les numéros en français? Lisez à haute voix les numéros qu'on doit composer pour les Grottes de Caugnac et la bibliothèque.

Soissons

La journée

TOURISME CULTURE - LOISIRS

L'UNION-HAVAS-VOYAGES. — Billets et réservations, 15, rue du Commerce, tél. 53.22.74.
BUREAU MUNICIPAL DU TOURISME. — A Saint-Jean-des-Vignes, tél. 53.17.37.
SYNDICAT D'INITIATIVE. — Place de la République, de 15 à 18 heures, tél. 53.08.27.
BIBLIOTHÈQUE MUNICIPALE. — De 13 h 30 à 18 heures.
MUSÉE. — Visites de 10 à 12 heures et de 14 à 17 heures.
M.J.C. — L'après-midi et le soir.
EXPOSITION DE PEINTURE. — A l'Imagerie, 9 rue du Collège.
PISCINE. — De 17 heures à 19 h 30.

PERMANENCES SOCIALES

CRÈCHE FAMILIALE. — De 8 h 30 à 9 h 30, 7, rue du Bois-Dupleix (tél. 53.22.15).
SERVICE SOCIAL FAMILIAL. — « Spécial jeunes », de 14 à 16 heures, 31, rue Anne-Morgan (tél. 53.04.52).
LA CROIX D'OR. — De 18 h 30 à 20 heures, 12, boulevard de Presles (tél. 59.27.45).
AFFAIRES SOCIALES MUNICIPALES. — Mme Moret, de 14 à 15 heures, à l'hôtel de ville.
ASSISTANTE SOCIALE. — Hôtel de ville, de 14 à 16 heures.
SERVICE SOCIAL ET DE SAUVEGARDE. — De 8 h 45 à 12 heures et de 14 à 17 heures, 20, rue Richebourg.

INFORMATIONS — RENSEIGNEMENTS

C.C.I.A. — De 8 à 12 heures et de 13 h 30 à 17 h 30, 15, rue Georges-Muzart (tél. 53.01.87).
C.S. DES FAMILLES. — De 17 à 19 heures, au Centre social Saint-Crépin.
F.J.T. — De 14 à 16 heures, 20, rue Mahieu.
LOISIRS 3. — De 10 à 12 heures et de 14 h 30 à 17 heures, 31, rue Anne-Morgan.

DE JOUR ET DE NUIT

POLICE-SECOURS. — Tél. 17.
SAPEURS-POMPIERS. — Tél. 18.
GENDARMERIE. — Tél. 53.12.85.
CENTRE HOSPITALIER. — Tél. 59.11.02.
POMPES FUNÈBRES. — Tél. 53.07.24 ou 59.36.17.
TAXIS. — Tél. 53.63.96, 53.32.09 et 53.32.98.

LES CINÉMAS

CLOVIS I. — 21 heures : « Tendres cousines ».
CLOVIS II. — 21 heures : « Terreur extra-terrestre ».
CLOVIS III. — 21 heures : « Inspecteur la Bavure ».
CLUB. — 21 heures : « Un drôle de flic ».
VOX. — 21 heures : « Animatrices pour couples déficients ». (interdit aux moins de 18 ans).

E8

You are trying to decide what to do in Soissons, your pen-friend's town. You want to visit the museum, go for a swim in the swimming pool, get some brochures from the tourist office, browse in the library, and see a film in the cinema, if possible. You will have from 3 p.m. till 7 p.m. to do what you want. Draw up an efficient timetable giving reasons for your order of doing things.

E9

You have some cassettes of English pop music to sell, and you wish to place an advertisement in the next edition of *'Le furet'*, the local free newspaper.

1 Name four ways in which an advertisement can be placed in *'Le furet'*.

2 How much does it cost to insert an advertisement?

3 How can payment be made?

4 When is the deadline for placing an advertisement in the next issue?

P

Composez une annonce pour le prochain numéro du «Furet».

B A la banque

E10

It is 6.15 p.m. on a Saturday, can you use this bank? If not when is the earliest you can change some money?

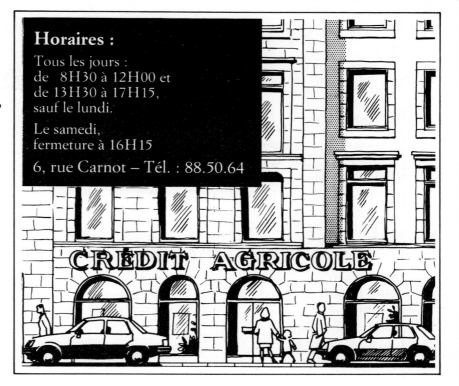

Horaires :

Tous les jours :
de 8H30 à 12H00 et
de 13H30 à 17H15,
sauf le lundi.

Le samedi,
fermeture à 16H15

6, rue Carnot – Tél. : 88.50.64

CRÉDIT AGRICOLE

E11

You need to change some travellers' cheques, and you consult this list of banks in and around Morlaix.

- **Fermeture habituelle :** dimanche et lundi. Mais le lundi des banques sont ouvertes à Saint-Pol-de-Léon, à Roscoff et à Guerlesquin.

- **Fermeture exceptionnelle les jours fériés :**

Fête du Travail	: Du mardi 30 avril après-midi au mercredi 1er Mai
Armistice 1945	: Du mardi 7 Mai après-midi au mercredi 8 Mai
Ascension	: Du mercredi 15 après-midi au jeudi 16 Mai
Pentecôte	: Du samedi 25 au lundi 27 Mai
Fête Nationale	: Le samedi 13 Juillet après-midi
Assomption	: Du mercredi 14 après-midi au jeudi 15 Août
Armistice 1918	: Lundi 11 Novembre
Noël	: Du mardi 24 après-midi au mercredi 25 Décembre
Jour de l'An	: Du mardi 31 Décembre après-midi au mercredi 1er Janvier

- **Change : en dehors des heures d'ouverture des banques**
  - à l'Hôtel d'Europe : 1, Rue d'Aiguillon, Morlaix, Tél. 98. 62.11.99
  - à la Gare Maritime de Roscoff : Crédit Agricole en saison
  - chez certains commerçants : Ex CIM à Morlaix
  - dans certains bureaux de poste.

List which of the following statements are true.

1 All banks are closed on Saturdays.

2 A bank at Roscoff is open on Mondays.

3 Banks are closed on Whit Monday.

4 The 13 July is a Sunday according to this leaflet.

5 The banks are closed longer over Christmas than in the New Year.

6 You cannot change money in post offices.

CRÉDIT AGRICOLE

CAISSE RÉGIONALE DU FINISTÈRE
7, Route du Loch   29101 QUIMPER

ACHAT DE DEVISES A LA CLIENTÈLE   041967

☒ **PAR CAISSE**

Pièce d'identité : *Passeport*
Nº : *L 378608 B*
Date de délivrance : *14 fev 1979*
Lieu de délivrance : *Liverpool*

M. *SYMONS. Jancher.*

Angleterre

ORIGINE *29 JB*

NUMÉRO DE COMPTE D A V

☐ **PAR DÉPOTS A VUE**
(Billets de Banque et Travellers Chèques uniquement)

NOUS VOUS ACHETONS

BILLETS DE BANQUE	DEVISE	NBRE	QUOTITÉ	MONTANT

COURS ___ CONTREVALEUR ___ COMMISSION – ▶

TRAVELLERS CHÈQUES	NBRE	QUOTITÉ	MONTANT
DEVISE *£ STERL*	*2*	*50*	*100*
Établ. Émetteur : *St. Chartered*			
Nos : *505302 et 303*			
			100

COURS *11,49* CONTREVALEUR *1149,00* COMMISSION *–7,60* ▶ *1141,40*

EUROCHÈQUES	DEVISE	Nº CHÈQUES	MONTANT
Nº Carte :			
Établ. Émetteur :			

COURS ___ CONTREVALEUR ___ COMMISSION – ▶

CLIENT *S. Symons*   B. P.

DATE OPÉRATION *24 07 84*

TOTAL GÉNÉRAL *1141,40*

Ex. 1 - CLIENT

ET.01200 -   05-82

E12

When you change money in a French bank you may get a receipt like this.

1 What was given as a means of identification?

2 How much money did the customer change from travellers' cheques to French francs?

3 How much commission was charged?

4 On what date was the money changed?

5 How much did the customer receive?

P

a) Imaginez que vous êtes dans une banque française. Vous êtes le/la client(e) qui veut changer des chèques de voyage, votre partenaire est l'employé(e). Jouez la scène.

b) Au cours du change actuel, combien de francs recevrez-vous si vous changez £20?

C   A la poste

... expédier vos envois

• **Les timbres-poste:** vous pouvez vous les procurer dans les bureaux de poste (où on vend également des aérogrammes), les bureaux de tabac ou les distributeurs automatiques jaunes disposés sur la façade de certains bureaux de poste.

• **Les boîtes de dépôt des lettres:** vous les trouverez à l'extérieur et à l'intérieur des bureaux de poste et dans les lieux de fort passage du public*.

• **Paquets:** les paquets adressés à d'autres pays jusqu'à 1 kg (ou 2 kg au tarif des lettres) acceptés par les bureaux de poste doivent porter extérieurement une étiquette verte de douane. Si vous voulez réaliser un envoi rationnel et pratique, utilisez les emballages préformés mis en vente dans les bureaux de poste.

• **Colis postaux:** ils sont acceptés au bureau de poste principal de chaque localité:
– "Avion" jusqu'à 10 ou 20 kg suivant la destination.
– "Voie de surface" jusqu'à 5 kg et jusqu'à un certain format (au-delà ils peuvent être confiés à la SNCF).

• **Service Posteclair:** national et international à votre disposition dans 500 points réseau PTT, si vous désirez envoyer tout document urgent (plans, graphiques, tableaux, schémas...).

E13

The French Post Office publishes several leaflets about the services it offers. You browse through one, since you have a birthday card and present to send from France to your mother.

1 Where, apart from post offices, can you buy stamps?

2 What do you have to complete when sending a small parcel from France to another country?

E14

For a surprise, you wish to telephone your mother on her birthday. Your pen-friend's family, however, have no phone in the house. You consult this extract from the Post Office leaflet.

1 If you can't find a public phone booth in the street, where else can you telephone from?

2 As it is a Saturday, when is the cheapest time to ring England?

3 Is there a French equivalent of English 'phone cards'?

Vous désirez téléphoner...

Utilisez l'une des 167 000 cabines placées dans les lieux publics:
– soit avec une TELECARTE qui vous permettra de téléphoner sans souci et sans monnaie à partir d'une cabine équipée d'un publiphone à cartes. Ces télécartes, de 50 et 120 unités s'achètent dans les bureaux de poste, guichets SNCF et revendeurs agréés reconnaissables à leur affichette "TELECARTE" (*).
– soit avec des pièces de monnaie (page 15).
Vous pouvez aussi vous adresser au guichet téléphone d'un de nos 17 000 bureaux de poste (*). Si vous appelez à partir de votre hôtel, d'un café ou d'un restaurant, votre facturation risque d'être supérieure à la taxe officielle (maximum 30 %).

Tarifs réduits:
– du lundi au samedi
de 20 h à 10 h pour le Canada et les Etats-Unis.
de 21 h 30 à 8 h pour Israël et les pays africains d'expression française.
de 23 h à 8 h pour l'Algérie, le Maroc et la Tunisie.
de 23 h à 9 h 30 pour le Portugal.
– du lundi au vendredi, de 21 h 30 à 8 h et le samedi, de 14 h à 18 h pour les autres pays de la CEE, la Suisse, l'Autriche et la Yougoslavie.
– les dimanches et jours fériés: toute la journée pour ces mêmes pays.

... télégraphier

Vous pouvez déposer votre texte au guichet d'un bureau de poste, ou le téléphoner depuis votre hôtel.

... recevoir votre courrier

• Votre adresse en France comporte un numéro de code à 5 chiffres; n'oubliez pas de le communiquer à vos correspondants.
• Le courrier adressé en "poste restante", dans une ville ayant plusieurs bureaux, est, sauf précision, disponible au bureau principal. Le retrait d'une correspondance donne lieu à paiement d'une taxe.
• Pour toute opération de retrait de courrier ou d'argent au guichet, on vous demandera votre passeport ou une pièce d'identité, pensez-y!

E15

You decide that you would like to travel around France on a touring holiday. You could use the *poste restante* section of the Post Office to receive mail. What do you need to do to obtain your letters?

E16

Your pen-friend is a keen stamp collector and you are amazed at his collection of modern French stamps. You wonder how he could have got hold of such a collection. He shows you details of a scheme run by the Post Office. Can you briefly explain it?

Pour constituer votre collection de timbres-poste, les PTT vous proposent un moyen simple et efficace:

LA RESERVATION AU BUREAU DE POSTE

Pour vous garantir la continuité de votre collection, pour vous éviter de nombreux déplacements et des pertes de temps, les PTT vous proposent de faire réserver vos timbres par le bureau de poste de votre choix.
Cette facilité concerne tous les timbres-poste de France.

Modalités pratiques

• Pour réserver vos timbres, il vous suffit de remplir un bulletin de réservation et de le remettre au guichet du bureau de votre choix.

• Celui-ci ouvre un dossier à votre nom et vous réserve systématiquement les timbres-poste que vous désirez, au fur et à mesure des émissions.

• Vous avez la possibilité de faire varier le nombre de timbres «réservés» selon leur catégorie (exemple: série artistique: 10 exemplaires, timbres-poste avec surtaxe: 5 exemplaires).
Dans toute la mesure du possible, votre bureau de poste pourra satisfaire également les services particuliers (découpage, bord de feuille, coin daté, etc.).

• Quand vous le voulez, mais au moins une fois par trimestre, vous allez au bureau de poste retirer vos timbres réservés contre paiement de la somme correspondante.

• Si vous désirez modifier les caractéristiques de votre réservation, et en cas de changement d'adresse ou d'état civil, informez sans retard votre bureau de poste: cela vous garantira le bon fonctionnement de votre réservation.

• Si vous décidez d'y mettre fin, faites immédiatement connaître votre résiliation par simple lettre adressée au receveur de votre bureau de poste.

E17

In cases of emergency you may have to send a telegram. Can you work out how to fill in this form?

➤ Nº 698	TÉLÉGRAMME	Étiquettes		Timbre à date	Nº d'appel : ....
					INDICATIONS DE TRANSMISSION

Ligne de numérotation

ZCZC   Nº télégraphique   **Taxe principale.**   Nº de la ligne du P.V. : ....

Ligne pilote   Taxes accessoires   Bureau de destination   Département ou Pays

Total . .

Bureau d'origine	Mots	Date	Heure	Mentions de service

Services spéciaux demandés :
(voir au verso)

Inscrire en **CAPITALES** l'adresse complète (rue, nº bloc, bâtiment, escalier, etc...), le texte et la signature (une lettre par case ; **laisser une case blanche entre les mots**).

Nom et adresse

TEXTE et éventuellement signature très lisible

728678 Y - Cy, Paris - 7/80.

Pour accélérer la remise des télégrammes indiquer le cas échéant, le numéro de téléphone (1) ou de télex du destinataire
TF _____ TLX _____

Pour avis en cas de non remise, indiquer le nom et l'adresse de l'expéditeur (2) :

1 Does the total number of words used have to be stated?

2 Is a postage stamp necessary?

3 How should you fill in the address and message?

4 Why are you advised to fill in your own name and address in the bottom right-hand corner?

4.200.000 personnes de 123 nationalités : telle est la population étrangère en France en 1983. Les principales communautés sont les suivantes : Portugais 860.000, Algériens 815.000, Italiens 450.000, Marocains 445.000, Espagnols 412.000, Tunisiens 195.000, Turcs 118.000, Pays Sud du Sahara 115.000.

E18
According to this article, from which continent do the majority of immigrants come?

You notice that French letter boxes are all very much the same.

This leaflet from the Post Office helps to explain why.

POURQUOI DES BOITES AUX LETTRES NORMALISEES ?

Vous avez déjà découvert votre courrier mouillé ou abîmé ? Des journaux ou des paquets vous ont été volés ?

C'est que votre boîte aux lettres est trop petite, peu étanche ou ne ferme pas...

Pour apporter une solution à ces mauvaises surprises, la Poste vous invite à vous équiper de nouvelles boîtes aux lettres aux normes PTT qui assurent à votre courrier sécurité et protection.

Les boîtes aux lettres normalisées, grâce à leurs dimensions et à l'ouverture totale de la porte, permettent le dépôt de toutes vos correspondances même volumineuses : journaux, revues, petits paquets... et vous évitent le cas échéant de vous déplacer au bureau de poste.

Pour protéger votre correspondance des actes de vandalisme, ces boîtes sont équipées de serrures de sécurité à combinaisons multiples agréées par les PTT : seul votre facteur dispose d'un passe-partout pour y déposer votre courrier.

Ces boîtes aux lettres normalisées sont obligatoires pour les constructions bâties après 1979.

COMMENT VOUS EQUIPER ?

– Si vous habitez un immeuble collectif :
Adressez-vous à votre syndic : c'est à lui de faire le nécessaire. Tous les renseignements pourront lui être fournis par la Direction Départementale des Postes en ce qui concerne les "batteries" de boîtes aux lettres.

– Si vous habitez en maison individuelle :
• Vous pouvez acheter les boîtes aux lettres normalisées chez les quincailliers, menuisiers ou grandes surfaces spécialisées (bricolage, jardinage...).

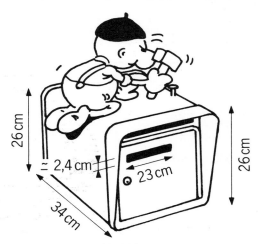

• Si vous êtes bricoleur, vous pouvez la fabriquer vous-même en respectant bien les bonnes dimensions (dimensions intérieures : 26 cm x 26 cm x 34 cm) et en posant une serrure agréée PTT que vous trouverez chez les revendeurs de boîtes.

1 What reasons are given for introducing standardised letter boxes?

2 Name three kinds of mail which can be delivered in a standardised letter box.

3 What precaution has been taken against vandalism?

4 The building you are staying in was built in 1947. Is it required to have such a letter box?

5 Where can you buy these letter boxes from?

6 What must you do if you make one yourself?

D A la douane

Your pen-friend's family have taken you on a day trip to Spain. On your return to France, you all have to pass through customs. Here is a leaflet that they have kept in their car which you glance through whilst waiting in the queue.

marchandises

1 A votre retour, les marchandises contenues dans vos bagages personnels sont admises sans rien payer à la douane dès lors que leur valeur ne dépasse pas les limites suivantes :

VOYAGEURS AGÉS DE	Marchandises de la CEE (2) TVA comprise	Marchandises des autres pays
15 ans et plus	**2 000 F** (4)	**300 F**
Moins de 15 ans	**400 F**	**150 F**

Dans ces limites, pour les achats d'appareils (photo, cinéma, magnéto-phones, transistors, électroménager, etc.) vous devez vous faire établir une carte de libre circulation par le bureau frontière des Douanes françaises, **cette carte ne pourra pas être établie après votre retour.**
Au-delà de ces limites (tableau ci-dessus) vous devez déclarer les mar-chandises achetées à l'étranger (même dans un pays de la CEE).
Vous paierez des droits de douane, éventuellement des taxes et la TVA, ou la TVA seulement sur les marchandises achetées dans la CEE.
ATTENTION : Les sommes indiquées au tableau ci-dessus ne peuvent être cumulées pour l'achat d'un même objet.
Exemple : Un groupe, ou une famille de quatre personnes ne peut rapporter un appareil d'une valeur de 8 000 F [4 × 2 000] (4).
L'objet devra être déclaré et vous acquitterez les droits et taxes, sans aucun abattement.
Vous rapportez plusieurs articles (achats ou cadeaux) : seront admis sans paiement les objets dont la valeur cumulée ne dépasse pas le montant indiqué au tableau ci-dessus.

2 **En plus**, vous pouvez rapporter les marchandises ci-dessous dans les limites suivantes.

MARCHANDISES		VOYAGEURS EN PROVENANCE DE	
		La C.E.E. (2)	Autres pays (3)
TABACS (1)	Cigarettes	**300** pièces	**200** pièces
	ou Cigarillos	**150** pièces	**100** pièces
	ou Cigares	**75** pièces	**50** pièces
	ou Tabac à fumer	**400** g	**250** g
et BOISSONS ALCOOLISÉES (1)	Vins de table	**4** litres	**2** litres
	et Boissons titrant plus de 22°	**1,5** litre	**1** litre
	ou titrant 22° ou moins	**3** litres	**2** litres
et PARFUMS	Parfums	**75** g	**50** g
	et Eaux de toilette	**37,5** centilitres	**25** centilitres
et CAFÉ	Café	**750** g	**500** g
	ou Extraits et essences de café	**300** g	**200** g
et THÉ	Thé	**150** g	**100** g
	ou Extraits et essences de thé	**60** g	**40** g

(1) *Seuls les voyageurs âgés de plus de 17 ans ont droit à ces quantités.*

1 What is the total value of goods your pen-friend's parents can each bring back into France from Spain, which is a Common Market country?

2 What can your pen-friend's sister aged eight , bring back?

3 If someone in the group doesn't use his allowance, can someone else use it for him?

4 How much coffee can your pen-friend bring back?

P

a) Avez-vous jamais passé par la douane? Où? Quand?

b) Imaginez un dialogue entre un douanier et un touriste qui semble cacher quelque chose de soupçonneux dans sa valise. Jouez la scène avec un partenaire.

E Au commissariat

MINISTÈRE DE L'INTÉRIEUR
PRÉFECTURE DE POLICE

RÉCÉPISSÉ DE DÉCLARATION
DE PERTE OU DE VOL DE PIÈCES D'IDENTITÉ

SERVICE	☐ **PERTE** ☒ **VOL** (1)
	DÉSIGNATION DES DOCUMENTS
	500 frs francais
	clefs voiture
Tél. :	carte EUROCHEQUE LLOYDS BANK
	carte retrait VISA B BARCLAY
(CACHET)	(Banque BARCLAY) factures

Imp. S T 3605 5-70

DATE 11 janvier 1981

DÉCLARATION REÇUE CE JOUR DE :

NOM	MME SYMONS
NOM DE JEUNE FILLE	EMMERTON
PRÉNOMS	Sandra
DATE DE NAISSANCE	2 juin 1949 à Plymouth GB
LIEU DE NAISSANCE	
ADRESSE	7 tregellas Road Mullion à CORNWALL

L'article 154 du Code Pénal punit d'un emprisonnement de trois mois à deux ans et d'une amende de 500 F à 5.000 F quiconque se sera fait délivrer indûment ou aura tenté de se faire délivrer indûment... un récépissé... soit en faisant de fausses déclarations, soit en prenant un faux nom ou une fausse qualité, soit en fournissant de faux renseignements. Les mêmes peines seront appliquées à celui qui aura fait usage d'un tel document.

DÉCLARANT	SIGNATURE	RÉDACTEUR	NOM MENDEZ	GRADE inspecteur
			SIGNATURE	

N.B. - En cas de vol ou de perte de pièces administratives ou d'identité la présente attestation ne peut être utilisée qu'en vue de la délivrance de duplicata et ne saurait remplacer la pièce elle-même.

(1) Cocher la case correspondante.

E21

You no doubt understand that you should insure your belongings before travelling abroad. If anything is lost or stolen you have to go to the police station and obtain a form like the one on the left in order to make an insurance claim.

1 Were the objects lost or stolen?

2 Name at least two things declared missing.

3 What warning does this notice carry for those who have given false information?

E22
Can you explain this pun?

E23

Here is an eye-catching title of a newspaper article. See how much of this item you can understand.

1 When did this incident take place?

2 What does the reporter say the man looked like?

3 What did the loaf of bread conceal?

4 How much money was involved?

5 What did the authorities wish he had left behind?

Hold-up à la baguette

NI BÉRET ni journal sous le bras, seulement une baguette croustillante à la main ; l'homme, âgé d'environ 25 ans, qui rentrait dans une agence du Crédit agricole de Lyon, jeudi, ne se distinguait en rien du Français moyen. Mais l'homme a rompu le pain qui dissimulait... une carabine. Plus riche de 25 000 F, le malfaiteur est reparti à pied, négligeant de semer des miettes de pain. Les enquêteurs ne disposaient donc d'aucune piste.

P

a) Qu'est-ce que c'est, un malfaiteur? Et un cambrioleur?

b) Imaginez et racontez à votre partenaire, une petite histoire qui s'intitule: «Incident à la banque».

Here is an article about a raid on a Post Office train.

Trois blessés dans un hold-up à Arles

LES TRUANDS RATENT LE TRAIN

*Puissamment armés, une dizaine de gangters ont été contraints
d'abandonner leur butin et de prendre la fuite après avoir attaqué un convoi postal*

COMMENCEE selon les meilleurs scénarios du genre, l'attaque du train postal 5038 Marseille-Lyon, entre Arles et Saint-Martin-de-Crau (Bouches-du-Rhône), s'est terminée lamentablement hier matin par la fuite sanglante d'une dizaine de malfrats violents et dangereux qui ont été contraints d'abandonner leur butin.

Hier matin, il était 0 h 40 environ, quand une dizaine d'hommes puissamment armés de revolvers et de mitraillettes, le visage dissimulé par des cagoules, ont arrêté le train postal en bloquant un signal par des barres de fer. Obéissant au « rouge » qui lui ordonne de stopper, le mécanicien a en effet immobilisé son convoi à hauteur de Raphèle-lès-Arles, dans une zone marécageuse.

Les truands, installés dans trois véhicules volés, se sont alors précipités sur le conducteur qu'ils ont contraint à descendre de sa motrice en le molestant. Communiquant entre eux par talky-walkies, ils se sont ensuite attaqués à plusieurs des huit wagons postaux dans lesquels travaillaient une quarantaine d'agents des PTT. Brisant les vitres, ils ont pénétré dans les voitures en blessant deux agents à coups de crosse, avant de s'emparer de vingt-trois sacs postaux contenant des valeurs déclarées, qu'ils ont transportés dans leurs véhicules.

Mais, lorsqu'ils se sont apprêtés à prendre la fuite, ils sont tombés sur un fourgon de gendarmerie qu'un témoin, intrigué par l'arrêt du train en pleine campagne, avait alerté. Les gangsters ont alors révélés leur véritable visage : celui de dangereux malfrats. Ils n'ont en effet pas hésité à mitrailler le fourgon « Trafic » des policiers avant de s'enfuir à pied, abandonnant la totalité de leur butin. Onze impacts de balles de gros calibre ont été relevés sur le véhicule des gendarmes.

A travers champs, les truands ont ensuite réussi à atteindre la RN 113 Arles-Salon où ils ont tenté d'arrêter une voi-

Le commando n'a pas hésité à molester le mécanicien de la motrice ainsi que deux agents PTT. (Photo AFP.)

ture, mais sans succès. Ils ont alors ressorti l'artillerie pour tirer sur un second véhicule dont le conducteur a été atteint d'une balle à la mâchoire. M. Serge Hermabessière, trente et un ans, a été conduit à l'hôpital d'Arles, où ses jours ne sont pas en danger.

Profitant de la confusion créée par l'accident du véhicule de M. Hermabessière, les malfaiteurs se sont emparés de quatre voitures à bord desquelles ils ont pris la fuite en direction de Lançon-de-

Provence. Un important dispositif policier était mis en place, mais seule, une 505 devait être interceptée peu après vingt kilomètres de Marseille, son conducteur réussissant à fuir à pied. Les enquêteurs du SRPJ de Marseille, à qui l'enquête a été confiée, sont convaincus qu'il s'agissait d'un des agresseurs du train.

Depuis le début de 1985, c'est la cinquième attaque de train qui se déroule dans la région, la dernière en date étant celle d'un convoi de messageries de la

Banque de France dans la nuit du 11 au 12 décembre. Dans un communiqué rendu public hier, le syndicat CGT-PTT de la Méditerranée a estimé « qu'en refusant les moyens nécessaires afin que le personnel des PTT puisse assumer ses fonctions en toute sécurité et en détournant les forces de police de leur mission première, la protection des biens et des personnes, les pouvoirs publics et l'administration portaient une lourde responsabilité » dans l'agression d'Arles.

L'HUMANITÉ/VENDREDI 22 AOUT 1986 - 13

1 How many robbers were involved in the raid?

2 How did they stop the train?

3 How did they get in the coaches?

4 What was their goal?

5 How had they planned their getaway? What problem did they encounter?

6 What is the reporter's attitude to the subsequent conduct of the gang?

7 How did they make their escape?

8 According to the Post Office worker's union, where can blame be laid for such attacks?

Chapter 8
La santé et le bien-être

Imaginez que vous tombez malade en France. Vous recevrez des ordonnances, des conseils de médecins et des médicaments en plusieurs formes. Ce chapitre vous montre une série de papiers, de panneaux, et de médicaments. Comment vous débrouiller? On va voir!

A Les maladies

Here are some important signs relating to your welfare abroad.

La Poste	80 m
Théâtre	150 m
Sécurité Sociale	200 m
Recette des Finances	200 m
Centre Hospitalier Général	
Gendarmerie	

E1

If you were involved in an accident,
why would this sign be of significance?

SANG = VIE!

- de 18 à 60 ans, toute personne en bonne santé peut donner son sang.

- Un intervalle de 2 mois doit être respecté entre 2 dons (les hommes peuvent donner 5 **fois par an**, les femmes 3 **fois**).

- Le volume prélevé ne représente qu'une goutte sur 14, l'organisme le reconstitue en moins de 3 **heures**.

Ne pas consommer de matières grasses avant le don, mais il est inutile de se présenter à jeun. Une collation est offerte **après le don du sang**.

E3

What does this sign encourage people to do?

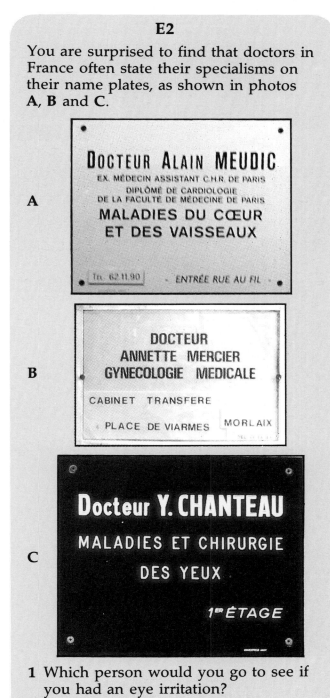

E2

You are surprised to find that doctors in France often state their specialisms on their name plates, as shown in photos **A**, **B** and **C**.

A

DOCTEUR ALAIN MEUDIC
EX. MÉDECIN ASSISTANT C.H.R. DE PARIS
DIPLÔME DE CARDIOLOGIE
DE LA FACULTÉ DE MÉDECINE DE PARIS
**MALADIES DU CŒUR
ET DES VAISSEAUX**

Tél. 62.11.90 · ENTRÉE RUE AU FIL ·

B

DOCTEUR
ANNETTE MERCIER
GYNECOLOGIE MEDICALE

CABINET TRANSFERE

· PLACE DE VIARMES   MORLAIX

C

Docteur Y. CHANTEAU

MALADIES ET CHIRURGIE

DES YEUX

1ᵉʳ ÉTAGE

1 Which person would you go to see if you had an eye irritation?

2 Where is the surgery?

Je t'écris maintenant que j'ai beaucoup de temps devant moi car figure-toi je suis malade. Je dois rester au lit toute la journée pendant au moins une semaine parce que j'ai la rougeole depuis deux jours! Aujourd'hui, j'ai un peu moins de fièvre mais hier, cela n'allait vraiment pas. En plus, j'ai un rhume et le docteur a bien peur que cela me devienne une grippe. Je n'ai vraiment pas de chance : j'ai tout attrapé en même temps. Remarque, comme ça, maman me chouchoute beaucoup et je ne vais pas à l'école... (seulement après, il va falloir que je rattrape les cours, ce qui est plus embêtant).

Bon, je vais te quitter. J'espère que cette lettre ne va pas t'apporter tous mes microbes !

E4

Your French pen-friend has just written a letter and she is suffering!

1 How long has she had measles?

2 For how long must she stay in bed?

3 What other complication does she have?

4 What will happen when she goes back to school?

E5

When you pay a doctor's bill in France, you can go to the local social security office for reimbursement. You are likely to obtain a form like the one on the right.

1 What is the name of the person who had received treatment?

2 Was she referred to a hospital?

3 How much had to be paid?

4 What piece of identification was produced?

Caisse Primaire de Sécurité Sociale du Nord-Finistère
N° 29 B - Square Marc-Sangnier - BREST

N° 2562

ACOMPTE

SUR PRESTATIONS DUES

Date : 25.7.87

ASSURÉ

N° | YH | 3 | 66 | 36 | B |

NOM SYMONS Ray

ADRESSE 7 Tregellas Rd Mullion Moon Heptor Cornwall England

BÉNÉFICIAIRE SYMONS JOANNA

Feuille de maladie du 21.7 87 au 23.7.87

Feuille de soins ou Prothèse Dentaire :

Pièce du Carnet de Maternité :

Facture Clinique :

Montant de l'acompte versé | 221 | 25 |

ch gu no 2917620
Pièce d'identité = Passeport L 150297 B

Deux Cent Vingt et Un francs
Vingt Cinq Centimes

Le présent acompte est versé sous réserve de vérification définitive des droits.

Pour le Directeur,	Pour l'Agent-Comptable,	Pour Acquit,
Cradec	95	Raymond RSymons
	AZOU ALBERT	

94

Britain considers itself to be a nation of animal lovers, and we may be blind to the more unhealthy aspects of keeping pets, as shown by this notice in a French street.

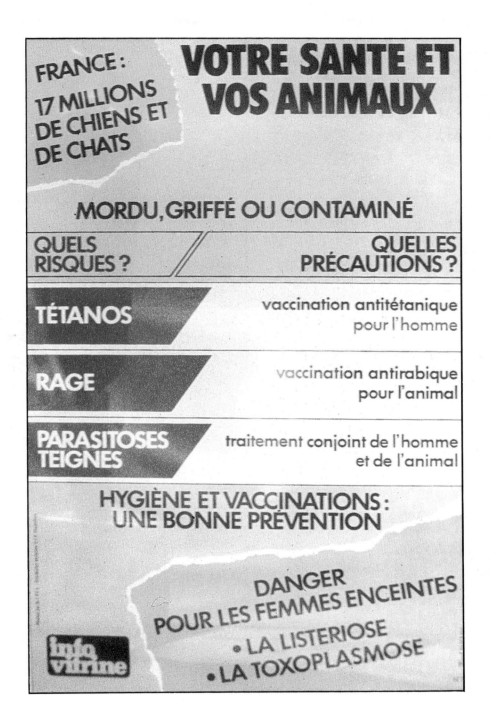

1 What, briefly, does the sign deal with?

2 How can these diseases be passed on?

P

a) Êtes-vous jamais allé(e) à un hôpital? Pourquoi?

b) Racontez ce que vous avez fait la dernière fois que vous étiez malade.

c) Avec votre partenaire, jouez la scène entre un(e) malade et un docteur.

B Les médicaments

Whilst looking for some aspirins in the medicine cupboard of your French family, you come across various medicine packets.

avibon® pommade

formule   pour 100 g

rétinol (vitamine A naturelle)   1.000.000 U.I.
excipient parfumé q.s.

visa NL 1.502

avibon® pommade

rétinol

théraPlix

tube
de 30 g

indications

plaies atones, ulcères de jambe, escarres de décubitus,
retard de cicatrisation, brûlures, engelures, gerçures,
coups de soleil, érythèmes fessiers des nouveau-nés,
dermatoses

posologie et mode d'emploi

se reporter à la notice jointe

COMPOSITION
- Phénacétine . . . . 100,00 mg
- Acide Ascorbique (Vit. C) . . . . 200,00 mg
- Chlorhydrate de quinine . . . . 72,59 mg
  (correspondant à 66 mg de chlorhydrate de quinine anhydre)
- Excipient . . . . q.s.p. un comprimé enrobé
A.M.M. n° 326 519.9   Visa Pc 326 Q 488

CÉQUINYL
100 mg

ETATS GRIPPAUX ET REFROIDISSEMENTS

ÉTATS GRIPPAUX
REFROIDISSEMENTS
COURBATURES
ÉTATS FÉBRILES ACCOMPAGNANT
LES AFFECTIONS RHINOPHARYNGÉES
LABORATOIRES LABAZ 33440 AMBARÈS FRANCE
Distribué par : LABORATOIRES LAFARGE 36000 CHATEAUROUX

Cette boîte contient un gramme de Bromure de Pinavérium.

dicetel
20 GELULES

INDICATIONS (adultes seulement) :
Colites, dyskinésies biliaires, dyskinésies œsophagiennes,
ulcères gastroduodénaux, préparation aux examens radiologiques.
POSOLOGIE : Suivant avis du médecin.
MODE D'EMPLOI :
**Avaler la gélule sans l'ouvrir avec une boisson
au milieu des repas.**   A.M.M. 319.323.5

TOPLEXIL

SIROP
CONTRE LA TOUX

FLACON DE 125 ml
VOIE ORALE

Il est recommandé de ne pas laisser les
médicaments à la portée des enfants.

Même dans les affections chroniques le
Toplexil sirop ne doit pas être administré
de façon continue.

The brand names of these medicines are listed below together with some common ailments.

	Sunburn	Stomach complaints	Colds and 'flu
Avibon			
Dicetel			
Toplexil			
Céquinyl			

Copy out the box and tick the treatment that can be used for each of the conditions mentioned.

TOTAPEN TOTAPEN

Ampicilline   Ampicilline

NOURRISSONS

MODE D'EMPLOI : introduire dans le flacon de l'eau minérale non gazeuse ou de l'eau bouillie refroidie jusqu'au trait indiqué.

Agiter à plusieurs reprises jusqu'à obtention d'un liquide homogène. Si besoin, compléter à nouveau avec de l'eau jusqu'au trait et agiter.

Le sirop obtenu se conserve une semaine à la température ordinaire.

AGITER AVANT L'EMPLOI

125 mg

POUDRE POUR SIROP

E8

Here is another label from a medicine bottle in the cupboard. List the sentences which are true about the medicine Totapen.

1 It is in tablet form.

2 It should be diluted with water.

3 It should be shaken before use.

4 It can be kept for one month at room temperature.

ÉTATS GRIPPAUX

LA RÉPONSE OSCILLOCOCCINUM®

Vous pensez avoir pris froid. Vous vous sentez fatigué. Peut-être avez-vous mal à la tête, des frissons, des courbatures...? Vous couvez quelque chose. Vous avez peur d'attraper la grippe.

OSCILLOCOCCINUM® est indiqué pour les états grippaux. Il sera d'autant plus efficace et rapide d'action qu'il sera utilisé dès les premiers symptômes.

BIEN PASSER L'HIVER

Il est conseillé de prendre une dose, matin et soir, pendant 1 à 3 jours.

On peut aussi le prendre de façon préventive à raison d'une dose par semaine pendant la période d'exposition grippale.

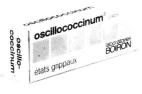

oscillococcinum®
PRÉPARATION HOMÉOPATHIQUE

---

théralène
pectoral

sirop composé
flacon de
150 ml

théraPlix

posologie

se conformer aux prescriptions du médecin traitant

adultes :
2 à 3 cuillerées à soupe par jour

enfants :
(à partir de 30 mois)
1 cuillerée à café
à 3 cuillerées à soupe
par jour
suivant l'âge.

indications

toux rebelles, trachéites, laryngites, coqueluche, bronchites aiguës et chroniques, complications pulmonaires de la grippe, pneumopathies, emphysème, dyspnées.

E10

If you are prescribed medicines in France you must make sure you understand the instructions!

1 Does this medicine come in tablet form?

2 Should this medicine be taken internally?

3 How many tablespoonfuls may an adult take a day?

4 Is this medicine suitable for children under two and a half years old?

5 Can this medicine be used to treat a range of throat infections and coughs?

E9

Here are details of a treatment that can be bought from a chemist.

1 Can you take this medicine to soothe muscle pain?

2 Would this medicine ease 'flu symptoms?

3 Is this medicine only effective when 'flu is diagnosed?

4 Does this packet suggest that the medicine will help you enjoy winter time?

5 May you take this product as a preventative medicine once a day?

E11

Here is a set of instructions for some tablets.

1 What is the recommended dosage for people suffering from 'flu?

2 What else is recommended during the treatment?

3 What is the longest period that you should use this drug continuously?

POSOLOGIE

- *Affections grippales :*
  Adultes : dès les premiers symptômes, 1 comprimé toutes les 4 heures.
  A partir du 2e jour, 1 comprimé 1 à 3 fois chaque jour.
  Enfants de 7 à 15 ans : 1 comprimé 1 à 3 fois par jour.

- *Refroidissements et courbatures fébriles,*
  Etats fébriles accompagnant les affections rhinopharyngées :
  1 comprimé 1 à 3 fois par jour pendant 3 jours.

MODE D'EMPLOI

Il est recommandé de boire plusieurs verres d'eau au cours de la journée pendant la durée du traitement.

MISE EN GARDE

Ce médicament contient de la phénacétine ; en cas de maladie rénale, ne pas l'utiliser sans avis médical.

PRECAUTIONS D'EMPLOI

- *L'utilisation abusive et prolongée des médicaments à base de phénacétine peut entraîner des lésions rénales graves et irréversibles.*
- *Ne pas dépasser la posologie journalière indiquée sauf avis médical.*
- *Ne pas utiliser ce médicament plus de 30 jours sans avis médical.*
- *Ne pas laisser à la portée des enfants.*

PRESENTATION
Etui de 12 comprimés enrobés.

A.M.M. N° 326 519.9
Visa Pc 325 Q 488

LABAZ *Laboratoires LABAZ 33440 AMBARÈS FRANCE*

SANOGYL enfant

FORMULE :

Acétarsol sodique	0,56 g
Monofluorophosphate de sodium	0,76 g
Phosphate dicalcique stabilisé	42,50 g
Excipient aromatisé à la fraise des bois q.s.p.	100,00 g

MODE D'EMPLOI :

Il est recommandé de pratiquer le brossage des dents après chaque repas, soit trois fois par jour, en tous cas après le petit déjeuner et le dîner. La durée moyenne du brossage doit être de UNE minute environ, en laissant la mousse au contact des dents et de la muqueuse buccale pendant environ TROIS minutes avant le rinçage de la bouche à l'eau froide ou tiède.

CONTRE-INDICATION :

Aucune contre-indication n'a été signalée.

PRÉSENTATION :

Tube de 60 g

Le **SANOGYL ENFANT** est vendu exclusivement en Pharmacie sous le numéro d'Autorisation de Mise sur le Marché :
A.M.M. n° 315-742-3

LABORATOIRES H. VILLETTE
5, rue Paul-Barruel - 75015 PARIS

E12

Regular brushing of teeth is a prerequisite for good health. Here is a wrapper for some special toothpaste.

1 Who is likely to use this sort of toothpaste?

2 Where can it be purchased?

3 What flavour is it?

4 How often should it be used?

5 How long should be spent on each brushing on average?

C La santé

French people are, like us, becoming increasingly health conscious. Here are some extracts from a magazine article about vitamin C.

Santé.

Manger mieux

Vitamine C au quotidien

Une alimentation riche en fruits et en légumes comble nos besoins quotidiens en vitamine C. Cette vitamine peut se dégrader facilement. Sachez la découvrir et la conserver.

CLAUDE JOUAIRE.

1 Où la trouver

● **Les fruits.** Ils sont la meilleure source de vitamine C. Les agrumes viennent en tête précédés du cassis (en saison). Pour 100 g, le cassis apporte 150 mg de vitamine C ; les citrons 50 à 60 mg ; les oranges 50 mg ; les mandarines 40 mg.

● **Les légumes.** Crus, ils gardent leur vitamine C, mais leur teneur varie. Par exemple, toujours pour 100 g, le chou vert contient 200 mg de vitamine C ; les épinards 50 mg ; le chou-fleur, les poireaux seulement 30 mg. Pensez à parsemer vos plats de quelques brins de persil haché, très riche en vitamine C (pour les autres légumes voir le tableau). Pour subvenir à vos besoins journaliers (la vitamine C n'est pas stockée par l'organisme), consommez chaque jour deux fruits entiers ou pressés en jus, un légume cru et un légume cuit et variez-les.

E13

1 Which fruit is the best source of vitamin C?

2 Which of the following vegetables should you eat to obtain the maximum vitamin C?
   a) Cauliflower
   b) Green cabbage
   c) Spinach
   d) Leeks

3 How can you ensure that you are receiving the right amount of vitamin C daily?

E14

Here is a list of vegetables that contain vitaminC. Below are four drawings of some of these vegetables.
What are their French names?

1   2

3   4

Teneur en vitamine C
en mg pour 100 g d'aliments
Légumes

Persil : 200 mg
Chou vert : 200 mg
Chou rouge : 70 mg
Chou blanc : 50 mg
P. de terre nouv. : 40 mg
Tomates : 38 mg
Haricots verts : 19 mg
Radis : 18 mg
Choucroute : 16 mg
Laitue : 10 mg
Salsifis : 9 mg
Concombre : 8 mg

E15

The article concludes with advice on how to obtain the highest amount of vitamin C in your cooking.

Are these statements true or false?

1 You should store vegetables in the bottom of your fridge.

2 You should peel vegetables well in advance.

3 You should not soak vegetables before cooking.

4 You can recover essential vitamins and minerals by using the water from boiling vegetables at a later date.

5 Frozen vegetables and fruit contain less vitamin C than fresh ones.

2 Pour bien la garder

Attention, la vitamine C est fragile. Elle s'oxyde à l'air, « file » dans l'eau de cuisson. D'où l'importance de garder vos légumes dans le bac de votre réfrigérateur (pas plus de deux jours) et de savoir les préparer et les cuire.

● **Épluchez les crudités** à la dernière minute avec un couteau inoxydable. Accommodez-les vite, l'acidité de l'assaisonnement favorise la stabilité de la vitamine C.

● **Ne laissez pas tremper vos légumes** avant cuisson. Une partie des vitamines serait perdue.

● **Préférez la cuisson à la vapeur** (10 à 20% de perte de vitamine C) ou à l'autocuiseur, à la cuisson à grande eau qui en perd 50%.

● **Gardez le bouillon,** si vous les cuisez à l'eau, et servez-le comme entrée le soir. Vous récupérerez ainsi une bonne partie des vitamines et des sels minéraux.

● **Autre solution : l'étuvage** dans une très petite quantité d'eau qu'on laisse s'évaporer. La perte est peu importante.
Les fruits et légumes crus surgelés n'ont pas « attendu » avant leur transformation industrielle. Leur teneur en vitamine C est donc la même que celle des produits frais. En conserve, les légumes ne subissent pas une grande perte. ■

Santé.

Manger mieux

Les laitages allégés

Yaourts et fromages blancs sont d'excellents aliments pour garder la ligne. En suivant nos conseils, vous saurez mieux les choisir et vous aurez plein d'idées pour les préparer.

C. JOUAIRE

Qu'ils soient à 0% de matière grasse ou à 20%, 30%, les laitages conservent à peu près la même teneur en protéines et en calcium. Ils laisseront votre corps ferme et musclé et vos os en bon état. Seuls changent leur goût et le nombre de calories qu'ils apportent.

Peu de matière grasse

Pour guider votre choix dans les rayons des supermarchés, voici un classement des principaux laitages « minceur », en commençant par les moins caloriques.

● **Yaourt ou fromage blanc, lait fermenté à 0% de matière grasse.** Totalement écrémés, riches en eau (plus de 82% dans la plupart des fromages blancs), ils sont d'excellents « coupe-faim » naturels et se digèrent facilement. Un yaourt maigre (120 g) apporte 50 Kcal soit 7 Kcal de moins qu'un yaourt normal ;

E16
Here is the first part of another article on health matters.

1 What is the difference in the protein and calcium levels of full and low-fat milk products?

2 What specific benefits does it say these products will bring to you?

3 How many Kcalories does an ordinary yoghurt contain?

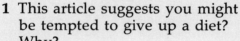

E17
When do you think this patient was having his X-ray taken?

Humour

RADIOLOGIE

BONNE ANNÉE

E18

1 This article suggests you might be tempted to give up a diet? Why?

2 What does this article advise you to drink?

3 What are you advised to eat before your evening meal?

4 What should you not do if you have a sedentary job?

5 To replace energy, what is suggested as an addition to your normal diet?

Santé

Manger mieux

Un régime en hiver

Vous suivez un régime ? Ne soyez pas tentée de l'arrêter à cause du froid. Adaptez plutôt votre nourriture à la saison et à votre mode de vie.

Pour vous réchauffer, ne cédez pas aux alcools chauds : grogs, vins... très riches en calories. Buvez plutôt des tisanes, du thé léger, des citronnades chaudes, des bouillons. Et commencez vos repas, au moins, celui du soir, avec un potage aux légumes.

Selon le mode de vie

Lorsqu'il fait moins 5°, vos besoins quotidiens en calories sont différents selon votre mode de vie.

● Si vous êtes sédentaire ou si vous travaillez dans un endroit bien chauffé, n'augmentez pas votre ration calorique mais buvez et mangez chaud.
● Si vous vous déplacez en moto, à bicyclette ou si vous marchez longtemps dans le froid, ajoutez un supplément à votre régime habituel. Un exemple : une heure de marche au froid occasionne une dépense de 200 kcal. Vous pouvez compenser cette perte en ajoutant une cuillerée à dessert d'huile (ou bien 2 mini-plaquettes de beurre allégé) et une pomme (ou bien deux morceaux de sucre) à votre ration calorique journalière.

P

a) Avez-vous jamais suivi un régime ?

b) Les régimes, pensez-vous qu'ils produisent de bons résultats ?

c) Composez un régime d'hiver à votre goût et aussi un régime d'été. (Ce menu d'hiver vous servira d'exemple, peut-être.)

Petit déjeuner
● The
● Pain grillé beurré
● Fromage blanc

Déjeuner
● Salade d'endives
● Langue de bœuf à la choucroute
● Tome à 10% de matière grasse
● Orange

Goûter
● Lait chaud au cacao amer
● 1 tartine beurrée

Dîner
● Pot-au-feu et ses légumes
● Fromage blanc
● Pomme rôtie

Le fromage constitue l'une des bases les plus nutritives et savoureuses de l'alimentation. C'est un aliment presque complet qui contient à peu près tout ce qui est nécessaire à la croissance et au développement du corps humain. Il est une source incomparable de protides et de calcium, il convient à tous les tempéraments et peut être consommé à tous les âges.

La France a la chance d'être le paradis des fromages puisqu'elle en possède plus de 365 sortes qui ont chacune leur caractéristique et leur saveur particulière.

La fromagerie française a su évoluer du stade familial et artisanal au stade industriel tout en gardant intacte ses recettes traditionnelles, sa garantie de pureté, de naturel et de gastronomie. Brillat Savarin, célèbre gastronome français, disait : "un repas sans fromage est comme une belle à qui il manque un œil".

This is an extract from a leaflet explaining the virtues of French cheeses.

1 What are the advantages of consuming cheese?

2 Can you explain Brillat Savarin's statement?

E20

If 'cleanliness is next to godliness' what do you make of this article in a French magazine?

Quatre savonnettes par an et par Français ! Chaque année, les résultats des enquêtes effectuées en France sur l'hygiène nous époustouflent. Ce n'est pas possible ! Les Français ne se lavent-ils pas ? De la même manière, 61 % des Français déclarent se laver les dents plusieurs fois par jour, on en déduit donc que 135 millions de brosses à dents devraient être vendues, alors qu'il ne s'en vend que 42 millions par an. Quelque chose cloche, mais quoi ? L'idée que l'on a de l'importance de l'hygiène probablement. Une notion qu'il vaut mieux de toute façon, sures- timer que sous-estimer. Pour sa propre santé d'abord, pour notre bien à tous ensuite...

LES MAINS

Là, il faut faire très attention. En effet, les mains, et l'on n'y pense jamais autant qu'on le devrait, représentent le véhicule idéal des microbes. N'oubliez donc jamais de les laver soigneusement en sortant des transports en commun, avant de passer à table, en sortant des toilettes, le soir avant de vous coucher. Toujours à l'eau chaude. En outre, n'ignorez pas la brosse à ongles qui elle aussi est indispensable. On doit brosser ses ongles sous le robinet chaque fois que l'on se lave les mains. Enfin, il faut impérativement s'empêcher de porter ses mains à la bouche. Ce réflexe risque de vous valoir des maladies inexpliquées qui pourraient si facilement être évitées.

LES DENTS

Après chaque repas, tout le monde sait qu'il faut se laver les dents. Tout d'abord pour éviter les caries, ensuite pour avoir bonne haleine, enfin pour garder ses dents blanches. Mais qui le fait effectivement ? Désormais, plus d'excuses avec ces bros- ses à dents pliables, enfermées dans un petit étui que l'on peut transporter n'importe où. Enfin, sachez qu'une brosse à dents se change très souvent : dès que les poils semblent se détacher, il est temps pour vous d'en racheter une autre.

SOUS LA DOUCHE

Une douche chaque matin, dès le réveil, représente un principe d'hygiène de base. Inutile d'y consacrer trois heures, ce serait exagérer. Après s'être mouillé des pieds à la tête, se savonner entièrement, puis rin- cer avec attention, en effet, le savon qui reste dans les replis de la peau, entre les orteils par exemple, risque d'irriter votre peau, et provoquer des réactions indésira- bles. Ensuite se sécher avec une serviette propre, minutieusement. A partir de quoi vous pourrez utiliser eau de toilette, lait pour le corps, et autres produits de toilette, mais jamais avant la douche. En été, nul ne vous interdit d'en prendre une le soir en ren- trant chez vous. Tout d'abord on dort mieux, ensuite, vous évitez les risques d'irritation et les désagréments provoqués par une transpiration trop abondante.

LE LINGE

Qu'il s'agisse du linge de toilette ou de sous-vêtements, il faut être méticuleux. Les serviettes de toilette ainsi que les gants, les éponges, les peignoirs, etc. sont des effets strictement personnels. Ils vous appartien- nent et nul ne doit s'en servir autre que vous-même. De la même manière que l'on n'emprunte jamais la serviette de quicon- que. Quant aux sous-vêtements, qui sont eux aussi personnels, ils se doivent d'être changés chaque jour. En été, voire plusieurs fois par jour, car la transpiration les salit beaucoup plus vite et les rend humides.

CONSEILS D'HYGIENE

• Préférez les savons crème ou gels dou- che aux traditionnelles savonnettes. En effet, des chercheurs ont découvert que les savons que l'on repose mouillés sur le bord du lavabo, contenaient énormément de microbes, ennuyeux pour la peau, et que l'on se transmettaient allègrement les uns aux autres par l'intermédiaire du même savon.
• Préférez les sous-vêtements en coton plu- tôt qu'en synthétique. Ils permettent une transpiration naturelle, et évitent de ce fait les désagréments des irritations et des démangeaisons.
• Peignes et brosses à cheveux doivent être lavés soigneusement chaque semaine, en procédant ainsi : débarrasser peignes et brosses des cheveux, ensuite les faire trem- per une demi-heure dans de l'eau chaude additionnée d'un peu de produit vaisselle, et d'une goutte d'eau de Javel, qui désin- fecte en profondeur.
• Ne jamais boire ni manger dans le verre ou l'assiette de qui que ce soit. En effet, même si cette personne est propre, cela ne l'empêche pas d'être porteuse de microbes, comme tout un chacun, et de vous le trans- mettre par cet intermédiaire.
• Préférez les mouchoirs ou serviettes en papier, que vous jetterez au bout d'une seule et unique utilisation.
• Dans les endroits publics, autant boire à la paille tout ce qu'il est possible de boire de cette façon (boissons gazeuses ou non), par prudence, tout simplement.

1 What are the five main headings for comment in the article?

2 When should you always wash your hands?

3 When should a toothbrush be thrown away?

4 When should you always take a shower?

5 What is said about:
   a) sharing crockery?
   b) using handkerchiefs?
   c) using drinking straws?

Chapter 9
Les voyages et le transport

La joie d'une visite à l'étranger, c'est l'art de voyager – et quelquefois, le voyage vaut mieux que l'arrivée! Qu'en pensez-vous?

A En voiture

As you drive around a French town, you will see many signs giving traffic instructions. Most can be guessed. Here is a selction of some you might find about parking, as this is one of the most common problems concerning cars.

E1
Can you park your car here?

E2
What can you not do here?

E3
What would happen to you if you were caught parking here? Why?

E4
Why are you not permitted to park here?

E5
Where exactly is parking allowed in this street?

E6
1 How much would it cost you to park here for one and a half hours?

2 Which coins would you have to put in the meter?

E7
1 Can you park your car here?

2 Which vehicles may not park here?

3 Where can these vehicles park?

E8

If you do not observe the law of the road, you may get a parking ticket from the police like the one below.

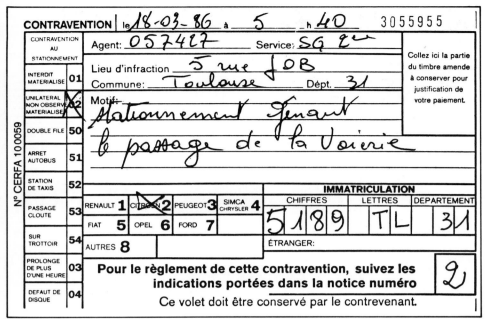

1 Which of the following statements are true?
   a) The owner has already paid an 'on the spot' fine for the offence.
   b) This form cannot be used for foreign visitors' cars.
   c) The offence was committed in Toulouse.

2 The ticket was issued because:
   a) the car was parked on or near a pedestrian crossing.
   b) the car was parked on the pavement.
   c) the car was blocking the street and restricting traffic.
   d) the car had no tax disc.

E9

Whilst on holiday with your family, your car develops a faulty headlight. You look through a local newspaper and find several garages mentioned.

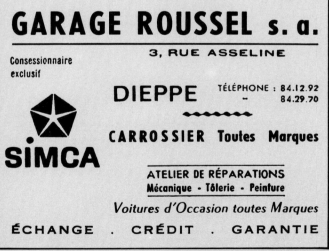

Which two garages (A–D) specialise in electrical faults?

Your family is spending a short holiday in Brittany and your parents have decided to hire a car so that you can all travel around and see the countryside and neighbouring towns. Your mother points out these two advertisements to you.

ÇA ROULE À 1/2 PRIX !

à partir de

59 F

par jour TTC
+ 0,60 F/Km
Contrat Mondial
Assistance inclus

ADA est le premier loueur de véhicules d'occasion (tourisme et utilitaires) en France. Ce nouveau service vous permet de couper la facture en deux par rapport aux loueurs traditionnels.

Toutes les voitures ADA sont parfaitement entretenues et régulièrement révisées.

ADA pratique la location de courte et longue durée, la location au kilomètre parcouru ou le forfait kilométrique illimité.

pam brest

ADA
LOCATION D'OCCASIONS

TARIF SPECIAL BRETAGNE
Hertz

FORFAIT "1 JOUR + 350 KMS"

CATEGORIES - TYPES		PRIX TTC par JOUR
A	SUPER 5 C ou similaire	**400 F**
B	PEUGEOT 205 ou similaire	**450 F**
C	RENAULT 11 ou similaire	**500 F**
D	RENAULT 21 ou similaire	**650 F**

T.V.A. 33,33 %. Tarifs valables jusqu'au 31.12.87

CONDITIONS

- Ces tarifs sont applicables uniquement dans les villes AFFAIRES & LOISIRS
- Le véhicule doit être obligatoirement restitué à la station de départ.
- Ces tarifs sont reconductibles mais non remisables.
- Le paiement s'effectue au comptant, au retour de la location.
- Age minimum : 21 ans.
- Le carburant n'est pas compris au tarif.
- Kms supplémentaires : suivant tarif HERTZ FRANCE.
- Le contrat comprend une assurance aux tiers illimitée, vol, bris de glaces, incendie et dégâts de la voiture avec une franchise de 5500 F pour les groupes A et B, 6000 F pour le groupe C et 6500 F pour le groupe D.
- La suppression de franchise et l'assurance personnes transportées peuvent être obtenues aux conditions du tarif HERTZ-FRANCE en vigueur.

S.A. AFFAIRES & LOISIRS Concessionnaire

Since your parents understand very little French, can you explain the conditions of hiring a car?

1 Can you leave the Hertz car in a different town from the pick-up place?

2 When do you pay for the hire of the Hertz car?

3 Why is the *ADA* hire charge so much lower?

4 Do you have to pay extra for each kilometer travelled with *ADA*?

You glance through a French magazine and see this review of a new small car, the *Innocenti Minimatic SE.*

La passe-partout
Une boîte automatique associée à un petit gabarit : une formule idéale pour rouler partout sans trop se fatiguer

FICHE TECHNIQUE

Cylindrée	993 cm
Puissance fiscale	6 C V
Puissance maxi	52 ch
Vitesse maxi	135 km/h
Roues motrices	avant
Longueur	3.160 m
Largeur	1.520 m
Poids	673 kg
Prix	47 900 F

Innocenti, le charme fou de la Minimatic SE

Pour vous mesdames ! Avec sa carrosserie sobre et moderne, son intérieur particulièrement raffiné, son moteur nerveux... et sa conduite reposante, grâce à la boîte automatique, la Minimatic SE a vraiment tout pour séduire... les femmes d'abord !

La Minimatic SE d'Innocenti chausse la même pointure que ses concurrentes : 316 cm ! Même profil, même tablier-bouclier à l'avant qui, en cas de distraction, permet de cogner un petit peu sans érafler la carrosserie. Mais passé le barrage d'ouverture des portières — pas moins de 3 clés prévues dans le trousseau — tout diffère !

Côté confort, c'est une véritable bonbonnière : tout a été fait pour rendre les séjours à bord agréables.

Intérieur de première classe

Au menu : portières recouvertes de velours damassé, sièges enveloppants, moquette bouclée tête-de-nègre, bandeau de suédine champagne pour souligner un tableau quadrillé sur fond bleu lumineux.

Les témoins de contrôle sont au grand complet : eau, température, niveau d'huile, on ne se salit plus les mains avec la jauge, le témoin s'allume en cas de besoin ! L'équipement est également haut de gamme : appui-tête, lève-glace électrique, montre digitale, disque de stationnement incorporé dans le pare-soleil qu'il suffit de baisser pour que la contractuelle puisse lire de l'extérieur. Un détail appréciable enfin : vide-poches et boîte à gants juste à hauteur du tableau de bord.

Dommage que l'on ne puisse faire profiter d'un tel confort toute sa famille. Il faut choisir : ou votre passager se retrouve tassé à l'avant, ou vos bambins n'ont pas la place de glisser leurs petites gambettes à l'arrière.

Peu de coffre, mais du souffle

On regrette une mauvaise distribution de l'espace à l'arrière, que l'on aurait pu réserver presque entièrement aux sièges : pour une bonne utilisation du coffre, un peu bâtard, il faut obligatoirement rabattre la banquette arrière dès lors que l'on décide d'aller faire un tour au supermarché.

La boîte automatique est à l'automobile ce que la machine à laver est à la lessive : le symbole d'une certaine libération. Plus de vitesse à passer, plus de débrayage, il suffit de placer le levier sur la position marche-avant pour que les vitesses s'enclenchent automatiquement dès que le moteur en redemande et vice versa, ce qui est appréciable dans les embouteillages. Le moteur est suffisamment nerveux pour emprunter gaiement la route ou l'autoroute. Aucune crainte des radars puisque sa vitesse de pointe ne dépasse guère 130 km/h. Dommage que la suspension ne fasse pas bon ménage avec les rues pavées et les dos d'âne ! Choisissez bien votre environnement.

Budget, bon rapport qualité-prix compte tenu du confort intérieur et de l'agrément de conduite. On lui pardonne d'être un tout petit peu gourmande : 6,45 l à 90 km/h, 9,57 l à 120 et 8,35 l en ville. On en veut au service des Mines qui lui a attribuée une puissance fiscale de 6 CV en raison de sa boîte automatique, ce qui porte la vignette à 350 F au lieu de 184 F pour les petites cylindrées habituelles, auxquelles elle est comparable. ∎

Annick Gaidoz

NOTRE AVIS

POUR
- boite automatique
- confort interieur
- maniabilite
- prix

CONTRE
- places arriere exigues
- suspension.

1 What features does the *Minimatic* have in common with its rivals?

2 How does one check on the oil level?

3 Name three features of the car's interior that can be considered top of the range.

4 What is the biggest single drawback of the car?

5 What is the car like to drive?

Minicopie. Réplique d'une véritable Suzuki, la Feber Suzuki 2 places trace la route aux enfants de 3 à 8 ans qui ont soif d'aventures « tout terrain » : roues en caoutchouc, changement de vitesse avant-arrière, accélérateur et frein à pied. La philosophie de Feber : créer des jouets originaux d'une qualité et d'une sécurité absolues. Magasins de jouets et grandes surfaces.

Here are details of a mini Suzuki.

1 What features does this car have?

2 What market is it aimed at?

3 Where can it be bought?

E13

Your French friends are conducting a survey on road accidents in the region for their school magazine. Here is an extract from the local press.

DES QUATRE OCCUPANTS de la R 20, écrasée jeudi soir par un poids lourd qui s'est retourné au Bignon-sur-Maine, en Loire-Atlantique, seul le conducteur M. Alain Blandel, de Rezé, en est sorti vivant, certes légèrement blessé. Sa femme, sa fille, sa nièce, qui avaient profité d'un voyage d'affaires à Poitiers pour visiter un zoo, ont été tuées. Tué, également, le conducteur de la 4 L, M. Jacky Bochand, de Nantes, qui avait perdu le contrôle de son véhicule, celui-ci se déportant sur la gauche au moment où survenait en face le poids lourd. Le routier, en tentant d'éviter le choc, s'est retourné, écrasant la R 20 et coupant la route à une troisième voiture, une Alfa-Roméo, qui survenait. Bilan à méditer au moment de prendre la route : quatre morts et sept blessés.

Their fact sheet asks for details of each accident. Copy out the table and try to complete it for the accident above.

Place of accident		Day and time of accident		
Details of Accident	vehicle 1	vehicle 2	vehicle 3	vehicle 4
Type of vehicle				
Number of people killed				
Total number of casualties				
Cause of accident				

P

a) Quelles sont les avantages et les dangers de posséder une voiture?

b) Comment serait-elle, votre voiture idéale?
Comparez-la à celle de votre partenaire et justifiez votre choix.

B En vélo

E14

You wish to explore the locality of your pen-friend's home.

1 Why should this advertisement appeal to you?

2 What special facility is available for a hire period of at least seven days?

E15

Another way of hiring a bicycle is through a scheme run in conjunction with French railways.

1 Where could you hire your bicycle?

2 How much deposit is usually required?

3 When do you pay for the hire charge?

4 How many types of bicycle are available?

5 How much would it cost to hire a touring bicycle for two days?

P

Quels sont les avantages, et les inconvénients, de faire des promenades à vélo dans les grandes villes de nos jours?

---

vous n'emportez pas votre vélo :

TRAIN + Vélo

La SNCF met à votre disposition dans 287 gares un service de location de vélos.

Il vous suffit de présenter une carte d'identité et de verser une caution de 250 F.

Si vous présentez :
– une Carte Bleue, une Carte Bleue Visa, Eurocard, Master Card, Access,
– une carte d'abonnement à libre circulation, carte demi-tarif, carte Vermeil, carte France Vacances, carte Jeune, vous ne payez pas cette caution.

Vous restituez le vélo à votre gare de départ ou dans une autre gare de la région (renseignez-vous auprès du personnel SNCF).

Vous payez la location en restituant le vélo.

La réservation est possible, dans la limite des disponibilités.

Trois types de bicyclettes vous sont proposés :
– des vélos, de type randonneur, à 10 vitesses, avec cadre homme ou mixte et, pour les vélos homme, guidon course et freins double poignée...
– des bicyclettes de type traditionnel : cadre mixte, guidon et selle à réglage instantané avec ou sans dérailleur.
– des bicyclettes "tous chemins" : cadre mixte, avec dérailleur 6 vitesses, amortisseur central. (Assimilées au type randonneur).

Vous trouverez ci-après la liste des 287 gares ouvertes au service Train + vélo.

En fonction de la durée de votre location, une tarification* dégressive vous est proposée.

	1/2 journée	journée
Vélo type traditionnel	25 F	35 F
Vélo type randonneur ou "tous chemins"	35 F	45 F

	3e au 10e jour		à partir du 11e jour	
	1/2 journée	journée	1/2 journée	journée
Vélo type traditionnel	19 F	27 F	13 F	18 F
Vélo type randonneur ou "tous chemins"	27 F	34 F	18 F	23 F

* Prix au 30/4/87.

E16

The *Tour de France* cycle race is keenly followed by the French. This article indicates that cycling is not just a spectator sport.

La bicyclette : plus qu'une mode

Aujourd'hui, on ne peut plus parler de mode. Le « vélo de grand-père » a retrouvé ses lettres de noblesse, un temps laissé pour compte d'une automobile en plein essor. les difficultés de circulation aidant, la voiture se transformant peu à peu en bête noire et obligatoire de la civilisation, le vélo est revenu, discrètement, au départ, franchement en masse à présent.

Et on ne peut pas ne pas connaître ces nouveaux sportifs du dimanche qui, au lieu — ou avant — de regarder leur petit écran, s'en vont (parfois) tôt le matin sur les routes de notre verte campagne, y disputer un peu d'air frais, d'impressions neuves, et de grande forme. lorsqu'on les fréquente du bout du pneu, on les comprend.

Retrouver le calme de la nature, se libérer de ce bruit, dont on s'habitue trop vite, en profitant de tout cela pour se désintoxiquer des pollutions citadines, voilà un programme qui séduirait les plus difficiles.

1 What is the reporter's attitude to the motor car?

2 What does he consider to be the essential virtues of cycling?

107

C En autocar

Service urbain : horaires du 1ᵉʳ juillet au 31 août (sauf dimanches et fêtes)

LIGNE : SAINT-MARTIN — KERFRAVAL

DÉPART de Saint-Martin		7.30	8.30	9.30	10.30	11.30		13.30	14.30	15.30	16.30	17.30	18.30
Hôtel de Ville		7.45	8.45	9.45	10.45	11.45	12.15	13.45	14.45	15.45	16.45	17.45	18.45
Kerfraval		8.00	9.00	10.00	11.00	12.00	12.30	14.00	15.00	16.00	17.00	18.00	19.00
DÉPART de Kerfraval ..		8.00	9.00	10.00	11.00	12.00		14.00	15.00	16.00	17.00	18.00	19.00
Hôtel de Ville		8.15	9.15	10.15	11.15	12.15		14.15	15.15	16.15	17.15	18.15	19.15
Saint-Martin		8.30	9.30	10.30	11.30	12.30		14.30	15 30	16.30	17.30	18.30	19.30

LIGNE : LA BOISSIÈRE — KERNEGUES (Hôpital)

DÉPART de La Boissière		7.30	8.30	9.30	10.30	11.30		13.30	14.30	15.30	16.30	17.30	18.30
Hôtel de Ville		7.45	8.45	9.45	10.45	11.45	12.15	13.45	14.45	15.45	16.45	17.45	18.45
Kernégues		8.00	9.00	10.00	11.00	12.00	12.30	14.00	15.00	16.00	17.00	18.00	19.00
DÉPART de Kernégues..		8.00	9.00	10.00	11.00	12.00		14.00	15.00	16.00	17.00	18.00	19.00
Hôtel de Ville		8.15	9.15	10.15	11.15	12.15		14.15	15.15	16.15	17.15	18.15	19.15
La Boissière		8.30	9.30	10.30	11.30	12.30		14.30	15.30	16.30	17.30	18.30	19.30

LIGNE DU BINIGOU

DÉPART du Binigou		8.00	9.00	10.00	11.00	12.00	13.30		14.30	16.30	17.00	18.00	
Place Cornic		8.15	9.15	10.15	11.15	12.15	13.45		14.45	16.45	17.15	18.15	
DÉPART Place Cornic		8.45	9.45	10.45	11.45	12.15		14.15	16.15	16.45	17.45		19.15
Le Binigou		9.00	10.00	11.00	12.00	12.30		14.30	16.30	17.00	18.00		19.30

LIGNE DE LA ROUTE DE CALLAC

DÉPART H.L.M. Rte Callac		8.30			
Hôtel de Ville		8.45			
DÉPART Hôtel de Ville				10.45	
H.L.M. Rte de Callac				10.55	

Pour les lignes St-Martin / Kerfraval et La Boissière / Kernéguez, le Samedi, le service se fera à la 1/2 heure - de 8 H 45 à 12 H 30.
Ligne de Ploujean : demander le dépliant horaire en gare routière

E17

You are staying in Morlaix near the town hall and decide to catch a bus to the swimming pool, which is in *La Boissière*.

It is 11.20 a.m. on Saturday 30 July, when is the next bus from the town hall to the swimming pool?

E18

Here is an old coach ticket which was used by a French friend in 1986.

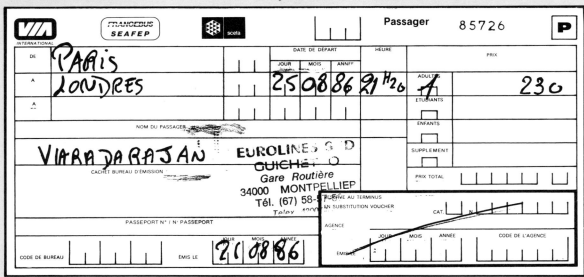

1 What time was the coach scheduled to leave?
2 On what route was the ticket valid?
3 Where was the ticket bought?

P

Préférez-vous le service de jour ou celui de nuit?
Comparez les deux en discutant avec votre partenaire.

Aller Simple (220F)

PARIS - LONDRES

Aller Retour (400F)

SERVICE REGULIER
PAS DE TRANSFERT DE BAGAGES
L'autocar embarque sur le Ferry

SERVICE NUIT

SERVICE JOUR

TOUS LES SOIRS

22.00	**PARIS** Gare Routière Internationale 3-5, av. de la Porte de la Villette Tél.: (1) 40 38 93 93	07.30
23.45	**AMIENS** Buffet de la Gare SNCF	05.30
03.00/03.30	**CALAIS** Gare Maritime	02.30
04.00	**DOUVRES** Eastern Docks	23.30/23.59
07.30	**LONDRES** Bay 20, Victoria Coach Station	21.00

TOUS LES MATINS

Toute l'année du 15.06 au 06.09			
09.00	12.30	**PARIS** Gare Routière Internationale 3-5, av. de la Porte de la Villette Tél.: (1) 40 38 93 93	18.45 21.45
12.30	16.30	**CALAIS** Gare Maritime	14.45 17.30
13.15	17.00		14.15
13.45	17.30	**DOUVRES** Eastern Docks	12.00 14.00
	18.00		11.30
17.00	20.00	**LONDRES** Bay 20, Victoria Coach Station	09.30 12.30
			du 15.06 Toute au 06.09 l'année

★ **DE PARIS** : Pas de départ les 24, 25 et 31 décembre 1987 et 1er janvier 1988.
★ **DE LONDRES** : Pas de départ les 24, 25, 26 et 31 décembre 1987 et 1er janvier 1988

★ **DE PARIS** : Pas de départ les 25 et 26 décembre 1987 et 1er janvier 1988
★ **DE LONDRES** : Pas de départ les 25 et 26 décembre 1987 et 1er janvier 1988

FORMALITES DE VOYAGE

– Les passagers sont priés de passer au contrôle à nos guichets avant embarquement.
– Respectez le numéro d'autocar qui vous est donné.
– Après le passage de la douane à DOUVRES, n'oubliez pas de récupérer tous vos bagages à la sortie et de les remettre avec l'aide du conducteur dans l'autocar que vous avez initialement pris.

TARIF BAGAGES :

1ere et 2e valise : gratuite.
Au-delà : gratuit sous réserve des places disponibles

TARIF ENFANT :

50 % de réduction pour les enfants de moins de 12 ans.

IMPORTANT : Convocation des Passagers 1 heure avant le départ.

BILLETS RETOUR « OPEN »

Attention : les places retour ne peuvent être garanties que dans la limite des places disponibles.

- *Pensez à réserver votre retour -*

BILLETS PERDUS OU VOLÉS

EUROLINES ne remplace ni ne rembourse les billets perdus, détruits ou volés.

BAGAGES

Les bagages sont l'objet de tous nos soins, et sont acceptés sur la base de 2 valises de dimension normale, par personne. Sur certaines destinations la 2e valise fera l'objet d'une taxation supplémentaire. Ils doivent être étiquetés au nom du voyageur pour pour faciliter les contrôles qui pourraient être effectués par les services de douane et de police.

En aucun cas ne seront acceptés les cartons, motos, vélos et produits inflammables.

11	12	13
21	22	23
31	32	33
41	42	43
51	52	53
61	62	63
71	72	73
81	82	83
91	92	93
101	102	103
111	112	113

E19

The coach company *Eurolines* has certain booking conditions. Do you understand them?

1 At what time must travellers report to the coach station?

2 What is the company's policy on lost or stolen tickets?

3 Why should suitcases be labelled?

4 Name the four items not allowed on the coach.

E20

You are considering making the return journey from Paris to London by coach. Which of the following statements are true?

1 The day service is cheaper than the night service.

2 The night service is longer than the day service.

3 You must pay for each suitcase.

4 Children under 12 pay half price.

5 The French coach travels across the channel on the ferry.

6 Passengers unload their cases and carry their luggage through British customs.

D   En bateau

You are travelling back to England with Brittany Ferries.

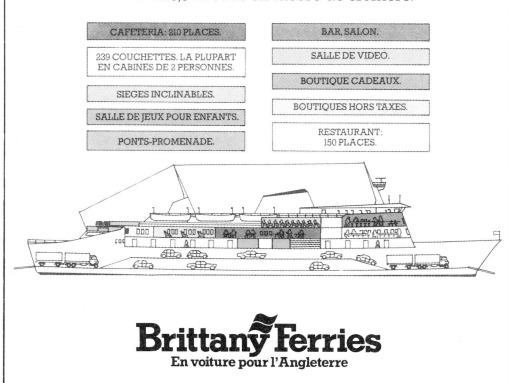

LE BÉNODET

POUR OFFRIR ENCORE PLUS DE PLACES ET ENCORE PLUS DE CONFORT

Notre ferry multiplie
les performances sur la ligne Roscoff-Plymouth. d
En capacité. En vitesse. En confort.
Le Bénodet (4250 tonneaux)
accueille 800 passagers et 250 voitures.
Il atteint 18,5 noeuds en vitesse de croisière.

CAFETERIA: 210 PLACES.	BAR, SALON.
239 COUCHETTES. LA PLUPART EN CABINES DE 2 PERSONNES.	SALLE DE VIDEO.
SIEGES INCLINABLES.	BOUTIQUE CADEAUX.
SALLE DE JEUX POUR ENFANTS.	BOUTIQUES HORS TAXES.
PONTS-PROMENADE.	RESTAURANT: 150 PLACES.

Brittany Ferries
En voiture pour l'Angleterre

You have decided on a list of things to do on the ferry to pass the time. Can you match these activities with the headings above?

1 Watch a video

2 Buy a fizzy drink

3 Buy duty free goods

4 Buy presents

5 Buy a snack

6 Walk around on deck

7 Have a snooze on a comfortable seat

8 Play bar football

9 Have a decent meal

Here are two special offers encouraging French people to visit England whilst they are on holiday in Brittany.

2 forfaits-Channel au départ de Roscoff et St-Malo

Cet été, profitez de votre séjour en Bretagne pour faire une mini-croisière avec Brittany Ferries, depuis Roscoff et St-Malo.

A des prix exceptionnels, embarquez sur l'un de nos confortables bateaux - Trégastel, Quiberon, Armorique, Prince of Brittany - avec, à bord : ponts-promenade, salles de jeux pour les enfants, boutiques hors-taxes, restaurants, bars, salons, cafeterias, film vidéo, tir aux pigeons (sur la ligne de St-Malo).

Profitez-en à l'aller comme au retour.

Si vous avez choisi notre forfait Channel avec nuit, débarquez à Portsmouth, pour passer une journée en Angleterre, avec hébergement à l'hôtel.

Traversez la Manche avec Brittany Ferries et mettez vos vacances en Bretagne à l'heure de la Grande-Bretagne !

Mini-croisière vers l'Angleterre

190F*

de Roscoff et St-Malo

(*prix par personne, aller/retour)

Du 01.07.87 au 06.09.87

Départ de Saint-Malo	Retour à Saint-Malo
Tous les jours 10 h 45	08 h 15 le lendemain

Du 02.07.87 au 29.08.87

Départ de Roscoff		Retour à Roscoff	
Jeudi	08 h 00	Jeudi	22 h 00
Samedi	08 h 00	Samedi	22 h 00

Du 19.07.87 au 16.08.87

Départ de Roscoff		Retour à Roscoff	
Dimanche	08 h 00	Dimanche	22 h 00

Mini-croisière

+

Journée en Angleterre avec excursion guidée

+

Nuit à l'hôtel

=

312F*

de Roscoff et St-Malo

(*prix par personne, aller/retour)

Les excursions en Angleterre sont accompagnées d'un guide.

Du 01.07.87 au 06.09.87

St-Malo/Portsmouth Jours et heures de départ		Excursions	Portsmouth/St-Malo Jours et heures de départ	
Jeudi	21 h 15	Vendredi matin	Samedi	09 h 30
Samedi	21 h 15	Dimanche matin	Lundi	21 h 00

Du 17.07.87 au 22.08.87

Lundi	21 h 15	Mardi matin	Mercredi	09 h 30

Excursion en Angleterre	• Nuit et petit déjeuner à l'hôtel à Portsmouth. • 1/2 journée en autocar - visite guidée à travers le vieux sud anglais dans la New Forest. • Repas libres et shopping dans Portsmouth.

Du 09.07.87 au 31.08.87

Roscoff/Plymouth Jours et heures de départ		Excursions	Plymouth/Roscoff Jours et heures de départ	
Lundi	16 h 30	Mardi matin	Mardi	23 h 30
Mardi	16 h 30	Mercredi matin	Mercredi	23 h 30
Jeudi	08 h 00	Jeudi après-midi	Vendredi	15 h 00
Samedi	08 h 00	Dimanche matin	Dimanche	23 h 30
Dimanche	16 h 30	Lundi matin	Lundi	23 h 30

Excursion en Angleterre	• 1/2 journée en autocar - visite guidée de Plymouth, du Devon à travers le Parc National du Dartmoor, de Torquay sur la "Riviera Britannique". • Repas libres et shopping dans Plymouth. • Nuit et petit déjeuner à l'hôtel à Plymouth.

1 How much would two adults and one child aged 12 pay altogether for a short break with one night's accommodation in Plymouth?

2 What else is included in this offer?

3 If the departure from Roscoff was on a Saturday at 8 a.m., when would they leave Plymouth?

E En avion

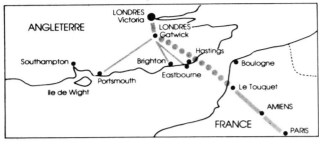

PARIS/LONDRES (GATWICK)
et vers LONDRES (VICTORIA) et la côte

					ALLER					
Paris-Nord	Amiens	Étaples Le Touquet	Le Touquet Aéroport	Londres Gatwick	Londres Gatwick	Londres Victoria	Brighton	Portsmouth H	Eastbourne (via Lewes)	Hastings
dép.	dép.	arr.	dép.	arr.	dép.	arr.	arr.	arr.	arr.	arr.
12 10	13 23	14 20	15 10	15 00	15 35	16 18				
					15 30(1)		16 16(1)			
	Train 405		Vol BR/UK 496		16 04(1)			17 35(1)		
					15 27				16 20	16 51(1)

E23

Your pen-friend's brother is explaining to you how he travelled to an English course in London. He shows you his old travel documents.

1 How did your pen-friend travel to Gatwick from Paris?

2 How long did it take him to go from the centre of Paris to the centre of London?

3 Could he have travelled on a Saturday?

Grand 53,62 m de long · 5,64 m de large · 251 passagers Airbus permet de répondre à l'augmentation du trafic sans augmenter le nombre des vols, donc l'encombrement de l'espace aérien.

Puissant (900 km/h vitesse de croisière · décollage sur piste de moins de 2000 m).

Economique moins de 4,5 l aux 100 km siège-passager sur 2000 km.

Silencieux surface atteinte par le bruit de l'Airbus en dehors de l'aéroport : 3,5 km² : c'est l'avion de grande capacité le plus silencieux du monde.

Agréable. Le décor est gai
Le service efficace
Les sièges vastes et confortables et vous pouvez garder plus de bagages avec vous !

Airbus pourrait accueillir 331 passagers, mais Air France a choisi d'installer 251 fauteuils seulement (26 en 1ᵉ, 225 en touriste).
Voici votre fauteuil.
Vous avez une place confortable.
Etendez librement vos jambes... elles ne buteront pas sur un sac ou une valise. Airbus est le seul moyen-courrier au monde à offrir à chaque passager un vaste coffre à bagages : on ne met plus sa valise sous son fauteuil !
Choisissez l'inclinaison de dossier qui vous convient pour lire, dormir ou déjeuner... si le fauteuil voisin du vôtre est inoccupé, abaissez-en le dossier : vous disposerez ainsi d'une table à votre côté.
Vous n'êtes jamais à plus d'un fauteuil d'une allée, grâce à la disposition : 2 sièges / couloir / 2 sièges / 2 accoudoirs / 2 sièges / couloir / 2 sièges.

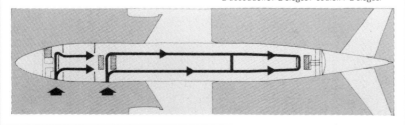

P

a) Avez-vous jamais pris un vol? Cela vous a plu?

b) Où êtes-vous allé(e)?

c) Si non, aimeriez-vous le faire? Pourquoi ou pourquoi pas?

E24

You come across this advertisement for the European Airbus.

1 Why has the Airbus been constructed with a wide body?

2 How has *Air France* modified the seating capacity of the aeroplane?

3 How has this given additional comfort?

F   Par le train

At a French railway station, you might be confronted by a variety of signs.

Each of the 30 signs above signify services at a French railway station.

The words below correspond to some of them.

Can you match them?

a)   Consigne automatique
b)   Bureau de poste
c)   Eau potable
d)   Bureau des objets trouvés
e)   Salle d'attente

f)   Guichet des billets
g)   Bureau de change
h)   Bains
i)   Toilettes (hommes)
j)   Sortie

k)   Buvette
l)   Bureau de renseignements
m)   Compartiment non fumeurs
n)   Buffet
o)   Enregistrement de bagages

E26

The French system of ticket control is markedly different from that of British Rail in the way that you must stamp (composter) your ticket.

● Vous devez le valider dans tous les cas en le compostant lors de l'accès au train.

— même si vous avez réservé;
— même si la date de départ est indiquée sur le billet.

Pour valider votre billet, il suffit d'utiliser les composteurs de couleur orange mis à votre disposition dans les gares ou les points d'arrêts.

○ Si votre billet est aller-retour, compostez-le à nouveau lors de l'accès au train de retour.
○ Si vous vous arrêtez en cours de route, n'omettez pas de composter votre billet une nouvelle fois au moment de reprendre le train.

1   Do you have to stamp your ticket if:
   a)   you have reserved a seat?
   b)   your ticket states the date of departure?

2   What colour are the ticket stamping machines?

3   What do you do if:
   a)   you have a return ticket?
   b)   you stop off in the middle of a journey?

E27

1 Which of the following facilities are offered by the *SNCF* in this region?
   a) Tourist information service
   b) Food and drink trolley service
   c) Special train and hotel packages
   d) Guaranteed seats
   e) Free return journeys
   f) Special group excursions
   g) Trains with bar and disco

2 Your train leaves today at 11 a.m. What is the latest time you can arrive to reserve your seat?

3 You want to make a reservation for a journey next week. How can you make it?

LA SNCF COMMUNIQUE :

Par suite de travaux en gare de Puteaux, la circulation des trains sera interrompue le 24 août 1986, toute la journée, entre La Défense et Suresnes-Mont-Valérien. Des autobus assureront la liaison entre ces deux gares avec desserte de Puteaux.

E28
What was this notice telling people?

LA SNCF MIDI-PYRENEES C'EST AUSSI

- **UN SERVICE DE TOURISME**

- **DES SEJOURS EN RESIDENCES**

- **DES FORFAITS TRAIN + HOTEL**

- **DES VOYAGES ET DES CIRCUITS TOURISTIQUES POUR LES GROUPES**

- **DES TRAINS ANIMES AVEC VOITURE BAR DANCING**

INFORMATIONS-RESERVATIONS

- Réservations immédiates au guichet.
- Par téléphone.

Quand doit-on retirer sa réservation ?

DEMANDE	RETRAIT
J-60 à J-9 J-8 à J	au plus tard 7 jours après la demande. au plus tard 2 jours après la demande, sans dépasser 30 mn avant le départ du train.

- par numéro de dossier : retrait dans tout point de vente de votre choix équipé d'un terminal de réservation.

P

a) Evaluez avec votre partenaire ou dans un groupe le service offert par la SNCF dans ce cas.

b) Ajoutez-y d'autres services que vous aimeriez peut-être voir à la SNCF.

c) Avez-vous jamais voyagé à l'étranger ou en Grande-Bretagne? Comment? Quand? Racontez l'expérience.

d) Nommez les différents moyens de transport. Lequel préférez-vous, et pourquoi?

e) Votre région, par quels moyens de transport est-elle desservie?

French railways have numerous schemes to enable certain types of traveller to take advantage of special discounts. Here is an extract from a leaflet.

Ce calendrier comporte trois périodes : bleue, blanche et rouge. Choisissez, de préférence, les jours bleus pour voyager plus confortablement et à des prix particulièrement avantageux.

Période bleue	Période blanche	Période rouge
en général, du samedi 12 h au dimanche 15 h, du lundi 12 h au vendredi 12 h	en général, du vendredi 12 h au samedi 12 h, du dimanche 15 h au lundi 12 h et quelques jours de fêtes.	les jours, peu nombreux, correspondant aux grands départs.

CARTE "COUPLE/FAMILLE", gratuite et valable 5 ans :
• lorsque 2 personnes figurant sur la carte voyagent ensemble et commencent chaque trajet en période bleue, l'une d'elles bénéficie de 50% de réduction, l'autre payant le plein tarif ;
• lorsqu'au moins 3 personnes figurant sur la carte voyagent ensemble et commencent chaque trajet en période bleue ou blanche, elles bénéficient de 50% de réduction dès la 2e personne, la 1re personne payant le plein tarif, les autres le tarif réduit. La réduction "Couple/Famille" s'applique même sur les allers simples.

CARTE "VERMEIL", 85 F au 30 avril 1987 et valable 1 an : 50% de réduction à tout titulaire de la carte. Il suffit de commencer chaque trajet en période bleue. Cette réduction est individuelle et valable à partir de 60 ans. La réduction "Vermeil" s'applique même sur les allers simples.

"CARRE JEUNE", 150 F au 30 avril 1987 et valable 1 an. Il permet d'effectuer 4 trajets, avec une réduction de 50% pour chaque trajet commencé en période bleue, et 20% de réduction pour chaque trajet commencé en période blanche. Cette réduction est individuelle et valable pour les jeunes de 12 à moins de 26 ans.

CARTE "JEUNE", 150 F en 1987, valable du 1er juin au 30 septembre : 50% de réduction pour chaque trajet commencé en période bleue, et d'autres avantages (1 couchette gratuite, réduction sur d'autres services SNCF...). Cette réduction est individuelle et valable pour les jeunes de 12 à moins de 26 ans.

BILLET "SÉJOUR", 25% de réduction pour un parcours aller et retour ou circulaire totalisant au moins 1000 km, le voyage retour ne pouvant être effectué au plus tôt qu'après une période comprenant un dimanche ou une fraction de dimanche (ou jour férié légal). Il suffit de commencer chaque trajet en période bleue.

REDUCTIONS "GROUPES", vous voyagez avec des amis ou vous organisez des voyages collectifs : renseignez-vous dans les gares et agences de voyages sur les possibilités de réduction que vous pouvez obtenir.

Toutes ces réductions sont applicables en 1re comme en 2e classe sur toutes les lignes de la SNCF à l'exclusion de celles de la banlieue parisienne.

To help you find the information you might need, make a chart like the one below and fill in as many details as you can.

Note that the details of the *carte vermeil* are given as an example.

Name of Railcard	People card applies to	Length of time valid	Cost of card	Reduction	First class	Second class	Single journeys	Return journeys	Restricted to blue off peak days
Carte vermeil	People over 60	1 year	85 F	50%	Yes	Yes	Yes	Yes	Yes
Carte couple/ famille									
Carte jeune									
Billet de sejour									

P

Si vous étiez en France pendant deux mois et vous vouliez faire des excursions en train, quelle carte acheteriez-vous? Essayez de justifier votre réponse.

Chapter 10
Le logement et les vacances

Si vous allez passer vos vacances en France, avec votre famille ou bien avec vos amis, il vous sera nécessaire de trouver des endroits au bord de la mer, à la campagne, ou en ville, et de trouver de la place dans un camping, dans un hôtel ou dans une pension. Cette section vous aidera à mieux comprendre les informations dont vous aurez besoin.

A Les hôtels

E1

When looking for a hotel you see this sign.

1 How much will it cost if you want a room with a shower and toilet for one night?

2 What facilities are available in the simplest room, if you wished to economise?

P

Avez-vous jamais passé des nuits dans un hôtel en Grande Bretagne ou à l'étranger? Racontez les détails de votre expérience.

PRIX DES CHAMBRES	
Équipement Sanitaire	Prix de la Chambre
EAU C. et F.	65F
CAB de T.	
CAB de T. et WC.	
DOUCHE	88F
DOUCHE et WC.	130F
BAIN	
BAIN et WC.	130F/150F

E2

Here are details of two hotels.

Hostellerie La Bouriane

Spécialités Quercynoises
vente et production de conserves maison
Place du Foirail - 46300 GOURDON-EN-QUERCY - Tél. 65.41.16.37

Dans un cadre agréable
Repos - Détente
Propriétaire : G. LACAM

CAFÉ-RESTAURANT   Chambres tout confort
NOUVEL-HÔTEL
Mme G. Cabianca, Propriétaire

Spécialités du Pays   Cuisine Soignée   Repas Gastronomiques
Boulevard de la Madeleine. 46300 GOURDON. Tél. 65.41.00.23

1 Which would you choose if you wanted a peaceful holiday?

2 Do they both offer local dishes?

E3

Here is a group of advertisements for food and accommodation.

Hôtel d'Europe

RESTAURANT   BRASSERIE

29204 MORLAIX   Tél. 62.11.99

●

2 Possibilités de Restauration

Brasserie: 21 h 45

Restaurant Gastronomique

Hôtel-Restaurant des Halles ★ NN

NICOLE VIARGUES

23, rue du Mur (à proximité de la Maison de la Reine Anne)

29120 MORLAIX   Tél. 88.03.86   Parking assuré

COUSCOUS le jeudi soir   V.R.P. restaurant fermé le dimanche

NORMANDY   Tél. 84.27.18

16, Rue Duquesne — (Près de la Plage)

RESTAURANT - BAR

— PRIX FIXE - SERVICE CARTE —

CUISINE BOURGEOISE —

Restaurant LA POTINIÈRE

Prat' al' lan   29234 PLOUIGNEAU

Tél. 98 88.35.31

HÔTEL LES BRUYÈRES ★★ NN

Salle de réunions - Parking

Départementale 712 - 4 km de Morlaix-Ville

Sortie Voie Express PLOUIGNEAU

Tél. 98 88.08.68

29234 PLOUIGNEAU

Auberge Saint-Antoine

M. et Mme LE GODEC

Salles pour Banquets et Séminaires

Spécialité de Fruits de Mer et de Homards Grillés

SAINT-ANTOINE   (6 km de Morlaix)

29252 PLOUEZOC'H   Tél. (98) 67.27.05

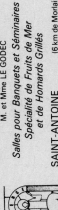

Which establishment(s) would you choose if you wanted:

1 to eat lobster?

2 a conference centre?

3 easy access to a main road?

4 to be near a beach?

5 one which serves both meals and snacks?

6 a North African dish?

E4

Your parents ask you to look at the details of the hotels on the right and to pick out one which will suit them. They want a quiet hotel that serves good food. Which one would you suggest?

P

Composez une lettre à l'hôtel de votre choix en précisant les détails de la visite de vos parents.

Discutez-les d'avance avec votre partenaire.

Your parents are planning a short visit to France and they wish to spend a night in Brittany close to the port before proceeding to Paris. Here are details of a suitable hotel.

Hostellerie du Castel ar Sal
Finistère

TARIFS CHAMBRES 1987	Juin et septembre	Juillet et août
Chambre 1 personne	210 F	350 F
Chambre 2 personnes	230 F	370 F
Lit supplémentaire	20 F	30 F
Petit déjeuner	25 F	25 F
REPAS pension	75 F	75 F

Route de la Plage - Primel Trégastel 29228 Plougasnou - Télex : 941624 F - Réservations : (16) 98 72 30 05
S.A. COGÉSELP au capital variable - R.C. 522 814 807

1 How much would one night's accommodation cost for your parents and yourself to share a room in August?

2 How much extra would it cost for the three of you to have breakfast?

P

a) Expliquez le terme «repas pension».

b) Jouez une petite scène avec votre partenaire entre un(e) client(e) et un(e) réceptionniste dans un hôtel. Le(la) client(e) a beaucoup de problèmes avec sa chambre.

E6

Your parents ask you to choose a hotel in Paris. Here are details of four hotels.

A HÔTEL FRANTOUR BROCHANT *NN
163 bis, avenue de Clichy - 75017 Paris - Tél. 42.28.40.40
Métro Brochant

A quelques minutes de Montmartre et du Sacré Cœur ou des Champs-Elysées. Etablissement moderne et fonctionnel où le maximum de confort vous est offert dans cette catégorie d'hôtel. Les 324 chambres à 2 lits comportent toutes une salle de bains complète avec W.C. Téléphone (possibilité de ligne directe).

B HÔTEL FRANTOUR SUFFREN ***NN
20, rue Jean Rey - 75015 Paris - Tél. 45.78.61.08   Métro Bir-Hakeim

Ce très bel hôtel est installé à l'ombre de la Tour Eiffel, dans le Paris des perspectives orgueilleuses du Champ-de-Mars et de Chaillot, tout près du Paris des affaires et des promenades. Ses 407 chambres, équipées d'une salle de bains et de toilettes privées, disposent en outre du téléphone direct, télévision en couleurs et radio, mini-bar, réveil automatique. Vaste hall avec boutiques. Bars et restaurant donnent sur les jardins privés de l'hôtel. Salles de conférences.

They want a medium sized hotel in a nice part of Paris and a room with a private bathroom and a colour television. Which of these hotels would you recommend to them? What other facilities does this hotel offer?

C HÔTEL FRANTOUR PARIS EST ***NN
Cour d'honneur de la gare de l'Est
4, rue du 8-Mai-45 - 75010 Paris
Tél. 42.41.00.33
Métro Gare de l'Est
Situé dans la gare même de Paris-Est, cet hôtel offre 33 chambres confortables, insonorisées, avec salle de bains ou douche, W.C., téléphone direct, radio, TV couleur. Salles magnifiques pour banquets et conférences.

D HÔTEL CONCORDE LA FAYETTE **** Luxe
3, place du Général Kœnig - 75017 Paris
Tél. 47.58.12.84
Métro Porte Maillot

Merveilleusement situé à 5 minutes de l'Arc de Triomphe et des Champs-Elysées, à 10 minutes de la Défense, un hôtel de 1000 chambres vous attend. D'accès direct avec l'hôtel, les 80 boutiques de prestige du Palais des Congrès sont à votre disposition.

B Les campings

You are thinking of going camping in the *Val de Loire*.

LA MEMBROLLE-SUR-CHOISILLE

CAMPING **

— *au bord de la Choisille*

— *ses ombrages*

— *ses tennis*

— *terrains de volley-ball et de pétanque*

— *sa pêche*

— *ses installations modernes*

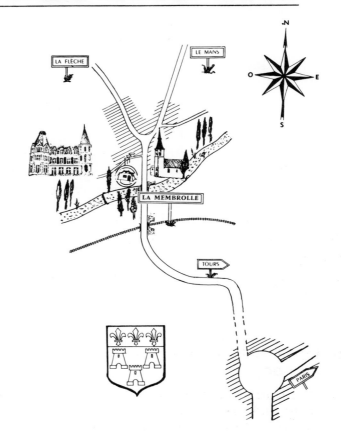

A deux cents mètres du village, à proximité des commerçants

Sa situation privilégiée pour la visite du Val de Loire

What features make this an attractive campsite?

un camping caravaning de très grande classe

Dans un site de rêve en bordure de l'Odet et à proximité de l'océan, le PARC DE KERVOUYENN vous offre la possibilité de profiter pleinement de vos vacances sans avoir les soucis de trouver le terrain habituellement surchargé des bords de mer. Soucieux de préserver le calme et le repos de chacun, notre architecte a aménagé le parc de 16 hectares en lots de 150 à 350 m², tout en vous réservant de vastes espaces verts (8 000 plantations). Chaque emplacement, parfaitement aménagé, possède l'eau et l'électricité. Vous trouverez sur place une alimentation, des plats cuisinés et à proximité, au sud de Quimper un Hypermarché

Here are details of *le Parc de Kervouyenn* in Brittany.

1 Your requirements are listed below.

a) To be near the sea
b) A spacious site
c) Sporting facilities nearby
d) Water and electricity points

How many of these would be satisfied here?

EQUIPEMENT ET CONFORT DU TERRAIN DE CAMPING

- Douches chaudes
- Emplacements délimités
- Branchements pour caravanes : eau
- Branchements pour caravanes : électricité
- Branchements pour caravanes : égouts
- Locations de tentes ou bungatoiles
- Locations de caravanes ou mobilhomes
- Locations de bungalows
- Commerces
- Plats cuisinés
- Restaurant
- Bar
- Centre de naturisme
- Garderie d'enfants
- Réservations d'emplacements
- Equipements spéciaux pour handicapés
- Laverie
- Chiens admis

ANIMATION DU TERRAIN DE CAMPING

- Piscine ou Baignade surveillée
- Tennis
- Locations de bâteaux et pédalos
- Sports hippiques
- Télévision
- Discothèque
- Bibliothèque
- Animation culturelle
- Animation sportive

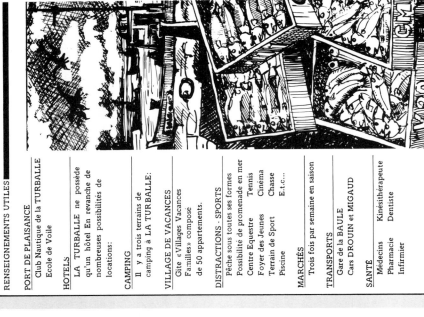

DORDOGNE

LOCALITÉS ÉQUIPEMENTS ET DISTRACTIONS SORTIE AUTOROUTE LA PLUS PROCHE	NOM - CLASSEMENT ADRESSE - TÉLÉPHONE DU TERRAIN DE CAMPING	RENSEIGNEMENTS			ÉQUIPEMENT du CAMPING	ANIMATION du CAMPING
		Dates d'ouverture	Nbre de campeurs	Situation géographique		
24300 ABJAT-BANDIAT K1	** NN Camping du Moulin de Masfrolet	15-5/30-9	390			
24480 ALLES-sur-DORDOGNE L5	** NN Camping « Port de Limeuil » Tél. (53) 61.42.10	1-5/15-9	270			

Campsite leaflets have their own special symbols for classifying facilities. Study the list at the top of this page.

E9

1 You will be in France in the last week of May. Will the campsite *Port de Limeuil* be open?

2 Which of the amenities listed below does this campsite have?

Electricity points Tent hire Cooked meals Launderette
Children's creche Marked-out sites Bar

3 Would pet owners be able to take their dogs with them?

4 Is there a swimming pool on the site?

5 What sports could you play here?

RENSEIGNEMENTS UTILES

PORT DE PLAISANCE
Club Nautique de la TURBALLE
Ecole de Voile

HOTELS
LA TURBALLE ne possède qu'un hôtel En revanche de nombreuses possibilités de locations:

CAMPING
Il y a trois terrains de camping à LA TURBALLE:

VILLAGE DE VACANCES
Gîte «Villages Vacances Familles» composé de 50 appartements.

DISTRACTIONS - SPORTS
Pêche sous toutes ses formes
Possibilité de promenade en mer

Centre Equestre	Tennis
Foyer des Jeunes	Cinéma
Terrain de Sport	Chasse
Piscine	E.t.c...

MARCHÉS
Trois fois par semaine en saison

TRANSPORTS
Gare de la BAULE
Cars DROUIN et MIGAUD

SANTÉ

Médecins	Kinésithérapeute
Pharmacie	Dentiste
Infirmier	

E10

You are planning a camping holiday with three friends next summer. You have received details of various resorts in Southern Brittany. Your friends, Nigel, Martin and Joanna all have different interests. To whom would *La Turballe* appeal the most?

Nigel likes fishing, windsurfing and rambling. Martin likes shooting, roller skating and swimming. Joanna like sailing, horse riding and films.

P

a) Vous aimez la chasse? La pêche? Les sports nautiques?

b) Est-ce que vous avez fait du camping? Où? Quand? Avec qui?

P

Discutez avec un(e) partenaire ce que vous écririez dans une lettre à un camping à La Turballe, en précisant les détails de vos exigences et les dates.

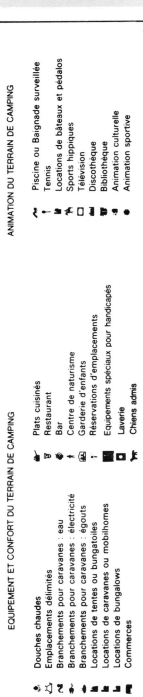

C Logement pour les jeunes

E11

Here are details of a *Foyer de Jeunes Travailleurs* in Morlaix which offers its facilities to young foreign visitors in the summer.

1 Who normally uses the *Foyer*?

2 Comment on the charges.

3 What accommodation is available and what is provided in each room?

4 What arrangements are there for eating?

5 What leisure activities are there?

RESIDENCE KER YAOUENNIC

FOYER DE JEUNES TRAVAILLEURS
=-=

FICHE DE CANDIDATURE
o-o-o-o-o-o-o-o-o-o-o-o-o-o-o-o-o-o-o-o-o-o

NOM: ....

PRENOM: ....

DATE DE NAISSANCE: ....

LIEU DE NAISSANCE: ....

ADRESSE DES PARENTS: ....

....

....

TELEPHONE: ....

Nº SECURITE SOCIALE: ....

E12

When you arrive at the *Foyer* you are given this form to fill in. Which of the following pieces of information does it ask for?

1 Parents' occupation

2 Place of birth

3 Parents' address

4 Your full name

5 Passport number

6 Length of stay

PUBLIC CONCERNE

Jeunes travailleurs de 16 à 25 ans ayant un emploi, ou à la recherche d'un emploi, en stage, en formation en apprentissage.

C'est la solution entre la vie en famille ou en pension et une autonomie de logement.

Le Foyer peut permettre de se stabiliser progressivement dans la vie active.

TARIFS

Les tarifs pratiqués et les aides dont peuvent bénéficier les personnes aux ressources faibles permettent à tous de prétendre à se loger au foyer

HEBERGEMENT

60 chambres individuelles meublées avec lavabos (eau chaude)
12 studios meublés pour deux personnes (avec salle de bains)
5 studios pour groupes (capacité 32 personnes)
Literie et draps fournis.

Pour les chambres, sanitaire à chaque étage (bac, baignoire, douche, WC).

Possibilité de laver son linge (bac ou machine)

RESTAURATION

Chaque studio est équipé d'un coin cuisine. Pour les hébergements en chambres, chaque étage dispose d'une cuisine collective qui permet à chacun de se faire son repas.

Service de petits-déjeuners au bar du Foyer sauf le dimanche.

Il est également possible de prendre son repas de midi au self service municipal (à 50 m. du Foyer) au tarif préférentiel accordé aux résidents.

Un service de restauration légère fonctionne le soir, avec la participation des résidents.

VIE SOCIALE, EDUCATIVE, ANIMATIONS

Le Foyer dispose d'un hall d'accueil centre de vie et de rencontres avec bar, jeux, ping-pong, baby, d'une salle de télévision et d'une salle d'activités.

- Soirées dansantes, soirées vidéo
- Expositions, débats
- Tournois
- Activités sportives (Tennis football)

E14

You are looking for cheap accommodation in France.

LES POINTS D'ACCUEIL JEUNES :

Les P.A.J. sont des terrains de camping équipés d'installations sanitaires. Il en existe pratiquement dans toutes les régions. Ils accueillent les jeunes randonneurs de 13 à 18 ans, seuls ou en groupe de moins de 10 pour une durée maximum de 5 nuits.
- prix par nuit et par personne : 4 Fr.
On peut trouver la liste des P.A.J. au Point Information Jeunesse ou auprès de la Direction Départementale Jeunesse et Sports des départements qui vous intéressent.

LES GÎTES D'ÉTAPE :

Les gîtes d'étape sont des hébergements exclusivement réservés aux randonneurs pédestres, équestres ou cyclotouristes, pour une durée de 2 nuits maximum.
Ils se composent :
• d'une salle commune avec coin cuisine équipée du matériel nécessaire.
• de sanitaires,
• d'un dortoir de 15 à 20 places.
Le relais est une formule plus sommaire.
Les prix : gîte : 18 F / personne et par nuit.
relais : 10 F / personne et par nuit.
La liste des gîtes et des relais vous sera fournie par :
l'A.B.R.I.
3, RUE DES PORTES MORDELAISES - 35000 RENNES
TEL : (99) 31.59.44
ou par : l'A.D.A.J.
RUE DE KERBRIAND - 29200 BREST
TEL : (98) 41.90.41
vous pouvez également la demander au P.I.J.

Here are two types of accommodation available to young people in France. You are trying to work out what each place offers, so you draw up the following grid. Copy this grid in your book. Give the information required or tick the box if the facility is available.

Types of Accommodation	Kitchen available	Toilets, showers etc.	Membership card needed	Age limit	Cyclists allowed	Time allowed to stay	Cheapest price per person per night	Meals available
Les points d'acceuil jeunes								
Les gîtes d'étape								

P

Êtes-vous jamais resté(e) dans une auberge de jeunesse? Où? Quand? Avec qui?

E13

Here is an interesting type of holiday – taking part in a work camp.

CHANTIERS

Participer à un chantier de travail est un moyen de passer des vacances à bon marché ; mais c'est aussi l'occasion de rencontrer des jeunes de toutes nationalités, origines sociales, confessions ou opinions politiques.

Le nombre d'heures de travail est d'environ 4 heures par jour pour les adolescents.

Parfois une contribution financière est demandée aux participants pour les frais d'hébergement et de nourriture, en plus de l'inscription à l'association.

On distingue trois types de chantiers :

• chantier de restauration de monuments et d'archéologie,
• chantiers de protection de la nature,
• chantiers d'aménagement de locaux à caractère social.

La fiche 7.12 vous fournira les adresses des organismes assurant des chantiers.

1 Name two advantages of a work camp.

2 You may have to pay for three things. What are they?

3 Which sort of work camp would you prefer to take part in? Give details of those available and give reasons why you would (or would not) like to take part.

Youth hostelling is a convenient and cheap way of travelling abroad.

LES AUBERGES DE JEUNESSE

La **F.U.A.J.**, association à but non lucratif, a été créée en Avril 1956. Mais le mouvement des Auberges de Jeunesse en France existe depuis 1929, inspiré de celui fondé en Allemagne en 1911.

La **F.U.A.J.** gère, en France, un important réseau d'Auberges de Jeunesse ouvertes à tous les jeunes.

La **F.U.A.J.** est restée fidèle à sa vocation : offrir des lieux d'hébergement économiques, et favoriser les rencontres entre jeunes de tous les pays, sans distinction de race, de nationalité, d'opinions politiques ou confessionnelles.

La **F.U.A.J.** est la seule association française affiliée à la **FEDERATION INTERNATIONALE DES AUBERGES DE JEUNESSE (INTERNATIONAL YOUTH HOSTEL FEDERATION/I.Y.H.F.)** offrant un réseau international de plus de 5.000 A.J. dans plus de 55 pays.

COMBIEN Y-A-T-IL D'AUBERGES DE JEUNESSE EN FRANCE ?
plus de 220 réparties dans toute la France : dans les villes, à la campagne, à la montagne ou au bord de la mer.

SONT-ELLES TOUTES IDENTIQUES ? non. Dans certaines, le confort y est très appréciable, dans d'autres, le caractère, le charme dont elles sont empreintes, compensent leur côté simple, voire sommaire.

A QUI SONT-ELLES OUVERTES ? à tous. Seul, avec des copains ou avec un groupe pour y passer une nuit... un week-end... des vacances... Une seule condition : être en possession de la carte de la F.U.A.J.

QUE PEUT-ON Y FAIRE ? en plus d'un hébergement très économique, on peut y pratiquer de multiples activités sportives, culturelles, de détente, de loisirs...

L'ACCUEIL

SEJOUR ET HORAIRES

Le séjour dans une A.J. n'est pas limité, sauf en cas d'affluence : 3 nuits maximum.
Le Bureau d'Accueil des A.J. est généralement ouvert de 7h.30 à 10h. et de 17h.30 à 20h.
Les A.J. sont ouvertes durant les mêmes horaires, et le soir jusqu'à environ 23h. l'été (22h. l'hiver). Certaines, à Paris et dans les grandes villes, le sont jusqu'à 1h. ou 2h. du matin.

TARIFS 87

HEBERGEMENT* (selon catégorie)		**REPAS** (boissons non comprises)	
Catégorie 🏨	32,00 F	Petit déjeuner	10,00 F
Catégorie 🏠	28,00 F	Déjeuner ou dîner	32,50 F
Catégorie ⚠	18,00 F	Plat unique (aux individuels seulement et dans certaines A.J.)	20,50 F

(*) Une "taxe de séjour" municipale est appliquée dans certaines localités. Elle s'ajoute au prix de l'hébergement de l'A.J.

Location draps / sacs couchage
(de 1 à 7 nuits) .... 11,00 F
Vente sac de couchage .... 65,00 F

• Dans certaines A.J., les tarifs sont plus élevés. Par exemple à PARIS "Jules Ferry", PARIS "D'Artagnan", PARIS/CHOISY-LE-ROI, STRASBOURG...

• Les centres d'hébergement associés figurés par le signe ■ ne sont pas gérés par la F.U.A.J. Il convient donc de les contacter directement pour connaître les conditions d'accueil, ainsi que les tarifs parfois différents de ceux appliqués dans les A.J.
ADHESIONS : voir "TARIFS" au dos.

DES "PLUS" POUR PAYER "MOINS"

• les **CHEQUES PLEIN AIR** alloués aux jeunes de 15 à 25 ans par la Direction Départementale de la Jeunesse et des Sports de votre lieu de résidence
• les **CHEQUES VACANCES** attribués par les employeurs aux salariés dont le revenu ne dépasse pas un seuil d'imposition fixé.
• la **CARTE JEUNE** : 25 % de réduction sur le prix de la carte INTERNATIONALE F.U.A.J.
• les **"CARRE JEUNE", "CARTE JEUNE", "CONGE ANNUEL", "SEJOUR", "MINI-GROUPES"**, et pour l'étranger : **"CARTE INTER-RAIL".** Renseignements auprès des Bureaux d'information SNCF.

INDIVIDUELS

Le réseau des Auberges de Jeunesse de la F.U.A.J. est constitué d'installations très différentes les unes des autres. Toutes les A.J. sont équipées de chambres collectives, parfois encore de petits dortoirs, salles à manger/séjour, salles de réunions. La plupart dispose d'une "cuisine individuelle", et certaines d'une cafétéria.
Une Auberge de Jeunesse, ouverte à tous, est la maison de tous les jeunes. C'est pourquoi il vous sera parfois demandé d'assurer quelques services.
Et nos animaux familiers ? Désolés, ils ne sont pas admis dans les A.J. !

GROUPES

La plupart des A.J. accueillent des groupes scolaires, sportifs, ou autres. Seuls les accompagnateurs doivent être porteurs d'une carte de "RESPONSABLE DE GROUPE" INTERNATIONALE. Les groupes peuvent participer aux activités de la F.U.A.J. l'été, l'hiver, ou durant les week-ends. (Réductions consenties hors périodes de forte fréquentation).

UNE CENTRALE DE RESERVATION
Quelque soit votre projet en France ou à l'étranger : voyages, séjours avec ou sans prestations... confiez-en l'organisation à notre Service "GROUPES", en appelant le (1) 45.53.51.14.

COUPLES ET FAMILLES

Les couples et les familles (avec enfants moins de 14 ans) peuvent être reçus dans certaines A.J. équipées de ch. de 1 à 3 lits, d'autres mettent des ch. collectives à disposition lorsque la fréquentation le permet. Avant de réserver, contacter l'A.J. Voir les tarifs "COTISATIONS" au verso.

HANDICAPES

Certaines A.J. peuvent accueillir les jeunes en fauteuil roulant. Pour la France, voir la liste au verso (colonne ♿) ; pour l'étranger, voir le guide international des A.J.

APPELES

"UN VRAI PLUS". La carte de la F.U.A.J. leur est délivrée GRATUITEMENT, sur présentation de leur carte de militaire.

Read the information above about French youth hostels and answer the following questions.

1 Who is eligible to stay in a youth hostel?

2 Briefly state the types of accommodation available.

3 What arrangements are there for families?

4 If you stayed for two nights in a well-equipped youth hostel, with breakfast and an evening meal on both days, and you have your own sleeping bag, how much would it cost you?

D Les gîtes

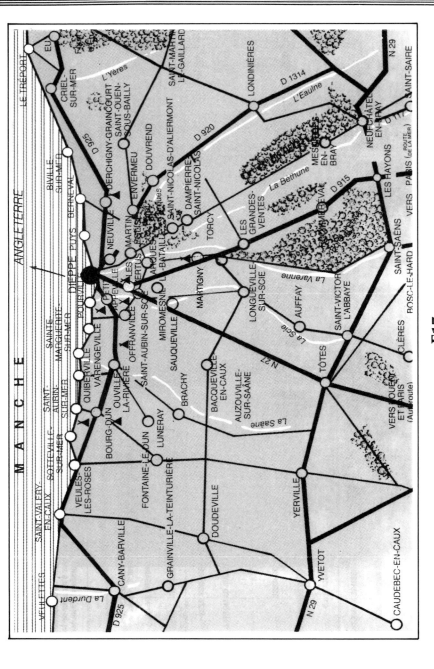

LE GÎTE RURAL

- Généralement réalisé dans les bâtiments anciens.
- Confortable et aménagé pour les vacances exprime la personnalité d'un terroir.
- Classé, contrôlé par le relais départemental en liaison avec la Fédération nationale des gîtes ruraux de France.
- Tous les gîtes sont pourvus de sanitaires (WC intérieur, lavabo, douche minimum), eau chaude, réfrigérateur.
- Bénéficie de 1 épi, 2 épis, 3 épis la qualité d'un gîte n'est pas fonction de son prix de location mais de son nombre d'épis.
- C'est l'accueil, l'originalité de ces vacances au vert.
- C'est le calme, l'espace, la verdure et l'air pur.
- Pour vos congés annuels, fêtes de fin d'année, vacances de Pâques et week-ends.

E16

Your family is thinking of spending some time in a French *gîte* and they have asked you to explain the information above.

Make a list of those facilities listed below which are normally available on a *gîte* holiday.

1 Fridge
2 Inside toilet
3 Shower
4 Fine old buildings
5 Welcome food pack
6 Hot water
7 Video recorder
8 Car hire
9 Short breaks

E17

Your family decide to hire a *gîte*. Here is the map sent to them by the French owners and a letter containing directions.

En quittant le Havre allez à Yvetot. Continuez tout droit et suivez la N29 jusqu'à Tôtes, où vous devez prendre la N27, direction Nord, vers Dieppe. A moitié-chemin, prenez la rue à droite pour Longueville-sur-Scie et Torcy. A Torcy, tournez à droite sur la D915 et puis aux Grandes Ventes tournez à gauche et suivez jusqu'à la D920. Tournez à droite sur la D920 (direction sud-est) et vous serez là au bout de quelques kilomètres.

What is the name of the village nearest to the *gîte*?

P

Aimeriez-vous passer des vacances en gîte? Justifiez votre réponse en vous référant à l'information ci-dessus.

124

E Les excursions

E18

Your *gîte* is near to Dieppe. Here are details of what the town has to offer.

You are on holiday in August.

1 How can you get from Dieppe to Paris?

2 When is the castle open?

3 When is the main office of the tourist information service open?

4 Which of the following sports could you do in Dieppe?

  a) Horse riding
  b) Offshore fishing
  c) Flying
  d) Ice-skating
  e) Go-kart racing
  f) Mini-golf
  g) Roller skating
  h) Parachuting
  i) Clay pigeon shooting
  j) Fresh water fishing

5 What is special about the swimming pool?

E19

From your *gîte* you visit Rouen.

1 Can you see the main sights by car?

2 How long do the guided tours take?

3 You are in Rouen on Wednesday 3 August. Would you be able to go on a guided tour?

4 Where does the tour start from?

5 You would particularly like to see the Old Market Square. Should you go on the morning or afternoon guided tour?

6 How much would it cost you? You are 16 years old.

7 List which of the following sights you could see:
  a) Cathedral
  b) Flaubert Museum
  c) Saint Maclou Church
  d) Law Courts
  e) Old Market Square
  f) The Old Clock
  g) Port

DIEPPE

RELATIONS

ROUTES D 915 (LA ROUTE DE LA MER) PARIS-DIEPPE 168 KM ET N 27 ROUEN-DIEPPE 58 KM ■ S.N.C.F. PARIS-DIEPPE ET ROUEN-DIEPPE ■ SERVICES DE CARS ROUEN-DIEPPE ET LITTORAL ■ DIEPPE VOYAGES, TÉL. 35 82 31 01 ■ CARS RENAULT, TÉL. 35 85 00 29 ■ CARS AUTIN, TÉL. 35 85 59 19 ■ AÉRODROME STATION AIR-ROUTE À 3 KM DU CENTRE URBAIN.

PLAGE

1 800 MÈTRES DE RIVAGE, 8 HECTARES DE PELOUSES, TRÈS VASTES PARKINGS GRATUITS ■ PISCINE OLYMPIQUE D'EAU DE MER CHAUFFÉE (24°) OUVERTE DU 15 MAI AU 30 SEPTEMBRE ■ GOLF MINIATURE ■ PING-PONG OUVERT DU 1er AVRIL AU 30 SEPTEMBRE ■ JARDIN D'ENFANTS GRATUIT OUVERT DE PÂQUES AU 30 SEPTEMBRE (NOMBREUX JEUX, PISTE DE PATINAGE À ROULETTES), MINI-KARTS ■ THALASSOTHÉRAPIE TOUTE L'ANNÉE. RENSEIGNEMENTS AU CENTRE DE CURES MARINES, ARCADES DU CASINO, TÉL. 35 84 28 67.

CAMPING

À CAMPING VITAMIN', LES VERTUS ****, OUVERT TOUTE L'ANNÉE, TÉL. 35 82 11 11 ■ À CAMPING MUNICIPAL DU POLLET **, OUVERT TOUTE L'ANNÉE, TÉL. 35 84 32 87 ■ À CAMPING DU PRÉ SAINT-NICOLAS **, ROUTE DE POURVILLE, OUVERT TOUTE L'ANNÉE, TÉL. 35 84 11 39.

DISTRACTIONS

VISITES GUIDÉES : PORT, DIEPPE-VILLE D'ART. RENSEIGNEMENTS : O.T.-S.I. ■ CASINO OUVERT TOUTE L'ANNÉE : BOULE, ROULETTE BACCARA, BANQUE OUVERTE, BLACK-JACK ■ CINÉMAS : CASINO, CLUB A, REX, ROYAL ■ DISCOTHÈQUES ■ MAISON POUR TOUS (M.J.C.) ■ MAISON JACQUES-PRÉVERT ■ CENTRE CULTUREL JEAN-RENOIR.

SPORTS

MAISON DES SPORTS (BASSIN DE NATATION, SALLES POLYVALENTES) ■ SAISON HIPPIQUE (10 RÉUNIONS DE JUILLET À SEPTEMBRE) ■ GOLF (18 TROUS) ■ ÉQUITATION ■ TIR À L'ARC ■ TIR AU PIGEON ■ AVIATION ■ PARACHUTISME ■ PÉTANQUE ■ AUTOMODÉLISME ■ PÊCHE SUR LE RIVAGE, EN MER, EN RIVIÈRE ET EN ÉTANG TOUTE L'ANNÉE ■ YACHTING ET ÉCOLE DE VOILE ■ "SLIP" : DESCENTE POUR DÉRIVEUR LÉGER ■ PERMIS BATEAU ■ TENNIS/SQUASH CLUB "5" (13 COURTS), TÉL. 35 84 00 04.

MONUMENTS

CHÂTEAU-MUSÉE (XVe) OUVERT TOUTE L'ANNÉE (FERMÉ LE MARDI DU 30 SEPTEMBRE AU 1er JUIN) ENTRÉE PAYANTE (PRIX SPÉCIAUX POUR GROUPES): IVOIRES, SALLE DE MARINE, ETC. EXPOSITIONS TEMPORAIRES ■ PORTE DES TOURELLES (XVe) ■ ÉGLISES SAINT-JACQUES (XIVe ET XVe) ET SAINT-RÉMY (XVIe ET XVIIe) ■ CHAPELLE DE BONSECOURS ■ VIEUX QUARTIERS DES PÊCHEURS "LE POLLET" ET "LE BOUT DU QUAI".

PORT

SERVICE QUOTIDIEN DIEPPE-NEWHAVEN PAR CAR-FERRIES (S.N.C.F.), EN SAISON, 4 ALLERS ET RETOURS PAR JOUR ■ PORT DE COMMERCE ■ PORT DE PÊCHE ET DE PLAISANCE ■ CHANTIER NAVAL ■ PROMENADES EN MER DU 1er MAI AU 20 SEPTEMBRE.

ACCUEIL & DOCUMENTATION

OFFICE DE TOURISME-SYNDICAT D'INITIATIVE ■ BUREAU PRINCIPAL OUVERT TOUTE L'ANNÉE SAUF DIMANCHE, TÉL. 35 84 11 77 ET 35 84 83 97, DU 14 SEPTEMBRE AU 30 AVRIL : 9 H À 12 H ET 14 H À 18 H ; DU 1er MAI AU 13 SEPTEMBRE : 9 H À 12 H ET 14 H À 19 H ■ BUREAU ANNEXE ROTONDE DE LA PLAGE, TÉL. 35 84 28 70, DU 1er JUILLET AU 31 AOÛT TOUS LES JOURS SAUF LUNDI : 10 H À 13 H ET 15 H À 20 H ; SAMEDI, DIMANCHE ET JOURS FÉRIÉS EN MAI ET JUIN, ET DEUX PREMIERS WEEK-END DE SEPTEMBRE.

ROUEN   VISITE DE LA VILLE

En raison du secteur central réservé aux piétons, la visite des quartiers historiques et des principaux monuments ne peut se faire qu'à pied.

Prix par personne : 21 F.
Moins de 25 ans et plus de 60 ans : 17 F.
Départ de l'Office de Tourisme - Syndicat d'Initiative, 25, place de la Cathédrale.

VISITES-CONFÉRENCES de la Caisse Nationale des Monuments Historiques et des Sites

  a) Pour visiteurs individuels

★ QUARTIERS HISTORIQUES :

Durée : 2 heures. Les samedis, dimanches et fêtes, du 18 avril au 8 juin. TOUS LES JOURS, du 13 juin au 30 septembre.

à 10 h : rue Saint-Romain, Aître et Église Saint-Maclou, rue Damiette, Abbatiale Saint-Ouen.

à 15 h : Cathédrale, rue du Gros-Horloge, Palais de Justice, Place du Vieux-Marché.

★ MONUMENT JUIF :

Durée : 1 heure. Le samedi à 14 h sous réserve d'inscription au moins deux jours à l'avance.

  b) Pour groupes constitués

★ QUARTIERS HISTORIQUES extérieurs des monuments : Cathédrale, rue Saint-Romain, Aître et Église Saint-Maclou, Palais de Justice, Gros-Horloge, Place du Vieux-Marché.

★ SUR LES PAS DE JEANNE D'ARC : Du Donjon au Vieux-Marché.

★ MONUMENT JUIF d'époque romane, situé dans la cour d'honneur du Palais de Justice.

★ MUSÉE DES BEAUX-ARTS

★ MUSÉE LE SECQ-DES-TOURNELLES

★ MUSÉE DE CÉRAMIQUE

CAP BLANC *se visite tous les jours...*

– Des RAMEAUX au 30 JUIN : De 10 h. à 12 h. et de 14 h. à 17 h.
– Du 1er JUILLET au 31 AOUT : De 9 h. 30 à 12 h. et de 14 h. à 18 h. 30.
– Du 1er SEPTEMBRE au 31 OCTOBRE : De 10 h. à 12 h. et de 14 h. à 17 h.
– L'hiver : Sur rendez-vous.

– Accès facile ;
– Parking ombragé ;
– Durée de la visite commentée : 30 minutes ;
– En été : Évitez l'affluence en visitant le matin.

Renseignements : Jean ARCHAMBEAU - Les Pechs - 24200 SARLAT — Téléphone : 53 59 21 74

Dessin de J.-G. MARCILLAUD

CAP BLANC

Situé à 7 km des Eyzies, ce site préhistorique daté du Magdalénien moyen (environ 14.000 ans avant nos jours), domine la vallée de la Grande Beune, face au château de Commarque.

En 1909, les fouilles dirigées sous l'abri par le Docteur Lalanne, permirent la découverte de nombreux vestiges (silex taillés et ossements travaillés), et la mise au jour d'une frise monumentale sculptée sur 14 mètres de paroi.

Chevaux, bisons, cervidés sont réalisés en bas et haut-relief, parfois de plus de 20 cm d'épaisseur.

Une sépulture humaine fut ensuite découverte à la base des dépôts archéologiques.

Cap Blanc est le plus important abri sculpté préhistorique ouvert au public.

E20

You have heard that the Dordogne area has famous prehistoric sites, as can be seen from this leaflet.

1 What is the main attraction at *Cap Blanc*?

2 Are there guided visits?

3 When is the quietest time of day to visit it in summer?

E21

Whilst on holiday in the Morlaix area, you see this poster.

1 What events are taking place?

2 What can you get to eat throughout the afternoon and evening of 20 July?

LOCQUIREC
19 Juillet A LA SALLE DES FETES
BAL
DU COMITÉ DES FETES

20 Juillet
FÊTE DE LA MER

14h.	JEUX de PLAGE
16h.	JEUX NAUTIQUE
19h.	CONCERT
20h.	DANSES FOLKLORIQUES

21h. Long John SYLVER
CHANTS de MARINS

22h30 à 2h. FEST NOZ

DEGUSTATION HUITRES, MOULES, SOUPE DE POISSONS, FRITES

E22

In the area where you are staying there are lots of saltworks where sea salt is reclaimed from sea water.

1 How can you find out more information about visiting these saltworks?

2 When do the tours take place?

3 What three facts about salt production can you learn from this visit?

4 Taking the Mesquer road from Guérande, how would you find the saltworks?

5 Can you buy salt here?

Dans le cadre de la Protection de la Nature

Visitez
une Saline
en exploitation

* HISTORIQUE DES MARAIS SALANTS
* FONCTIONNEMENT D'UNE SALINE
* TECHNIQUE DE RECOLTE

tous les jours de 16 h. à 19 h.

3 F par personne — Enfants **2 F**
A Guérande *Route de* à Mesquer :
suivre les Flèches
Vente de sel régional :
— Sel gris et " Fleur de Sel "

Pour tous renseignements :
☎ 61-91-68 le matin

F Les vacances des Français

Where do French people spend their holidays? This section gives you some ideas.

E23

These are details of special offers. Where does the holiday to Tunisia that costs 2050 F depart from?

Corse

Exemple de forfait :

7 jours en Alta Rocca

Hébergement. Demi-pension en hôtel familial : de 525 à 574 F/pers. Chez l'habitant : de 350 à 420 F la chambre (petit déjeuner compris). En gîte rural : de 3 à 6 personnes, de 420 à 840 F. Pour groupes : en dortoirs de 6/8 personnes (petit déjeuner compris), de 161 à 175 F/pers.

Location de voiture (obligatoire) : forfait de 7 jours, Renault 4 ou 2 CV Citroën avec kilométrage illimité, assurance passagers et véhicules : 750 F.

Forfait « multi-activités » (facultatif) comprenant ski de fond, randonnée équestre et pédestre, visites archéologiques, avec encadrement : 450 F.

Transport (facultatif) : vols vacances Air France Paris/Ajaccio/Paris, départ le dimanche, retour le samedi : 780 F.

E24

Corsica is another popular resort with French people.

Make out a chart like the one below in your answer book. Fill in as much information as you can about this holiday.

Name of resort	Types of accommodation offered	Car hire details	Activities offered	Day of departure and day of return

---

P

a) L'été dernier, êtes-vous allé(e) en vacances? Où? Avec qui?

b) Si non, qu'est-ce que vous avez fait pendant le mois d'août?

c) Préférez-vous aller en vacances avec votre famille ou avec vos amis? Pourquoi?

Excursions d'un jour à partir de Londres

Pour une excursion d'un jour par chemin de fer, demandez un billet aller-retour spécial (Awayday Return), qui vous permettra d'économiser jusqu'à 45% du tarif aller et retour normal et de voyager n'importe quel jour de la semaine. Vous pouvez prendre la plupart des trains sauf certaines lignes pendant les heures de pointe du lundi au vendredi. (Veuillez vérifier les détails lorsque vous achetez votre billet). Les enfants de moins de trois ans voyagent gratuitement ; les enfants de 3 ans et de moins de 14 ans paient demi-tarif.

Voici quelques suggestions de lieux à visiter avec un billet Awayday.

ARUNDEL
Ravissante ville, dominée par le magnifique château des Ducs de Norfolk. Ouverture du château : lundi–jeudi 13.00–17.00 (jusqu'au 26 mai) ; lundi–vendredi 12.00–17.00 (30 mai – 30 septembre) et le dimanche en août de 12.00 à 17.00.

BATH
Ville romaine d'Aquae Sulis. Voyez les thermes, l'abbaye médiévale et les bâtiments du dix-huitième siècle à l'architecture élégante.

BOURNEMOUTH
Station balnéaire anglaise typique possédant 9 km de plages de sable, de grands parcs de grandes pelouses et de ravissants jardins.

BRIGHTON
Station balnéaire favorite du Prince Régent (Georges IV) qui fit construire l'unique et splendide Pavillon Royal. (Ouvert tous les jours de 10.00 à 17.00 heures jusqu'au 30 juin, et de 10.00 à 20.00 heures de juillet à septembre. Fermé les 24 et 25 juin). Attractions foraines traditionnelles sur la plage et la jetée du Palais ; promenez vous dans les "Lanes", ruelles tortueuses pleines de petites boutiques. dont beaucoup de magasins d'antiquités.

CAMBRIDGE
Un monde tranquille consacré à la culture qui n'a guère changé depuis le Moyen Age. Visitez certains des 23 collèges, dont le plus vieux remonte à 1281 et n'oubliez pas la célèbre Chapelle de Kings College. Promenez-vous le long des "Backs", calmes jardins et pelouses bordant la rivière ou mieux, exercez-vous à manier un "punt", bateau plat conduit à la perche.

HASTINGS
Station balnéaire, attractions foraines traditionnelles sur la jetée, vieille ville pittoresque et château normand en ruines.

HATFIELD
Hatfield House, construit entre 1607 et 1611 pendant le règne de Jacques I, possède de beaux salons d'apparat et est entouré d'un grand parc. La reine Elisabeth I passa son enfance dans l'ancien Palais Royal, maintenant en ruines. Hatfield House est ouvert du 25 mars au 7 octobre. Mardi – samedi 12.00–17.00 ; dimanche 14.00–17.30. Fermé le lundi sauf les jours fériés. Jardins ouverts le lundi seulement 14.00–17.00. Parcs ouverts tous les jours 10.30–20.00.

OXFORD
Ville universitaire d'une grande richesse architecturale, célèbre dans le monde entier. Visitez les collèges, du plus vieux, University College, au plus grand, Christ Church, qui possède sa propre cathédrale. Chemins tranquilles au bord de la rivière, cours cloîtrées fraîches, cours carrées au doux tapis d'herbe parfaitement entretenue. Possède également un centre commercial très vivant. Une promenade avec guide d'environ 2 heures commence au Centre d'information touristique de St. Aldates, la plupart des jours de la semaine à 10.45 et 14.15.

RYE
Ancien port de mer important, un des "Cinque Ports" de défense et aujourd'hui à 3 km de la mer, cette ravissante petite ville en haut d'une colline possède des rues pavées, des vieilles maisons et des vieilles auberges.

E25

Britain is another popular holiday destination. Here is an extract from a British Rail publication.

1 What according to the information given are the attractions of:

a) Bath?　　*b*) Bournemouth?　　*c*) Oxford?

2 Which town, a former seaport, has picturesque cobbled streets?

P

Jouez, avec votre partenaire, une scène dans le syndicat d'initiative de votre ville, entre un(e) employé(e) et un(e) touriste français(e). Suggérez un programme de visites à faire dans votre région, selon les intérêts mentionnés par le (la) touriste.

G La météo

E26

Holidays in Britain depend very much on the weather and you can see that the French, too, follow weather forecasts closely!

Monsieur météo : partout un week-end à l'heure de l'automne

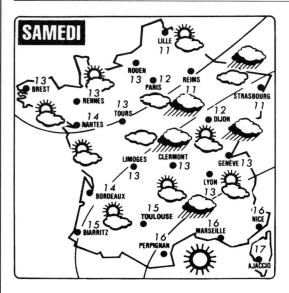

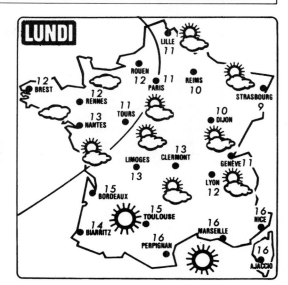

BEL effort des anti-cyclones pour ce long week-end du 11 novembre.

Ils ont réussi à faire un mur de hautes pressions en travers de l'océan et sur la France pour coincer les dépressions et le mauvais temps sur le nord de l'Atlantique où le vent souffle en tempête et où les averses sont assez violentes. Si les nuages réussissent par moments à passer au travers du mur et à se glisser sur la France, c'est seulement pour renforcer un peu plus la grisaille des brumes du matin et pour donner de faibles brumes éparses ou de petites pluies passagères.

Nous allons partout vivre à l'heure de l'automne, de la fraîcheur et de la grisaille du matin. Les après-midi nous réservent de bons moments ensoleillés avec des températures de saison.

● **Aujourd'hui : partout la matinée sera brumeuse et il fait à nouveau très frisquet au lever du jour.** De l'air maritime humide dans un ciel plus sombre sur la côte Atlantique et le Sud-Ouest.

● **Samedi, pas de changement pour la moitié sud, la journée sera encore très agréable. Sur la moitié nord, ce sera plus incertain.**

● **Dimanche : cette fois beaucoup mieux sur la moitié nord.** Ce sera à peu près le même temps qu'aujourd'hui, avec de belles heures de soleil pour l'après-midi et, toujours, des petites gelées le matin.

● A partir de lundi, les nuages vont faire un pressing plus soutenu et venir par l'ouest nous apporter un peu de pluie. Mais lundi, l'anticyclone répondra encore présent et gardera les menaces de mauvais temps en mer

● **Mardi, la France semble vouloir se partager en deux.** Sur la moitié ouest, la pluie rentrera finalement en cours de journée. Sur la moitié est, pas de changement, le soleil persiste et signe dès la fin du brouillard.

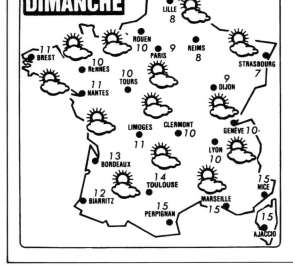

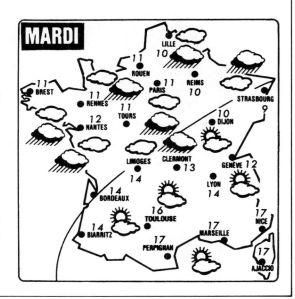

It is Friday 10 November

1 Briefly summarise the forecast for the weekend.

2 If you were living in Paris, would you expect better weather on Saturday or Sunday?

3 What changes are predicted from Monday?

METEO

Aujourd'hui, le temps va devenir progressivement nuageux sur la moitié nord de la France. Le matin, il fera frais et il y aura souvent du brouillard, que le soleil dissipera vite sur la majeure partie des régions, mais le ciel commencera à être plus chargé sur le Nord-ouest, et même couvert en Bretagne.

Dans l'après-midi, il pleuvra légèrement en Bretagne et sur le Cotentin, mais le soleil se montrera encore par endroits sur la moitié nord.

E27

Read through this weather forecast and see if you can compose a version of it in English. Try and make it sound like a television forecast and don't forget to use all the technical jargon of the weathermen!

Chapter 11
Mock examination

Level One

1

Apart from newspapers and drinks what else can be obtained from this bar? (2)

2

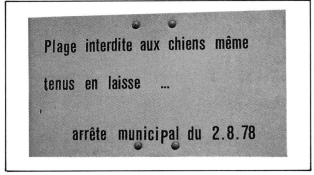

What by-law is being enforced here? (1)

3

What is this car used for? (1)

4

Name four types of product on sale here. (4)

5

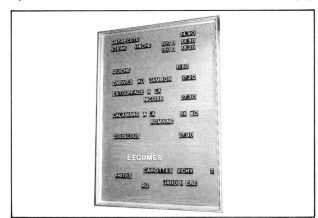

What bathing conditions are indicated by the three types of flags? (3)

6

Prix des chambres		
COMPLET	lavabo-bidet	80.00 (2 pers.)
	douche-w.c.	125.00 (2 pers.)
	douche	150.00 (4 pers.)
	bains-w.c.	180.00 (4 pers.)
	petit déjeuner	16.50 fr.

a) How much would it cost for bed and breakfast in a room with a private bathroom for two people? (2)

b) Is accommodation still available? (1)

7

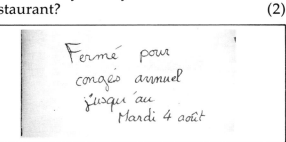

What could you buy for 15F in this restaurant? (2)

8

Fermé pour congés annuel jusqu'au Mardi 4 août

What does this sign tell you? (1)

9

a) How much would it cost to park here from 10 a.m. to 11 a.m. on a Saturday? (1)

b) When is free parking possible? (5)

10

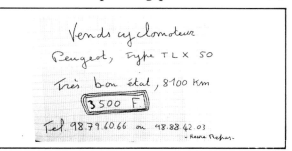

a) What is being advertised for sale here? (1)

b) When should you ring for details? (1)

11

These signs are at the entrance to a supermarket. What do they tell customers? (3)

12

Where would you find this notice? (1)

13

What is on offer here? (1)

14

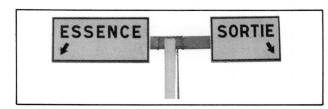

If you wanted petrol would you go left or right? (1)

15

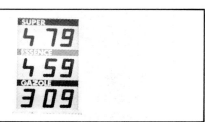

How much is four star petrol? (1)

16

How can you pay at this checkout? (1)

17

Here is a sign outside a restaurant.

Apart from steak what else is on offer? (4)

18

Nos Crêpes

Le Froment :

- nature au beurre	4 F
- au beurre et au sucre	5 F
- au beurre et au sucre *sans couverts*	4 F 50
- à la compote de pommes	6 F
- à la confiture de fraises	6 F
- au chocolat maison	8 F
- à la confiture de myrtilles	8 F
- au citron	8 F

a) What does this restaurant specialise in? (1)

b) Name three different varieties available. (3)

19

la champagne

LA GRANDE BRASSERIE DE LA MER

10 bis, Place Clichy

Réservation : (1) 48 74 44 78

Huîtres
Fruits de Mer
Homards
Langoustes
Bouillabaisses

```
LA CHAMPAGNE
  SERVICE 15 0/0 COMPRIS MERCI
  2 1                       2
SEPTEMB 10,1987
TABLE     14     CLIENT   4
   2 SALADE FR. MER   116.00
   1 MUSCADET 1/2       43.00
   1 1/2 EAU            14.00
   2 FILET GRILLE      210.00
   1 GARNI NOUILLES     25.00
   1 GARNIT.H.VERTS     36.00
   1 FILET DE SOLE     105.00
   1 ESCALOPE SAUM.     99.00
   1 BANANE FLAMBEE     57.00
   1 CAFE               11.00
   3 THE CREME          43.50
     H.SERV.           759.50
  21 TOTAL   759.50
```

Here is a receipt from a restaurant in Paris.

a) What did the customers have to drink? (4)

b) Was the service charge included? (1)

20

COLLECTIONNEZ
LES CARTES POSTALES

IRIS

PROCÉDÉ MEXICHROME

Théojac

ADHÉREZ GRATUITEMENT AU

Club **IRIS**

Association des Collectionneurs de Cartes Postales
102, Avenue Denfert Rochereau
PARIS (XVᵉ)

●

Présentez-vous à nos bureaux,
ou bien envoyez sur une carte postale
vos nom, prénoms, profession, adresse.

After buying some postcards, you notice these details about a special club printed on the paper bag.

a) What exactly is the *Club Iris*? (1)

b) What is the charge to join this club? (1)

c) What personal details do you need to give to join? (4)

21

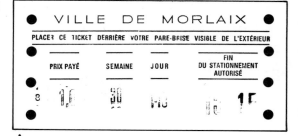

A

VILLE DE MORLAIX

PLACER CE TICKET DERRIÈRE VOTRE PARE-BRISE VISIBLE DE L'EXTÉRIEUR

PRIX PAYÉ	SEMAINE	JOUR	FIN DU STATIONNEMENT AUTORISÉ

D

LA CLUSAZ
SKI PASS
FORFAIT PERSONNEL
0265313

0903 991   88F 21 387 01

JOURNÉE

09.3

La possession du présent billet comporte la connaissance et l'acceptation intégrale du Règlement des Transports.

G

MUSÉES NATIONAUX
TARIF RÉDUIT
**ENTRÉE
11 F**

A	B
C	D

2219306

MOORE PARAGON   ARGENT

B

Trains Touristiques d'Avignon

G. EISENREICH

Circuit en ville

à conserver et
à présenter à tous contrôles
non remboursable

Nº 12293   **PRIX : 20 F.**

E

VILLE DE SIZUN (FINISTÈRE)

PISCINE MUNICIPALE

ADULTE

Nº 003582

H

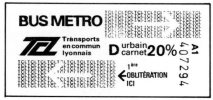

BUS METRO

TCL Transports en commun lyonnais

D urbain 20% carnet

1ère
◄OBLITÉRATION
ICI

A1 407294

Here is a selection of tickets.

Which tickets (**A–H**) would have been issued for:

a) an adult swimmer?

b) skiing?

c) parking?

d) a sightseeing tour?

e) entrance to a museum?

f) travelling on the underground?   (6)

C

– COMMUNE DE MORLAIX –

PISCINE MUNICIPALE DE LA BOISSIÈRE

ENTRÉE
Enfants: Nº 002593
7 F 30

Bon de perception à présenter à toute réquisition

F

PARKING **10** F

Journée ou Fraction

L'ESTEL s.a.r.l.

" Les Esclamandes "
83600 St AYGULF

Décline toute responsabilité en cas de vols ou détériorations

Nº 000523

22

Aujourd'hui c'était le deuxième jour d'école.
Mon école se trouve à 10 minutes en voiture de la maison – Elle vient juste d'être construite.
Nous n'avons pas encore travaillé car les emplois du temps ne sont pas encore au point. Cette année j'ai choisi les maths comme option – C'est ma matière préférée. Mais j'aime bien l'anglais et le français aussi. Tous les matins l'école commence à 9 heures. Nous avons cours jusqu'à 10 h 30 et puis nous avons une récréation. Ensuite nous avons cours jusqu'à midi. Nous reprenons à 2 heures jusqu'à 4 heures moins 10 et de 4 heures à 5 heures. À midi, je reste manger à l'école car mes parents travaillent tous les deux. Mais je n'aime pas la nourriture de la cantine.
As-tu beaucoup de devoirs à faire à la maison?
Il paraît qu'ici les profs en donnent beaucoup.
J'espère que ta rentrée s'est bien passée.
À bientôt
Corinne

This is an extract from a letter from a pen-friend.

a) In what month do you think this letter was written?   (1)

b) How does your pen-friend get to school?   (1)

c) Name three subjects she studies?   (3)

d) What happens at 10.30 a.m.?   (1)

e) Why does she have school dinner?   (1)

f) When does she finish school?   (1)

Chapter 12
Mock examination

Level Two

1

If you were keen on water sports why should this sign interest you? (2)

2

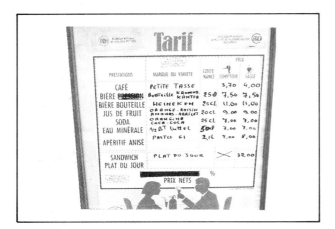

How much would an orange juice and a coffee cost for you and your friend sitting down at this café? (1)

3

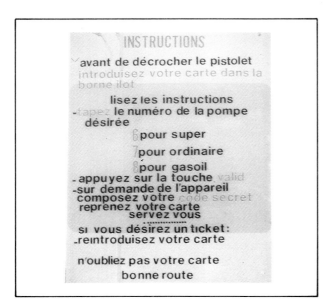

This modern petrol station uses credit cards. Briefly summarise how to use it. (6)

4

```
        BASCULE  A  TICKETS
           10 a 130 KILOS
   •  1º MONTEZ SUR LA PLATE—FORME  •
      2º ATTENDEZ L'ARRET DU DISQUE
      3º INTRODUISEZ VOTRE MONNAIE
```

What sort of machine is this sign? (1)

5

'IL EST INTERDIT'

DE CIRCULER EN PATINS A ROULETTES ET EN VEHICULES A 2 ROUES DANS LES BALLA DOIRS . DE GARER LES VEHI-CULES A 2 ROUES DANS LE SAS D'ENTREE DU CENTRE COMMERCIAL

LES EUROMARCHANDS

What three regulations apply in this shopping precinct? (3)

6

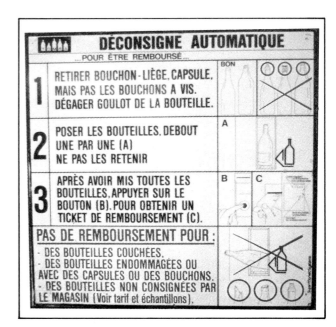

What service is offered in this hypermarket for its customers? (2)

CONSIGNE

Dans la plupart des gares existe une consigne où vous pouvez laisser vos bagages en dépôt. (Prix forfaitaire par bagage et par période de 24 h). Dans un nombre important de gares des armoires consignes automatiques sont également à votre disposition. Vous y déposez vous-même vos bagages. Le prix dépend du type d'armoire et de la durée d'utilisation.

Par précaution, n'y mettez pas d'objets de valeur.

Consigne manuelle : 10 F par bagage et par 24 h.
Armoires-consignes automatiques, selon les dimensions :
– à fonctionnement mécanique, 5 ou 10 F par 24 h.
– à fonctionnement électronique, 10, 15 ou 20 F pour 48 h.
– case-skis, à fonctionnement mécanique, 5 F pour 24 h.

You find this information in a French railways booklet.

a) What service is described here? (1)

b) How are charges calculated? (2)

Comment occuper les longs moments que vous passez dans les transports en commun pour vous rendre à votre travail ? Les Anglais, eux, ont trouvé la bonne solution... en prenant des cours dans le train. C'est ainsi qu'on trouve sur la ligne Brighton-Londres des cours de français pour les voyageurs en mal de formation professionnelle permanente. Il existe même un diplôme agréé par l'université du Sussex et les chemins de fer britanniques.
Tout a commencé en 1977 lorsque Mme Le Pelley, so-

Rude tâche pour Madame Challand : enseigner la langue de Molière aux descendants de Shakespeare... dans un wagon des chemins de fer britanniques.

fesseur a trouvé un remède astucieux, le suçage des bonbons distribués gratuitement, suivi d'une séance d'articulation qui, selon les étudiants en chapeau melon, relève d'un sadisme à la limite du supportable.
En tout cas, l'expérience porte peu à peu ses fruits. Certains ex-élèves ont pu, grâce à ses cours, obtenir

Compartiment en folie sur le Brighton-Londres

cio-anthropologiste, réussit à monter le premier cours de ce genre. Depuis, beaucoup d'élèves sont venus s'ajouter à la liste, sur d'autres lignes de banlieue...
La classe de français est menée par Mme Challand, une énergique quinquagénaire. Les devoirs sont remis pendant les pauses tunnel et commentés tout au long des

vertes collines du Sussex. Dès les premiers pavillons de banlieue, on passe à la poésie. Puis, un quart d'heure avant l'arrivée, on aborde le chapitre musique. Car cet ancien professeur du lycée français insiste pour que ses élèves (directeurs de banques de la City, responsables de relations publiques, et autres cadres supérieurs)

chantent à chaque cours (en français, cela s'entend). Au répertoire, notamment, *Une demoiselle sur une balançoire* ! Le résultat s'avère parfois peu convaincant mais le cœur y est tout de même... Le plus important selon Mme Challand, c'est la gymnastique de la mâchoire, quasi inexistante selon elle chez les Anglais. Mme le pro-

des postes dans des pays francophones. D'autres ont pu découvrir les joies de la lecture de Madame Bovary ou des gazettes financières, en français dans le texte. La SNCF tente une expérience semblable sur quelques lignes.
De quoi vous remettre sur les rails si vous vous sentez une âme d'étudiant. ■

A French friend points out this article on British life.

a) Where does Mme Challand do her teaching? (1)

b) What exactly does she teach? (1)

c) Who started the trend? (1)

d) What are the professions of Mme. Challand's pupils? (3)

e) What happens a quarter of an hour before arrival? (2)

f) Why does Mme Challand give her students sweets? (1)

g) What particular successes have her former students had? (3)

9

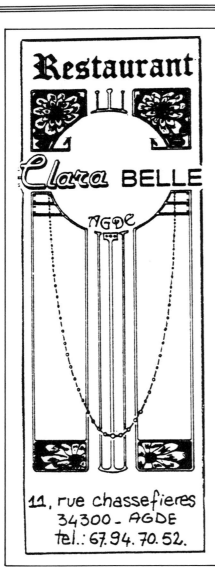

Restaurant
Clara BELLE
AGDE

11, rue chassefières
34300 - AGDE
tel.: 67.94.70.52.

Menu à 69,- frs

La soupe de poissons avec sa rouille et ses croutons
L'œuf en cocotte au crabe et aux champignons
La terrine maison au poivre vert

∘ ∘ ∘

La Daurade au four à la Provençale
Le Sauté d'agneau aux aubergines
L'émincé de volaille au curry

∘ ∘ ∘

Brie ou tarte aux pommes

Study this menu.

a) What is available as a main course apart from fish? (2)

b) What is the choice to follow? (2)

10

INFOS VACANCES été

VILLAGE DE
capbreton

Pour vos repas

Les petits déjeuners sont pris en famille dans votre appartement. A votre arrivée, vous trouverez chez vous les denrées nécessaires pour préparer votre café, chocolat ou thé. Tous les matins, nous déposons devant votre porte le pain frais.

A l'« Airial », salle à manger des adultes, les repas sont servis entre 12 h 30 et 13 h 45 et 19 h 30 et 20 h 45 par table de 6 personnes.

Les enfants de 5 à 10 ans prennent entre eux leurs repas sous la surveillance des monitrices du club, à 12 h 30 pour le déjeuner et à 19 h 30 pour le dîner (salles de la Palombière et de la Bergerie). Les enfants de moins de 5 ans prennent leur repas sous la surveillance des parents entre 11 h 30 et 12 h 45 et entre 18 h 30 et 19 h 45, au Mini-Club.

Vous pouvez, si vous le désirez, demander des paniers-repas (pique-nique) certains jours pour le midi ou le soir. Les commandes sont faites la veille à la réception. Il n'est pas possible de servir des plats de régime.

Your parents have booked in at a holiday village and have been given details of the meal arrangements.

As you are the only one who can understand French, they ask you the following questions.

a) Where is breakfast to be taken? (1)

b) What will it consist of? (2)

c) What are the dining arrangements for:
   i) you and your parents? (2)
   ii) your nine-year-old sister? (2)

d) When can picnic lunches be ordered? (1)

e) Can your mother continue her calorie controlled diet whilst on holiday? (1)

11

_ CHOISISSEZ VOTRE PLAT

_ DEMANDEZ A NOTRE
CAISSIERE

_ VENEZ LE PRENDRE CHAUD
AUPRES DE NOTRE CHEF
QUAND VOUS LE DESIREZ

You see the following sign in a cafeteria.

How does this sign tell you to order and receive your food? (2)

12

If you were rich enough, you could consider buying property in France for your holidays by the sea or in the mountains. Here are details of four holiday property complexes at:

1   Samoens
2   Sables d'Olonne
3   Villeneuve-Loubet
4   Val-Cenis.

Which resort (**1**, **2**, **3** or **4**) would you send for details if you wanted a place for:

a) skiing holidays. (2)

b) swimming holidays. (1)

c) sailing holidays. (1)

13

SAMEDI 17 DECEMBRE — 21 heures
DIMANCHE 18 DECEMBRE — 15 heures

JEAN-CLAUDE DROUOT - NITA KLEIN

jouent **PHÈDRE**

de **RACINE**

Mise en scène de Marcelle TASSENCOURT
et Thierry MAULNIER

Costumes de Georges TOUSSAINT
Musique de RAMEAU

avec **JEAN DAVY**

Créée sur l'initiative de M. le Bâtonnier André Damien, Maire de Versailles, pour le Festival, devant la Colonnade du Grand Trianon, cette nouvelle présentation du chef-d'œuvre de Racine trouve tout naturellement sa place au Théâtre Montansier.

A l'issue de la représentation du dimanche, vers 17 h 15, **Thierry MAULNIER** signera ses livres, notamment **"Lecture de Phèdre"**, **"Les Vaches Sacrées"**, **"Le Sens des Mots"**.

Here are details of two performances of *Phèdre*.

a) Who wrote the play *Phèdre*? (1)

b) How long does the performance last? (1)

14 The following card gives travel concessions in Paris.

CARTE ORANGE
RATP SNCF APTR

nom

prénom

signature

U 413944 ◆ N° à reporter sur le coupon

rangez ici votre coupon

prenez-en soin

ne le pliez pas et ne l'introduisez pas dans les composteurs des autobus

1 - LA CARTE ORANGE EST RIGOUREUSEMENT PERSONNELLE, ELLE EST CONSTITUÉE D'UNE PART DE CETTE CARTE NOMINATIVE ET D'AUTRE PART D'UN COUPON HEBDOMADAIRE (COUPON JAUNE), MENSUEL (COUPON ORANGE) OU ANNUEL EN COURS DE VALIDITÉ.

2 - La carte orange permet, à l'intérieur de la Région des transports parisiens, dans la classe, les zones et pendant la période de validité indiquées sur le coupon, d'effectuer un nombre illimité de déplacements sur les réseaux de la RATP et de la SNCF, ainsi que sur les lignes agréées des entreprises de l'APTR.

3 - AVANT D'UTILISER VOTRE CARTE ORANGE VOUS DEVEZ **OBLIGATOIREMENT** SUR VOTRE CARTE NOMINATIVE :
- Inscrire vos nom et prénom, signer, coller votre photographie d'identité (récente, de face, tête nue), puis y faire apposer le cachet d'authentification à un point de vente ;
SUR VOTRE COUPON :
- reporter à l'encre (stylo à bille) le numéro de votre carte nominative. Tout coupon sur lequel le numéro de la carte nominative n'aura pas été reporté sera considéré comme non valable et son porteur se trouvera en situation irrégulière.

4 - COMMENT VOYAGER AVEC VOTRE CARTE ORANGE
Présentez ensemble votre carte nominative et votre coupon, dans leur étui transparent, aux agents du contrôle (y compris les conducteurs d'autobus ou d'autocars). Ceux-ci peuvent exiger la présentation d'une pièce d'identité ou une signature de contrôle. Le coupon doit être utilisé pour franchir les postes de contrôle magnétique des réseaux ferrés.

POUR TOUT RENSEIGNEMENT COMPLÉMENTAIRE, vous pouvez vous adresser aux points de vente.

* *

Le non-respect d'une quelconque des prescriptions ci-dessus rend le voyageur passible du paiement d'une amende.

Toute utilisation frauduleuse de la carte nominative ou du coupon entraîne la résiliation immédiate de l'abonnement et le retrait de ces pièces sans préjudice de poursuites devant les tribunaux. Les sommes versées correspondant à la période de validité du coupon restant à courir sont acquises au transporteur à titre de dommages-intérêts.

* *

Votre coupon mensuel ou annuel ne peut être remboursé en totalité ou partiellement que dans les conditions limitativement fixées par les documents tarifaires de la RATP et de la SNCF.

La RATP et la SNCF déclinent toute responsabilité quant à l'utilisation qui pourrait être faite de cette carte en tant que pièce justificative d'identité.

* *

Adresse du titulaire (mention facultative) _____

Téléphone du bureau recueillant les coupons perdus et récupérés ☎ 257 56 85   Mod. 006 8002 P - 3-83 3 000 000

a) For how long was it valid? (1)

b) How many journeys could be made within this time? (1)

c) What means of transport are included in this scheme? (2)

SNCF-RATP 413944 COUPON JAUNE
CARTE N° 413944 HEBDOMADAIRE
SEMAINE DU **2**CL
220CT 1 2 **3** ZONES
149036 662

15

Pour votre voyage en TGV, vous devez être muni :
● du billet qui correspond au trajet effectué,
● de la réservation, obligatoire.

Outre ces deux titres, peuvent être délivrés en même temps l'un ou l'ensemble des titres suivants :
● le supplément, à payer dans certains cas (TGV circulant aux heures de pointe), qui correspond au parcours que vous effectuez.

Il existe des carnets de suppléments à coupons, que vous pouvez utiliser au fur et à mesure de vos voyages en TGV ou dans tout autre train à supplément sur n'importe quel parcours intérieur français. Ces suppléments à coupons ont une validité illimitée et vous évitent d'acquérir le supplément au coup par coup. Ils sont vendus en carnets de 6, 10 ou 15 coupons. A titre d'exemple, les carnets de 6 et 10 coupons permettent un aller-retour (2e ou 1re classe) entre Paris et Lyon en TGV à supplément.
● la réservation pour un repas en 1re classe, si vous le désirez.
● le supplément spécifique "Jeune Voyageur Service" –JVS– (cf p.9).

Votre billet et votre réservation obligatoire, ainsi que le ou les titres ci-dessus, vous sont délivrés joints en une seule et même pochette.

LA RESTAURATION

1 - LE BAR

Dans chaque rame, le bar est ouvert pendant toute la durée du trajet. Ce bar offre aux voyageurs des deux classes : ● des plats simples chauds et froids ● des sandwichs ● des boissons chaudes et froides.

2 - LA RESTAURATION
A LA PLACE EN 1re CLASSE

Un service à la place est assuré dans les voitures 1re classe réservées à la restauration de tous les TGV circulant aux heures habituelles des repas.

Ce service propose :
● le matin, un petit déjeuner,
● à midi et le soir un menu complet avec choix entre plat du jour chaud ou froid ou une grillade.

Les menus sont souvent renouvelés à l'intention des voyageurs se déplaçant fréquemment en TGV.

Réservez votre repas dans ces voitures en même temps que votre place.

LES AUTRES SERVICES

Un coin boutique situé dans le bar vous propose :
● tabac
● journaux et revues.

Handicapés

Une place dans une voiture de 1re classe peut être réservée pour une personne handicapée désireuse de voyager sur son fauteuil roulant. Cette personne paye le tarif de 2e classe.

Jeune Voyageur Service (JVS)[1]

Pour les enfants voyageant seuls (de 4 à moins de 14 ans) un service particulier (JVS) est mis à votre disposition dans certains TGV : une hôtesse prend en charge les enfants, de la gare de départ à la gare d'arrivée, moyennant un supplément spécifique.

You have heard about the French high speed train service, the *TGV*. Here is some information about the *TGV* from a guide published by French railways.

a) Are seat reservations necessary? (1)

b) Why is there sometimes an additional charge? (1)

c) How can this charge be reduced? (1)

d) What special service is offered to first class travellers? (2)

e) Explain briefly how young people travelling alone are catered for. (2)

Acknowledgements

I would like to express my gratitude to Peter Lupson, author of Echt Deutsch, for allowing his book to be used as a model for En Direct de la France; to Bozena Bannon for typing the original manuscript; and to friends for providing some of the authentic material.

My grateful thanks also to the following for kindly granting permission to reproduce copyright material:
Astroscope, Paris for the advertisement on page 7 • Brittany Ferries, Roscoff for details of 'Le Benodet' on page 110 and for the advertisement '2 forfaits – Channel' on page 111 • Centre régional de documentation pédagogique de Grenoble for the extract 'Des droits' on page 21 • Collège Lamartine, Soissons for various extracts from their 'Règlement intérieur' on pages 16, 19, 20 and 21 • M. et Mme. Dauguet, M. et Mme. Durose for their birth announcement cards on page 2 • Educatel, Rouen for the advertisement on page 28 • Eurolines, 75019 Paris for the ticket on page 108 and details of their Paris-London service on page 109 • Fédération unie des auberges de jeunesse, Paris, for their information on page 123 • Le Figaro for the article 'Laurent Fignon: le coup dur' on page 39 • France-Soir for the article 'Kriter Brut de Brut' on page 77 and the 'Météo' on page 129 • Le Grand Livre du mois, Paris for their advertisement on page 42 • L'Humanité for the article 'Les Truands ratent le train' on page 92 • M. et Mme Julien for their birth announcement card on page 2 • Laboratoires Labaz for the medicine instructions on page 98 • Libération for the following articles 'Les chemises et les jeans' on page 65; '. . .et l'essence s'achète. . .' on page 66 and the 'Meteo' on page 129 • Office du Tourisme, Dieppe for the map on page 124 and details of local attractions on page 125 • Office du Tourisme, Perros-Guirec for extracts from their guide on pages 34 and 39 • Office du Tourisme, Rouen for details of visits on page 125 • ONISEP (Ministère de l'éducation nationale) Paris for extracts from various documents: 'L'entrée en classe de sixième' on pages 16, 17, 18; 'Orientation après la troisième' on pages 25, 27; 'Cahier des métiers' on pages 26, 28–31 • Ouest France, for 'Les Forbans' on page 9; 'Chute d'une télécabine à la Plagne' on page 41; 'Un menu complet à 5F. . .' on page 74; 'Hold-up à la baguette' on page 91; 'Des quatre occupants. . .' on page 106; and the artist Larrosse for the cartoon on p 3 • La Poste (P.T.T.), Paris for extracts from their leaflets on pages 87, 89 and telegramme form on page 88 • Radio Nostalgie (Radio Corsaire), Morlaix for their advertisement on page 83 • Rallye Hypermarché, Morlaix for extracts from their consumers' advice leaflets on pages 80, 81 • Residence Ker Yaouennic, Morlaix for the 'Foyer de jeunes travailleurs' information on page 121 • Restaurant de la Reine Anne, Morlaix for the menu on page 73 • Nathalie Sanchez for her identity card and student card on page 1; voting card on page 2; school reports on pages 22, 23 • Télé Sept Jours for the extract 'Commissaire Moulin' on page 44 • Télé Star for the TV extract on page 43 • Théâtre Montansier (M. Tassencourt), Versailles for information on page 137 •

Every effort has been made to contact copyright holders. We apologise if any have been overlooked, and we would be pleased to recognise sources in the normal way if approached subsequently.

Finally, I would like to thank my wife, Sandra, for encouraging me throughout, and for dedicating much time and hard work in the production of this book.

Ray Symons

First published in 1988 by
Stanley Thornes (Publishers) Ltd
Old Station Drive, Leckhampton,
CHELTENHAM Gl53 0DN

Reprinted 1989
Reprinted 1991

British Library Cataloguing in Publication Data

En direct de la France: reading materials
from authentic sources.
1. French language. Readers—for schools
I. Symons, Ray   II. Bowey, Zina
III. Donaldson, Fiona
448.6'421

ISBN 0–85950–720–3

Typeset by Tech-Set, Gateshead, Tyne & Wear.
Printed and bound in Great Britain at The Bath Press, Avon.

Other modern language books from Stanley Thornes include:

FRENCH

M and E Bonnea *A la découverte de la France*
E-P Davoust *Danger de mort*
J Hall *Escalier* (Pupils' Books, Teacher's Book, Flashcards, Cassettes)
K Heurin *A la découverte de Paris*
Inner London Education Authority *Studio 16* (Students' Books, Teacher's Books, Cassettes)
C Neamat *Scènes de France*
M Nicoulin *The French Verb*
J S Oudot *French Verbs and Essentials of Grammar*
J S Oudot *Guide to Correspondence in French*
J S Ravisé *Tableaux culturels de la France*
R Steele and J Gaillard *Ainsi va la France* (Course Book, Cassettes)

GERMAN

G Cumming *Kommissar Schlaufuchs*
P Lupson *Echt Deutsch* (Reading materials from authentic sources)
P Lupson *Everyday German Idioms*
P Lupson *Schreiben ohne Leiden!*
P Lupson, H Aufderstraße et al *Los geht's!* (Course Books, Teacher's Books, Cassettes)
P Smith *Einfach toll!* (Course Books, Teacher's Books, Flashcards, Cassettes)

ITALIAN

D Aust and C Shepherd *Lettere Sigillate*
R Brambilla, A Crotti et al *Avanti!* (Course Book, Teacher's Book, Cassettes)
G Dekovic *Vita Italiana*
C Flynn *Attenzione Prego!* (Book, Cassettes)

SPANISH

T Connell and J Kattán-Ibarra *Spain after Franco*
T Connell and J Kattán-Ibarra *Working with Spanish* (Course Books, Teacher's Notes, Cassettes)
T Connell and E Heusden *The Spanish Verb*
Jaguar Readers (*La herencia* by R H de Escobar, *El enredo* by A M Kosnik, *Un verano misterioso* by A M Kosnik, and *El ojo de agua* by A Schrade)
M Montoro-Blanch *Premio* (Pupils' Books, Teacher's Books, Flashcards, Cassettes)
J Noble and J Lacasa *Complete Handbook of Spanish Verbs*
S Rouve and R Symons *En Directo desde España*